FEMALE OFFENDERS

Critical Perspectives and Effective Interventions

Edited by

Ruth T. Zaplin, MA, MPA, DPA

Manager
Management Consulting Division
KPMG Peat Marwick
Washington, DC
Formerly, Executive Director
THE PROGRAM for Women and
Families, Inc.
Allentown, Pennsylvania

AN ASPEN PUBLICATION®
Aspen Publishers, Inc.
Gaithersburg, Maryland
1998

Library of Congress Cataloging-in-Publication Data

Female offenders: critical perspectives and effective interventions/
edited by Ruth T. Zaplin.
p. cm.
Includes bibliographical references and index.
ISBN 0-8342-0895-4 (hardbound)
1.Female offenders—United States. 2. Female offenders—Rehabilitation—
United States. 3. Womeen prisoners—United States.
I. Zaplin, Ruth T.
HV6789.F47   1998
364.3´74´0973—dc21
98-22000
CIP

Orders: (800) 638-8437
Customer Service: (800) 234-1660

About Aspen Publishers • For more than 35 years, Aspen has been a leading professional publisher in a variety of disciplines. Aspen's vast information resources are available in both print and electronic formats. We are committed to providing the highest quality information available in the most appropriate format for our customers. Visit Aspen's Internet site for more information resources, directories, articles, and a searchable version of Aspen's full catalog, including the most recent publications: **http://www.aspenpublishers.com**
Aspen Publishers, Inc. • The hallmark of quality in publishing
Member of the worldwide Wolters Kluwer group.

Editorial Services: Ruth Bloom
Library of Congress Catalog Card Number: 98-22000
ISBN: 0-8342-0895-4

Printed in the United States of America

1 2 3 4 5

This book is dedicated with love to my mother, Sylvia Zaplin Lovit, and in loving memory of Joshua Zim and Chögyam Trungpa, Rinpoche, the teacher who continues to guide my steps.

Table of Contents

Contributors

Emilie Allan, PhD
Professor, Department of Behavioral
  Sciences
St. Francis College
Loretto, Pennsylvania

Susan Baugh, MCP
Executive Director, Atkins House
York, Pennsylvania
President, Community Corrections
  Association of Pennsylvania

Joanne Belknap, PhD
Associate Professor, Sociology Depart-
  ment
University of Colorado
Boulder, Colorado

Lorry Bradley, MA
Northampton County Project Director
Turning Point
Bethlehem, Pennsylvania

Tim Brennan, PhD
Research Associate, Psychology Depart-
  ment
University of Colorado
Institute for Cognitive Science
Boulder, Colorado

Susan Bull, MS
Psychologist, York Guidance Center
York, Pennsylvania

Kathy Cohen, Master's Candidate
Department of Community Psychology
Pennsylvania State University
Harrisburg, Pennsylvania

Stephanie S. Covington, PhD
Co-Director, Institute for Relational
  Development
La Jolla, California

Joyce Dougherty, PhD
Associate Professor, Sociology & Crimi-
  nal Justice
Chair, Sociology Department
Director, Criminal Justice Program
Moravian College
Bethlehem, Pennsylvania

Frank B. W. Hawkinshire, PhD
Professor and Director (retired), Applied
  Social Psychology and Social Policy
  Program
Center for the Study of Human Relations
New York University
New York, New York

Zelma Weston Henriques, PhD
Professor, Department of Law and Police
    Science
John Jay College of Criminal Justice
The City University of New York
New York, New York

Kristi Holsinger, MS
Doctoral Candidate, Division of Criminal
    Justice
University of Cincinnati
Cincinnati, Ohio

Delores Jones-Brown, PhD
Assistant Professor, Department of Law
    and Police Science
John Jay College of Criminal Justice
The City University of New York
Post-Doctoral Fellow, Teachers College
Columbia University
New York, New York

Kathleen Kendall, PhD
Lecturer, Department of Sociology
University of Reading
Reading, Berkshire, England

Lori Moschella, MSW
Therapist, THE PROGRAM for Women
    and Families, Inc.
Allentown, Pennsylvania

Darrell Steffensmeier, PhD
Professor, Department of Sociology
The Pennsylvania State University
University Park, Pennsylvania

Carolyn Swift, PhD
Director (retired), The Stone Center for
    Developmental Services and Studies
Wellesley College
Wellesley, Massachusetts

Angela Velasquez, BS
Director of Community, Educational, and
    Institutional Programs, THE
    PROGRAM for Women and
    Families, Inc.
Allentown, Pennsylvania

Bernard Weitzman, PhD
Associate Professor, Graduate Faculty,
    Department of Psychology
New School for Social Research
New York, New York

**Ruth T. Zaplin, MA, MPA, DPA
    (Editor)**
Manager
Management Consulting Division
KPMG Peat Marwick
Washington, D.C.
Former Executive Director, THE
    PROGRAM for Women and
    Families, Inc.
Allentown, Pennsylvania

Foreword

Meda Chesney-Lind

Why a book on women's crime and effective strategies for working with girl and women offenders? Because what used to be a relatively "boutique" subspecialty within feminist criminology now faces an extraordinary challenge—one that makes a collection that brings together perspectives and strategies both timely and welcome.

The 1980s signaled a fundamental change in women's imprisonment in our country. At the beginning of that period, there were just over 12,000 women in U.S. state and federal prisons. By 1996, there were almost 75,000. Since 1985 the annual rate of growth of female prisoners has averaged 11.2 percent, higher than the 7.9 percent average increase in male prisoners (Bureau of Justice Statistics 1997). In less than two decades, the nation has seen the number of women in U.S. prisons increase six-fold.

As a result of this surge in the numbers of women being sentenced to prison, our country has fundamentally altered its approach to women's crime. Prison historian Nicole Hahn Rafter observes that between 1930 and 1950 roughly two or three prisons were built or created for women each decade. In the 1960s, the pace of prison construction picked up slightly with seven units opening, largely in southern and western states. During the 1970s, 17 prisons opened, including units in states such as Rhode Island and Vermont that once relied on transferring women prisoners out of state. In the 1980s, 34 women's units or prisons were established. This figure is ten times larger than the figures for earlier decades (Rafter 1990, p. 181–2), and there is no question that this trend to build women's prisons continued in the 1990s.

To put this dramatic shift in another important historical context, consider the fact that only 20 years earlier the majority of states did not operate separate women's prisons. In 1973, only 28 states (including Puerto Rico and the District of Columbia) had separate institutions for women. Other states handled it differently; women were either housed in a portion of a male facility or, like Hawaii, Rhode Island, or Vermont, women were imprisoned in other states (Singer 1973, p. 298).

Looking backward, this pattern was very significant. Indeed, the official response to women's crime during the 1970s was heavily influenced by the relative absence of women's prisons, despite the fact that some women were, during these years, committing serious crimes.

What has happened in the last few decades, then, signals a major and dramatic change in the way the country is responding to women's offending. Without much fanfare and certainly with little public discussion, the male model of incarceration has been increasingly used in response to women's offending. Some of this punitive response to women's crime can be described as "equality with a vengeance"—the dark side of the equity or parity model of justice that emphasizes the need to treat women offenders as though they were "equal" to male offenders. But beyond this, it is clear that even well-intended programs and procedures developed around the needs of male offenders need to be completely revised so that they can respond to the unique needs of girls and women.

For this reason, it is clear that a book on the special needs of women offenders, complete with some very practical materials, was never more necessary and timely. A book that brings together both scholarly and programmatic perspectives on women's unique problems also demonstrates, as Adrian LeBlanc so eloquently put it, that a "woman behind bars is not a dangerous man" (LeBlanc 1996, p. 34). Specific strengths of this volume include the recognition that girls' problems lead to women's involvement with the criminal justice system, that women offenders' pathways to crime are distinct from male pathways, and that male violence and the experience of victimization are central to an understanding of women's crime.

Because the increase in women's imprisonment has fallen so disproportionately on women of color, the development of culturally appropriate programming is also vital. This work also includes a detailed effort to work from within the strengths of a woman's cultural background to help her rebuild, or in some cases, build her life.

Hopefully, this book will also prompt readers to imagine an approach to women's crime that does not rely so heavily on incarceration. As all the work in this volume clearly shows, women are incarcerated overwhelmingly for nonviolent offenses and that, in essence, the "war on drugs" has become a largely unannounced war on women, particularly women of color.

Indeed, if history is read correctly, we could imagine revisiting the nonincarcerator response to women's offending, not only for this decade's women inmates but also for their male counterparts. Recall that the United States now shares with the new state of Russia, a dubious distinction: the world's highest incarceration rates. Perhaps it is time to rethink the pattern of mindless incarceration that both our nations appear to be pursuing just as we rethought the equally mindless and destructive cold war.

Putting women offenders, and their needs, on the nation's agenda as this volume does, gives us an important position from which to begin imagining a more humane and nurturing response to crime and punishment, not only for girls and women but also for their brothers and sons.

REFERENCES

Bureau of Justice Statistics. 1988. *Profile of state prison inmates, 1986*. Washington, D.C.: U.S. Department of Justice.

Bureau of Justice Statistics. 1997. *Prisoners in 1996*. Washington, D.C.: U.S. Department of Justice: 34–40.

Rafter, N. H. 1990. *Partial justice: Women, prisons and social control*. New Brunswick, NJ: Transaction Books.

Singer, L. R. 1973. Women and the correctional process. *American Criminal Law Review* 11: 295–308.

Meda Chesney-Lind is Professor of Women's Studies at the University of Hawaii at Manoa. She is the author of many books, *Girls, Delinquency and Juvenile Justice: Toward a Feminist Theory of Young Women's Crime* and *The Female Offender: Girls, Women, and Crime*, and numerous articles on women and crime.

Preface

Female offenders are often seen in the eyes of society as women and girls who have betrayed our idealistic image of what women and girls should be. That is to say, they do not appear to be like us, or our sisters, daughters, or wives. They have broken the law and displayed errant behavior. They have spent time in prisons, jails, and/or detention centers. This "gender betrayal" somehow makes them seem less worthy in the eyes of many. Who are they really?

This book is for people who want to learn about who female offenders are and about what services and support can be offered to women and girls in conflict with the law. Hopefully this audience includes, but is not limited to: faculty members and students in criminal justice, practitioners who work in the criminal justice system—line officers, wardens, managers and staff who work in programs for female offenders, including volunteers—treatment providers, researchers, legislators who develop and vote on criminal justice policy issues, and funding decision-makers. Anyone else who is looking to have a better understanding of the fastest growing population in the criminal justice system today—women and girls—should be interested in this book as well.

While the subject of this book is female offending, many of the issues discussed are equally predictive of and relevant to male offending. For example, the planned change model presented in Chapter Four and power-belief theory presented in Chapter Six are not female-specific. They provide a context within which the criminality of men and boys can be understood. This is not to say that gender is not a crucial variable in responding to females who come in conflict with the law. Rather, it is to say that this book is also relevant to those interested in learning about and/or advancing a gender-specific theory of male offending. Steffensmeier and Allan in Chapter One suggest that both female and male crime may be better understood by taking into account the ways in which the continued profound differences between the lives of women and men shape the different patterns of female and male offending.

The wishful thought that female offenders currently institutionalized will somehow just "pull themselves up by their bootstraps" upon their release like so many others have done will only ensure that the "revolving door of justice" syndrome becomes a mainstay in our society. Metaphorically speaking, many of the female offenders described throughout this book, have no boots, more accurately, most of them have no feet. They have nothing to stand on, no base on which to redirect their lives. Had we encountered these girls and women through preventive systemic responses before they entered the criminal justice system and became burdened by the stigma of "gender betrayal," they most certainly would have been easier to help. Individuals and agencies are more willing to support help for innocent girls than adult women offenders with chronic problems. After they are "damaged" and it is "too late" in the eyes of society, the task is both more daunting from a treatment and program perspective and less popular, albeit necessary.

The first, most compelling reason for reading this book is to learn innovative ways to rehabilitate female offenders. The second, most compelling reason for reading this book is that female offenders have children. Consider that whatever form a family takes, the mother is the core, the nurturer, frequently the central and often the only adult role model. What happens to these girls and women is tantamount to determining what happens for generations to come.

Acknowledgments

I am particularly indebted to Joyce Dougherty, Angela Velasquez, and my friend and secretary, Frances Toto. I am indebted to all the contributors for their expertise, diligence, and patience. They did much to shape my thinking about female offenders. I would like to thank the Board of Directors at THE PROGRAM for Women and Families in Allentown, Pennsylvania, for their continued support and encouragement. I would also like to thank Mike Brown, Susan Beauchamp, and Kathleen McGuire-Gilbert at Aspen Publishers. Finally, I thank John Hexem who endured me throughout the project.

Introduction

This book contains theory, guidelines, as well as "nitty gritty," treatment and program considerations and strategies designed to rehabilitate and empower female offenders to re-enter society in a meaningful and productive way. This information, taken together and applied skillfully, can significantly reduce the incidence of female offenders being institutionalized and then recidivating upon their release.

With respect to the term institutionalization used throughout this book, one point of clarification is necessary. The institutionalization of juvenile girls is inclusive of the placement of juveniles in detention centers, residential drug and alcohol rehabilitation facilities, and/or residential mental health facilities. The institutionalization of women is inclusive of the placement of women in detention, residential drug and alcohol rehabilitation facilities, residential mental health facilities and/or jails or prison. Thus the term institutionalization is used throughout this book to refer to both juvenile placement and women's detention and incarceration.

This book does not cover all of the critical, feminist perspectives that pertain to female offending. In general, these perspectives would focus more on the socioeconomic context of why females come into conflict with the legal system rather than the rehabilitation needs of female offenders, the focus of this book. This book also does not offer a quick fix for the female offender problem in this country. Rehabilitation is necessarily long-term and therefore not consistent with the notion of a quick fix. Simply put, there is no one, easy solution that will address the high-risk behaviors of female offenders. Wishful thinking alone will not make the reality go away. While selected feminist perspectives are presented, the main focus of this book, as stated, is on the rehabilitation needs of female offenders and on the comprehensive rehabilitative services inclusive of long term support designed to meet their needs. The focus of this book is rooted in the logic that, while some women and girls break laws for reasons such as excitement, breaking gender norms, and economic desires unrelated to drug addiction or street life needs, most female offenders have very real and unmet needs often related to their violent pasts that spiral them into deviant behavior.

ORGANIZATION OF THE BOOK

To facilitate the book's use and enhance the reader's understanding of the material, introductions to each of the four parts of the book are provided. In addition, explanatory remarks and analyses precede each chapter and cross-references are provided.

Important theoretical considerations to use as a basis for developing programs that positively correct the maladaptive behaviors of female offenders are presented in Part One, The Theoretical Perspective. It is noteworthy that the preponderance of theory presented in this section, while not all female-specific, is *not* part of the traditional criminal justice literature largely based on studies of men and boys. For example, relational theory, the subject of Chapter Five, describes women's psychological development and comes out of the field of psychology. An understanding of relational theory is important as a basis not only for taking gender into account. It is most important in a correctional setting as a means of understanding and avoiding the same kinds of growth-hindering relationships that these girls and women typically experience. Further, relational theory provides the ground for understanding how the victimization of women has permitted men's violence to be more easily linked to some of the more salient features of patriarchal societies, especially power, the theory discussed in Chapter Six. All of the theories presented in this section are critical for the purpose of designing rehabilitative programs for female offenders.

Extensive treatment issues are presented in Part Two, Treatment Considerations and Strategies. The chapters are arranged in this section from the most theoretical—applying systems theoretical insights to psychotherapy—to the most basic treatment considerations and strategies related to needs assessment and goal planning with female offenders. Issues regarding institutional classification, mental health, childhood maltreatment and battering are also discussed in this section.

Detailed programmatic considerations related to rehabilitative interventions are presented in Part Three, The Program Perspective. Chapter Thirteen, the first chapter in Part Three, dispels myths commonly held by the general public and politicians which negatively influence and create major obstacles to developing, implementing, and funding effective rehabilitative programs for female offenders. These myths are at the root of the pervasive public and political sentiment that "nothing works" when it comes to crime in general and female offenders in particular. As Hawkinshire explains in Chapter Four, the "nothing works" attitude is largely due to the fact that many of the promising efforts of the early pioneers in social treatment programs for offenders were not elaborated on, refined, improved, or even maintained. Velasquez, the author of Chapter Thirteen, argues that the "nothing works" attitude will be perpetuated if the current human service delivery systems—inclusive of justice, education, and public behavioral health systems—continue to act as single entities, not integrated either on a policy or a functional level. The chapter provides methods to achieve system integration through a comprehensive change strategy. The following chapters will describe model programs that work with female offenders, looking specifically at those offenders who are African American, mothers, and prostitutes.

These programs will significantly impact the targeted subpopulations to the extent that they incorporate the broad-based design and implementation strategy recommended, are theoretically grounded, and are outcome driven.

It is important to emphasize here that while some factors discussed in this section of the book have been found to be particularly acute among certain female offender subpopulations, e.g., African American women, mothers, and prostitutes, these factors usually contribute to the institutionalization of all girls and women. Further, while some chapters in this section and in other sections of the book focus on women offenders and others focus on delinquent girls, it is recognized that there is a great deal of overlap in the kinds of problems experienced by both groups. Therefore, the recommendations and strategies presented are, with possible theoretical and methodological adjustments, applicable to all female offenders.

The major themes of this book, delineated briefly below, are discussed in Part Four, Future Directions, in relation to relevant management considerations. These considerations are increasingly urgent. The multifaceted problems of female offenders require a multifaceted program response that promotes a sense of well-being, enhances the ability to take action, and increases self-worth in participants. This response also requires that the staff members that design and provide these programs be creative. In order to be creative, they must manifest a commitment to constant growth and learning. Such staff members increase the likelihood that the female offender will receive those rehabilitative services that ultimately inspire her to acquire the skills and take advantage of the opportunities that she needs to be successful in reintegrating into society.

The themes of this book, explicitly discussed and/or implicitly embedded within the logic of the chapters, are delineated as follows.

- The importance of adopting a rehabilitative perspective rather than a punitive perspective when working with female offenders. This approach does not preclude the use of rules and restitution for crimes committed.
- The importance of adopting a broad-based perspective to treatment that addresses the core issues of the female offender's maladaptive behaviors, as opposed to a single-focus approach targeting one risk factor alone, e.g., substance abuse.
- The importance of adopting a broad-based perspective to program development and implementation in order to institute comprehensive, interdisciplinary service delivery across justice, education, and public behavioral health systems.
- The importance of developing programs that are both grounded in theory that is relevant to female offenders and outcome driven. A program must be outcome driven in order to demonstrate the impact of services provided through systematic program evaluation of key performance areas and goals.
- The importance of gender-specific services. These services are not possible if program development efforts focus exclusively on providing the same programs to both males and females—what Chesney-Lind in the Foreword to this book calls, "equality with a vengeance."

- The importance of being culturally sensitive to the rehabilitative needs of female offenders. Like male offenders, the majority of female offenders are disproportionately African American or Hispanic.
- The importance of developing and implementing comprehensive, long-term aftercare as part and parcel of rehabilitative efforts based on the reality that planned change is neither linear nor short-term in nature.
- The importance of doing all of the above, if possible, while the offender is in a community-based setting, preferably in the least restrictive environment possible. The reality is that girls and women are institutionalized overwhelmingly for non-violent offenses and therefore pose far lower institutional risks than males.

Finally, the reader is encouraged to consider the following: in the case of girls, the onset of delinquency is often the result of running away to escape violence at home. Then, because of poor role models at home and without adequate education and basic living skills, the first step is taken on the road to a lifetime of dependence on criminal activity to survive. This is often the scenario, not only for them but for the children they have or will have. Hopefully this book will be a major step toward breaking this pernicious cycle.

PART I

The Theoretical Perspective

Defined in the context of crime research by J. David Hawkins (1996, p. vii), theory is "an internally consistent set of assumptions and propositions that organizes the evidence on the wide range of predictors of crime." Academic criminologists have been theorizing about the question "why does crime occur?" for a long time, and they have come up with a variety of answers mostly based on studies of men and boys. However, as Dougherty points out in the introduction of Chapter Six, for decades those interested in the study of female offenders have not been content to accept the inadequacies of traditional (prefeminist) criminological theories. While both the traditional theories of crime, particularly those deemed "gender-neutral," and feminist theories of crime are discussed in this section, the preponderance of theory is being presented for the first time in the context of female offending. Thus, this section represents a significant departure in scope and content not only from traditional primers of criminological theory but from primers of crime based exclusively on feminist perspectives.

It is important to emphasize here why theories are important. Theories do inform and influence the policies and practices found in the adult and juvenile criminal justice systems. Different theories suggest different ways to reduce crime. According to Lilly et al. (1995), depending on what is proposed as the cause of illegal behavior, certain criminal justice policies and practices will seem reasonable, others will seem irrational and perhaps dangerously irresponsible. Additionally they argue that support for criminal justice policies will collapse eventually if the theory on which they are based no longer makes sense. According to Senge et al. (1994, p. 30), "without underlying theory, you get tools which might work in one situation, but you don't know why. They might fail in other situations, but you don't know why either. Further, with no underlying theory, we may not always appreciate the limitations of a tool, or even its counterproductiveness if used inappropriately."

In Chapter One, "The Nature of Female Offending: Patterns and Explanation," Steffensmeier and Allan review the nature and patterns of female offending. On one hand, the authors adopt the position that in spite of their androcentric origins, traditional structural and social process theories, even though they are based on studies of men, are more or less gender neutral and help explain female and male crime at a general level. On the other hand, the authors also contend that many of the subtle and profound differences between female and male offending patterns may be better understood by a gendered approach. They advance a gendered paradigm of female offending that builds on existing theory and on the growing body of work on gender. The paradigm is used to illuminate the nature and context of female offending.

In Chapter Two, "An Overview of Delinquent Girls: How Theory and Practice Failed and the Need for Innovative Changes," Belknap and Holsinger adopt the position that "the sexist and inaccurate representation of female offenders has been part-and-parcel of the majority of theories about crime, whether they included females or not." They explore the child-abuse-victim-to-offender link in order to present an accurate representation of female delinquents, specifically addressing which girls are most at risk of becoming delinquents. The authors contend that this is necessary not only because the theories and media have either ignored or misrepresented these girls, but because a realistic understanding of them is critical to most effectively treat them.

In Chapter Three, "Female Offenders: A Systems Perspective," Zaplin encourages those who work with female offenders to adopt a systems theoretical perspective. This perspective is concerned with problems of structure and interdependence from the female offender herself, services designed for her, the institutions and organizations that deliver these services, and the external political environment as well as the social milieu of offenders. The author explains that it is only from this perspective that the complex social reality encompassing the female offender's relationships, personal history, and the many contextual, sociological forces inducing her criminality can be properly understood.

In Chapter Four, "Social Treatment—A Multiphased Event," Hawkinshire presents a very different conceptual perspective that describes ways for theoreticians to formulate, and practitioners and therapists to employ, notions about human behavior. The context and past policies and practices of social treatment of offenders are reviewed in order to examine the record rather than merely relying on misleading reports to determine what was learned over time. The author concludes from this examination that no standard extramural or intramural treatment models exist, that consist of specified elements with previously demonstrated efficacies. After this overview, a model of planned change is presented for criminologists and others to use in their designs of social treatment for female offenders.

In Chapter Five, "The Relational Theory of Women's Psychological Development: Implications for the Criminal Justice System," Covington writes from the academic discipline of psychology rather than criminology. In essence, relational theory purports that men and women are socialized differently. In addition to having programmatic implications, this theory has important implications in regard to both female crime and delinquency and the victimization of women.

In Chapter Six, "Power Belief Theory: Female Criminality and the Dynamics of Oppression," Dougherty suggests that by focusing on the oppression of women and children, in particular girls, important explanatory insights into female criminality are revealed. Central to power-belief theory is the contention that within the structural and ideological context of oppression, as women and girls struggle to cope and in some instances simply survive, they develop a matrix of beliefs about themselves, about their own power, and about the legitimacy of the patriarchal order. The author suggests that the development of these beliefs represents the essence of the dynamics of oppression from which rule violating (criminal, and/or delinquent) behavior manifests itself.

It is interesting to note that it was not until the late 1960s and early 1970s that significant explanations of female crime were developed—Adler's *Sisters in Crime* (1975) and Simon's *Women and Crime* (1975) are based on analyses of female arrest trends. Both books attracted critical attention and have been reviewed extensively in the literature. However, they did not consider the nature of planned change or relational theory. They also did not consider the impact of power relations in patriarchal societies where the social structure institutionalizes men's control over women's labor and sexuality (Lilly et al. 1995). It is hoped that the explanatory value of the theories presented in this section hold great promise for contemporary criminologists interested in the nature and patterns of female offending.

REFERENCES

Adler, F. 1975. *Sisters in crime: The rise of the new female criminal.* New York: McGraw-Hill.

Hawkins, J., ed. 1996. *Delinquency and crime.* Cambridge: Cambridge University Press.

Lilley, J., et al. 1995. *Criminological theory,* 2nd ed. Thousand Oaks, CA: Sage Publications.

Senge, P.M., et al. 1994. *The fifth discipline fieldbook.* New York: Doubleday.

Simon, R.J. 1975. *Women and crime.* Lexington, MA: Lexington Books.

CHAPTER 1

The Nature of Female Offending: Patterns and Explanation

Darrell Steffensmeier and Emilie Allan

Editor's Notes

Chapter One reviews the nature of female offending and advances a gendered paradigm of criminality that builds on existing theory and on the growing body of work on gender. In terms of patterns and trends in female offending, the authors highlight the fact that rather than equality between the sexes leading to more female crime, it is female *inequality* and economic vulnerability that most shape female offending patterns. They also cite increased formalization of law enforcement, increased opportunities for "female" types of crime, and trends in female drug dependency as an explanation for gains in the female percentage of arrests. These issues are discussed in detail.

In terms of theory, Steffensmeier and Allan adopt the position that, in spite of their androcentric origins, traditional structural and social process theories are more or less gender neutral, and, therefore, are as useful in understanding female crime as they are in understanding overall male crime. On the other hand, the authors also contend that many of the subtle and profound differences between female and male offending patterns may be better understood by a gendered approach. The authors expound on the underlying issues for this rationale and follow the overview of patterns of female offending and what they call the gender "gap" with a gendered paradigm to illustrate more specifically the nature and context of adult female offending.

Chapter One, along with the chapter on juvenile offenders that follows, provides an accurate representation of women offenders and delinquent girls respectively. This foundation is necessary to understand the current patterns and trends in female crime and delinquency. This knowledge also provides the contextual foundation necessary to utilize all of the theory presented in this section as a basis for developing innovative ways to rehabilitate female offenders and ultimately break the cycle of intergenerational criminality.

No single article can do justice to the vast literature on gender and crime, both the old but especially the new writings. If criminologists were ever indifferent to female crime, this is steadily changing. A great deal is now known about the nature and extent of female offending, as well as about gender differences in crime.

Our goal in this chapter is to review the nature of female offending and advance a gendered paradigm of female offending that builds on existing theory and on the growing body of work on gender. We begin by presenting an overview of patterns of female offending and the gender gap, after which we introduce a gendered paradigm for explaining female crime first sketched elsewhere. That paradigm is then used to illuminate more specifically the nature and context of female offending.

FEMALE (AND MALE) OFFENDING PATTERNS

There are both similarities and differences in patterns of offending by men and women. Both are more heavily involved in minor property and substance abuse offenses than in serious crimes like robbery or murder. However, men offend at higher rates—usually much higher—than women for all crime categories except prostitution. This gender gap in crime is greatest for serious crime and least for mild forms of lawbreaking such as minor property crimes.

Many sources provide data that permit comparison of male and female offending. We review FBI arrest statistics (U.S. Department of Justice 1995) for males and females, and draw upon offender information from the National Crime Victimization Survey. We also draw upon findings from surveys on self-reported crime, from studies of criminal careers and delinquent gangs, and from case studies that provide a wealth of qualitative data on the differing contexts of male and female offending.

FBI's Uniform Crime Reports

Table 1–1 summarizes a variety of information drawn from 1995 (also 1960 and 1980) male and female arrest data for all FBI offense categories except rape (a male crime) and runaway and curfew (juvenile offenses): male and female arrests rates per 100,000 population (columns 3 and 6), the female percent of arrests (column 9), and the offending profile of males and females (columns 11and 13). All calculations in Table 1–1 adjust for the sex composition in the population as a whole and are based on all ages (versus, for example, using ages 10–64 as the population most at risk for criminal behavior).

Arrest Levels

For both males and females, arrest rates are higher for less serious offenses. Female rates are highest for the minor property crimes like larceny and fraud, and for substance abuse (driving under the influence, or DUI; drugs; and liquor law violations). Arrest rates for prostitution-type offenses are comparatively smaller, a pattern that largely reflects nonen-

Table 1–1 Male and female arrest rates/100,000 (all ages), female percentage of arrests, and male and female arrest profiles (1960–1995 *Uniform Crime Reports*)

Offense	Male rates			Female rates			Female percentage (of arrests)			Offender profile percentage* Males		Females	
	1960 (1)	1980 (2)	1995 (3)	1960 (4)	1980 (5)	1995 (6)	1960 (7)	1980 (8)	1995 (9)	1960 (10)	1995 (11)	1960 (12)	1995 (13)
Against persons													
Homicide	8.7	15.3	16.6	1.8	2.3	1.7	17.2	12.8	9.2	0.1	0.2	0.2	0.1
Aggravated assault	99.5	215.7	367.5	16.0	29.2	70.3	13.8	11.9	16.0	1.4	3.9	1.9	3.2
Weapons	68.2	135.3	190.5	4.1	10.2	15.6	5.7	7.0	7.6	1.0	2.0	0.5	0.7
Simple assault	263.7	368.2	790.7	28.8	55.4	174.0	9.9	13.1	18.0	3.8	8.5	3.5	7.8
Major property													
Robbery	64.2	123.5	132.0	3.2	9.0	12.6	4.8	6.8	8.7	0.9	1.4	0.4	0.6
Burglary	268.8	428.4	281.7	8.8	27.0	31.4	3.2	5.9	10.0	3.9	3.0	1.1	1.4
Stolen property	21.1	96.2	114.0	1.9	11.0	17.0	8.2	10.2	12.9	0.3	1.2	0.2	0.8
Minor property													
Larceny-theft	390.6	728.1	810.1	77.8	300.7	381.8	16.6	29.2	32.0	5.6	8.7	9.4	17.3
Fraud	69.3	146.2	195.2	12.6	90.2	125.8	15.4	38.2	39.2	1.0	2.1	1.5	5.7
Forgery	43.0	47.8	58.8	8.1	19.8	30.8	15.9	29.4	34.4	0.6	0.6	1.0	1.4
Embezzlement	—	5.6	6.6	—	1.9	4.5	—	25.3	40.6	—	0.1	—	0.2
Malicious mischief													
Auto theft	122.2	125.4	140.4	4.7	11.2	19.0	3.7	8.2	11.9	1.8	1.5	0.6	0.9
Vandalism	—	202.1	217.5	—	17.7	30.6	—	8.0	12.3	—	2.3	—	1.4
Arson	—	15.3	13.5	—	2.0	2.3	—	11.3	14.5	—	0.1	—	0.1
Drinking/drugs													
Public drunkenness	2499.5	946.0	499.2	207.8	72.3	62.0	7.7	7.1	11.0	35.9	5.4	25.1	2.8
DUI	340.8	1078.5	948.4	21.2	99.1	150.8	5.9	8.4	13.7	4.9	10.2	2.6	6.8
Liquor laws	182.7	316.3	342.8	28.0	51.8	78.0	13.3	14.1	18.5	2.6	3.7	3.4	3.5
Drug abuse	48.5	456.2	897.5	8.2	67.6	168.8	14.5	12.9	15.8	0.7	9.6	1.0	7.6

continues

Table 1–1 continued

Offense	Male rates			Female rates			Female percentage (of arrests)			Offender profile percentage* Males		Females	
	1960 (1)	1980 (2)	1995 (3)	1960 (4)	1980 (5)	1995 (6)	1960 (7)	1980 (8)	1995 (9)	1960 (10)	1995 (11)	1960 (12)	1995 (13)
Sex/sex related													
Prostitution	13.6	26.2	32.1	35.9	52.7	50.5	72.6	66.9	61.1	0.2	0.3	4.3	2.3
Sex offenses	80.5	56.3	73.4	16.2	4.5	6.4	16.8	7.3	8.0	1.2	0.8	2.0	0.3
Disorderly conduct	744.7	566.5	462.7	113.5	99.8	118.2	13.2	15.0	20.4	10.7	5.0	13.7	5.3
Vagrancy	251.8	27.6	18.3	22.1	8.1	3.6	8.1	21.2	16.8	3.6	0.2	2.7	0.2
Suspicion	206.9	14.3	9.1	26.4	2.2	1.6	11.3	13.2	14.8	3.0	0.1	3.2	0.1
Miscellaneous													
Against family	88.1	44.6	76.1	8.1	4.7	18.3	8.4	9.6	19.3	1.3	0.8	1.0	0.8
Gambling	193.0	44.3	13.3	17.0	4.4	2.2	8.0	9.1	14.1	2.8	0.1	2.0	0.1
Other except traffic	867.4	1382.7	2418.9	154.0	222.3	509.4	15.1	13.9	17.4	12.5	26.0	18.6	23.0
Indices													
Violent	188.4	387.4	545.1	21.1	40.6	85.0	10.0	9.5	13.5	2.7	5.9	2.5	3.8
Property	781.6	1286.4	1245.8	91.3	339.5	434.5	10.5	20.8	25.9	11.2	13.4	11.1	19.6
Index	974.0	1668.2	1790.9	112.7	380.1	519.4	10.4	18.5	22.5	14.0	19.3	13.6	23.5
Total													
All Offenses	6956.8	7757.1	9305.6	826.7	1372.7	2214.1	10.6	15.0	19.2	—	—	—	—

*1960 columns don't quite add to 100% because rape (a male offense) is omitted. 1995 columns don't add to 100% because runaways and curfew/loitering also are omitted; prior to 1964 (i.e., including 1960) the UCR lumped arrests for these two juvenile-status offenses into "other except traffic."

Source: Reprinted from U.S. Department of Justice, 1960–1995. *Uniform Crime Reports*, Federal Bureau of Investigation, Washington, D.C.: U.S. Government Printing Office.

forcement police practices. Other data sources indicate that prostitution continues to be a chief form of female offending, especially on the part of drug-dependent women and women facing adverse economic circumstances.

Arrest Profiles

Both similarities and differences are evident in the profiles of male and female arrest patterns displayed in columns 8 and 10. These profiles reflect the percentage of total male and total female arrests represented by each crime category. The homicide figures of .18 for men in 1995 and .08 for women mean, respectively, that only about two-tenths of 1 percent of all male arrests were for homicide, and only one-tenth of 1 percent of all female arrests were for homicide. In comparison, a whopping 23 percent of all male arrests and 26 percent of female arrests are "other-except-traffic"—a residual category that includes mostly criminal mischief, harassment, public disorder, local ordinance violations, and assorted minor crimes. For both males and females, the five most common arrest categories in 1995 are other-except-traffic, DUI, larceny-theft, drug abuse, and other assaults. As we discuss later, the offense category "other assaults" (also called simple assault) includes mostly minor, even trivial, incidents of threat or physical attack against another person such as scratching, biting, throwing objects, shoving, hitting, or kicking. Because of growing citizen concerns about violence and aggression in American society, enhanced reporting and policing have resulted in rising rates of arrest of both males and females for other assaults in recent years. Together, these five offenses account for 63 percent of all male arrests and 62 percent of all female arrests. Note, however, that after "other except traffic," larceny arrests are the most numerous category (17 percent in 1995) for females; but that for males, DUI arrests are more important (10 percent). Arrests for murder, arson, and embezzlement are relatively rare for males and females alike, while arrests for offenses such as liquor law violations (mostly underage drinking), simple assault, and disorderly conduct represent "middling ranks" for both sexes.

The most important gender differences in arrest profiles involve the proportionately greater female involvement in minor property crimes (collectively, about 25 percent of female arrests in 1995, compared to 12 percent of male arrests), and the relatively greater involvement of males in the more serious person or property crimes (16 percent of male arrests, but only 6 percent of female arrests).

Female Percentage of Arrests and Recent Trends in Female Crime

The female share of arrests for most categories is 15 percent or less, and is typically smallest for the most serious offenses (column 6) The female share of arrests is the largest for prostitution (including disorderly conduct and vagrancy statutes that are used in arresting females for prostitution) and for minor property crimes (larceny, fraud, forgery, and embezzlement).

The female share of arrests has tended to rise over the past 2–3 decades—most notably in the property crime categories (compare columns 7–9; also columns 1–6 for arrest rate trends). When total arrests across all offenses are considered, the female percentage rose substantially—from 11 percent in 1960 to 15 percent in 1975 and to 19 percent in 1995. However, the bulk of that rise is due to the sharp increase in the numbers of women arrested for minor property crimes like larceny, fraud, and forgery. The female share averaged about 15 percent in 1960 and between 30–40 percent of arrestees for these crimes in 1995. On the other hand, for a number of offenses, the female percentage has held steady or declined slightly, including arrests for drug law violations, aggravated assault, and homicide. Particularly noteworthy is the decline in the female share of arrests for murder (from 17 percent in 1960 to 9 percent in 1995). That decline appears due to two main factors: (1) large increases in male arrests for felony murders connected with the drug trade and the increased availability of guns; and (2) stable or declining rates of murders committed by women because of the growth in domestic abuse shelters and abuse protection statutes—both of which protect women from abusive males and diminish the opportunity context for victim-precipitated mate slayings involving females as the homicide offender). It also is worth noting that, while the female-to-male percentage of arrests for illegal drug use has not been rising—drug arrest rates have been rising for both sexes and the impact of drugs on offending levels is greater among females than males (see discussion below).

Some criminologists have attributed the increases in the female share of arrests to gains in gender equality and the women's movement. The media during the 1970s (and even in the 1990s) enthusiastically embraced this interpretation of the "dark side" of female liberation. It is plausible to argue that greater freedom has resulted in more female participation in the public sphere (work, shopping, banking, driving, and the like), and could help account for some of the increases in the female share of arrests for minor property offenses like larceny (shoplifting, employee theft), fraud (misuse of credit cards), or forgery (writing bad checks). But do such behaviors as shopping, banking, or working in shops really reflect female emancipation? More in-depth analysis shows that typical arrestees for these offense categories do not commit white collar crimes but that these are petty offenses committed by economically marginal women (Chesney-Lind 1986; Daly 1989; Steffensmeier 1980, 1993). Rather than gender equality, a variety of alternative explanations provide more plausible and more parsimonious accounts for those increases in the female percent of arrests that did occur.

Increased Economic Vulnerability for Many Women. Some feminists (and others) point to the peculiarity of considering "a hypothesis that assumed improving girls' and women's economic conditions would lead to an increase in female crime when almost all the existing criminological literature stresses the role played by discrimination and poverty (and unemployment or underemployment) in the creation of crime" (Chesney-Lind and Shelden 1992, p. 77; see also Chesney-Lind 1989; Daly 1989; Miller 1986; Richie 1995; Steffensmeier 1980).

Patriarchal power relations shape gender differences in crime (see Chapter Six by Dougherty), pushing women into crime through victimization, role entrapment, economic marginality, and survival needs. Nowhere is the gender ratio more skewed than in the great disparity of males as offenders and females as victims of sexual and domestic abuse. Rather than equality between the sexes leading to more female crime, it is female *in*equality and economic vulnerability that most shape female offending patterns. For example, recent increases in property crimes among females is due not so much (if at all) to workforce gains but to adverse economic pressures on women that have been aggravated by heightened rates of divorce, illegitimacy, and female-headed households, coupled with greater responsibility for children.

The "liberated female crook" hypothesis also is undermined by the prevalence of traditional gender-role definitions among most male and female offenders (Bottcher 1995). A few studies report a relationship between non-traditional or masculine gender-role attitudes and female delinquency on a given item but not on other items (Heimer 1995; Shover et al. 1979; Simpson and Ellis 1995). The bulk of studies, however, report that traditional rather than nontraditional views are associated with greater delinquency (see reviews in Chesney-Lind and Shelden 1992; Pollock-Byrne 1990; Steffensmeier and Allan 1995).

In addition to increased economic insecurity among large subgroups of adolescent girls and adult women within the overall female population, several other factors—including the increased formalization of law enforcement, increased opportunities for "female" types of crime, and trends in female drug dependency—help explain gains in the female percentage of arrests in some offense categories (e.g., other assaults, fraud).

Increased Formalization of Law Enforcement. Some increases in female arrests may have been an artifact of improved records processing that provided more complete tabulation of female arrests for some categories of arrest, particularly during the 1960s. Also, the expanded use of informants has increased the utility of female suspects who are charged with offenses as a pressure point for gaining incriminating evidence against male offenders with whom they are associated, particularly for male-dominated crimes such as burglary, robbery, fencing stolen property, and drug dealing (Steffensmeier and Terry 1986; Commonwealth of Pennsylvania 1991). Additionally, changes in laws and enforcement toward targeting less serious forms of lawbreaking (e.g., lowering the blood alcohol content in arrests for DUI; broadening the definition of "assault" to include minor scrapes and trivial acts of hitting, scratching, etc.) has increased the risk of arrest for female offenders. The ability of authorities to dip more deeply into the pool of offenders will tend to increase the female share of arrests, because females tend to be involved disproportionately in the less serious forms of lawbreaking even within a specific offense category. How changes in the organizational management of crime have affected female arrest patterns for assault is reflected in this quote from a veteran police officer.

> We [the police] bust people for assault a lot quicker today than we used to. Whole lot quicker. Especially women. If it's a domestic case involving a man and a woman, or one female fighting with another female over a boyfriend, chances are the lady will be arrested. Even if she is the one reporting a domestic violence situation but the guy claims that she threw things at him or scratched him bad, then we'd be inclined to arrest them both. Same with two ladies who get into a

scuffle—one hits the other or pulls her hair, if there is a complaint, we'd arrest one or maybe both of them. Years ago, we didn't do that. Maybe charge disorderly or just give them a warning. Another example is "resisting arrest"—say it's a man or woman who is stopped for a traffic violation or whatever, maybe the person is drinking and hassles the officer, maybe there is some pushing or shoving. More and more times today, the officer will tack on an assault charge. On account of society being so uptight about violence, it's a different ballgame today—you can get busted for assaulting someone, even aggravated assault, very easily. The same thing is happening in some other areas like driving while drinking—the surveillance and the amount needed to be "under the influence" has changed, so there are more arrests but is there really more drunk driving?

Increased Opportunities for "Female" Types of Crime. The increased female percent of arrests for (minor) property crimes reflects not only economic marginalization, but also an increase in opportunities for these crime categories (Steffensmeier 1993). Largely excluded from lucrative forms of crime (Steffensmeier 1983) female increases in share of arrests for economically motivated crimes have come largely in those categories that (1) require little or no criminal "skill"; (2) have expanded due to changes in merchandising and credit; and (3) are easily accessible to women in their roles as consumers and heads of families. Together, growing economic adversity among large subgroups of women has increased the pressure to commit consumer-based crimes (likewise expanding) such as shoplifting, check fraud, theft of services, and welfare fraud.

Trends in Female Drug Dependency. Rising levels of illicit drug use by females appear to have had a major impact on female crime trends, even though female drug arrests have not outpaced male arrests over the past several decades. Drug dependency amplifies income-generating crimes of both sexes, but more so for females because they face greater constraints against crime and need a greater motivational push to deviate (Anglin and Hser 1987; Inciardi et al. 1993). Female involvement in burglary and robbery, in particular, typically occurs after addiction and is likely to be abandoned when drug use ceases (Anglin and Hser 1987).

Drug use is also more likely to initiate females into the underworld and criminal subcultures and to connect them to drug-dependent males who use them as crime accomplices or exploit them as "old ladies" to support their addiction (Miller 1986; Pettiway 1987, Steffensmeier and Terry 1986). The drug trends also help explain the small rise in the female percentage of incarcerated felons, from about 3 percent in the 1960s to 6 percent in the 1990s (but compare to 6 percent in the 1920s).

Other Evidence of Female Offending

Evidence from other sources corroborates the relatively low female involvement in serious offending and also shows more stability than change in female crime relative to male crime over the past several decades. Data from the *National Crime Victim Survey* (NCVS)—in which victims of personal crimes like robbery and assault are asked the sex of offender—reveal female-to-male totals that turn out to be quite close to those found in Uniform Crime Reports (UCR) data (Bureau of Justice Statistics 1994). In 1994, for example, women are reported to be responsible for about 8 percent of robberies, 12 percent of aggravated assaults, 15 percent of simple assaults, 5 percent of burglaries, and 5 percent of motor vehicle thefts reported by victims. These percentages have held unchanged since the NCVS began in the mid-1970s.

The pattern of a higher female share of offending for mild forms of lawbreaking and a much lower share for serious offenses is confirmed by the numerous self-report studies in which persons (generally juveniles) have been asked to report on their own offenses (Canter 1982; Steffensmeier and Allan 1996). These results hold both for prevalence of offending (the percent of the male and female samples that report any offending) and especially for the frequency of offending (the number of crimes an active offender commits in a given period). Gender differences are smallest for offenses such as shoplifting and minor drug use.

Statistics on males and females incarcerated in state and federal prisons reveal that from roughly the mid-1920s to the present, the female percentage of the total prison population varied between 3 and 6 percent. The female percentage was about 5 percent in the 1920s, about 3 percent in the 1960s, and is about 6 percent today. As with male incarceration rates, female rates have risen very sharply—more than tripled—over the past two decades. Most women in prison today were convicted of homicide and assault (usually against spouse, lover, or child) and increasingly in recent years for drug offenses or for property crimes that are often drug related. A much larger percentage of female new court commitments than of male new court commitments are entering prison today for a drug offense. Also, a higher percentage of female prison inmates than male inmates was under the influence of drugs or alcohol at the time of the offense (Greenfeld and Minor-Harper 1991).

Studies of gang participation indicate that girls have long been members of gangs (Thrasher 1927), and some girls today continue to solve their problems of gender, race, and class through gang participation. At issue is not their presence but the extent and form of their participation. Early studies, based on information from male gang informants, depicted female gang members as playing secondary roles as cheerleaders or camp followers, and ignored girls' occasionally violent behavior.

Recent studies, which rely more on female gang informants, indicate that girls' roles in gangs have been considerably more varied than early stereotypes would have it. Although female gang members continue to be dependent on male gangs, the girls' status is determined as much or even more so by her female peers (Campbell 1984). Also, relative to the past, girls in gangs appear to be fighting in more arenas and even using many of the same weapons as males, and the gang context may be an important source of initiating females into patterns of violent offending. The aggressive rhetoric of some female gang members notwithstanding, their actual behavior continues to display considerable deference to male gang members, avoidance of excessive violence, and adherence to traditional gender-scripted behaviors (Campbell 1990; Chesney-Lind and Shelden 1992; Swart 1991). Ganging is still a predominantly male phenomenon (roughly 85 percent). The most common form of female gang involvement has remained as auxiliaries or branches of male gangs (Miller 1980; Swart 1991), and females are excluded from most of the economic criminal activity (Bowker et al. 1980).

Research on criminal careers—the longitudinal sequence of crimes committed by an individual offender—has become an increasing focus of criminology. The limited research comparing male and female criminal careers is limited mainly to violent career offenders and has found substantial gender variation: (1) although violent offenses comprise only a small percentage of all the offenses committed by offenders in any population, females participate in substantially less violent crime than males during the course of their criminal careers; (2) the careers of violent females both begin and peak a little earlier than those of males; (3) females are far less likely than males to repeat their violent offenses; and (4) females are far more likely to desist from further violence (see reviews in Denno 1994; Kruttschnitt 1994; Weiner 1989). In brief, long-term involvement in crime—an extensive criminal career—is extremely rare or virtually nonexistent within the female offender population.

Case studies and interviews, even with serious female offenders, indicate no strong commitment to criminal behavior (Arnold 1989; Bottcher 1995; Miller 1986). This finding stands in sharp contrast to the commitment and self-identification with crime and the criminal lifestyle that is often found among male offenders (Sutherland 1924; Prus and Sharper 1977; Steffensmeier 1986; Commonwealth of Pennsylvania 1991). Case studies also show, for example, that the career paths of female teens who drift into criminality are typically a consequence of running away from sexual and physical abuse at home (see Chapter Two by Belknap and Holsinger). The struggle to survive on the streets may then lead to other status offenses and crimes (Gilfus 1992; Chesney-Lind 1989), including prostitution and drug dealing (English 1993). Especially when drug abuse is involved, other criminal involvements are likely to escalate (Anglin and Hser 1987; Inciardi et al. 1993). Other researchers have chronicled how female vulnerability to male violence may drive women into illegal activities (Miller 1986; Richie 1995). Despite histories of victimization or economic hardship, many of these women display considerable innovation and independence in their "survival strategies" (Mann 1984).

Finally, female involvement in professional and organized crime continues to lag far behind male involvement. Women are hugely underrepresented in traditionally male-dominated associations that engage in large-scale burglary, fencing operations, gambling enterprises, and racketeering. The 1990 report on organized crime and racketeering activities in the state of Pennsylvania during the 1980s revealed that only a handful of women were major players in large-scale gambling and racketeering, and their involvement was a direct spin-off of association with a male figure (i.e., the woman was a daughter, spouse, or sister). Moreover, the extent and character of women's involvement was comparable to their involvement during the 1960s and 1970s (Commonwealth of Pennsylvania 1991).

EXPLAINING FEMALE OFFENDING

Most theories of crime were developed by male criminologists to explain male crime. Recent decades have seen a lively debate concerning whether such theories are equally useful in explaining female crime, or whether female crime can only be explained by gender-specific theories.

Some criminologists argue that the "traditional" theories are in fact male-specific theories and therefore not well-suited to the explanation of female crime. We take the position that, in spite of their androcentric origins, traditional structural and social process theories are more or less gender neutral. These theories are as useful in understanding overall female crime as they are in understanding overall male crime. They can also help explain why female crime rates are so much lower than male rates.

On the other hand, we also contend that many of the subtle and profound differences between female and male offending patterns may be better understood by a gendered approach. To illustrate the underlying issues a bit more clearly, let us take a brief look at the so-called "traditional" theories and how they can be used to explain female crime and the gender gap in crime.

Approaches like anomie theory and conflict theory suggest that structural factors such as poverty and inequality, particularly in the face of societal emphasis on success/profits, underlie much of conventional crime. Consistent with these approaches, both male and female criminals come disproportionately from the ranks of the poor and disadvantaged. These approaches would explain the gender gap in crime as a consequence of the lesser relevance of success/profit goals to women compared to men.

Social process approaches like differential association theory and labeling theory tend to explain conventional crime in terms of differential opportunities for the learning of criminal values and skills; or in terms of self-fulfilling prophecy effects of labels imposed by social control processes. Such theories would explain the gender gap as a consequence of lower access by females to criminal learning opportunities and/or the greater consistency between male stereotypes and negative behavioral labels.

Control theory argues that weak social bonds account for much crime. Consistent with this approach, both male and female delinquents and criminals come disproportionately from dysfunctional families, have lower levels of academic achievement, or exhibit other evidence of having weak stakes in conformity. The gender gap would be explained by greater female socialization toward bonding behavior.

The utility of the traditional theories is supported by evidence of considerable overlap in the causes of female and male crime. First, like males, female offenders (especially those with frequent contact with criminal justice agencies) come from social backgrounds that disproportionately involve low-income, poor education, and minority status (see reviews in Chesney-Lind and Shelden 1992; Denno 1994; Steffensmeier and Allan 1995). The key difference is that female offenders are more likely to have dependent children (see Chapter Fifteen by Zaplin and Dougherty).

Second, evidence that female rates respond to the same societal forces as male rates is also found in the close parallel between female rates and male rates across time, offense categories, social groupings, or geographic areas: female rates are high where male rates are high, and low where male rates are low (Steffensmeier and Allan 1988; Steffensmeier et al. 1989; Steffensmeier and Haynie 1998).

Third, both aggregate and self-report studies identify structural correlates that are similar for female and male crime; and causal factors identified by traditional theories of crime such as anomie, social control, and differential association appear equally applicable to female and male offending (Steffensmeier and Allan 1996). Measures of bonds, associations, learning, parental controls, perceptions of risk, and so forth have comparable effects across the genders.

In the face of such evidence, a gender-specific theory of female crime appears unnecessary at best, a hindrance at worst. On the other hand, while existing theories help understand female and male crime at a general level, they are less adept at explaining a number of persistent differences between female and male offending patterns. Compared to male offenders, females are far less likely to commit serious crimes (whether against persons or property) or to participate in or to lead criminal groups. When involved with others, women typically act as accomplices to males who both organize and lead the execution of crime; more organized and highly lucrative crimes are dominated overwhelmingly by males (Steffensmeier 1983; Daly 1989; Commonwealth of Pennsylvania 1991).

Additionally, females are far more likely than males to be motivated by relational concerns and to require a higher level of provocation before turning to crime. Situational pressures such as threatened loss of value relationships play a greater role in female offending. The saying, "She did it all for love" is sometimes overplayed in reference to female offending, but the role of men in initiating women into crime—especially serious crime—is a consistent finding across research (Gilfus 1992; Miller 1986; Pettiway 1987; Steffensmeier and Terry 1986). Similarly, "doing crime for one's kids or family" plays a greater role in female than male offending (Daly 1994; Miller 1986; Steffensmeier 1983; Zeitz 1981). Such findings also suggest that women are not necessarily less risk-oriented than men, but that women's risk-taking is less prone to lawbreaking and more protective of relationships and emotional commitments. These issues are discussed in detail in Chapter Five.

Further, although many factors are as predictive of female as male offending, female offenders are more likely to have been victims of abuse as children or adults, and they are more likely to have had records of neurological and other biological or psychological abnormalities. Female felons nevertheless tend to be more conventional in other aspects of their life—more likely to have greater responsibilities for children, commitment to education or job training, legitimate sources of income, and so forth—and thus more amenable to rehabilitation or reform (Daly 1994; Steffensmeier et al. 1993).

These and other differences in female and male offending patterns often involve subtle issues of context that are not well explained by other theories and that are nearly invisible to quantitative analysis. However, both traditional criminological literature and recent feminist analyses provide a wealth of qualitative data that illuminate such contextual issues.

TOWARD A GENDERED THEORY OF FEMALE OFFENDING

A gendered theory (Steffensmeier and Allan 1995, 1996) can advance our knowledge not only of female crime but of male crime as well (although this chapter focuses on female crime). A gendered theory is quite different from gender-specific theories that propose causal patterns for female crime that are distinctly different from theories of male crime.

Rather, both female and male crime may be better understood by taking into account the ways in which the continued profound differences between the lives of women and men shape the different patterns of female and male offending. The traditional theories shed little light on the specific ways in which gender differences in the type, frequency, and context of criminal behavior are shaped by differences in the lives of men and women.

Gender differences in crime may be better understood by taking into account gender differences in at least four key elements:

1. The organization of gender (differences in norms, moral development, social control, and relational concerns, as well as reproductive, sexual, and other physical differences).
2. Access to criminal opportunity (underworld sexism, differences in access to skills, crime associates, and settings).
3. Motivation for crime (differences in taste for risk, self-control, costs-benefits, stressful events, and relational concerns).
4. The context of offending (differences in the circumstances of particular offenses, such as setting, victim-offender relationship, use of weapons).

We elaborate on each of these four areas below. Figure 1–1 provides a graphic depiction of how these elements interact to mold gender differences in crime.

The Organization of Gender

We use the term "organization of gender" to refer broadly to many areas of social life that differ markedly by gender. Coupled with differences in physical and sexual characteristics, the organization of gender blunts the probability of crime on the part of women but increases that probability for men.

At least five areas of life tend not only to inhibit female crime and encourage male crime, but also to shape the patterns of female offending that do occur:

1. gender norms
2. moral development and relational concerns

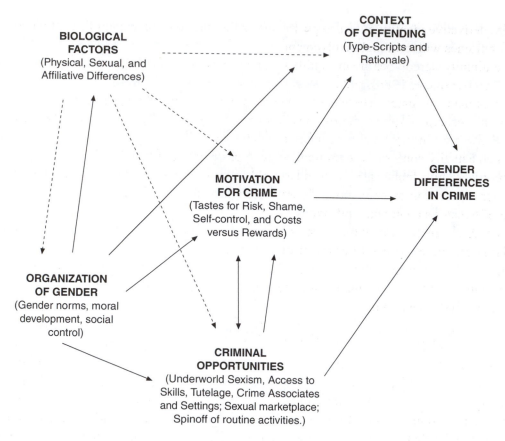

Figure 1–1 Gendered model of female offending and gender differences in crime. Broken line indicates weak effect; solid line signifies strong effect.

3. social control
4. physical strength and aggression
5. sexuality

These five areas overlap and mutually reinforce one another. They also condition gender differences in motivations, criminal opportunities, and contexts of offending.

Gender Norms

Female criminality is inhibited by two powerful focal concerns ascribed to women: (1) role obligations and the presumption of female nurturance; (2) expectations of female beauty and sexual virtue. Such focal concerns pose constraints on female opportunities for illicit endeavors. Women, much more than men, are rewarded for building and maintaining relationships and for nurturance of family, and the constraints posed by child-rearing responsibilities are obvious. Moreover, female identity often derives from that of the males in their lives. If those males are conventional, female deviance is restrained. On the other hand, derivative identity may also push females into the roles of accomplices of husbands or boyfriends with criminal involvements.

Femininity stereotypes are the antithesis of those qualities valued in the criminal subculture (Steffensmeier 1986), and crime is almost always more destructive of life chances for females than for males. The cleavage between what is considered feminine and what is criminal is sharp—crime is almost always stigmatizing for females—whereas the dividing line between what is considered masculine and what is criminal is often thin. Whether women actually conform to femininity stereotypes is irrelevant. Male acceptance of such stereotypes limits female access to underworld opportunities by virtue of being subjected to greater supervision by conventional parents and husbands as well as by criminal devaluation of females as potential colleagues.

Female internalization of the same stereotypes heightens fear of sexual victimization and reduces female exposure to criminal opportunity through avoidance of bars, nighttime streets, and other crime-likely locations (McCarthy and Hagan 1992; Steffensmeier 1983). Expectations of female sexuality also shape the deviant roles available to women, such as sexual media or service roles.

Moral Development and Amenability to Affiliation

Compared to men, women are more likely to refrain from crime due to concern for others. This may result from gender differences in moral development (Gilligan 1982) and from socialization toward greater empathy, sensitivity to the needs of others, and fear of separation from loved ones. From an early age, females are encouraged to cultivate interpersonal skills that will prepare them for their roles as wives and mothers (Beutel and Marini 1995; Brody 1985; Rossi 1984).

This predisposition toward an "ethic of care" restrains women from violence and other behavior that may injure others or cause emotional hurt to those they love. Such complex concerns also influence the patterns and contexts of crime when women do offend.

Men, on the other hand, are more socialized toward status-seeking behavior. When they feel those efforts are blocked, they may develop an amoral ethic in which the ends justify the means. The likelihood of aggressive criminality is especially heightened among men who have been marginalized from the world of work, but such individuals may be found in the suites as well as on the streets. Their view of the world becomes one in which "people are at each other's throats increasingly in a game of life that has no moral rules" (Messerschmidt 1986, p. 66).

Social Control

The ability and willingness of women to commit crime is powerfully constrained by social control. Particularly during their formative years, females are more closely supervised and their misbehavior discouraged through negative sanctions. Risk-taking behavior that is rewarded among boys is censured among girls. Girls' associates are more carefully monitored, reducing the potential for influence by delinquent peers (Giordano et al. 1986), while attachments to conventional peers and adults are nurtured. Even as adults, women find their freedom to explore worldly temptations constricted (Collins 1992).

Physical Strength and Aggression

The weakness of women relative to men—whether real or perceived—puts them at a disadvantage in a criminal underworld that puts a premium on physical power and violence. Muscle and physical prowess are functional not only for committing crimes, but also for protection, contract enforcement, and recruitment and management of reliable associations.

Females may be perceived by themselves or by others as lacking the violent potential for successful completion of certain types of crime, or for protection of a major "score." This can help account for the less serious and less frequent nature of female crime. Female criminals sometimes deliberately restrict themselves to hustling small amounts of money in order not to attract predators. Perceived vulnerability can also help explain female offending patterns such as women's greater restriction to roles as solo players, or to dependent roles as subordinate accomplices, as in the exigencies of prostitute-pimp dependency (James 1977).

Sexuality

Reproductive-sexual differences, coupled with the traditional "double standard," contribute to higher male rates of sexual deviance and infidelity. They also reinforce the gender differences in social control described above. On the other hand, the demand for illicit sex creates opportunities for women for criminal gain through prostitution. This in turn may reduce the need for women to seek financial returns through serious property crimes that remain a disproportionately male realm.

At the same time that male stereotypes of female sexuality open certain criminal opportunities for women, within criminal groups these same stereotypes close opportunities for women that are not organized around female attributes. The sexual tensions that may be aroused by the presence of a woman in a criminal group may force her to protect herself through sexual alignment with one man, becoming "his woman."

Despite our reference to prostitution as a criminal opportunity that women may exploit, it is of course a criminal enterprise that is controlled by men. Pimps, clients, police, and businessmen who employ prostitutes; all control in various ways the working conditions of prostitutes, and virtually all are men.

Access to Criminal Opportunity

All the above factors contrive to limit female access to criminal opportunity and to shape the patterns of female crime. Limits on female access to legitimate opportunities put further constraints on their criminal opportunities, because women are less likely to hold jobs such as truck driver, dockworker, or carpenter, that would provide opportunities for theft, drug dealing, fencing, and other illegal activities. In contrast, abundant opportunities exist for women to commit and/or to be caught and arrested for petty forms of theft and fraud, for low-level drug dealing, and sex-for-sale offenses.

Like the upperworld, the underworld has its glass ceiling. The scarcity of women in the top ranks of business and politics limits their chance for involvement in price fixing conspiracies, financial fraud, and corruption. If anything, women face even greater occupational segregation in underworld crime groups—whether syndicates or more loosely structured organizations (Steffensmeier 1983; Commonwealth of Pennsylvania 1991). Just as in the legitimate world, women face discrimination at every stage from selection and recruitment to opportunities for mentoring, skill development, and, especially, rewards.

Motivation

The same factors that restrict criminal opportunities for women also limit the subjective willingness of women to engage in crime. Gender norms, social control, lack of strength, and moral and relational concerns all contribute to gender differences in criminal motivation: tastes for risk, likelihood of shame, level of self-control, and assessment of costs and benefits of crime.

Although motivation is different from opportunity, opportunity can amplify motivation. Being able tends to make one more willing. The opposite is also true. Female as well as male offenders tend to be drawn to those criminal activities that are easy, within their skill repertoire, a good payoff, and low risk.

Women have risk-taking preferences and styles that differ from those of men (Hagan 1989; Steffensmeier 1980; Steffensmeier and Allan 1995). Men will take risks in order to build status or gain competitive advantage, while women may take greater risks to protect loved ones or to sustain relationships. Overall level of criminal motivation is suppressed in women by their greater ability to foresee threats to life chances and by the relative unavailability of female criminal type scripts that could channel their behavior.

Context of Offending

Female and male offending patterns differ profoundly in their contexts. "Context" refers to the circumstances and characteristics of a particular criminal act (Triplett and Myers 1995), such as the setting, presence of other offenders, the relationship between offender and victim, the offender's role in initiating and committing the offense, weapon (if any), the level of injury or property loss/destruction, and purpose of the offense.

Even when the same offense is charged, the "gestalt" of offending is often dramatically different for females and males (Daly 1994; Steffensmeier 1983, 1993). Moreover, female/male contextual differences increase with the seriousness of the offense.

Spousal murders provide a striking example of the importance of context. The proposition that wives have as great a potential for violence as husbands has had some currency among criminologists (Steinmetz and Lucca 1988; Straus and Gelles 1990). Although in recent years husbands have only comprised about one-fourth of spousal victims, the female share of offending has approached one-half in earlier decades. But, as Dobash, et al. (1992) observe, the context of spousal violence differs dramatically for wives and husbands. Wives are far more likely to have been victims, and turn to murder only when in mortal fear, after exhausting alternatives. Husbands who murder wives, however, have rarely been in fear for their lives. Rather, they are more likely to be motivated by rage at suspected infidelity, and the murder often culminates a period of prolonged abuse of their wives. Some patterns of wife killing are almost never found when wives kill husbands: murder-suicides, family massacres, and stalking.

Another area where female prevalence often approximates that of males is in common forms of delinquency such as simple theft or assault. Here again we find important contextual differences: girls are far less likely to use a weapon or intend serious injury (Kruttschnitt 1994), to steal things they cannot use (Cohen 1966), to break into buildings, or steal from building sites (Mawby 1980).

Similarly, with traditional male crimes like burglary, females are less likely to be solitary (Decker, et al. 1993), more likely to be an accomplice, and less likely to share equally in the rewards ((Steffensmeier and Terry 1986). Females more often engage in burglaries that are unplanned, in residences where they have been before as maid or friend but where no one is at home (Steffensmeier 1986, 1993).

UTILITY OF GENDERED PERSPECTIVE

The real test of any approach is in its ability to predict and explain female (and male) offending patterns as well as gender differences in crime. In general, the perspective correctly predicts that female participation is: highest for those crimes that are most consistent with traditional gender norms and for which females have greater opportunity; and lowest for those crimes that diverge the most from traditional norms and for which females have little opportunity.

The potential contributions of this gendered approach can be illustrated with examples of property, violent, and public order offending patterns.

Among property crimes, two offenses that are consistent with the traditional female roles of family shopping include shoplifting, misuse of credit cards, and bad checks, categories (larceny, fraud, forgery) for which the percent of female arrests is very high. The pink collar ghetto—the high concentration (90 percent) of women in low-level bank teller and bookkeeping positions—helps account for the high female percent of arrests for embezzlement. Embezzlement arrests are less likely to occur among higher-level accountants or auditors where women are less represented in employment (less than half). The perspective also correctly predicts gender differences in motives for embezzlement: women tend to embezzle to protect their families or relationships, while men are more often trying to protect their status (Zeitz 1981).

A gendered approach also correctly predicts the low level of female involvement in serious property crimes, whether on the "streets" or in the "suites" (Steffensmeier and Allan 1995). Such crimes are most at odds with female stereotypes and/or present few opportunities for female participation. When women do engage in such crimes, the "take" is likely to be small, or they are acting as accomplices (as is the case with female burglaries, described above). Solo robberies by women typically involve small sums, such as "wallet-sized" thefts by prostitutes or addicts (James 1977; see also Covington 1985; Pettiway, 1987). As accomplices, female roles in robberies often simultaneously exploit their sexuality (e.g., as decoys) and reinforce male domination (American Correctional Association 1983; Miller, 1986; Steffensmeier and Terry 1986).

Lack of opportunity helps explain the negligible female involvement in serious white collar crime (Daly 1989; Steffensmeier 1983). Female representation in high-level finance, corporate leadership, and politics, is simply too limited to provide much chance for women to become involved in insider trading, price-fixing, restraint of trade, toxic waste dumping, fraudulent product production, bribery, official corruption, or large-scale governmental crimes such as the Iran-Contra affair or the Greylord scandal. In lower-level occupations, even where women have the criminal opportunities, they are less likely to commit crime.

Our discussion above of gender differences in spousal murders provides an example of how our gendered approach can advance the understanding of female violence. Other forms of female violence are also shaped by the organization of gender. Female violence is less likely to be directed at strangers, and female murders of strangers or even casual acquaintances are rare. Victims of women are likely to be either a male intimate or a child. Furthermore, violent women are likely to commit their offenses within the home against a drunk victim, and they frequently cite self-defense or depression as their motive (Dobash, et al. 1992). Women appear to require greater provocation to reach the point they are willing to commit murder.

In the area of public order offenses, the gendered paradigm can predict with considerable accuracy those categories with a high percent female involvement, particularly prostitution and juvenile runaways, the only categories where the rate of female arrests exceeds that of males (see Chapter Two for more discussion of this issue). These are easily accounted for by gender differences in the marketability of sexual services and the patriarchal double standard. For example, customers must greatly outnumber prostitutes, yet they are less likely to be sanctioned. Similarly, concerns about sexual involvement increase the probability of arrest for female runaways, even though self-report data show that actual male runaway rates are just as high (Chesney-Lind and Shelden 1992).

The organization of gender also shapes gender differences in substance abuse. The importance of relational concerns are reflected in the fact that women are often introduced to drugs by husbands or boyfriends (Inciardi, et al. 1993; Pettiway 1987). Female abuse patterns reflect less integration into drug subcultures or the underworld (Department of Health and Human Services 1984). Because women typically are less likely to have other criminal involvements before addiction, the crime amplification effects are greater in terms of being driven to theft or other income-generating crimes by the need for money to purchase drugs. As the paradigm would predict, female addict crimes are likely to be nonviolent (Anglin and Hser 1987).

Although we have concentrated on demonstrating the utility of a gendered paradigm in explaining female crime, it can do the same for male crime. For example, violence draws on and affirms masculinity, just as prostitution draws on and affirms femininity. For both men and women, "doing gender" can direct criminal behavior into scripted paths (although for women it more often pre-empts criminal involvement altogether).

As both women and men move increasingly into nontraditional roles, it will be difficult to predict the impact on levels and types of criminal involvement. Because traditional female stereotypes appear to constrain most women from crime, some have been tempted to predict that female crime rates would increase to the level of male crime rates as women's roles become more like those of men. However, entrapment in traditional roles may actually increase the likelihood of criminal involvement for some women. For example, it is wives playing traditional roles in patriarchal relationships who appear to be at greatest risk, not just for victimization but also for committing spousal homicide. Similarly, emotionally dependent women are more easily persuaded by criminal men to "do it all for love." Among gypsies, where traditional gender roles prevail and male dominance is absolute, gypsy women do practically all the work and earn most of the money, and the culture dictates a large female-to-male involvement in thievery (Maas 1973).

CONCLUSION

Our knowledge about fundamental issues in the study of gender and crime has expanded greatly with the proliferation of studies over the past several decades, although significant gaps still exist. Our coverage of patterns and etiology of female offending has necessarily been selective and cursory. We conclude by restating and enlarging on some key points.

Women are far less likely to be involved in serious crime, regardless of data source, level of involvement, or measure of participation. The girls and women who make up the bulk of the criminal justice workload involving the female offender (and are the grist of female offender programs) commit ordinary crimes—mostly minor thefts and frauds, low-level drug dealing, prostitution, and simple assaults against their mates or children. They are likely to have at least one adult conviction for theft, prostitution, or drug/alcohol involvement but return to further crime commission afterward. Some of them commit crime over several years and serve multiple jail or prison terms in the process. But they are not career criminals.

Oftentimes the lives of many of these women are intertwined with the men who are persistent thieves or, in other ways, are "losers." Along with their children, these men are the principal focus of these women's lives. The world of these men tends to be an extremely patriarchal one in which women are relegated to subordinate roles. Exploited or treated with indifference by their male partners, the women lead lives that often are miserable and difficult. Routinely, it is they who are left to cope with the consequences of men's unsuccessful escapades and the incarceration these can bring.

Despite some shifts in attitudes toward greater acceptance of women working and combining career and family, the two major focal concerns of women, beauty and sexual virtue and nurturant role obligations, persist. For example: Though increasingly represented in the labor force, women continue to be concentrated in traditional "pink collar"—teaching, clerical and retail sales work, nursing, and other subordinate and "help-mate" roles—that reflect a persistence of traditional gender roles. In fact, the number of occupations that are filled largely or exclusively by women—nearly always at lower salaries than "male" occupations—has actually increased in recent years.

There has been little change over the past several decades in: gender-typing in children's play activities and play groups (Fagot and Leinbach 1983; Stoneman et al. 1984; Maccoby 1985); the kinds of personality characteristics that both men and women associate with each sex (Leuptow and Garovitch 1992; Simmons and Blyth 1987); the importance placed on the physical attractiveness of women and their pressure to conform to an ideal of beauty or "femininity" (Leuptow and Garovitch 1992); risk-taking preferences and value orientations toward competition versus cooperation, and so forth (Beutel and Marini 1995).

The most significant evidence, perhaps, that core elements of gender roles and relationships have changed little is the continuing dominance of women as "caretakers"—for the sick, elderly parents, children, and so forth. At the group level, women today are more responsible for child rearing than two or three decades ago. The "degendering" of family roles—in which fathers and mothers share breadwinning and caregiving roles equally—has not gone smoothly. Men have increased their participation in child care over the last 30 years, but the amount of change has been small (Coltrane 1995, Amato 1996). A more significant trend is the rise in single-mother households (due to increases in divorce and nonmarital birth) that has reduced the amount of time that men spend living with children over the life course (Eggebeen and Uhlenberg 1985). Furthermore, many nonresident fathers see their children infrequently and pay no child support or less than they should (Seltzer and Bianchi 1988; Furstenberg 1988). A recent review of the research in the area concludes as follows: "Increasingly, American children are being raised with little or no assistance from fathers. These changes in behavior and family structure have led to a contradictory situation. At a time when some men are becoming more involved with children, men (as a group) are spending *less* time with children than ever before" (Amato 1996, p. 2).

A growing body of historical research indicates that the gender differences in quality and quantity of crime described here closely parallel those that have prevailed since at least the 13th century (Beattie 1975; Hanawalt 1979). Even where variability does exist across time, the evidence suggests that changes in the female percentage of offending (1) are limited mainly to minor property crimes or mild forms of delinquency (Hagan 1989; Steffensmeier 1980, 1993; and (2) are due to structural changes other than more equalitarian gender roles such as shifts in economic marginality of women, expanded availability of female-type crime opportunities, and greater formalization of social control (Beattie 1995;

Steffensmeier 1993). The considerable stability in the gender gap for offending can be explained in part by historical durability of the organization of gender and by underlying physical/sexual differences (whether actual or perceived). Human groups, for all their cultural variation, follow basic human forms.

The gendered perspective that we offered has implications both for understanding the nature of female offending and for developing female offender programs. Both theory and programmatic approaches to female offenders should include at least four key elements. The first is the need to take into account how the organization of gender deters or shapes delinquency by females but encourages it by males. We use the term "organization of gender" to refer broadly to gendered-norms, identities, arrangements, institutions, and relations by which human sexual dichotomy is transformed into something physically and socially different.

The second is the need to address not only gender differences in type and frequency of crime, but also differences in the context of offending. Even when men and women commit the same statutory offense, the "gestalt" of their offending is frequently quite different (Daly 1994). The differing gestalt of female offending (and its link to the organization of gender) was reviewed earlier but is further reflected in this comment from an ex-female offender who now works in a drug treatment program for "serious" female offenders:

> A lotta what is called "serious" crime that is committed by women is hardly that. The other day two women were referred because they were busted for armed robbery. What happened is, they were shoplifting and had a guy as a partner. The security person spotted them and confronted them as they is [sic] leaving the store. This causes the guy partner to spray the security man with mace. They all get away but not before the security man gets the license number of the van they is driving. They all gets arrested—not for shoplifting now but for armed robbery on account of the mace.

> What female robbery there is, is because a guy has them be a distraction or the watcher. Or it's a prostitute who maybe steals from a john, or it's a woman so heavy into dope that she crosses the line. I did a couple of robberies when I was heavy into drugs but it was not my thing. Selling dope, shoplifting, and prostitution were my main activities. This goes for most of the women I've known who get involved in crime on account of having to support themselves or their kids or some sponge [male] they is hooked up with (personal communication).

Finally, theory and programmatic approaches to female offending need to address several key ways in which women's routes to crime (especially serious crime) may differ from those of men. Building on the work of Daly (1994) and Steffensmeier (1983, 1993), such differences include: (1) the more blurred boundaries between victim and victimization in women's than men's case histories; (2) women's exclusion from the most lucrative crime opportunities; (3) women's ability to exploit sex as an illegal moneymaking service; (4)

consequences (real or anticipated) of motherhood and child care; (5) the centrality of greater relational concerns among women, and the manner in which these both shape and allow women to be pulled into criminal involvements by men in their lives; and (6) the frequent need of these women for protection from predatory or exploitative males.

In sum, recent theory and research on female offending have added greatly to our understanding of how the lives of delinquent girls and women continue to be powerfully influenced by gender-related conditions of life. Profound sensitivity to these conditions is the bedrock for preventive and remedial programs aimed at female offenders.

REFERENCES

Amato, P. 1996, November. More than money? Men's contributions to their children's lives. Paper presented at Men in Families Symposium, The Pennsylvania State University, University Park.

American Correctional Association 1983. *Female inmate classification: An examination of the issues*. Washington, D.C.: Government Printing Office.

Anglin, D., and Hser, Y. 1987. Addicted women and crime. *Criminology* 25: 359–397.

Arnold, R. 1989. Processes of criminalization from girlhood to womanhood. In *Women of color in American society*, eds. Zinn, M., and Dill, B., 88–102. Philadelphia: Temple University Press.

Beattie, J. 1975. The criminality of women in eighteenth century England. In *Women and the law: A social historical perspective*, ed. Weisberg, D.K., 168–191. Cambridge, MA: Schenkman Publishing Co.

Beattie, J. 1995. Crime and inequality in 18th century London. In *Crime and inequality*, eds. Hagan, J., and Peterson, R., 240–273. Stanford, CA: Stanford University Press.

Beutel, A., and Marini, M. 1995. Gender and values. *American Sociological Review* 60: 436–448.

Bottcher, J. 1995. Gender as social control: A qualitative study of incarcerated youths and their siblings in greater Sacramento. *Justice Quarterly* 12: 33–57.

Bowker, L., et al. 1980. Female participation in delinquent gang activities. In *Women and crime in America*, ed. Bowker, L., 158–179. New York: MacMillan Publishing USA.

Brody, L. 1985. Gender differences in emotional development: A review of theories and research. *Journal of Personality* 14:102–149.

Bureau of Justice Statistics 1973–1994. *Criminal victimization in the United States, 1991*. Washington, D.C.: Department of Justice.

Campbell, A. 1984. *The girls in the gang*. Oxford: Basil Blackwell.

Campbell, A. 1990. Female participation in gangs. In *Gangs in America*, ed. Huff, C., 32–55. Newbury Park, CA: Sage Publications.

Canter, R. 1982. Sex differences in delinquency. *Criminology* 20: 373–398.

Chesney-Lind, M. 1986. Women and crime: The female offender. *Signs* 12: 78–96.

Chesney-Lind, M. 1989. Girls' crime and woman's place: Toward a feminist model of female delinquency. *Crime & Delinquency* 35: 5–29.

Chesney-Lind, M., and Shelden, R. 1992. *Girls, delinquency, and juvenile justice*. Pacific Grove, CA: Brooks/Cole Publishing.

Cohen, A. 1966. *Deviance and control*. Englewood Cliffs, NJ: Prentice-Hall.

Collins, R. 1992. Women and the production of status cultures. In *Cultivating differences*, eds. Lamont, M., and Fournier, M., 70–89. Chicago: University of Chicago Press.

Coltrane, S. 1995. The future of fatherhood. In *Fatherhood: Contemporary theory, research, and social policy*, ed. Marsiglio, W., 255–274. Thousand Oaks, CA: Sage Publications.

Commonwealth of Pennsylvania 1991. *Organized crime in Pennsylvania, The 1990 report*. Conshohocken, PA: Pennsylvania Crime Commission.

Covington, J. 1985. Gender differences in criminality among heroin users. *Journal of Research in Crime and Delinquency* 22: 329–353.

Daly, K. 1989. Gender and varieties of white-collar crime. *Criminology* 27: 769–794.

Daly, K. 1994. *Gender, crime and punishment.* New Haven, CT: Yale University Press.

Decker, S. et al. 1993. A woman's place is in the home: Females and residential burglary. *Justice Quarterly* 10: 1–16.

Denno, D. 1994. Gender, crime, and the criminal law defenses. *The Journal of Criminal Law and Criminology* 85: 80–180.

Department of Health and Human Services 1984. *Drug abuse and drug abuse research.* Rockville, MD: National Institute on Drug Abuse.

Dobash, R., et al. 1992. The myth of sexual symmetry in marital violence. *Social Problems* 39: 71–91.

Eggebeen, D., and Uhlenberg, P. 1985. Changes in the organization of men's lives. *Family Relations* 34: 251–257.

English, K. 1993. Self-reported crime rates of women prisoners. *Journal of Quantitative Criminality* 9: 357–382.

Fagot, B., and Leinbach, M. 1983. Play styles in early childhood: Social consequences for boys and girls. In *Social and Cognitive Skills: Sex Roles and Children's Play,* ed. Miss, D., 93–116. New York: Academic Press.

Furstenberg, F. 1988. Good dads-bad dads: Two faces of fatherhood. In *The changing American family and public policy,* ed. Cherlin, A.J., 193–218. Washington, D.C.: Urban Institute.

Gilfus, M. 1992. From victims to survivors to offenders: Women's routes of entry and immersion into street crime. *Women & Criminal Justice* 4: 63–89.

Gilligan, C. 1982. *In a different voice: Psychological theory and women's development.* Cambridge, MA: Harvard University Press.

Giordano, P., et al. 1986. Friendships and delinquency. *American Journal of Sociology* 91: 1170–1203.

Greenfeld, L., and Minor-Harper, S. 1991. *Women in prison.* Washington D.C.: U.S. Department of Justice, Bureau of Justice Statistics

Hagan, J. 1989. *Structural criminology.* New Brunswick, NJ: Rutgers University Press.

Hagan, J., et al. 1993. The power of control in sociological theories of delinquency. In *Advances in criminological theory,* ed. Adler, F., and Laufer, W., 18–34. Vol. 4. New Brunswick, NJ: Transaction.

Hanawalt, B. 1979. *Crime and conflict in English communities, 1300–1348.* Cambridge: Harvard University Press.

Heimer, K. 1994. Gender, race, and the pathways to delinquency: An interactionist explanation. In *Crime and inequality,* eds. Hagan, J., and Peterson, R., 211–234. Stanford, CA: Stanford University Press.

Inciardi, J., et al. 1993. *Women and crack cocaine.* New York: MacMillan Publishing USA

James, J. 1977. Prostitutes and prostitution. In *Deviants: Voluntary action in a hostile world,* eds. Sagarin, E., and Montanino, F., 191–211. New York: Scott, Foresman & Co.

Kruttschnitt, C. 1994. Gender and interpersonal violence. In *Understanding and preventing violence: Social influences,* ed. Roth, J., and Reiss, A., Vol. 3, 295–378. Washington, D.C.: National Academy Press.

Lueptow, L., and Garovich, L. 1992, August. The persistence of sex stereotypes amid the reconstruction of women's role. Paper presented at the annual meeting of the American Sociological Association, Pittsburgh, PA.

Maas, P. 1973. *King of the gypsies.* New York: Bantam.

McCarthy, B., and Hagan, J. 1992. Mean streets: The theoretical significance of situational delinquency and homeless youths. *American Journal of Sociology* 98: 597–627.

Maccoby, E. 1985. Social groupings in childhood: Their relationship to prosocial and antisocial behavior in boys and girls. In *Development of antisocial and prosocial behavior: Theories, research and issues,* eds. Olweus, D., et al., 141–165. New York: Academic Press.

Mann, C. 1984. Female Crime and Delinquency. Birmingham, AL: University of Alabama Press.

Mawby, R. 1980. Sex and crime: The results of a self-report study. *British Journal of Sociology* 31: 525–543.

Messerschmidt, J. 1986. *Capitalism, patriarchy, and crime: Toward a socialist feminist criminology.* Totowa, NJ: Rowman & Littlefield.

Miller, E. 1986. *Street women.* Philadelphia: Temple University Press.

Miller, W. 1980. The molls. In *Women, crime, and justice*, eds. Datesman, S., and Scarpitti, F., 111–119. New York: Oxford University Press.

Pettiway, L. 1987. Participation in crime partnerships by female drug users. *Criminology* 25: 741–767.

Pollock-Byrne, J. 1990. *Women, prison, & crime*. Belmont, CA: Brooks/Cole Publishers.

Prus, R., and Sharper, C.R.D. 1977. *Road hustler*. Lexington, MA: Lexington Books.

Richie, B. 1995. *The gendered entrapment of battered, Black women*. London: Routledge.

Rossi, A. 1984. Gender and parenthood. *American Sociological Review* 49: 1–19.

Seltzer, J., and Bianchi, S. 1988. Children's contact with absent parents. *Journal of Marriage and the Family* 50: 663–677.

Shover, N, et al. 1979. Gender roles and delinquency. *Social Forces* 58: 162–175.

Simmons, R., and Blyth, D. 1987. *Moving into adolescence*. New York: Aldine.

Simpson, S., and Ellis, L. 1995. Doing gender: Sorting out the caste and crime conundrum. *Criminology* 33: 47–77.

Steffensmeier, D. 1980. A review and assessment of sex differences in adult crime, 1965–77. *Social Forces* 58: 1080–1108.

Steffensmeier, D. 1993. National trends in female arrests, 1960–1990: Assessment and recommendations for research. *Journal of Quantitative Criminology* 9: 413–441.

Steffensmeier D. 1983. Sex-segregation in the underworld: Building a sociological explanation of sex differences in crime. *Social Forces* 61: 1010–1032.

Steffensmeier, D. 1986. *The fence: In the shadow of two worlds*. Totowa, NJ: Rowman & Littlefield.

Steffensmeier, D., and Terry, R. 1986. Institutional sexism in the underworld: a view from the inside. *Sociological Inquiry* 56: 304–323.

Steffensmeier, D., and Allan, E. 1988. Sex disparities in crime by population subgroup: residence, race, and age. *Justice Quarterly* 5: 53–80.

Steffensmeier, D., and Allan, E. 1995. Gender, age, and crime. In *Handbook of contemporary criminology*, ed. Sheley, J., 88–116. New York: Wadsworth.

Steffensmeier, D., and Allan, E. 1996. Gender and crime: Toward a gendered theory of female offending. *Annual Review of Sociology* 22: 459–487.

Steffensmeier, D., et al. 1989. Modernization and female crime: A cross-national test of alternative explanations. *Social Forces* 68: 262–283.

Steffensmeier, D., et al. 1993. Gender and imprisonment decisions. *Criminology* 31: 411–446.

Steffensmeier, D., and Haynie, D. 1998. Structural sources of urban female violence: Does gender (and age) make a difference? Paper presented at Annual Meeting of the American Sociological Association, August, San Francisco.

Steinmetz, S., and Lucca, J. 1988. Husband beating. In *Handbook of family violence*. ed. Hassselt, R., et al., 233–246. New York: Plenum Press.

Stoneman, A., et al. 1984. Naturalistic observations of children's activities and roles while playing with their siblings and friends. *Child Development* 55: 617–627.

Straus, M., and Gelles, R. 1990. *Physical violence in American families*. New Brunswick, NJ: Transaction.

Sutherland E. 1924. *Criminology*. Philadelphia: J. B. Lippincott Co.

Swart, W. 1991. Female gang delinquency: A search for "acceptably deviant behavior." *Mid-American Review of Sociology* 15:43–52.

Thrasher, F. 1927. *the Gang*. Chicago: University of Chicago Press.

Triplett, R., and Myers, L. 1995. Evaluating contextual patterns of delinquency: Gender-based differences. *Justice Quarterly* 12: 59–79.

U.S. Department of Justice. 1960–1993. *Uniform crime reports*. Washington, D.C.: Government Printing Office.

Udry, J.R. 1995. Sociology and biology: What biology do sociologists need to know? *Social Forces* 73 :1267–1278.

Weiner, N. 1989. Violent criminal careers and "violent career criminals." In *Violent crime, violent criminals,* eds. Weiner, H., and Wolfgang, M., 35–138. Newbury Park, CA: Sage Publications.

Zeitz, D. 1981. *Women who embezzle or defraud*. New York: Praeger Publishers.

CHAPTER 2

An Overview of Delinquent Girls: How Theory and Practice Have Failed and the Need for Innovative Changes

Joanne Belknap and Kristi Holsinger

Editor's Notes

In terms of theory, Belknap and Holsinger in Chapter Two contend that in order to comprehend the etiology and treatment of female delinquents, it is necessary to understand both the traditional sexist criminological theorizing (prefeminist theories) as well as the more recent feminist research focusing on girls, women, or addressing gender differences (feminist perspectives). The authors contend that the traditional theories are important to understand and acknowledge because they have had a significant impact not only on how scholars have addressed female (and male) offending, but also how girls (and women) have been responded to and treated differently than boys (and men) by professionals in the system, usually to the disadvantage of girls (and women). The authors then introduce a representation of female delinquents that addresses those girls who are most at risk of becoming delinquents. Specifically they delineate the pattern of a girl moving from victim (sexual and/or physical abuse) to survivor (utilizing criminal survival skills such as running away from home, using drugs, and prostitution) to offender. The authors deem this accurate representation is necessary not only because the theories and media have either ignored or misrepresented these girls, but because a realistic impression of them is necessary to most effectively treat them. The chapter also presents an overview and three possible hypotheses regarding the effect of gender on processing alleged offenders—the equal treatment hypothesis, the chivalry hypothesis, and the evil woman hypothesis. The chapter concludes with recommendations to enhance systemic responses to female delinquents. First and foremost, Belknap and Holsinger stress the need for preventive measures aimed at identifying and responding to children from abusive homes. Early intervention with high-risk youths and their families is needed to effectively address their problems and troubled behavior before the cycle of criminality becomes firmly established.

INTRODUCTION

In many ways, the most significant and potentially useful criminological research in recent years has been the recognition of girls' and women's pathways to offending. Specifically, a number of researchers since the 1980s have identified a pattern of female offending that begins with their victimization and eventually results in their offending. Female offenders report an extreme and disproportionate risk for incest, other child sexual and nonsexual abuse, and acquaintance and stranger rapes as adolescents and young women, and battering from intimate male partners. While such an explanation does not fit all female offenders (and also fits some male offenders), the recognition of these risks appears to be essential for understanding the etiology of offending for many girls and women. Yet this link between victimization and offending has largely been invisible or deemed inconsequential by the powers that be in criminology theory-building and by those responsible for responding to women's and girls' victimizations and offenses. The idea that child abuse might be related to subsequent juvenile delinquency is not necessarily new. It is interesting and somewhat disturbing, however, how little attention the child-abuse-victim-to-offender link has received and how it has often focused on boys, even though they are less likely than girls to be victimized. (For an overview of the research on the mainstream child abuse-delinquency connection, see Gray 1988).

It is often difficult to separate offending issues for adult females (women offenders) from childhood and adolescent female offenders (delinquent girls). Indeed, childhood experiences can and often do affect women much later on in their lives. For the purposes of this chapter, the terms *female offender* and *female offending* will be inclusive, referring to females of all ages, both women and girls. The term *delinquent* is meant to specifically represent individuals under the age of 18 years old. Much of the research discussed in this chapter was collected on adult female offenders (women) about their childhood experiences; some was collected directly from delinquent girls. While both types of research are useful, it is significant that only a small portion of this research has been conducted on girls while they are still girls. More research needs to take this approach.

There are four main goals of this chapter. First, in order to comprehend the etiology and treatment of female delinquents, it is necessary to understand both the traditional sexist criminological theorizing (referred to herein as the "prefeminist" theories) as well as the more recent feminist research focusing on girls, women, or addressing gender differences (referred to in this chapter as feminist perspectives). The traditional theories are important to understand and acknowledge because they have had a significant impact not only on how scholars have addressed female (and male) offending, but also how girls (and women) have been responded to and treated differently than boys (and men) by professionals in the system, usually to the disadvantage of girls (and women). The second goal of this chapter is to present an accurate representation of female delinquents, specifically addressing which girls are most at risk of becoming delinquents. This is necessary not only because the theories and media have either ignored or misrepresented these girls, but also because a realistic impression of them is necessary to most effectively treat them. Third, this chapter presents an overview of the systemic processing, treatment, and punishment of alleged female delinquents. Finally, the chapter closes with recommendations regarding improved understanding of delinquent girls in order to enhance systemic responses to them.

THE PREFEMINIST THEORIES

Feminist reviews of criminological theories have pointed to a number of disturbing patterns (see Belknap 1996; Feinman 1986; Leonard 1982; Morris 1987; Naffine 1987; Smart 1976, 1982). The early theorists, such as Lombroso, Freud, and Pollak, basically viewed females as victims of their biological (including psychological) make-up. They proposed that this limited "construction" of women and girls explained gender differences in offending, as well as variations among females regarding who was likely to offend. After these earliest theorists on offending behavior, most other researchers attempting to determine the etiology of crime focused almost exclusively on explaining why *males*, usually boys, offend. To these theorists (e.g., Robert Merton, Albert Cohen, Richard Cloward and Lloyd Ohlin, Edward Sutherland and Donald Cressey, and Howard Becker), females as potential offenders were either invisible (never accounted for), or like their biological theorist predecessors, when they did address female offending, did so in extremely sexist and simplistic manners. The same representations of female offending, either ignoring it and viewing it as inconsequential or presenting interpretations of female offending in a sexist manner, were exhibited by theorists attempting to explain why most people (read males) *follow the law* (as opposed to why some break the law) (e.g., Travis Hirschi and Michael Gottfredson). Even the conflict, radical, and Marxists theorists, for the most part, ignored gender and females (e.g., Ian Taylor, Paul Walton, and Jack Young). In contrast, John Hagan and his colleagues attempted to develop a theory, power-control theory, which included a gender and class analysis of families. This theory is more concerned with the level of equality between youths' parents in predicting their crime, however, than in how parental abuse of these youth might contribute to their offending. Rita Simon's and Freda Adler's theories designed to explain female offending in the 1970s, centered around how gender equality would *increase* female offending, a hypothesis at odds with the existing strain theory, and one that has not been confirmed by research and statistics (Feinman 1986; Steffensmeier and Allen 1988).

The fact that female offending and gender differences simply did not matter to most of these theorists is apparent. Furthermore, the sexist and inaccurate representations of female offenders have been part and parcel of the majority of theories about crime, whether they included females or not. Some of these theorists proposed that their theories were gender-neutral, and yet failed to collect data on girls (or women), or if they did, chose to leave these data out of their analyses (e.g., Hirschi). Moreover, given the recent historical documentation (Odem 1995; Shelden 1981) and present day documentation (e.g., Arnold 1990; Chesney-Lind and Rodriguez, 1983; Daly 1992; Gilfus 1992; Silbert and Pines 1981) of the high risk of incest and other abuse that runaway-come-delinquent girls experience, it is ironic that strain theorists viewed finding boyfriends and husbands as girls' greatest strain. The strains these victimized girls experience(d) are extreme, not only in the actual incident(s) of violation and violence, but also in their often futile reporting of it to the police and others. The strains of basic survival for many abused girls when they run away from these abusive homes are invisible and apparently unknown in traditional strain theorizing. These theorists' contention that the only strain girls experience is finding male mates would be laughable if the ramifications were not so serious. Chesney-Lind's (1989) attempt to model a feminist explanation of delinquency posits:

> The extensive focus on male delinquency and the inattention to the role played by patriarchal arrangements in the generation of adolescent delinquency and conformity has rendered the major delinquency theories fundamentally inadequate to the task of explaining female behavior. There is, in short, an urgent need to rethink current models in light of girls' situation in a patriarchal society (p. 10).

FEMINIST PERSPECTIVES ON FEMALE OFFENDING

A needed and refreshing change to theorizing about female offending has been advanced by feminist scholars in the 1980s and 1990s. These studies identify a pattern among many delinquent and adult female offenders, where childhood victimization (often incest) frequently results in girls, (and some boys,) running away from home. The childhood victimization might also be related to subsequent drug and alcohol use or abuse. Drug selling and prostitution often follow girls' (and boys') running away from home, as means of surviving on the street and/or supporting drug habits. Robbery as a means to survive, and often to support drug addictions, may also occur. Anywhere in this sequence of behaviors, a girl may be criminalized for running away and alcohol use (status offenses), using drugs, selling drugs, robbery, and/or prostituting.

It is worth noting that not *all* sexually abused (or otherwise abused) girls become delinquent. Furthermore, not all delinquent girls are survivors of sexual (and other forms of) abuse. Incarcerated females, however, represent disproportionately high rates of sexual abuse compared to females who have not been incarcerated. For example, Wyatt, et al.'s (1993) review of research on the prevalence of child sexual abuse among "community" (noninstitutionalized) females reported that prevalence rates ranged from 5 to 45 percent among the various studies. Chesney-Lind and Shelden's (1992) review of similar studies on delinquent (noncommunity) girls reported a range of physical and sexual abuse rates from 40 to 73 percent. Finally, Dembo et al. (1992) found that 65 percent of female and 24 percent of male juvenile detainees reported sexual abuse victimization. Thus, although sexual and other abuse does not necessarily result in a girl becoming a delinquent or adult offender, there is no denying the fact that childhood abuse places girls at increased risk of becoming offenders.

Moreover, some of the research discussed below documents these girls' increased risks as adults of being in relationships where they are battered by their intimate male partners, which in turn may lead to their offending. Some of this research documents how battered women may be coerced or forced to commit crimes such as selling drugs, robbing, and prostituting by their abusive male partners. Finally, there is the very real threat of some small portion of these girls (and women) *becoming* quite violent; which is hardly surprising given the extreme violence experienced in their childhoods and the inadequate systemic responses and treatment they received after experiencing such violence. Indeed, many women in the U.S. are in prison for killing or attempting to kill their highly abusive husbands and boyfriends (e.g., Browne 1987; Walker and Browne 1985).

Some of the studies documenting the victimization-to-offending cycle of females draw directly from the girls themselves. The majority of this documentation, however, is through data collected from adult females (women) tracing their childhood and other life-experiences, examining how these experiences might be related to their subsequent criminal activity. Again, it is necessary that more research is conducted in the future on the girls *while* they are still girls, rather than the more common approach of having women recounting childhood experiences. One of the first articles published directly linking women's childhood victimizations with their criminalizations, by Mimi H. Silbert and Ayala M. Pines (1981), was the result of 200 interviews with current and former female prostitutes in the San Francisco Bay area. Notably, the interviewers in this study were former juvenile or adult prostitutes themselves, which enhanced gaining the trust of and credibility with potential interviewees. (All interviewers took part in intensive interviewer training.) No official agency was used to recruit women and girls into the sample; they largely came by word of mouth and Public Service Announcements. The sample ranged in age from 10 to 46 with an average age of 22. The sample was diverse: 69 percent white, 18 percent Black, 11 percent Hispanic, 2 percent American Indian, and 1 percent Asian. Although two-thirds of the sample came from middle or higher income families, almost 90 percent reported their financial situation at the time of the interview as "just making it" or "very poor" (p. 408).

Silbert and Pines' (1981) findings are profound. Sixty percent of the sample reported being sexually abused before the age of 16 (although most were first abused at much younger ages), by an average of two sexual abusers each. Two-thirds of the sexual abuse victims were abused by fathers or father figures (stepfathers, foster fathers, and mothers' common law husbands). "Only" 10 percent of the victims were sexually abused by strangers. The sexual abuse was almost always followed by running away from home, which led to prostitution and other street work. "The average age of starting prostitution was 16…[although] a number were 9, 10, 11, and 12" (1981, p. 410). The authors cite that while the sexual abuse was undoubtedly the main reason for running away from home, the causes listed for running away were a variety of "home problems." "Eighty-nine percent of the juveniles said, 'Needed money; was hungry,' when asked why did they start prostituting. Almost all the juveniles felt they had no other options available to them at the time they started" (p. 410). Silbert and Pines (1981) warn that their findings should not be interpreted as evidence that the majority of sexually abused girls will become prostitutes. Rather, they emphasize the need to stop the "cycle of victimization" by providing the urgently needed "intervention services for juveniles running away from sexually abusive homes before they are solicited for prostitution" (p. 410).

The second study examining childhood victimizations and female offending was published in 1983 by Meda Chesney-Lind and Noelie Rodriguez. They conducted intensive interviews with sixteen incarcerated women. Among their findings was the prevalence of severe nonsexual child abuse experienced by ten of the women. "Clearly these reports of violence and physical brutality go beyond the question of discipline. What was obviously missing from the homes of most of the inmates was affection and physical security" (1983, p. 53). Fourteen (88 percent) of the women reported involvement in prostitution, and for most this was an outgrowth of running away from home and started in their teens. Similar to Silbert and Pines (1981), their reasons for becoming prostitutes were "largely financial" (p. 55). Half of the women in Chesney-Lind and Rodriguez's (1983) study reported having been raped as children, and 63 percent had experienced some form of child sexual abuse, with a pattern of multiple victimizations. Chesney-Lind and Rodriguez (1983) also found a strong theme of drug dependency, which often led to their entanglement with the law. Furthermore, there was an "obvious connection between prostitution, burglary, and robbery... explicit in most of the interviews" (p. 57).

Another of the early scholars linking females' childhood victimizations with their later offending is Regina A. Arnold. From her intensive data collection involving interviews, participant observation, and questionnaires of sixty African American women prisoners, Arnold (1990, p. 154) explains how these women "as young girls, are labeled and processed as deviants—and subsequently as criminals—for refusing to accept or participate in their own victimization." Moreover, she identifies how these girls' refusal to accept or participate in their own victimization serves to influence their structural dislocation from three primary socialization institutions: the family, the educational system, and occupational systems. This dislocation, in turn, leads to their entry into "criminal life." Arnold convincingly discusses how patriarchal families and family violence, economic marginality, racist teachers, and a poor educational system may individually or collectively produce environments leading to the criminalization of girls, making them feel alienated in their own homes, schools, and communities. Not surprisingly, Arnold (1990) reports that women and girls with these violent experiences and pasts often resort to drug use as a type of "self medication."

This finding is important, and consistent with other studies on drugs, and we will therefore momentarily digress from the early feminist studies linking childhood victimization with subsequent offending, to discuss this important phenomenon. Understanding chemical use and abuse as correlates of psychological problems and antecedents of abuse is crucial in the history of female (and male) victimization-to-offending life courses. One study on female and male delinquents found psychiatric disorders often go hand in hand with substance abuse (Milin et al. 1991), and a study on adult women found a *combined* history of incest and alcoholism (more so than incest or alcoholism in isolation) is related to psycho-logical adjustment problems and more negative characteristics of temperament (Carson, et al. 1988). Another study found that both female and male substance abusers report rates of childhood sexual victimization much higher than what is common in the public at large, and that relapse from sobriety back into chemical abuse was more common for those with a history of child sexual abuse victimization than for those who had no such history (Rohsenow, et al. 1988). In a study comparing gender differences in illicit drug use, Inciardi et al. (1993) found that males are more likely than females to use drugs for pleasure, thrill seeking, or due to peer pressure, while females are more likely than males to use drugs as "self-medication" to relieve their depression. Moreover, female drug users were more likely than their male counterparts to report having been depressed before developing a drug problem (Inciardi et al. 1993).

Returning to the early studies linking victimization with offending, Mary E. Gilfus (1992) conducted intensive interviews with twenty incarcerated women. Their life histories were analyzed in an attempt to understand their "routes of entry and immersion" into street crime. Among the women's reports there was a pattern of moving from victim, to survivor, to offender. Indeed, the best routes available to many of these women when they were physically and sexually abused as girls involved survival skills that are criminal: running away from home, using drugs, and prostitution. The women came from economically dis-advantaged backgrounds, and this was more apparent for the African American women. Another theme prevalent among the women's childhoods was educational neglect; teachers who verbally or even physically berated them, students who were abusive to them, and educational authorities who wanted to ignore the obvious abuse they experienced at home and, likewise, ignored the drugs in their schools. Additionally, Black women reported sig-nificant racial violence they experienced as children, including one girl witnessing her uncle murdered by two White men (Gilfus 1992). Many of these women reported *revictimization* in their lives on the street, including rape, assault, and attempted murder. This is consistent with a finding from another study, that delinquent activity increases a youth's risk of victimization (Jensen and Brownfield 1986), and numerous others who found that childhood sexual victimization, particularly incest, drastically increases a girl's likelihood of sexual abuse in the future by a different perpetrator (e.g., Jacobs 1994; Russell 1984; Wyatt et al. 1993). Many of the women in Gilfus' (1992) sample also reported having been in battering relationships as adults, consistent with Daly's (1992, 1994) findings, where battered women were frequently expected (often coerced or forced) to prostitute, shoplift, rob, and sell drugs by their battering husbands or boyfriends. Gilfus concludes that although the women in her study "were victims of an overwhelming amount of violence as children and adults…they were on the whole committed to not harming others in their criminal activities" (1992, p. 85).

Kathleen Daly (1992, 1994), drawing on presentence investigation reports (PSIs) and transcripts of court cases and remarks made on the sentencing day, analyzed data on men and women processed through felony court in one jurisdiction for a five-year period. Although Daly notes remarkable similarities in many of the women's histories, she was able to distinguish the following five categories of offenders, differentiated by the specific feature believed to bring the woman to felony court:

1. street women
2. harmed-and-harming women
3. battered women
4. drug-connected women
5. "other" women

Street women have typically experienced considerable abuse, which is why they are living on the street, which, in turn, results in a significant record of arrests for prostitution, theft, drug-selling, and drug using. *Harmed-and-harming women* were abused or neglected as children and subsequently identified as "problem children." These women are often drug addicted and tend to get violent when drinking alcohol or using drugs, may have psychological problems, and are unable to cope with their current life situation. *Battered women* are currently in or recently out of a relationship with a violent man. Unlike the battered women in Daly's other categories, women in this category went to felony court as a result of their battering relationships, often for harming, or even killing, their batterers. The *drug-connected woman* uses or sells drugs in connection with her family members or intimate male partner. Most of these women's criminal records and drug using were reported as recent, and the felony for which they went to court was related to a family member or boyfriend, such as selling drugs with or for a boyfriend or family member. The women Daly classifies as *other*, are basically all those who do not fit into the other four categories. The "other" women's offenses are motivated by economic desires unrelated to drug addiction or street life needs. These crimes were often "greedy" in nature, for example embezzling funds for reasons beyond the most basic financial needs.

In addition to the feminist perspectives presented thus far, it is useful to briefly mention some other related research. For example, an older study found that a female's likelihood of being convicted of a crime of personal violence was significantly related to histories of injurious parental punishments, deviant paternal punishments, parental alcoholism, and early abandonments by one or both parents (Felthous and Yudowitz 1977). Widom's (1989a) study comparing abused and nonabused children's juvenile and adult records found that girls who were abused and neglected were significantly more likely than their nonabused, nonneglected counterparts to have both a formal juvenile delinquency record *and* a formal adult criminal record. Notably, however, the abused and neglected girls were no more likely than the nonabused, nonneglected girls to have a record for *violent* crimes. In another study Rivera and Widom (1990) found that abuse and neglect of boys did not increase their likelihood of becoming violent juveniles, but abused and neglected girls showed a tendency for increased risk of arrest for a violent crime while still a juvenile. In yet another study, Widom (1989b) reported that although abused and neglected children had higher rates than a control group for subsequent adult criminality and arrests for violent crimes, they were not significantly more likely to be arrested as adults for committing child abuse or neglect. Another study found that for both girls and boys, a child's history of being physically harmed by an adult increases the likelihood of later aggressive behavior and an inability to process social information and generate competent solutions to interpersonal problems (Dodge et al. 1990).

A study focusing on women convicted of killing children found that these women had very violent pasts, including extreme nonsexual and sexual victimizations (Crimmins et al. 1997). Documenting high levels of victimization in general among imprisoned women, one study found that abuse by an intimate male partner was the most prevalent form of victimization reported (70 percent), followed by robbery (41 percent), physical assault by a stranger (37 percent), sexual assault by a stranger (30 percent), physical abuse by a parent (29 percent), and sexual assault by a relative (18 percent) (Lake 1993). Dembo et al.'s (1992) analysis of female and male juvenile detainees found family background/problems, and sexual and physical abuse experiences were related to substance use and delinquent behavior. Scholars have also noted that lesbian, gay, and bisexual youth (see D'Augelli and Dark 1994 for a review), and children with disabilities (see Levey and Lagos 1994 for a review) are at increased risk of physical and sexual abuse. These findings are pertinent for this chapter given the research linking child abuse with chemical use or abuse and delinquency.

Finally, in reviewing the existing research on pathways to criminality, it is useful to examine some of the more recent attempts to understand girls' lives in general, and female delinquency, specifically. For example, Mary Pipher's (1994) popular book, *Reviving Ophelia*, stresses that even girls raised in loving and healthy homes are at risk of "acting out" and delinquency in a culture such as ours where the media and schools frequently devalue and sexualize girls. Pipher stresses the agony, frustrations, and self-hate that U.S. culture currently fosters in many adolescent girls. This is related to Chapter Five in this book, by Stephanie Covington, in terms of the different ways girls and boys are socialized to view themselves and others. Another chapter in this book, Chapter Six, by Joyce Dougherty, promises a theoretical approach addressing the omissions for which the prefeminist theories have been criticized. *Power-belief theory*, discussed by Dougherty, contends that patriarchal dynamics cannot be reduced simply to the persistent and mutually supportive roles of structural barriers and ideological forces. Rather, it is necessary to examine the degree to which girls and women internalize a sense of themselves as objects (rather than subjects) and powerful (rather than powerless) in understanding female crime.

The purpose of this chapter is not to discredit the violent childhood histories of many boys, which preceded their delinquent behaviors, nor is it to say that all girls who are abused become delinquent. It does not imply that abused and delinquent boys receive adequate attention and treatment by the system. Rather it is to point out the realities of many delinquent (and nondelinquent) girls' lives, and how girls' increased risk of violence is necessary to understand in order to more effectively respond to both their victimizations and their offending. Wells (1994) believes that girl delinquents are more invisible than boy delinquents because "young men are more likely to act out in ways the community can see, [although] it may be the invisible delinquent and troubled girls who actually experience earlier and more serious damage" (p. 5). Thus, it is not surprising that a national study of state prisoners states that females are far more likely than males to report prior physical and sexual abuse before the age of 18 (Snell and Morton 1994).

In summary, the earliest theorists on crime presented women and girls in a biology-as-destiny manner, with their followers either ignoring women and girls, or minimizing, stereotyping, and sexualizing them and their experiences. Unfortunately, but perhaps not surprisingly, this theoretical approach has been translated into practice. Chesney-Lind (1989) convincingly describes how the juvenile processing system has actively *sexualized* female delinquents and how girls are *criminalized* for their survival strategies. The findings reported in this section document how girls who have run away from abusive homes have often been criminalized for their efforts to survive, and how incarcerated and delinquent girls and women have exceptionally high rates of childhood victimizations. The following section presents information on the types of offenses for which girls are likely to be formally processed. It is important to keep in mind that their "pathways" to the offenses for which they are charged were likely to be antecedents to childhood abuse that were often quite severe.

GIRLS' OFFENSES AND GENDER DIFFERENCES IN DELINQUENT OFFENSES

While a troubled boy may steal cars, vandalize property, or slash tires, a troubled girl who has experienced similar neglect or abuse will show her distress quite differently. She is more likely to commit what the justice system will call a "status offense," "just a misdemeanor," or no crime at all when she runs away, self-endangers, abuses substances, becomes a gang affiliate, involves herself in prostitution or promiscuity, or becomes pregnant. The troubled boy often leaves behind an agitated victim who will demand and often obtain swift intervention. The only victim the girl will leave behind is herself. No one will demand and obtain intervention for her because in our country it is more often slashed tires, not slashed wrists, that are noticed (Wells 1994, p. 4).

There has been a significant amount of research attempting to identify gender differences and similarities in types of crimes committed. Most research suggests that boys are at least as likely as girls to commit most status offenses. It is evident, however, that girls are treated more harshly for status offenses. A recent overview of juvenile offending and processing in Ohio found that girls are much less likely to be charged with delinquent crimes than boys, and much less likely to have dispositions for delinquent crimes than boys, yet are more or equally likely as boys to be charged with or given dispositions for *unruly behavior* (Belknap, et al. 1997). This is certainly curious; one cannot help but wonder whether girls and boys are equally likely to be unruly, but girls are simply more likely to be processed for this behavior because it violates their stereotypic gender norms. We are also curious as to where promiscuity fits in to unruly. Is unruly the new catchall for promiscuity and poor demeanor and other activities that boys are equally or more likely to "commit"?

One review of research on girls' and boys' offending found that gender similar rates in offending are most apparent (1) for less serious offenses, (2) in self-reported offenses, and (3) in more recent studies (Belknap 1996). Self-report studies on youth in recent years report a similarity in female and male offending for status, drug, and less serious offenses, although boys have considerably higher offending rates for serious property crimes and all violent crimes (Canter 1982; Feyerherm 1981; Figueira-McDonough et al. 1981; Richards 1981). Unfortunately, much of the data on offending fails to control for race *and* gender at the same time. Those which have, typically report no strong gender-racial differences (Canter 1982; Cernkovich and Giordano 1979; Datesman and Aickin 1984; Jensen and Thompson 1990), except that in some cases African American males tend to exhibit more delinquency than the remaining gender-racial categories (Black females, White females, and White males), and these remaining categories sometimes clump together (Hindelang 1981; Laub and McDermott 1985; Young 1980). A recent study by Shelden and Chesney-Lind (1993) of youth referred to juvenile court in 1980 reported that the role of gender and race in delinquency is "complex and significant" (p. 87). This study found that regardless of race, girls typically commit different and less serious offenses than boys. Although there were distinct and strong racial differences among boys, there were no strong racial differences among girls. Finally, Shelden and Chesney-Lind (1993) attempted to distinguish "chronic nuisance offenders" from "delinquent careers" (the difference between these two chronic offending types should be self-evident), and found that the chronic nuisance offenders were disproportionately girls, particularly for status and minor property offenses. On the other hand, "[d]elinquent careers that involve chronic commission of serious offenses are essentially a male phenomenon. (Shelden and Chesney-Lind 1993, p. 88).

It is worth noting that most juvenile offenses, whether committed by boys *or* girls, are minor, often without a clear victim (Chesney-Lind and Shelden 1992). Although research has typically found delinquent groups to be same-sex groups, and like males, females are usually led into delinquent behavior by an "instigator" of their own sex, a recent study found that "females are far more likely to follow males than males are to follow females" in committing delinquent acts (Warr 1996, p. 29). A study following delinquent girls committed to the California Youth Authority in the 1960s found that two-thirds formally entered the juvenile system through an arrest for a status offense (Warren and Rosenbaum 1986). Most of the sample, arrested as youth, continued to be arrested into adulthood, primarily (as adults) for a property offense, followed by prostitution, and then drug offenses.

Table 2–1 in this chapter is a presentation of the top ten offenses for which youth were arrested in the United States in 1995. It is interesting to note that the "top ten" offenses largely comprise fairly minor offenses for both girls and boys. There are, however, some interesting gender comparisons. First, boys and girls were arrested for the same offenses as their top ten except that aggravated assaults were among girls' top ten (ranked ninth), but

Table 2–1 Top 10 Crimes for which Youth under 18 Years Were Arrested in 1995

	Girls			Boys	
Offense	**Number of arrests**	**Arrests (%)**	**Offense**	**Number of arrests**	**Arrests (%)**
1. Larceny-theft	120,911	23.6	1. Larceny-theft	251,659	16.9
2. Running away	104,098	20.4	2. All other offenses*	237,394	15.9
3. All other offenses*	68,443	13.4	3. Drug abuse	124,540	8.3
4. Other assaults†	43,306	8.5	4. Other assaults†	113,696	7.6
5. Curfew and loitering	33,039	6.5	5. Disorderly conduct	95,045	6.4
6. Disorderly conduct	30,957	6.1	6. Vandalism	88,989	6.0
7. Liquor law violations	24,167	4.7	7. Burglary	88,870	6.0
8. Drug abuse	17,935	3.5	8. Curfew and loitering	78,676	5.3
9. Aggravated assault	12,160	2.4	9. Running away	77,464	5.2
10. Vandalism	10,683	2.1	10. Liquor law violations	59,267	4.0

*"All other offenses" includes all other nonindex offenses except traffic offenses of those listed in crime reports.
†"Other assaults" includes assaults which are not the "aggravated assaults" classified under the violent crime index. "Other assaults" are classified under the nonindex offenses.

Source: Data from Federal Bureau of Investigation, *Crime in the United States,* 1995, (Washington, D.C.: U.S. Government Printing Office, 1996).

not boys', and burglary was in boys' top ten (ranked seventh), but not girls'. It is important to note, however, that aggravated assaults, although not among boys' top ten, still constitute a greater frequency of boys' overall arrests (3.5 percent) than girls' (2.4 percent). Second, for both boys and girls, larceny-theft was the number one offense for which they were arrested. The following offenses were similarly ranked in both boys' and girls' arrests: other nonindex offenses besides those listed in the government reports, assaults other than aggravated assaults, and disorderly conduct. Vandalism was ranked tenth for girls and sixth for boys, curfew and loitering was ranked fifth for girls and eighth for boys, and liquor law violations were ranked seventh for girls and tenth for boys. Perhaps the most noticeable gender comparison from Table 2–1 is that running away was the second most frequent reason for which girls were arrested, and the ninth most frequent reason for boys. Indeed, running away constitutes one-fifth of girls' overall arrests and only one-twentieth of boys'. Simply comparing the percentages of boys' and girls' arrests suggests that boys are more eclectic in the offenses they commit. A final point regarding Table 2–1 is given that the nonindex offense category "all other offenses" constitutes such a high percentage of both girls' (13.4 percent) and boys' (15.9 percent) arrests, it would be useful if governmental documents further divided this category for juvenile offenses.

Chesney-Lind and Shelden's (1992) overview of gender differences in delinquency rates reports that the overall male-female arrest ratio is 4:1, with the biggest gender gap in property crimes (11:1) and violent crimes (9:1). Notably, even larceny-theft, commonly thought of as a "girl's" crime (also known as shoplifting), is predominantly committed by males (3:1). According to Chesney-Lind and Shelden (1992), status offenses, particularly running away, continue to account for far more of girls' than boys' arrests, and half of girls' arrests are for larceny-theft and running away, while boys are more eclectic in the types of offenses they commit. A study by Joe and Chesney-Lind (1995) on gangs reported that boys and girls join gangs for many of the same reasons: to alleviate boredom, for an alternative family, solidarity, and a social outlet. Consistent with other research on gender and delinquency, Joe and Chesney-Lind (1995) found that girls in gangs committed fewer and less serious offenses than their male counterparts, and were judged more harshly for staying out all night.

Media and political obsession with violent juveniles in recent years has increased, where particular incidents of heinous juvenile-committed crimes receive considerable media attention. One result of this is the move by many politicians and others to endorse the death penalty for juveniles and to increase the likelihood of juvenile offenders being tried as adults. Chesney-Lind and Brown (1998) have addressed this focus on the violent girl, examining arrest trends for boys and girls between 1985 and 1994. They note that, while girls' arrest rates increased by 39.5 percent during this time period, compared to a 25.1 percent increase for boys, the arrest rates of girls for serious crimes of violence have "essentially remained unchanged." A recent publication by the Office of Juvenile Justice and Delinquency Prevention (Poe-Yamagata and Butts 1996) highlighting the increase in girls' violent crime rate arrests received significant media play. A closer look, however, provides interesting distinctions. For example, although boys' violent arrest rates increased by 33 percent compared to girls' 55 percent increase between 1989 and 1993, girls' rates increased at a much smaller pace (a 35 percent increase) than boys' (a 45 percent increase) for murder/nonnegligent manslaughter, and girls' arrests for rape decreased by 10 percent, while boys' rates *increased* by 10 percent during this time (1996, p. 3). Furthermore, girls' percent of juvenile arrests for violent crimes only climbed from 11 to 13 percent between 1983 and 1993, with a significant decrease (from 11 percent to 6 percent) for murder/ nonnegligent manslaughter, an increase of 1 to 2 percent for forcible rape, an increase of 7 to 9 percent for robbery, and an increase from 16 to 18 percent for aggravated assault (p. 4). Indeed, the graphs presented in the document by Poe-Yamagata and Butts (1996) suggest that boys' and girls' rates are changing in very similar patterns over time, with some exceptions. Another indication that gender changes may be exaggerated is that girls' percent of juvenile cases waived to criminal courts between 1985 and 1994 has remained quite stable, hovering between 4 and 5 percent, with the exception of 1986 when girls represented 6 percent of such cases (DeFrances and Stron 1997, p. 5). In Poe-Yamagata and Butts' (1996, p. 3) analysis, the offenses for which girls' arrest rates appear to be growing significantly faster than boys' are aggravated assaults, motor vehicle theft, arson, possession of a weapon, vagrancy, and curfew and loitering violations.

Table 2–2 in this chapter is a presentation of the female percentage of juvenile arrests in the United States for the past 15 years. Browsing over this table, one can see the types of offenses for which females are more and less predominantly represented, and the changes in female representation in juvenile arrests over time. In examining this table, there are seven offenses for which girls constitute 30 percent or more of the juvenile arrests in 1995. These are somewhat predictable, and listed in order of highest representation to lesser representation of girls; they are running away (57 percent), prostitution and commercialized vice (48 percent), embezzlement (42 percent), offenses against family and children (37 percent), forgery and counterfeit (35 percent), larceny-theft (32 percent), and curfew and loitering (30 percent). By examining changes over time, it appears that there has been a slow but steady increase in girls' percentage of overall juvenile arrests. The percent of girls' *total* arrests increased 4 percent between 1980 and 1995, while their percent of the total crime index arrests increased 6 percent, their portion of the total violent crime index arrests increased 5 percent, total property index crime arrests increased 7 percent, and total nonindex offense arrests increased 4 percent. Some trends about specific offenses are worth noting. For example, while girls' arrests for aggravated assaults increased 5 percent (from 15 percent to 20 percent) between 1980 and 1995, there is a slight (2 percent) decrease in girls' percentage of arrests for murder/nonnegligent manslaughter. Girls' portion of robbery arrests slightly increased (2 percent), while girls' portion of forcible rape arrests have remained a negligible 2 percent for every year. A closer look at the property crime arrests suggests that girls' increase is most influenced by larceny-theft arrests. This is consistent with research by Chilton and Datesman (1987) suggesting that the increase in female offending is likely related to the "feminization of poverty." Similarly, in Chapter One,

Table 2–2 Female proportion of juvenile arrests: 1980, 1985, 1990, 1995

Offense	Female proportion of arrests of persons under age 18; %			
	1980	1985	1990	1995
Total	21	22	23	26
Crime index total	18	20	20	24
Violent crime index	10	11	12	15
Murder/nonnegligent manslaughter	8	9	6	6
Forcible rape	2	2	2	2
Robbery	7	7	9	9
Aggravated assault	15	16	15	20
Property crime index	19	21	22	26
Burglary	6	7	8	10
Larceny-theft	26	27	28	32
Motor vehicle theft	10	11	11	15
Arson	10	10	10	12
Nonindex offenses	22	24	24	26
Other assaults	21	23	23	28
Forgery and counterfeiting	30	32	33	35
Fraud	29	22	30	26
Embezzlement	27	30	40	42
Stolen property	9	9	9	12
Vandalism	8	9	8	11
Weapons	6	7	6	8
Prostitution and commercialized vice	72	70	55	48
Sex offenses (except prostitution and forcible rape)	7	8	7	7
Drug abuse violations	17	15	11	13
Gambling	5	5	4	5
Offenses against the family and children	36	36	35	37
Driving under the influence	10	13	14	16
Liquor law violations	23	26	28	29
Drunkenness	14	16	15	16
Disorderly conduct	18	19	20	25
Vagrancy	16	16	16	11
All other offenses (except traffic)	20	21	21	22
Curfew and loitering violations	24	25	28	30
Running away	58	57	56	57

Sources: Data from Federal Bureau of Investigation, *Crime in the United States, 1980,* (Washington, D.C.: U.S. Government Printing Office, 1981). Federal Bureau of Investigation, *Crime in the United States, 1985,* (Washington, D.C.: U.S. Government Printing Office, 1986). Federal Bureau of Investigation, *Crime in the United States,* 1990, (Washington, D.C.: U.S. Government Printing Office, 1991). Federal Bureau of Investigation, *Crime in the United States, 1995,* (Washington, D.C.: U.S. Government Printing Office, 1996).

Steffensmeier and Allen suggest that the increase in the percentage of female arrests is largely shaped by "economic vulnerability" and "female inequality."

Notably, the offense with the biggest change in gender arrest rates over this 15-year period represented in Table 2–2 is prostitution and commercialized vice. Girls' rates for this offense decreased from 72 percent in 1980 to 48 percent in 1995. The authors have no explanation for this drastic decrease, except that some states have implemented laws to crack down on prostitution in less sexist manners. It is also worth noting that there has been a slow but steady *decrease* in girls' proportion of drug abuse violations (from 17 to 13 percent), but that girls' rates of driving under the influence of alcohol, liquor law violations, and drunkenness show varying degrees of steady increases.

Finally, recent research identifies the need to address gender differences in offending from a myriad of references. For example, Triplett and Myers (1995) found that simply examining incidence and prevalence rates of delinquent offending ignores the greater gender difference: the *context* of offending. Specifically, females are less likely than males to hurt their victims, have their victims hospitalized, attack their victims with weapons, and to be on drugs at the time of the offense. Similarly, Bottcher (1995) argues that the *dimensions* of gender (e.g., range, timing, pace, definition, and focus) must be included in analyses of gender differences in delinquency. Finally, in Chapter One, Steffensmeier and Allan concur with Triplett and Myers (1995) and Bottcher (1995) in emphasizing the need for a gendered paradigm to explain crime, which recognizes the profound differences in females' and males' lives.

THE PROCESSING OF DELINQUENTS

Unfortunately, like most criminology theorists, academics are not the only ones who view male and female delinquents differently. This section of the chapter documents a considerable amount of sexism in the processing of juvenile offenders. These responses often reinforce gender roles and include differential responses by the police, juvenile and adult court workers, and correctional workers. Belknap (1996) previously identified the three possible hypotheses regarding assessments as to whether the justice system is gendered in decision making. First, the *equal treatment hypothesis* states that the system is *not* gendered, and therefore females and males are processed similarly for the same offenses. The *chivalry hypothesis* is based on the assumptions that society is paternalistic and chivalrous toward females, and therefore the police, prosecutors, judges, parole reviewers, and other decision makers will be chivalrous, as well. Thus, the chivalry hypotheses states that females are treated more leniently than males who commit similar offenses. This perspective is rooted in the belief that women are placed on pedestals and protected by men, even when they commit crimes. Finally, the *evil woman hypothesis* states that because females are stepping outside of both law-abiding *and* appropriate gender roles when they commit offenses, they are treated more harshly than males charged with the same offenses.

A number of studies have been conducted in order to determine which of these three hypotheses (equal treatment, chivalry, or evil woman) most accurately reflects the influence of gender on systemic decision making. Before examining the various studies addressing gender differences in the processing of alleged offenders, however, it is important to address that the hypothesis best reflecting reality may depend on the type of crime and stage of the system where the decision is made (i.e., policing, courts, and corrections). Furthermore, an assessment of whether the processing of offenders is gendered cannot group all females together. It is necessary to examine differences *among* females (not just comparing their processing to males) given that various females' likelihood of receiving chivalrous treatment is often related to their age, race, and class. Other extra-legal characteristics that may affect how justice is meted out include the female's marital and dependent child status and her sexual orientation.

When evaluating whether justice is gendered by the type of crime, Nagel and Hagan (1983) do not view chivalrous and evil woman approaches as necessarily at odds with each other. Rather, they suggest they work in tandem depending on the type of crime and the defendant's demeanor. More specifically, Nagel and Hagan (1983) believe that females are treated more leniently than males as long as they are committing less serious offenses and exhibit behaviors consistent with their "appropriate" gender role: acting passively. If the offense is serious in nature, on the other hand, Nagel and Hagan (1983) propose that the deviation from the female role is too extreme, and thus evil woman responses are more likely. Naffine's (1987) review of studies on the processing of offenders confirmed Nagel and Hagan's (1983) declaration regarding the type of offense and the systemic response: overall, chivalry was more common when women committed minor offenses, and the evil woman approach was more likely when females committed more serious offenses. Others also report variations in whether males or females are treated more leniently depending on the type of offense (Chesney-Lind 1987; Sarri 1987; Wilbanks 1986). An important caveat to this approach, however, is that although status offenses are generally considered minor offenses, they are a definite exception to the "rule" that minor offenses are those most likely to be processed chivalrously. In fact, Chesney-Lind's (1987) research review found that chivalrous treatment is *more* common for those charged with serious offenses. An abundance of research, discussed in more detail below, confirms that females have historically been and continue to be treated far more harshly than males for status offenses.

As pointed out previously, it is also necessary to recognize that there are variations *among* females, largely based on race, class, and age, as to their likelihood of receiving chivalrous or evil woman responses. Research has fairly consistently found that women and girls of color are afforded chivalry far less frequently than Anglo females in juvenile and criminal justice decision making (Krohn et al. 1983; Kruttschnitt 1981; Spohn et al. 1987; Visher 1983). Indeed, people of color are even more disproportionately represented in women's than men's prisons (Binkley-Jackson, et al. 1993; LaPrairie, 1989; Goetting and Howsen, 1983; Rafter 1985), and this overrepresentation may be increasing over time (Sarri 1987). Similarly, research on class and economic status has found that poorer women and girls and those on welfare are treated more harshly than their wealthier counterparts (Kruttschnitt 1981; Worrall 1990). Like race and class, age is also an important factor in reflecting differences among females in experiencing chivalrous versus evil woman responses by decision makers. Various studies assessing gender differences in responses to offenders found that girls and young women are *less* likely than older women to be afforded chivalrous treatment by the criminal and juvenile processing systems (Chesney-Lind and Shelden 1992; Farrington and Morris 1983; Hiller and Hancock, 1981; Krohn et al. 1983; Nagel and Hagan 1983; Visher 1983). In sum, chivalrous treatment by juvenile and criminal justice system decision makers is least likely for younger and poorer women and girls, and females of color.

Regarding the *stage* in the criminal and juvenile systems, two reviews of research on the processing of female offenders both found that chivalry is least common in the earlier stages of the system (e.g., the police) and most common in the latter stages of the system (e.g., sentencing) (Belknap 1996; Chesney-Lind 1987). In fact, of the three options in gender differences in sentencing outlined earlier, the evil woman approach is most apparent in the beginning stage (the police), equal treatment is most evident in the middle stages (decisions to prosecute, dismiss charges, and convict), and chivalrous treatment is most common at the end of the decision-making process (the decision to incarcerate and the sentence severity). A closer examination of this research, however, suggests that for juvenile offenders, the evil woman response by crime decision makers is more likely than for older females at *every* stage of the system. A more detailed account of the research on whether the systemic response to juveniles is gendered when broken down by the stage of processing follows.

Focusing on police decision making, the evil woman response has been most apparent for girls who are status offenders, that is, girls whose offenses would not be considered offenses if they were adults (Chesney-Lind and Shelden 1992; Hiller and Hancock 1981; Sarri 1983; Teilmann and Landry 1981). In fact, in a landmark study, Chesney-Lind (1974) found that it was routine for the police to question girls, but not boys, about their sexual experiences. Chesney-Lind's (1973) study of juvenile court cases between 1929 and 1964 found that one-quarter of boys and three-quarters of girls were arrested for status offenses, and approximately three-quarters of those girls arrested for status offenses were forced to have gynecological exams to determine whether they were virgins and whether they had any venereal diseases. (Not surprisingly, then, these girls were not only more likely to be sent to detention than boys, but spent three times as long in detention). Although there has historically been little concern by the criminal and juvenile authorities for girls who were sexually abused in their homes, girls who reported consensual sexual activity after being questioned by the police, ended up with sexual offense charges added to their original offense (Chesney-Lind 1974). On the other hand, Wells (1994) posits that the police take girls less seriously than boys because girls are less of a threat to the community than boys and more likely "only" a threat to themselves. Similar to statements from some institutionalized delinquent girls in the focus groups in our study (Belknap et al. 1997), Wells (1994) reports that girls will escalate the seriousness of their delinquent behavior as a cry for "help" or to come back to delinquent institutions because that was the safest they ever felt. Some of these girls in both Wells (1994) and our own research (Belknap et al. 1997) wished that the police had responded to their offending earlier, before it escalated to the point where they were in "really big trouble."

A review of studies on gender and decision making at the detention and pretrial release stages reveals that chivalrous treatment appears to be reserved for adult women who are not prostitutes, whereas the treatment of juveniles (and prostitutes) at these stages is more consistent with the evil woman hypothesis (Bernat 1985; Frazier and Cochran 1986; Kruttschnitt 1984; Kruttschnitt and Green 1984; Teilmann and Landry 1981). A study on the decision of whether to refer a youth to juvenile court reported that the systemic responses depended on the type of crime: for delinquent acts that were not status offenses, the response was more consistent with chivalry, but for status offenses, the response was more consistent with the evil woman approach (Datesman and Aickin 1984). Similarly, Chesney-Lind's (1973) analysis of juvenile offenses in Honolulu between 1929 and 1964 found that girls were more likely than boys to be referred to court, and three times as likely to be institutionalized. Moreover, most of these girls were forced to have pelvic exams to assess whether they were virgins. A study on the charge dismissal decision of juveniles reported that race and gender interacted in important ways: African American boys were most likely to be formally processed, African American girls were most likely to receive probation, Anglo girls were most likely to receive diversion, and Anglo boys were most likely to have their charges dismissed (Sarri 1983). Finally, a longitudinal study of ten European countries' juvenile courts found that girls' chances of being incarcerated and the length of their sentences when incarcerated were rising in seven of the ten countries studied (Cain 1989).

When examining incarceration rates in secure public facilities, Krisberg and Austin (1993) report that for both males and females, African Americans have the highest rates and Asian Americans the lowest rates. Moreover, this study found that at each stage of the system, youth of color were increasingly disproportionately represented, while Anglo youth were "proportionately filtered out of the juvenile justice system as the severity of the sanction increase[d]" (p. 125). They also found that "youth placed in private facilities tend to be disproportionately young women, white, and charged or adjudicated more for less serious property and person crimes" (p. 116). To date, however, there is a paucity of research addressing gender differences in processing delinquents at the latter stages of decision making, particularly the likelihood of pleading guilty or negotiating pleas, convictions, incarceration (especially studies on juvenile incarcerations in the U.S.), and probation rates. Most of these studies have been conducted on adults or lumped adults and juveniles together. As mentioned before, however, two reviews of the existing studies (which included studies on adults) suggest that if females receive chivalry at any stages, it is most likely to be the latter ones (Belknap 1996; Chesney-Lind 1987). Future research needs to continue to examine this, and to include in the analysis stage, age, race, and class, as well as gender.

Another finding from prior research on the processing of adults is that women who have dependent children are more likely than women without dependent children to receive chivalrous treatment by the crime-processing system (Daly 1989a, 1989b; Eaton 1986; Steffensmeier et al. 1993; Worrall 1990). Given the media's and politicians' focus on un-wed teenage mothers, it would be interesting and useful to determine whether *juveniles'* dependent child and pregnancy status are related to whether they receive chivalrous, equal, or "evil woman" processing, and if this differs among girls based on their race/ethnicity and class. This is another area which future research needs to address.

THE PROBLEMS WITH STATUS OFFENSES

Any examination of the female delinquent must carefully address the issue of status of-fenses. Status offenses have been mentioned earlier, particularly regarding documentation that females are treated more harshly than males for status offense violations. The reality is that most girls who enter the crime-processing system do so for these types of offenses: running away from home, incorrigibility, truancy, sexual activity, waywardness, and cur-few violations. As Chesney-Lind (1981) has stated, although females constitute a small proportion of the system, when they are in the system, it is most likely for status offenses. Moreover, research on the type of offense and the pattern in the juvenile system response found that girls were treated chivalrously for property crimes, but more harshly than males (as evil women) for status offenses (Hiller and Hancock 1981). Similarly, a study of family court records found that while boys received harsher dispositions than girls for felony and misdemeanor criminal offenses, girls received harsher dispositions than boys for status of-fenses (Datesman and Scarpitti 1980). A study conducted in England and Wales on a court punishment requiring juveniles to check in with a supervisor for two to three years, found that girls were far more likely to be forced to do this for trivial offenses (Webb 1984). Notably, consistent with race and gender stereotypes, other studies on family courts re-ported that Anglo girls are mostly likely to receive official intervention for status offenses, and African American boys are least likely for these same offenses (Datesman and Aickin 1984; Datesman and Scarpitti 1980). Other research on the juvenile court has consistently found that girls have historically been treated as or more harshly for *status* offenses than boys are treated for *criminal* offenses (Chesney-Lind 1973, 1981, 1987; Conway and Bogdan 1977; Schlossman and Wallach 1982). In the conclusion of her study on juvenile courts in Europe, Cain states that "girls are still punished more severely than boys for ac-tivities which put them at risk of an unauthorized sexual encounter, for status offenses, although boys engage in these activities at least as often as girls" (1989, p. 232).

This brings us back, again, to the issue of the double standard in processing juveniles for consensual (hetero)sexual experiences. Girls have historically been treated more harshly for consensual sex ("promiscuity") "offenses" than for nonsexual offenses (Terry 1970). Even more troubling is the finding that girls' sexual victimizations often get mixed up with their consensual sexual offenses. In a study on Memphis, Tennessee, court records between 1900 and 1919, sexual victimizations (rapes) of girls were treated the same by the juvenile courts as their consensual sexual activity: with excessively harsh sanctions (Shelden 1981). Sarri's (1983) more recent research found that females are often treated identically whether their sexual "crimes" were being sexually abused or participating in consensual sexual activity. Gelsethorpe's (1989) study of British youth found that girls' sexual activity is still monitored and treated more harshly than boys'. Additionally, the girls' running away from home was attributed to their "promiscuity," which resulted in their harsh treatment.

The Juvenile Justice and Delinquency Prevention Act (JJDPA) of 1974 was instituted in an effort to deinstitutionalize and divert status offenders from secure facilities in the United States. In theory, states were to discontinue placing status offenders in "training schools," detention centers, and adult jails in order to receive federal funds for delinquency programs. Individual states were expected to devise plans to treat status offenders outside of secure facilities. As expected, because girls had been highly disproportionately sanctioned for status offenses, the immediate effect of this act was greater on girls than boys (Chesney-Lind 1986, 1988; Sarri 1983). Following the implementation of JJDPA, girls' institutionalization rates for status offenses fell by 44 percent, while the corresponding rate for boys was 20 percent (Krisberg and Schwartz 1983).

Unfortunately, this initial success in the gendered effects of deinstitutionalization have been tempered with compounding findings. (1) The decline in the institutionalization of status offenders leveled off between 1979 and 1982, making the gains against judicial sexism "very much in jeopardy" (Chesney-Lind 1986, p. 90). Indeed, both male and female arrests for running away increased between 1983 and 1986 (Chesney-Lind 1988). (2) The diversionary process may be failing when one considers alternative juvenile placements, and how extra-legal characteristics of the juveniles might be related to their placement. Some believe that the JJDPA may not have decreased the stigmatizing of juvenile offenders (Datesman and Aickin 1984). One study found that youth who would typically have gone to secure facilities (such as training schools) before the JJDPA, have been institutionalized in more "hidden" institutions since 1974 (Schwartz et al. 1984). These alternative placements have included mental illness institutions, private juvenile "correctional" facilities, and chemical dependency programs. A study by Federle and Chesney-Lind (1992) assessing the impact of JJDPA documents how Anglo boys have been deinstitutionalized while girls have been "transinstitutionalized into mental health facilities for behaviors labeled 'inappropriate' since the early decades of the juvenile court. Indeed, sexually and physically abused girls may find their self-protective behaviors (like running away) criminalized, just as female status offenders may be placed in child welfare facilities for their 'protection.'" (p. 165). This same study reported that African American youth are "warehoused in the public system of juvenile institutions," and thus they conclude that "[d]einstitutionalization appears to have benefitted only white males" (pp. 165 and 189).

Schwartz et al. (1984), although not specifically addressing gender, believe that for many of these placements outside of the "training schools," the referrals are made by parents and the admissions "are not as 'voluntary' as one might think" (p. 382). This finding on parents is particularly relevant for gender regarding a substantial amount of documentation that parents play a significant role in many juveniles' first formal contact with the system, and that parents are far more likely to turn their daughters than their sons in to the police and juvenile courts (Chesney-Lind 1989; Chesney-Lind and Shelden 1992; Hiller and Hancock 1981; Sarri 1983; Teilmann and Landry 1981). Moreover, similar to the juvenile and criminal processing systems, parents are less tolerant of their daughters than their sons for the same behaviors, whether they are status or other offenses.

Another issue regarding parenthood and delinquency is how parents influence their children's likelihood of *becoming* offenders. In our own research conducting focus groups with delinquent girls, many of the girls discussed strained relationships with parents, and often alluded to or mentioned how abuse by their parents was related to their offending (Belknap et al. 1997). Many of them, not surprisingly, also listed numerous other family members who were incarcerated, including mothers, fathers, sisters, brothers, aunts and uncles. Notably, a recent national study of prisoners reported that women in prison were more likely than their male counterparts to report having an immediate family member incarcerated (Snell and Morton 1994). This is particularly important given another recent study that found that criminal convictions of a parent increase the likelihood of criminal convictions for a child, with family environment doing little to mitigate this relationship (Rowe and Farrington 1997). Finally, our research (Belknap et al. 1997), similar to others (Sommers and Baskin 1994; Howell and Davis 1992), emphasizes the problem of delinquent girls who have family members, including their parents, who are the ones who "turn them on" to drugs in the first place.

Reports from other countries are useful to examine as well. For example, a study of institutionalized delinquent youth in England found that many of these girls were institutionalized due to *emotional and family problems*, such as their *parents'* fighting, and had not themselves committed any delinquent acts (Gelsethorpe 1989). Thus, similar to the U.S., it appears that some girls are warehoused in delinquent institutions simply because their parents do not want to be bothered with them. On a more positive note, a study from South Australia of a policy implemented in 1979, very similar to the United States' JJDPA, found that this policy was successful in curbing the criminalization and institutionalization of status offenders, and appears to have resulted in more equal treatment for female and male youth, particularly regarding sexual "offenses" (consensual sex) (Naffine 1989).

The discussion about retracking youth who may have gone to "training schools" before the JJDPA in 1974, to mental illness/health institutions after this Act, is not complete without acknowledging that many of these youth indeed have significant mental health problems. First, there is documentation of serious mental and developmental disorders among institutionalized youth. For example, Hollander and Turner's (1985) study of institutionalized delinquent boys found not only significant psychological and developmental disorders, but that these disorders were related to their violent offending. Additionally, a study of institutionalized delinquent girls and boys found their psychological and psychiatric profiles very similar to youth who have been psychiatrically hospitalized, and that these institutionalized delinquents had a significant combination of emotional and behavioral problems (Davis et al. 1991).

Moreover, while it has been established that there is a link between child abuse and subsequent delinquency (for a review of the traditional research in this area see Gray 1988), only recently has research focused on how family violence can affect a child's mental health. A recent study on abusive families (that did not examine delinquency) found that children of battered women were at risk for child abuse (usually by the father), and "total" family violence, including woman battering of mothers and sexual and nonsexual physical parental abuse of children, "has a direct influence on children's mental health" (McCloskey, et al. 1995, p. 1257). Another study found sexually abused children have exceptionally high rates of post-traumatic stress disorder (PTSD), and that younger children were more symptomatic (Wolfe, et al. 1989). Interestingly, these studies found that mothers reported both a greater likelihood of *and* more extensive psychological disorders of their children, than the children reported of themselves (McCloskey et al. 1995; Wolfe et al., 1989). Similarly, a study of adult women reporting to a health center crisis service found that women reporting childhood sexual victimization were more likely than their nonabused counterparts "to be currently taking psychoactive medication, to have a history of substance addiction, to have been revictimized in an adult relationship, and to have made at least one suicide attempt in the past" (Briere and Runtz 1987, p. 370). In sum, it is logical to conclude from a review of this research that children from abusive homes are at risk for mental health problems *and* delinquency, and their psychological well being and delinquency levels might be very much related. Therefore, attending to the abuse in homes is key to deterring both delinquency *and* mental health problems of youth.

TREATING AND PUNISHING DELINQUENT GIRLS

Given the sexism in theories on crime and sexism in the processing of youth, it is not surprising that the "correctional" responses to treating and punishing sentenced and convicted youth are also sexist. To some extent, this was covered in the section on processing. (It is sometimes difficult to separate out sentences meted out by judges from punishments and treatments in institutional facilities.) In the mid-1800s separate facilities for women were developed in the United States; however, separate facilities for girls date from the early 1900s (Sarri 1987). A historical overview of juvenile institutions in the southern United States by Vernetta D. Young (1994), highlights how, once again, gender and race have interacted in the response to alleged youthful offenders:

> Although the refuge movement [for juveniles out of adult facilities] in the South began before the Civil War, the real demand for juvenile reformatories came 30 years later, in the decade of the 1890s….The literature suggests that the development of juvenile institutions in the South was precipitated by the need to control

the different segments of society. In the case of White male youth, once their delinquent activities became intolerable the pattern of placing these juveniles in institutions with adults was established. This soon became a bone of contention, and institutions to separate White male youth from White male adults were mandated....In the case of Black male youth, before the Civil War they were controlled by the institutions of slavery and the adult penal system. After slavery ended, Black youth remained in the adult penal system and were handled through the convict lease system. Once these mechanisms became untenable the juvenile institution was introduced to maintain social control, mainly by supplying needed laborers. In the case of White female youth, the institutions developed to save poor White girls from sexual immorality by providing a conduit for instruction in 'women's work.' In the case of Black female youth, they were remanded to adult institutions or handled out of state until it became either practically or fiscally prohibitive, then special institutions were developed. (pp. 261–262)

Chesney-Lind and Shelden (1992) point out that even now, women and girls sent to *jail* are essentially being sent to male facilities, and for arrested girls this is often a sentence of solitary confinement. Additionally, girls are more likely than boys to end up in jail for trivial and status offenses, and the conditions for girls in jail are significantly worse than those for boys. In 1989, 22 percent of girls and 3 percent of boys in public juvenile facilities were there for nondelinquent reasons, such as status offenses, abuse, neglect, and voluntary commitment (U.S. Department of Justice 1991). There is also documentation that girls are four times more likely than boys to be incarcerated for contempt of court charges (Criminal Justice Newsletter 1992, p. 4). These gender differences are further exacerbated by studies indicating that the nation's detention centers and training schools may be not only neglecting juvenile girls' needs, but sometimes, further victimizing them (Chesney-Lind and Shelden 1992, p. 164). For example, research on both jails and delinquent girls' institutions reports that girls appear to be at considerable risk for sexual assault by male staff and other inmates (Chesney-Lind and Rodriguez 1983; Faith 1993).

Regarding programming, institutions for delinquent girls are well known for reinforcing stereotypical gender roles (e.g., Gelsethorpe 1989; Kersten 1989: Smart 1976). Delinquent girls are subjected to greater rule rigidity and offered fewer vocational, educational, and athletic programs than boy delinquents (Kersten 1989; Mann 1984). A British study found that even though the policies were gender-neutral, the application of the policies was quite sexist: girls were rewarded for feminine behavior (e.g., crying and acting sensitive, maternal, and affectionate) (Gelsethorpe 1989). Additionally, activities were gendered: boys swam, jogged, and played volleyball, ping-pong, darts, and soccer, while the girls were relegated to watching from the sidelines. Girls who attempted to join the boys in these activities were pejoratively labeled "tomboys" and "unladylike." Girls' activities were limited to exercises to keep slim, cooking, sewing, and other practices to prepare them to be "acceptable" wives and mothers (Gelsethorpe 1989).

A recent overview of delinquent girls points out that "downsizing" of the juvenile "corrections" system has not been gender-neutral; "in application [downsizing] often means releasing and reducing services to those delinquents who pose the *least threat of harm to the community*—girls" (Wells 1994, p. 4). Wells (1994) states that the reason that girls' programs are often "the last funded and the first cut" is because they have no one advocating on their behalf, "creating the phenomenon of throwaway services for throwaway girls" (p. 4). Some mistakenly assume, according to Wells (1994), that because these girls are not being served by the juvenile "corrections" system they are being served elsewhere. Instead, she states, we are only offering these girls "fragments of services. The truth is that in the United States there are far more shelters and services for our country's abused and neglected animals than for girls and young women" (p. 4).

THE MOVEMENT FOR CHANGE: IMPROVING RESPONSES TO DELINQUENT GIRLS

In 1992 there was a reauthorization of the 1974 JJDPA. One aspect of this reauthorization was that Congress heard the concerns of some professionals who worked with juveniles that girl offenders had some "gender-specific needs." To this end, the final act of the reauthorization legislation provided that each state should (1) conduct an analysis of the need for and assessment of existing treatment and services for delinquent girls, (2) develop a plan to provide needed gender-specific services for the prevention and treatment of juvenile delinquency, and (3) provide assurance that youth in the juvenile system are treated fairly regarding their mental, physical, and emotional capabilities, as well as on the basis of their gender, race, and family income (Belknap et al. 1997). States across the U.S. have been receiving federal monies in attempts to secure these three provisions outlined in the 1992 Reauthorization of the JJDPA. Most of this work is in progress, so it is too early to make conclusive statements.

It is, however, prudent to examine the potential of these efforts across the United States. This chapter has highlighted the most important issues facing delinquent girls, as well as girls at risk of becoming delinquent. These factors are often interrelated and the order of causality is not always clear, but it is certainly clear that girls' high risk of victimization in their homes, particularly incest, are strongly related to their subsequent offending. The interrelationships of the many involved factors are often complex. For example, how do running away, psychological problems, drug and alcohol (ab)use, prostitution, larceny/theft, drug selling, robbery, assault, manslaughter, and homicide interrelate, or do they, for a given individual girl? This chapter has emphasized the sexualization of girls and the punishment of girls for their sexuality, whether it was consensual sex with another person or they were raped. Therefore, it seems evident that there is a need for "revamping" the treatment of not only delinquent girls, but also delinquent boys (because many of them come from abusive homes as well), and to pay more attention to youth in these abusive homes in order to "derail" them from their pathways to offending.

It is important to point out that designing and appropriating treatment and punishment based on gender *differences* might be tricky; and that biological (sex) differences have been routinely used against women and girls. Indeed, many gender differences (such as the ability to raise children) have been considered biological (sex) differences by the courts (see Epstein 1988; Rhode 1989; Smart 1989). Feminist legal scholars have agonized over the "equality vs. difference" (also known as the "sameness vs. difference") debate (e.g., Rhode 1989; Smart 1989). In a nutshell, the dilemma whether to acknowledge biological differences (e.g., the ability to get pregnant) in order to try to get better conditions for women (e.g., maternity leave without losing one's job), and/or gender differences (in the form of sexism; e.g., the likelihood of incest victimization) in order to improve conditions for females (e.g., treatment for survivors). If these issues are acknowledged, is something then lost by saying that females are different than males? In regard to this chapter, there is fear that highlighting some important gender differences will reinforce the notion that males and females are different, and that some policy makers may use this information to excuse unnecessary or even sexist gender differences in programming and treatment. Historically, both biological and socially structured differences between females and males have been used to provide less and worse treatment for females. There is concern about this approach being perpetuated with scholars' findings regarding girls' special needs.

Reformers in any movement usually have the best intentions, but it is important to recognize that some implemented policies that initially appear as important achievements to feminists and others who advocate for women and girls, have often backfired. Specifically, many policies implemented originally to help women and girls, have often been applied in sexist manners. Examples of this include penal reform movements to separate women from men in prison that resulted in sexist treatment and punishment for women (Freedman 1982); movements to make changes in sentencing for males and females that resulted in exceptionally long sentences for females (Belknap 1996; Feinman 1992; Temin 1980); and the mandatory arrest policy in domestic violence that has resulted in numerous women victims being arrested for resisting their batterers' abuse (Stanko 1985).

A historical evaluation of a reform movement directed at delinquent girls is a case in point. Odem's (1995) historical account of this reform movement in the U.S. between 1885 and 1920 exemplifies the sexism, racism, and classism referred to throughout this article, but also identifies the unexpected and sexist responses by the juvenile and criminal processing systems. While these largely White, middle-class women reformers were invested in *protecting* White, working-class girls and women from sexual exploitation, through implementing policies on the age of consent for sex, protection was not the end result. Their goal was to preserve the chastity of White (but not Black) women and prevent "illegitimate" (and biracial) offspring. The result, however, was a male-dominated system of police officers, judges and legal officials who treated the young women and girls passing before them as "immoral seductresses" rather than as victims of male exploitation. "In such hands, the law was used to humiliate and punish young women who did not conform to dominant standards of female respectability. In addition, because the court officials reserved the harshest punishments for African American men, the law became a tool for reinforcing racial discrimination within the criminal justice system" (Odem 1995, pp. 185–186). The second phase of this moral reform movement was to appoint more women into official decision-making positions, such as police officers, judges, and probation officers. But these appointed women were relegated to only working with females, leaving the male offenders to male officials. The result was a long-standing juvenile court bias of male officials treating males charged with sexual offenses far more leniently than females charged with such offenses, and female workers treating girls more harshly than male workers treated the boys (Odem 1995).

The following recommendations are made in hopes that changes can be implemented that have meaningful impact on girls' lives. While recognizing that gender-specific needs are useful to identify, it is also worth stating that many of these policies can be applied to boys as well. Particularly, youth from abusive homes, in school systems that are not concerned about drugs and violence, in school systems fraught with racism and classism (in addition to sexism), in communities with no sense of community, are at risk. The remainder of this chapter will list changes needed to help girls at risk of becoming delinquent or who have already become delinquent.

The first area of recommendations regarding female delinquency has to do with preventive measures. First and foremost, educational, social welfare, medical, and juvenile and criminal processing system personnel must become better equipped to identify and respond to children from abusive homes. Numerous studies cited in this chapter found a strong link between childhood victimization and the risk of becoming delinquent. Certainly not all abused children become delinquent (Falshaw et al. 1996; Widom 1989a), but the fact that abuse is a likely predecessor to delinquency underscores the need for more meaningful responses by the police, courts, schools, and communities against the *parents*, and more fruitful emotional help for children who have experienced or witnessed this violence. Dembo et al. stated that "early intervention with high-risk youths and their families is needed to address effectively their problems and troubled behavior before drug use and delinquent careers become firmly established" (1992, p. 245). This would require training of police and court workers, as well as the educators in our school system, about the risk of abuse in the homes, the effects of this abuse, and how best to respond to it. Relatedly, school systems need to be changed to empower girls and to provide less sexist environments. For example, the curriculum needs to include more information on women, girls, gender, and policies need to be in place and enforced regarding sexual harassment and other sexist behaviors (see Pipher 1994). In addition to the sexism in schools, numerous scholars on delinquent girls and incarcerated women have reported intensely racist experiences in the schools (e.g., Arnold 1990; Gilfus 1992).

These points were made at the recent annual meetings of the Academy of Criminal Justice Sciences by Christine Alder (1997). Alder noted that there is a need for policies for delinquent girls that do not undermine their independence, but instead empower and enable them to live independent lives. Currently, Alder stated, there is a lack of the necessary educational and employment resources for girls. Finally, Alder professed her concern for the sexual view of girls, and stated that sexuality has been created as a way for girls to resist and rebel (by being sexually active). Everyone, including the girls, needs to understand that sexuality is not bad, but rather girls need to learn who they are sexually in order not to see themselves as sexual objects (Alder 1997). The refocus on preventive measures, including the utility of providing services to young, poor women and girls with a myriad of psychological and emotional problems, could be funded by the money saved by decarcerating many of these girls who do not benefit from incarceration in the first place (Chesney-Lind 1995).

The second area of recommendations has to do with statistics and data gathering. Widom (1989a) has called on scholars to conduct research with multivariate models that can examine sex, race, and age to help understand how "victimization begets criminal behavior" (p. 163). Clearly more research needs to be conducted on the many variables related to delinquency and offending, that includes an account of individuals' childhood victimizations and exposure to violence and offending in the home. Furthermore, municipality, county, state, and national agency personnel responsible for collecting and publishing data on juvenile offending need to separate sex/gender and race *simultaneously*. In order to understand the processing of youth by the system, it is necessary to understand how racism and sexism may interact. This cannot be understood by simply looking at race and gender alone. The processing of females may vary depending on whether the individual is African American, Hispanic, Asian American, Native American, or Anglo. Related to these two areas of data gathering, more research needs to examine whether, and if so, how, justice is gendered. A close eye on the processing and institutionalizing of status offenders must be maintained, particularly regarding gender and the criminalization of girls (and boys) for running away from abusive homes. This research needs to be conducted at every stage of the system: the police, courts, and probation and parole decision-making stages. Moreover, this research needs to account for how a youth's gender, race, age, class, sexual preference, marital status, pregnancy status, dependent child status, and other "extra-legal" characteristics might impact decision making.

The final area of recommendations has to do with the treatment of girls once they have been institutionalized or processed as delinquents. At a recent conference on juvenile delinquents in Ohio (Ohio Department of Youth Services 1997), these authors participated in a special caucus on delinquent girls. Many of those working with delinquent girls spoke up on the importance of having the *girls* themselves take part in designing their own programs. As noted in this chapter and by these workers, these girls have entire lives filled with having power taken away from them and limited opportunities to express what they need. Although not empirically tested, these workers' enthusiasm about the significantly improved effectiveness of girls completing programs and achieving positive behavioral changes when they took part in designing their own programs, points to the need to try this innovative change. One worker noted that consistent weekly support groups, where it was up to the girls what they talk about, are more successful than ordering girls into structured programs. She believed that this was due to these girls' experiences of having been violated so severely that they could not trust something that they had no power over, and that taking part in their own rehabilitation was itself empowering. Linda Albrecht, who has considerable history working with delinquent girls, warned during this conference that simply making a "bad" program "gender-specific" was not going to make the program "good." Indeed, she warned that delinquent girls must be approached as a "whole package," not in a compartmentalized way, so that in addition to trying to educate girls about gender issues, you are also working on their acting out and violent behavior. (See Chapter Three by Zaplin for discussion of a systems approach.)

If in fact girls are becoming more violent, more programs need to assess the causes of this violence. Warehousing girls convicted of violent and other offenses in institutions while failing to adequately treat them for incest, nonsexual physical abuse, witnessing the battering of their mothers, witnessing general violence (including murder) in their neighborhoods, and so on, is not going to have a serious impact on deterring future problems, including delinquency. In addition to more proactive and individual and group counseling for survivors of these violent homes and communities, policies need to be implemented to address the revictimization some girls receive *while* institutionalized. The research reviewed above also points to the need for adequate programs for chemical abuse and dependency.

Given the overall gendered differences girls and boys experience in their families, schools, and the work force, it makes sense that services for juveniles, delinquents, and potential delinquents address the sexism and gender differences in the "real" world. It is necessary that class and racial differences and classism and racism are addressed, as well. Finally, the educational, vocational, and recreational programming available to incarcerated youth must be monitored to ensure that delinquent institutions are not providing unfair access to girls and are not working to reinforce gender stereotypes. Girls need education, vocations, exercise, and other activities as much as boys. Institutions need to be held more accountable for gender differences in access to programming.

CONCLUSION

This chapter has reviewed the many avenues through which girl delinquents have been ignored or treated in sexist manners. This has been the case in theorizing about delinquency, in the processing of delinquents through the formal system, and in the institutions warehousing delinquent girls. Research in the last fifteen years has documented the heretofore ignored relationship between high rates of violence in the home and the criminalizing of girls for running away from these abusive homes. Scholars must continue to examine the relationship between childhood abuse and subsequent mental health, chemical abuse, and delinquency problems. Juvenile and criminal processing system decision makers must be more informed about the link between childhood victimization and subsequent delinquency. Finally, institutions for delinquents cannot ignore and decide it is too late for these delinquents with chronic problems often related to their violent pasts. Although it may be too late to stop the youth from offending, and it is not ideal to wait until the youth has an official record, it is better to provide treatment after the offending starts, than none at all. In sum, improving systemic responses to female delinquency requires that more innovative preventive measures be taken, and that programs for institutionalized girls be improved and strengthened, recognizing gender differences, sexism, and the real life experiences of delinquent girls.

REFERENCES

Alder, C. 1997. Where have all the young girls gone: Programs and policies for delinquent young women. Paper presented at the Annual meeting of the Academy of Criminal Justice Sciences, Louisville, KY, March.

Arnold, R.A. 1990. Women of color: Processes of victimization and criminalization of black women. *Social Justice* 173: 153–166.

Belknap, J. 1996. *The invisible woman: Gender, crime, and justice.* Cincinnati: Wadsworth Publishing Company.

Belknap, J., et al. 1997. *Moving toward juvenile justice and youth-serving systems that address the distinct experience of the adolescent female.* A Report to the Governor. Office of Criminal Justice Services, Columbus, OH.

Bernat, F.P. 1985. New York State's prostitution statute: Case study of the discriminatory application of a gender neutral law. In *Criminal justice politics and women,* ed. Chaneles, S., 103–120. New York: Haworth Press.

Binkley-Jackson, D., et al. 1993. African-American women in prison. In *Women prisoners: A forgotten population,* ed. Fletcher, B.R., 65–74. Westport, CT: Praeger Publishers.

Bottcher, J. 1995. Gender as social control: A qualitative study of incarcerated youths and their siblings in greater Sacramento. *Justice Quarterly* 12: 33–58.

Briere, J., and Runtz, M. 1987. Post sexual abuse trauma. *Journal of Interpersonal Violence* 2: 367–379.

Browne, A. 1987. *When battered women kill.* New York: Free Press.

Cain, M., ed. 1989. *Growing up good: Policing the behavior of girls in Europe.* Newbury Park, CA: Sage Publications.

Canter, R.J. 1982. Sex differences in self-report delinquency. *Criminology* 20: 373–393.

Carson, D.K., et al. 1988. Temperament, adjustment, and alcoholism in adult female incest victims. *Violence and Victims* 3: 205–216.

Cernkovich, S., and Giordano, P. 1979. A comparative analysis of male and female delinquency. *The Sociological Quarterly* 20: 131–145.

Chesney-Lind, M. 1973. Judicial enforcement of the female sex role: The family court and the female delinquent. *Issues in Criminology* 8: 51–69.

Chesney-Lind, M. 1974. Juvenile delinquency: The sexualization of female crime. *Psychology Today,* 8: July, 43–46.

Chesney-Lind, M. 1981. Judicial paternalism and the female status offender: Training women to know their place. In *Women and crime in America,* ed. Bowker, L.H., 354–366. New York: Macmillan USA Publishing.

Chesney-Lind, M. 1986. Women and crime: The female offender. *Signs* 12: 78–96.

Chesney-Lind, M. 1987. Female offenders: Paternalism reexamined. In *Women, the courts, and equality,* eds. Crites, L.L., and Hepperle, W.L., 114–140. Newbury Park, CA: Sage Publications.

Chesney-Lind, M. 1988. Girls in jail. *Crime and Delinquency* 34: 150–168.

Chesney-Lind, M. 1989. Girls' crime and woman's place: Toward a feminist model of female delinquency. *Crime and Delinquency* 35: 5–29.

Chesney-Lind, M., and Brown, M. 1998. Girls and violence: An overview. In *Youth violence,* eds. Flannery, D.J., and Huff, C.T. In press.

Chesney-Lind, M., and Rodriguez, N. 1983. Women under lock and key. *Prison Journal* 63: 47–65.

Chesney-Lind, M., and Shelden, R.G. 1992. *Girls, delinquency and juvenile justice.* Pacific Grove, CA: Brooks/Cole Publishing.

Chesney-Lind, M. 1995. Rethinking women's imprisonment: A critical examination of trends in female incarceration. In *The criminal justice system and women: Offenders, victims, and workers*, eds. Price, B.R., and Sokoloff, N.J., 105–117. New York: McGraw-Hill.

Chilton, R., and Datesman, S.K. 1987. Gender, race, and crime: An analysis of urban trends. *Gender and Society* 1: 152–171.

Conway, A., and Bogdan, C. 1977. Sexual delinquency: The persistence of a double standard. *Crime and Delinquency* 23: 131–135.

Criminal Justice Newsletter. 1992. Florida supreme court bars detention to punish contempt. *Criminal Justice Newsletter* 23: 3–4.

Crimmins, S., et al. 1997. Convicted women who have killed children. *Journal of Interpersonal Violence* 12: 207–228.

Daly, K. 1989a. Rethinking judicial paternalism: Gender, work-family relations, and sentencing. *Gender and Society* 3: 9–36.

Daly, K. 1989b. Neither conflict nor labeling nor paternalism will suffice: Intersections of race, ethnicity, gender, and family in criminal court decisions. *Crime and Delinquency* 35: 136–168.

Daly, K. 1992. A women's pathway to felony court. *Review of Law and Women's Studies* 2: 11–52.

Daly, K. 1994. *Gender, crime and punishment*. New Haven, CT: Yale University Press.

Datesman, S.K., and Aickin, M. 1984. Offense specialization and escalation among status offenders. *Journal of Criminal Law and Criminology* 75: 1246–1275.

Datesman, S.K., and Scarpitti, F.R., eds. 1980. Unequal protection for males and females in the juvenile court. In *Women, crime, and justice*, 300–319. New York: Oxford University Press.

D'Augelli, A.R., and Dark, L.J. 1994. Lesbian, gay, and bisexual youths. In *Reason to hope: A psychological perspective on violence and youth*, eds. Eron, L.D., et al., 177–196. Washington D.C.: American Psychological Association.

Davis, D.L., et al. 1991. Prevalence of emotional disorders in a juvenile justice institutional population. *American Journal of Forensic Psychology* 9: 5–17.

DeFrances, C.J., and Strom, K.J. 1997. Juveniles prosecuted in state criminal courts. *Bureau of Justice Statistics Selected Findings*, NCJ-164265.

Washington, D.C.: U.S. Department of Justice Office of Justice.

Dembo, R., et al. 1992. The role of family factors, physical abuse, and sexual victimization experiences in high-risk youths' alcohol and other drug use and delinquency: A longitudinal model. *Violence and Victims* 7: 245–266.

Dodge, K.A., et al. 1990. Mechanisms in the cycle of violence. *Science* 250: 1678–1683.

Eaton, M. 1986. *Justice for women? Family, court and social control*. Milton Keynes, England: Open University Press.

Epstein, C.F. 1988. *Deceptive distinctions: Sex, gender, and the social order*. New Haven: Yale University Press.

Faith, K. 1993. *Unruly women: The politics of confinement and resistance*. Vancouver: Press Gang Publishers.

Falshaw, L., et al. 1996. Victim to offender: A review. *Aggression and Violent Behavior* 1: 389–404.

Farrington, D.P., and Morris, A.M. 1983. Sex, sentencing and reconviction. *British Journal of Criminology* 23: 229–248.

Federle, K.H., and Chesney-Lind, M. 1992. Special issues in juvenile justice: Gender, race, and ethnicity. In *Juvenile justice and public policy: Toward a national agenda*, ed. Schwartz, I.M., 165–195. Indianapolis, IN: Macmillian USA Publishing.

Feinman, C. 1986. *Women in the criminal justice system* 2nd ed. New York: Praeger Publishers.

Feinman, C. 1992. Criminal codes, criminal justice, and female offenders: New Jersey as a case study. In *The changing roles of women in the criminal justice system*, ed. Moyer, I.L., 2nd ed., 5768. Prospect Heights, IL: Waveland Press.

Felthous, A.R., and Yudowitz, B. 1977. Approaching a comparative typology of assaultive female offenders. *Psychiatry* 40: 270–276.

Feyerherm, W. 1981. Gender differences in delinquency: Quantity and quality. In *Women and crime in America*, ed. Bowker, L.H., 82–93. Indianapolis, IN: Macmillan USA Publishing.

Figueira-McDonough, J., et al. 1981. Normal deviance: Gender similarities in adolescent subcultures. In *Comparing female and male offenders*, ed., Warren, M.Q., 17–45. Newbury Park, CA: Sage Publications.

Frazier, C.E., and Cochran, J.C. 1986. Detention of juveniles: Its effects on subsequent juvenile court processing decisions. *Youth and Society* 17: 286–305.

Freedman, E. 1982. Nineteenth century women's prison reform and its legacy. In *Women and the law: A social historical perspective,* ed. Weisberg, D.K., Vol. 1, 141–157. Cambridge, MA: Schenkman Publishing.

Gelsethorpe, L. 1989. *Sexism and the female offender.* Aldershot, England: Gower Publishing.

Gilfus, M.E. 1992. From victims to survivors to offenders: Women's routes of entry and immersion into street crime. *Women and Criminal Justice* 4: 63–90.

Goetting, A., and Howsen, R.M. 1983. Women in prison: A profile. *The Prison Journal* 63: 27–46.

Gray, E. 1988. The link between child abuse and juvenile delinquency: What we know and recommendations for policy and research. In *Family abuse and its consequences,* eds., Hotaling, G.T., et al., 109–125. Newbury Park, CA: Sage Publications.

Hiller, A.E., and Hancock, L. 1981. The processing of juveniles in Victoria. In *Women and crime,* eds. Mukherjee, S.K., and Scutt, J.A., 92–126. North Sydney, Australia: Allen and Unwin.

Hindelang, M.J. 1981. Variations in sex-race-age specific incidence rates of offending. *American Sociological Review* 46: 461–474.

Hollander, H.E., and Turner, F.D. 1985. Characteristics of incarcerated delinquents: Relationship between development disorders, environmental and family factors, and patterns of offense and recidivism. *Journal of American Academy of Child Psychiatry* 24: 221–226.

Howell, N., and Davis, S.P. 1992. Special problems of female offenders. *Corrections Compendium* 17: 5–20.

Inciardi, J., et al. 1993. *Women and crack-cocaine* Indianapolis, IN: Macmillan USA Publishing.

Jacobs, J.L. 1994. *Victimized daughters: Incest and the development of the female self.* New York: Routledge.

Jensen, G.F., and Brownfield, D. 1986. Gender, lifestyles, and victimization: Beyond routine activities. *Violence and Victims* 1: 85–99.

Jensen, G.F., and Thompson, K. 1990. What's class got to do with it: A further examination of power control theory. *American Journal of Sociology* 95: 1009–1023.

Joe, K.A., and Chesney-Lind, M. 1995. "Just every mother's angel": An analysis of gender and ethnic variations in youth gang membership. *Gender and Society* 9: 408–432.

Kersten, J. 1989. The institutional control of girls and boys. In *Growing up good: policing the behavior of girls in Europe,* ed. Cain, M., 129–143. Newbury Park, CA: Sage Publications.

Krisberg, B., and Austin, J.P. 1993. *Reinventing juvenile justice.* Newbury Park, CA: Sage Publications.

Krisberg, B., and Schwartz, I. 1983. Rethinking juvenile justice. *Crime and Delinquency,* 29: 333–365.

Krohn, M., et al. 1983. Is chivalry dead? An analysis of changes in police dispositions of males and females. *Criminology* 21: 417–437.

Kruttschnitt, C. 1981. Social status and sentences of female offenders. *Law and Society Review* 15: 247–265.

Kruttschnitt, C. 1984. Sex and criminal court dispositions: The unresolved controversy. *Research in Crime and Delinquency* 21: 213–232.

Kruttschnitt, C., and Green, D.E. 1984. The sex-sanctioning issue: Is it history? *American Sociological Review* 49: 541–551.

Lake, E.S. 1993. An exploration of the violent victim experiences of female offenders. *Violence and Victims* 8: 41–51.

LaPrarie, C.P. 1989. Some issues in Aboriginal justice research: The case of Aboriginal women in Canada. *Women and Criminal Justice* 1: 81–92.

Laub, J.H., and McDermott, J.M. 1985. An analysis of serious crime by young Black women. *Criminology* 23: 81–98.

Leonard, E. 1982. *Women, crime and society.* New York: Longman.

Levey, J.C., and Lagos, V.K. 1994. Children with disabilities. In *Reason to hope: A psychological perspective on violence and youth,* eds. Eron, L.D., et al., 197–213. Washington, D.C.: American Psychological Association.

Mann, C.R. 1984. *Female crime and delinquency.* University, Alabama: University of Alabama Press.

McCloskey, L.A., et al. 1995. The effects of systemic family violence on children's mental health. *Child Development* 66: 1239–1261.

Milin, R., et al.. 1991. Psychopathology among substance abusing juvenile offenders. *Journal of American Academy of Child and Adolescent Psychiatry* 30: 560–574.

Morris, R.R. 1987. *Women, crime and criminal justice.* Oxford: Basil Blackwell.

Naffine, N. 1987. *Female crime: The construction of women in criminology.* Sydney, Australia: Allen and Unwin.

Naffine, N. 1989. Towards justice for girls: Rhetoric and practice in the treatment of status offenders. *Women and Criminal Justice* 1: 3–20.

Nagel, I.H., and Hagan, J. 1983. Gender and crime: Offense patterns and criminal court sanctions. In *Crime and justice,* eds. Tonry, M., and Morris, N., Vol. 4, 91–144. Chicago: University of Chicago Press.

Odem, M.E. 1995. *Delinquent daughters: Protecting and policing adolescent female sexuality in the United States, 1885–1920.* Chapel Hill: The University of North Carolina Press.

Ohio Department of Youth Services. 1997. The Female Offender Caucus of the Fourth Annual RECLAIM Ohio Conference. Columbus, Ohio, June 2–4, 1997.

Pipher, M.E. 1994. *Reviving Ophelia: Saving the selves of adolescent girls.* New York: Ballantine Books.

Poe-Yamagata, E., and Butts, J.A. 1996. *Female offenders in the juvenile justice system: Statistics summary.* Washington, D.C.: Office of Juvenile Justice and Delinquency Prevention.

Rafter, N.H. 1985. *Partial justice: Women in state prisons, 1800–1935.* Boston: Northeastern University Press.

Rhode, D.L. 1989. *Justice and gender.* Cambridge, MA: Harvard University Press.

Richards, P. 1981. Quantitative and qualitative sex differences in middle-class delinquency. *Criminology* 26: 151–170.

Rivera, B., and Widom, C.S. 1990. Childhood victimization and violent offending. *Violence and Victims* 5: 19–35.

Rohsenow, D., et al. 1988. Molested as children: A hidden contribution to substance abuse? *Journal of Substance Abuse Treatment* 5: 13–18.

Rowe, D. C., and Farrington, D.P. 1997. The familiar transmission of criminal convictions. *Criminology* 35: 177–201.

Russell, D. 1984. *Sexual exploitation: Rape, child sexual abuse, and workplace harassment.* Newbury Park, CA: Sage Publications.

Sarri, R. 1983. Gender issues in juvenile justice. *Crime and Delinquency* 29: 381–398.

Sarri, R. 1987. Unequal protection under the law: Women and the criminal justice system. In *The trapped woman: Catch-22 in deviance and control,* eds. Figueira-McDonough, J.R., and Sarri, R., 394–426. Newbury Park, CA: Sage Publications.

Schlossman, S., and Wallach, S. 1982. The crime of precocious sexuality: Female juvenile delinquency in the progressive era. In *Women and the law,* ed. Weisberg, D.K.,Vol. 1, 45–84. Cambridge, MA: Schenkman.

Schwartz, I., et al. 1984. The hidden system of juvenile control. *Crime and Delinquency* 30: 371–385.

Shelden, R.G. 1981. Sex discrimination in the juvenile justice system: Memphis, Tennessee, 1900–1917. In *Comparing female and male offenders,* ed. Warren, M.Q., 55–72. Newbury Park, CA: Sage Publications.

Shelden, R.G., and Chesney-Lind, M. 1993. Gender and race differences in delinquent careers. *Juvenile and Family Court Journal* 44: 73–90.

Silbert, M.H., and Pines, A.M. 1981. Sexual child abuse as an antecedent to prostitution. *Child Abuse and Neglect* 5: 407–411.

Smart, C. 1976. *Women, crime and criminology: A feminist critique.* London: Routledge and Kegan Paul.

Smart, C. 1982. The new female offender: Reality or myth? In *The criminal justice system and women,* eds. Price, B.R., and Sokoloff, N., 105–116. New York: Clark Boardman.

Smart, C. 1989. *Feminism and the power of the law.* London: Routledge and Kegan Paul.

Snell, T.L., and Morton, D.C. 1994. *Women in prison.* Washington, D.C.: Bureau of Justice Statistics.

Sommers, I., and Baskin, D.R. 1994. Factors related to female adolescent initiation into violent street crime. *Youth and Society* 25: 468–489.

Spohn, C., et al. 1987. The impact of the ethnicity and gender of defendants on the decision to reject or dismiss felony charges. *Criminology* 25: 175–191.

Stanko, E.A. 1985. *Intimate intrusions: Women's experiences of male violence.* London: Routledge and Kegan Paul.

Steffensmeier, D., and Allen, E.A. 1988. Sex differences in patterns of adult crime, 1965-77: A review and assessment. *Social Forces* 58: 1080–1108

Steffensmeier, D., et al. 1993. Gender and imprisonment decisions. *Criminology* 31: 411–446.

Teilmann, K.S., and Landry, P.H. 1981. Gender bias in juvenile justice. *Journal of Research in Crime and Delinquency* 18: 47–80.

Temin, C.E. 1980. Discriminatory sentencing of women offenders: The argument for ERA in a nutshell. In *Women, crime, and justice,* ed. Datesman, S.K., 255–276. New York: Oxford University Press.

Terry, R.M. 1970. Discrimination in the handling of juvenile offenders by social control agencies. In *Becoming delinquent,* eds. Garabedian, P.G., and Gibbons, D.C., 78–92. Chicago: Aldine Press.

Triplett, R. and Myers, L.B. 1995. Evaluating contextual patterns of delinquency: Gender-based differences. *Justice Quarterly* 121: 59–84.

U.S. Department of Justice. January 1991. *Children in custody, 1989.* Office of Juvenile Justice and Delinquency Prevention. NCJ-127189. Washington, D.C.: Government Printing Office..

Visher, C.A. 1983. Gender, police arrest decisions, and notions of chivalry. *Criminology* 21: 5–28.

Walker, L.E., and Browne, A. 1985. Gender and victimization by intimates. *Journal of Personality* 53: 179–195.

Warr, M. 1996. Organization and instigation in delinquent groups. *Criminology* 34: 11–38.

Warren, M.Q., and Rosenbaum, J.L. 1986. Criminal careers of female offenders. *Criminal Justice and Behavior* 13: 393–418.

Webb, D. 1984. More on gender and justice: Girl offenders on supervision. *Sociology* 18: 367–381.

Wells, R. H. 1994. America's delinquent daughters have nowhere to turn for help. *Corrections Compendium* 19: 4–6.

Widom, C.S. 1989a. The cycle of violence. *Science* 244: 160–166.

Widom, C.S. 1989b. Child abuse, neglect, and adult behavior: Research design and findings on criminality, violence, and child abuse. *American Journal of Orthopsychiatry* 59: 355–367.

Wilbanks, W. 1986. Are females treated more leniently by the criminal justice system? *Justice Quarterly* 3: 517–529.

Wolfe, V.V., et al. 1989. The impact of sexual abuse on children: A PTSD formulation. *Behavior Therapy* 20: 215–228.

Worrall, A. 1990. *Offending women: Female lawbreakers and the criminal justice system.* New York: Routledge.

Wyatt, G.E., et al. 1993. *Sexual abuse and consensual sex: Women's developmental patterns and outcomes.* Newbury Park, CA: Sage Publications.

Young, V.D. 1980. Women, race, and crime. *Criminology* 18: 26–34.

Young, V.D. 1994. Race and gender in the establishment of juvenile institutions: The case of the south. *Prison Journal* 732: 244–265.

CHAPTER 3

Female Offenders: A Systems Perspective

Ruth T. Zaplin

Editor's Notes

In the concluding portion of Chapter Two, Belknap and Holsinger cited Linda Albrecht, who warned that: "making a 'bad' program 'gender-specific' was not going to make the program 'good'..." Albrecht also stressed the need to approach delinquent girls "as a 'whole package,' not in a compartmentalized way..." In this chapter, Zaplin describes how the systems perspective and the tools of systems thinking, particularly the feedback loop, can greatly facilitate seeing the female offender not in a compartmentalized way but as a "whole package."

Systems thinking is a conceptual framework, a body of knowledge and tools, like the feedback loop, that has been developed over the past 50 years for the purpose of helping us see holistically. The logic of systems thinking is straightforward: if we can see patterns of interrelationships clearly, we can change unhealthy patterns effectively thereby producing long-lasting improvement. It is an extremely useful perspective for looking at a myriad of complex issues such as how female offenders, the criminal justice system, and the larger society are bound by interrelated actions that often take years to fully play out their effects on each other. Without the systems perspective, there is no understanding of these links. Nor can there be an understanding of other important interrelationships that foster crime such as the link between violence, learning disabilities, and the associated impulsiveness that can lead to juvenile delinquency. Ultimately, without this perspective, there is no understanding of the interplay of forces that must be mastered to educate female offenders about gender issues and working on their acting out and criminal behavior.

According to Senge (1994, p. 61), "The long term, most insidious consequence of applying nonsystemic solutions [to problems], is increased need for more and more of the solution," what Senge calls "short-term improvements leading to long-term dependency." Senge explained (1994, p. 61) that "the phenomenon of short-term improvements leading to long-term dependency is so common, it has its own name among systems thinkers—it's called 'Shifting the Burden to the Intervenor," In the case of female crime and delinquency, as a society, we have shifted the burden from, in the words of Belknap and Holsinger (Chapter Two), "failing to adequately treat them for incest, nonsexual physical abuse, witnessing the battering of their mothers, witnessing general violence (including murder) in their neighborhoods, and so on..." to institutions. Without the systems perspective we continue to fail to address the pattern of interrelationships between high rates of violence in the home, criminalizing of girls for running away from these abusive homes, and the consequences of institutionalization. In this case, more and more of the solution means that the revolving door of crime will become a mainstay in our society.

Ultimately what happens if, as a society, we choose not to learn the tools of systems thinking? Not only will we not address the root causes of female offenders' maladaptive behaviors often exacerbated by warehousing them in institutions, we will fail to have a lasting impact on deterring future crime and delinquency.

REFERENCE

Senge, P. M. 1994. *The fifth discipline*. New York: Currency Doubleday.

INTRODUCTION

One statement from a case study of a woman offender reads as follows, "My mother's sister's husband use to molest me from the ages of 9 to 11 during the summers and I felt at that point, when those things were happening, I felt ashamed....I felt dirty...I didn't know at that point that I could do something about it. I should have told somebody."

Having run away from home at age 16, this woman offender, in order to survive, engaged in prostitution and petty property crimes. She used drugs as a coping mechanism. Another statement from her case reads as follows, "What I like about it [using drugs]? —the escape. Why did I like an escape? Because all my life I disassociated without a drug, it [the disassociation] was familiar, it was safe, it was a coping mechanism...[then] I used a chemical and that chemical helped me to disassociate without me even trying to."

One statement from another case study of a woman offender reads as follows, "I always say that while growing up, the only consistency in my family was the inconsistency. There was none [consistency] and I know these things now because I've done the research within myself but while growing up I wasn't aware of them....My Dad left when I was 3 [years old]. When I was 5 [years old], I was raped."

While these statements do not allow valid generalizations to the entire population of female offenders, they highlight variables that are not atypical of the responses female offenders give when asked about their life experiences. Helping interventions rarely arise in their childhood. Often, when an option for help is available, because of the dynamics of abuse, their needs are misunderstood or ignored. Most of them however, never even know that help is available. And most are from dysfunctional families where, as described in previous chapters, they have been traumatized by physical, sexual, and/or emotional abuse.

Suffice it to say here, most are from social environments that support criminal values, attitudes, and behavior. Their family life is typically characterized by a lack of adequate care and positive support or good role models. There is inconsistent use of discipline, poor supervision, and often loss or absence of parent(s)—all of which are factors that have been related to poor attachment between parent and child.

It is not surprising that girls who grow up in this type of environment experience poor school performance, low educational aspirations and expectations, low involvement in school activities and low school-related satisfactions and ties of affection. In addition to not developing healthy relationships with their parent(s), they did not develop healthy relationships with their peers. Rather, longing for kinship ties, these same juvenile girls bonded to delinquent peers; one of the most important proximate causes of delinquency (Sampson and Laub 1993). While in this society girls are generally socialized toward greater empathy toward others than boys (see Chapter Five), the life experiences of female offenders give them a distorted view of empathy and caring. As a result of their childhood experiences, they do not feel self-worth. They are not able to develop empathic and caring attitudes towards themselves. Nor are they able to develop empathic and caring attitudes towards others. The relationships they do have are characterized by unhealthy, codependent attitudes (Zaplin 1998, p. 130).

The emotional deprivation experienced by female offenders in their interactions with others coupled with the absence of empathic attitudes towards themselves, particularly when it is combined with serious economic and social deprivation, leads to a condition of ongoing emotional stress. When they talk about themselves, they usually express strong feelings of self-hatred, worthlessness, joylessness, dread, anxiety, and depression. When in these emotional states, their behaviors are often aggressive, and impulsive. They act before they think. According to Goleman (1995), these behaviors are manifestations of both severe stress and what he calls "deficits" in emotional competencies. The result of this combination is that they often feel helpless to deal with their emotions because they lack emotional awareness.

Because female offenders lack healthy support systems, external resources to help with the emotional toll of stress, these women and girls remain in stressful states for prolonged periods of time. In these states, working memory does not function properly; they do poorly at the task at hand, be it job assignments or homework assignments. According to Goleman (1995), when emotionally upset, people cannot attend, learn, or make decisions clearly. This is one reason why female offenders often have an inability to concentrate even in "remedial" situations, e.g., a class in basic living skills. It is not surprising that as adults, for example as single mothers, they have great difficulty acquiring new job skills, establishing a home, or achieving economic stability. Thus, their stressful states are exacerbated by the fact that they remain either unemployed or work only sporadically for wages. Many turn to drugs because they have no healthy internal resources for dealing with their emotions. The fact is that most female offenders have become, or are on the road to becoming, acutely socially, politically, and economically marginalized individuals. Thus, it is extraordinarily difficult for them to remain substance-free and to maintain crime-free lifestyles.

Ironically, society's response has, for the most part, not been a rehabilitative one. Rather, society's response has been to place them in institutions that, for reasons elaborated upon below, do not offer social treatment programs that adequately address their rehabilitative needs. While, in the short term, institutionalization temporarily does take them out of the violence and abuse at home and on the street, without programs that adequately address their rehabilitative needs, institutionalization does not modify their unhealthy behavior patterns such as drug use, or have long-term positive impact on recidivism rates. In point of fact, institutionalization that does not contribute to the positive alteration of the behavioral repertoires of female offenders often exacerbates their situations especially if they experience violence and abuse within the institutions themselves. Given their maladaptive coping skills, poor self-esteem, and emotional stress, most female offenders find it impossible to change themselves positively in these environments. It follows then, that they are not likely to change themselves, returning to the environments from which they came upon their release. They remain in emotional states characterized by feelings such as anxiety and depression and their behaviors remain aggressive and impulsive—a state conducive to continued pathological behavior including repeated criminal activity. Once released from an institutional environment that does not address their rehabilitative needs, female offenders demonstrate a marked tendency to resume their criminal careers and to participate in what has come to be known as "the revolving door of justice"—crime, arrest, conviction, incarceration or institutionalization, release, and return to crime—and the cycle continues (National Task Force on Correctional Substance Abuse Strategies 1991). Thus, there is evidence that institutionalization is causing unintended consequences that actually contribute to increased crime (Butterfield 1997).

The institutionalization of female offenders in this country cannot be separated from the broader sociopolitical environment in which a "get tough" approach to crime exists. As a result, sentences have increased for many crimes. For example, women sentenced for drug offenses only (not charged with any other type of crime) account for a substantial growth in the prison population. Parole boards have also become much more sensitive to the public's demand for harsher treatment of criminals (Butterfield 1997). Thus, the result of the major thrust of crime policy in this country is, increasingly, simply to institutionalize people regardless of age or seriousness of the crime (Sampson and Laub 1993). This approach, while popular, has had deleterious effects on female offenders in terms of addressing their rehabilitative needs.

The general public's desire for a more punitive correctional environment, also known as "zero tolerance," coupled with changes in sentencing laws, has placed pressure on corrections departments to also "get tough." These facts, and the increased costs of running a constantly expanding prison system, portend a decreased probability that programs designed to address the rehabilitative needs of female offenders will be offered in institutional environments.

The problem of institutionalization that is not inclusive of treatment goes beyond the fact that they fail to rehabilitate. Female offenders are often sent to facilities that cannot even accommodate them properly, let alone begin to rehabilitate them. The environments in which they are housed are punishing in their own right (National Criminal Justice Association [NCJA] 1997). In addition, because most states have fewer facilities for female offenders than are available for male offenders, they are often relocated hours away from their homes. This logistical separation from their families can be particularly problematic when mothers are moved far from their children. Institutionalized women are most often mothers, consider themselves the primary nurturers for their children, and therefore suffer severe psychological consequences when confronted with the loss of love and family (see Chapter Fifteen for further discussion).

It is also troubling that, although rehabilitation programs may exist for women in prison and delinquent girls in juvenile institutions, they are usually not comparable in quality to those provided to male offenders and delinquent boys. Even in those cases where female offenders appear to be receiving lighter sentences, it must be borne in mind that they generally commit less serious crimes than male offenders, and, by virtue of the inadequate facilities and rehabilitative services that are characteristic of their terms of institutionalization, they are in fact being sentenced more harshly. That is to say, female offenders are punished more severely then are their male counterparts because of *how* they are institutionalized (NCJA, 1997). They are not even provided with the same opportunities as male offenders who have committed more serious offenses and have longer sentences.

It is important to emphasize here that the use of institutionalization *solely* as a punishment and not as an opportunity to rehabilitate, defines a set of relations between these female offenders and their social worlds. Obviously, the relations between those institutionalized, usually against their will (a small percentage of female offenders want to be institutionalized, e.g., for protection from a battering partner), and their keepers are structured by unequal power status. Although this fact may be unavoidable, the unequal power status reinforces the alienation of these female offenders from society. The lack of autonomy, the loss of identity, and powerlessness associated with institutionalization also creates an exaggerated dependency on those in authority for female offenders. This situation results in women and girls leaving institutions being less able to assume responsibility for themselves and their children.

Additionally, power relations are not consistent with or supportive of rehabilitative environments, nor do they foster the development of self-respect or empowerment (Hannah-Moffat 1995, p. 154). It is not surprising that in such circumstances, female offenders will typically not be receptive to treatment. That is to say, even if multifaceted, rehabilitative programs are developed, their efficacy will likely be undermined by the social structure of the institutional environment as it exists today. Thus, for most female offenders, punishments rendered in institutional environments are not conducive to addressing their rehabilitative needs even in the best of circumstances.

While a strong argument can be made on humanitarian and social welfare grounds alone to develop social treatment programs that will positively correct the maladaptive behaviors of female offenders, there are also pressing practical reasons to do so. The logic is simple.

These maladaptive behaviors, if not corrected, often produce unintended criminogenic effects because the marginality of the offender is exacerbated. Institutionalization of female offenders without social treatment programs to address maladaptive behaviors actually contributes, as previously stated, to the increasing numbers of women and juveniles involved in the revolving door of the criminal and juvenile justice systems. The larger the number of female inmates, the bigger the number of females who will someday be released, and then, if their maladaptive behaviors were not addressed, will be likely to commit new crimes and be rearrested (Butterfield 1997). Thus, institutionalization has created its own growth dynamic.

Another factor contributing to the growth dynamic of institutions are criminal justice policy shifts described earlier. It is interesting to note that these policy shifts, while they have resulted in more and more females being institutionalized, do not reflect significant changes in females' criminal behavior over time, i.e., increases in institutionalization cannot be explained by increases in female crime patterns. Even in light of this fact, it is unlikely that the public's feelings about crime and criminals will bring about changes in sentencing laws for the simple reason that, for the past five straight years, crime has been falling even as more and more tough sentencing laws take effect. With the expected huge influx of inmates over the next few years as more and more tough sentencing laws take effect, institutional beds will become an even more scarce and expensive resource that should be allocated in a judicious manner for those who need this level of control and sanction (Zaplin 1998). Therefore, on a very practical level, it is urgent that the maladaptive behaviors of female offenders are corrected.

A SYSTEMS PERSPECTIVE

Clearly, the life of the female offender is embedded in a complex social reality encompassing her relationships, personal history, and the many contextual, sociological forces inducing her criminality. The prospects for her rehabilitation and reintegration into society cannot validly be disentangled from this context. If the complexity is ignored, the purposes of any intervention program will be frustrated. On the other hand, the complexity can appear to be overwhelming for treatment providers.

The systems perspective based on general systems theory described below, provides powerful language, concepts, and tools that make it possible to think and talk in a disciplined and detailed manner about female offenders without undo simplification, i.e., not only in the context of her individual characteristics—how she "hangs together"—but in the context of complex systems of interactions, interventions, and influences. This perspective is inclusive of, among other things, the interrelationship of the characteristics of the female offender herself, the impact of informal social controls, the nature of her criminal offenses, services designed for her, the characteristics of the correctional institutions and agencies that deliver these services, and the external environment of these institutions and agencies, including the role of policymakers and legislators, and the society at large. It is suggested here that this systems perspective represents a necessary mind-set that criminologists, practitioners, therapists and others working with female offenders must learn if they are going to develop theory based programs that are efficacious in altering behavioral repertoires (see Chapter Four).

By adopting a systems perspective, beyond seeing the pattern of interrelationships inclusive of the attributes of people, institutions, agencies, and the society at large, those working with female offenders will also be able to see how these forces interact, shape, affect, and condition one another reciprocally. It also becomes possible to see patterns of causality—the cycles of cause and effect that make up systems (Senge et al. 1994). These circles or spirals of interaction are characterized by constant feedback and adjustment. In such a perspective, details come to be understood as aspects of a coherent picture of forces at play.

As stated, this perspective is based on general systems theory. General systems theory grew out of the effort to understand phenomena displaying a multiplicity of variables—and to understand them, not by analyzing the variables as separate entities but by attending to the interaction of these variables (Macy 1991). Specifically, it came out of biology and the work of von Bertalanffy (1968), who needed to go beyond the one-way causal paradigm of classical science to an understanding of whole processes as they naturally occurred in the phenomenal world. Von Bertalanffy found that wholes, be they animal or vegetable, cell, organ, or organism, could best be described as systems. A system is less a thing than a pattern consisting of a dynamic flow of interactions between variables including the larger environment (Macy 1991).

Other examples of systems include (Senge et al. 1994, p. 90) "biological organisms (including human bodies), the atmosphere, diseases, ecological niches, factories, chemical reactions, political entities, communities, industries, families, teams—and all organizations." These systems are consistent with the concepts of patterns, totality, feedback, self-stabilization and differentiation, information flow, and transformation (Macy 1991, p. 82) and what Senge et al. (1994 p. 87) calls "the world as if through a wide angle, not a telephoto lens." Thus it means looking at the female offender from a nonreductive point of view, i.e., not focusing exclusively on the symptoms of her drug problem, for example, but pushing beyond to assess the underlying causes of her drug problem.

The field of systems theory also includes: cybernetics and chaos theory, gestalt theory, the work of Gregory Bateson, Russell Ackoff, Eric Trist, the Santa Fe Institute, and the dozens of practical techniques for "process mapping" flows of activity at work. All of these diverse approaches have one guiding premise in common: behavior of all systems follows certain common principles, the nature of which can be discovered and articulated (Senge et al. 1994, p. 89).

Because of their utility, systems-cybernetic concepts have rapidly spread beyond the natural and life sciences and the work of von Bertalanffy, Norbert Wiener, and others, to the worlds of psychology and sociology. More and more areas of life were seen as manifesting systemic properties, and the system, as a new way of seeing, was found applicable to the human being—not just as a biological phenomenon but as a social and cognitive entity

(Macy 1991, p. 79). In terms of psychology, individuals could be seen as systems comprised of inner experiences in open interaction with their worlds, and, ultimately, being transformed by this interaction. The world of inner, subjective experience, is accepted by systems theorists as a given that must be understood in its own right, and the processes of which can be made intelligible.

The tools of systems thinking are causal loop diagrams, archetypes, and computer models. They are useful in bringing the relatively abstract notions presented here down to earth by enabling us to talk about rehabilitative interventions with respect to female offenders readily, as one common process. For the purposes of talking about the female offender, one tool of systems thinking, the feedback model (see Figure 3–1), provides a theoretical framework that is extremely useful for constructing a coherent description of the female offender herself, her interrelationship with the key components of the criminal justice and human services systems that she necessarily encounters, and how she is transformed (positively or negatively) by these encounters, as a single process. It is also useful for constructing a coherent description of the female offender and her world as a process that is ongoing. For example, the process would include how she moves through a single system (e.g., a jail or a detention center) and enters another (e.g., a day reporting program), and how various components within a single system must coordinate with and be aware of other components' strategies toward the rehabilitative intervention to ensure effectiveness.

Translating this theoretical perspective into viable programs that address the rehabilitative needs of female offenders on a practical level requires a broad-based, intra- and interagency approach guided by distinctive policies and practices. Female offenders are often on the caseloads of one or more human service providers when they become involved with the justice system. Efforts to change errant behavioral repertoires often require services and treatment that are provided by noncriminal justice agencies. For this reason, the systems perspective is inclusive of a wide circle of potential community corrections partners, described below, extending beyond traditional corrections and inclusive of public human service agencies, e.g., public health, private treatment and service providers, schools, religious organizations, and other community groups.

THE CASE FOR COMMUNITY CORRECTIONS

Given the nature of crimes committed by the majority of female offenders, community-based sanctions that address individual needs and require a greater commitment on the part of the offender than is required by institutionalization, can optimally challenge *most* women and girls to learn to cope with the community environment. In general, community corrections provide graduated levels of supervision. They range from simple probation at the least restrictive end of the criminal justice continuum and include a variety of community-based sanctions, such as work release, electronic monitoring, day reporting, and community service.

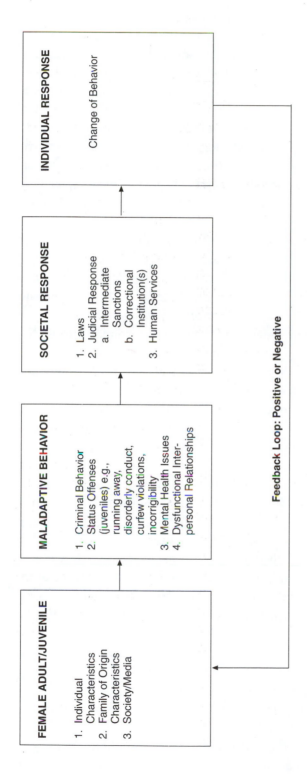

Figure 3–1 A systems theoretical framework

Community corrections programs can address the maladaptive behaviors of the female offender using the least intrusive interventions designed to change the behaviors that lead to criminal activity. It is suggested here and throughout this book that these kinds of programs have the greatest potential for addressing the rehabilitative needs of the female offender because they can provide the most comprehensive continuum of care. This continuum of care, to be optimally effective, should encompass gender-specific and culturally competent services inclusive of the female offender's complex health, educational, and social needs. These services should be delivered in a systematic and integrated fashion through, as stated, cooperative efforts of a broad range of community constituencies and agencies whose goal it is to achieve a rehabilitative societal response to maladaptive behavior (see Chapter Thirteen for discussion). This response needs to occur, as previously stated, at both a policy and an operational level.

For example, at the policy level, constituencies and agencies should develop memoranda of understanding or more formal interagency agreements regarding their respective roles and responsibilities. They should develop guidelines for sharing information and coordinating activities that address the rehabilitative needs of female offenders. These agreements should include a commitment to conduct joint, informational meetings, ongoing formal forums among correctional and treatment providers, and joint or cross training efforts (National Task Force on Correctional Substance Abuse Strategies 1991).

At the operational level, staff linkages among constituencies and agencies are important, not only to implement policy agreements, but to develop channels for enhanced working relationships. Enhanced working relationships can often mean the difference between successful and unsuccessful rehabilitative outcomes for female offenders. Joint staff meetings, mutual goal setting for female offenders, and case staffings are excellent opportunities to develop linkages at the operational level. In small agencies, in particular, cooperative arrangements with a variety of entities may be the only way to ensure that needed rehabilitative services can be provided (National Task Force on Correctional Substance Abuse Strategies 1991).

The ultimate purpose of adopting a systems perspective is to ensure that female offenders receive interventions that are consistent with their individual rehabilitative needs, while, at the same time, correcting errant behavior, thus meeting the collective safety needs of the community. Adopting a systems perspective will also ensure that service delivery is not hampered by opposing treatment philosophies; it allows for the placement of multiple philosophies into a single model.

A distinctive quality of a systems perspective is the coordination of a multidisciplinary staff. Treatment providers should be required, on a regular basis, to jointly discuss assessment findings and develop treatment services based on each individual's rehabilitative needs. At these meetings, each treatment plan should be updated to ensure that female offenders are receiving the optimum level of service delivery.

According to the National Task Force on Correctional Substance Abuse Strategies (1991), it is counterproductive to place individuals in programs that are not designed to meet their individual rehabilitative needs in terms of, for example, substance abuse severity, mental health disorders, criminality, etc. Overprogramming and underprogramming of individuals can also yield negative results. Excessive programming for a specific individual can cause the individual to drop out of treatment as well as waste limited treatment resources. Insufficient programming may allow the individual to complete treatment without receiving sufficient intervention for real change.

Unfortunately, because of the "get tough" approach to crime described earlier, few jurisdictions can boast at this time, the long-term effectiveness of a graduated range of community corrections, needs-based options developed from a systems perspective. According to McGarry (1993, p. 11),

> It is not the failure of the programs—in number, inventiveness, or sophistication—that has produced ineffective and frustrating results, but rather the failure of the system that surrounds them to behave as a system. These failures include: lack of communication among the actors and agencies about the capabilities and limitations of sentencing options; the absence of an agreement on specific populations and outcomes for which these options are best suited; a lack of information about the sentencing process and of hard data about the offenders who come through it; and most importantly, the absence of a vision or articulated mission for the entire sanctioning enterprise.

Thus, creating these systems of rehabilitative service delivery in a jurisdiction requires consistent communication focused on the development of both a range of rehabilitative program options and a coherent policy to guide their use (McGarry 1993, p. 12). In order to foster positive rehabilitative outcomes, this policy needs to emphasize that programs for female offenders should promote personal dignity, honor diversity, and support families and communities, while promoting public safety (Intermediate Sanctions For Female Offenders Policy Group 1995). In summary, community corrections programs are needed that are sensitive to women's and girls' unique needs and strengths and guided by an articulate policy framework.

It is important to emphasize here that increased research and knowledge of gender differences in behavioral, cognitive, moral, and emotional development has provided new frameworks for understanding female development and should be incorporated into both policy development and rehabilitative programs for female offenders (Coll and Duff 1995). A principle contribution of the systems perspective is to identify ways in which effective programs can integrate needed rehabilitative components that are gender-specific. One factor associated with failure of rehabilitative programs for female offenders has to do with the fact that often they are incorporated into generic programs that make no gender distinctions. This is sometimes because of lack of funding and sometimes results from the impracticality of creating programs for relatively small numbers of female offenders. Too often, however, the generic approach reflects a lack of knowledge and a failure to grasp the importance of services that address gender-specific, rehabilitative needs.

It is imperative at this time to consider female and male offenders separately when developing and implementing rehabilitative programs and the policy that guides them. That this is of particular relevance in developing community corrections options for women and girls is supported by theories of moral development. Kohlberg's (1981) model of moral development, which has been effective in elucidating the attitudes of men, for example, is demonstrably deficient in encompassing the moral attitudes of women. Carol Gilligan (1982) has provided a model of an independent, developmental moral pathway for women. Given the growing numbers of female offenders in criminal justice systems across the country, such considerations are increasingly urgent.

At this time, some generalizations can be made with respect to gender-specific, rehabilitative interventions for female offenders. In general, these types of interventions should:

- deal with the effects of early physical, sexual, and emotional abuse and the resulting trauma
- increase awareness of feelings, thoughts, and behaviors of themselves and others
- transmit shared cultural values
- help to mainstream them into the society at large by strengthening their membership in family and community

Specifically, these types of interventions should raise their level of (1) social and emotional competencies, and (2) education/employability. Raising their level of social and emotional competencies encompasses teaching: self-awareness, personal decision-making, handling stress, communications, personal responsibility, and resolving conflict creatively. Self-awareness includes learning how to identify, express, and manage feelings, as well as building a vocabulary for them. Personal decision-making includes examining actions and knowing their consequences. Handling stress includes learning stress reduction techniques as well as how to manage emotions. Communications includes learning how to take the perspective of others and how to talk about feelings effectively. Personal responsibility includes recognizing the consequences of decisions and actions. And finally, resolving conflict creatively includes being assertive rather than angry or passive and learning the arts of cooperation, conflict resolution, and negotiating compromise.

Because most female offenders did not complete high school, raising their educational level encompasses the basic General Equivalency Diploma (GED) curriculum and other basic, educational curriculums inclusive of life skills classes, and job readiness training. For those female offenders who have their high school diploma and/or basic job skills, college courses as well as more technical and advanced job training should be made available. This will help women to get out of the lower-paying, gender-stereotyped jobs. Because most female offenders are (or will be) mothers, who grew up in dysfunctional families, their education should also include parenting classes and parent support groups (see Chapter Fifteen). Last, and definitely not least, rehabilitative programs must integrate and provide for long-term hurdle-help (described in Chapter Four) including substance abuse education and treatment—an essential factor to address female offenders' chemical dependency problems effectively.

To facilitate the rehabilitative process, staff and mentors who exemplify individual strength and growth while also providing caring support can be extremely important in helping female offenders to build healthy connections and remove barriers to their rehabilitation. Staff and mentors will be successful in understanding the behavior and needs of the women and girls they work with to the extent that they can respond empathetically to the inner subjective experience of each female offender's construction of *her* world. They need emotional support and an understanding of the cultural and relational contexts in which they grow, develop, and change (Coll and Duff 1995, p. 14).

Finally, if there is no tolerance in the system for relapse and relearning as part and parcel of the rehabilitative process, individual transformation will be thwarted, resulting, from a systems perspective, in a negative feedback loop. In a positive feedback loop, in order to make new data meaningful and usable, new constructs must evolve over time. With these new constructs, the system—the female offender in this case—can alter and refine her map of the world. This corresponds to the process of learning. This learning is enhanced when the female offender is provided the opportunities to participate in treatment and is ready to try an alternative lifestyle.

In conclusion, the community-based rehabilitative options described can offer a positive learning opportunity in the life of the female offender. It can be more than just a time for her to "clean up, detox and stabilize" (Intermediate Sanctions for Female Offenders Policy Group 1995, p. 27). It can be a time for her to grow.

MANAGEMENT CONSIDERATIONS

Female offenders, as part of their rehabilitative process, need to be empowered and made confident about their capacity to deal with the larger social world. This is not an easy task. Multiple trauma histories create multifaceted problems. From a systems perspective, multifaceted problems require a holistic, multifaceted response in terms of rehabilitative programming and opportunities designed to address them. Designing effective, multifaceted programs for female offenders that promote a sense of well-being, ability to take action, and increase self-worth in participants, also requires creativity. Specifically, it requires that the staff that design these programs maintain a systems perspective incorporating the relevant management principles.

The heart of the approach to management suggested is that the effective and responsible agency be designed so that it can learn from its own experience and is, therefore, able to manifest constant growth in the quality of the services it delivers. Such an agency has the highest probability of delivering those services that will ultimately integrate the female offender into society as a contributing member. Agencies that are oriented in this way are organized as horizontal systems of racially and ethnically diverse individuals, rather than as vertical systems of racially and ethnically homogeneous individuals, so common in hierar-chically structured management organizations.

Horizontal, systems-oriented agencies enable team members to manifest a commitment to constant growth and learning. Toward this end, both teamwork and the taking of indi-vidual initiatives are stressed. In point of fact, one cannot maintain a systems perspective as an individual, not because systems thinking is so difficult, but because good results in a complex system depend on bringing in as many perspectives as possible (Senge et al., 1994). Team members are encouraged to take responsibility, to propose and implement crossfunctional solutions, and to be the inspiration for the organization. The result is that team members on the front line are constantly refining existing services and implementing new projects and new directions of development with community-wide support and re-sources.

Although this might seem to some an idealistic and impractical requirement, in practice, experiences with such organizational structures are quite positive. Such organizations in-crease the likelihood that the female offender will receive those rehabilitative services guided by a policy framework that ultimately inspires her to acquire the skills and take advantage of the opportunities that she needs to be successful in reintegrating into society.

Workers at such agencies respond to the opportunities and challenges with eagerness. This response is the path of growth both for the workers and for the agency. Participants find creative means to pool their diverse functions and talents, contributing to a con-stantly evolving, integrative, supportive whole—what Senge et al. (1994) call a learning organization.

CONCLUSION

Antisocial behavior in children is one of the best predictors of antisocial behavior in adults. However, most antisocial children do not become antisocial as adults (Sampson and Laub 1993). Further, while adult criminality seems to be preceded by the characteristic of childhood misconduct, research has established large variations in later adolescent and adult criminal behavior that are not directly accounted for by childhood propensities (Sampson and Laub 1993, p. 15). These facts imply that individuals do not remain constant in their behavior over time and further imply that intra-individual change is possible. It follows that if intra-individual change is possible, it is critical that female offenders have the opportunity to integrate into an appropriate array of rehabilitative services that address individual needs in order to facilitate positive change.

When attempting to elicit this positive change, one concept must be remembered: how female offenders respond to their environment is determined by their individual life experi-ences, which are embedded in a broader sociological context. Therefore, when developing rehabilitative programs for this population, a systems perspective is recommended to en-sure that the interventions—and the policies that guide them—adapt and change to meet the individualized needs of each female offender within the broad spectrum of her interrelationships. This is a difficult and arduous task to undertake. Yet, we have no choice. Without adopting and implementing a systems perspective, programs will continue to fall short of meeting the specific needs of female offenders.

REFERENCES

Butterfield, F. September 28, 1997. Crime keeps on falling but prisons keep on filling. *The New York Times* 4: 1, 4.

Coll, C. G., and Duff, K. M. 1995. Reframing the needs of women in prison: A relational and diversity perspective. *Final report of the women in prison pilot project.* Wellesley, MA: The Stone Center Working Paper Series.

Gilligan, C. 1982. *In a different voice: Psychological theory and women's development.* Cambridge, MA: Harvard University Press.

Goleman, D. 1995. *Emotional intelligence.* New York: Bantam Books.

Hannah-Moffat, K. 1995. Feminine fortresses: Woman-centered prisons? *The Prison Journal* 75: 135–164.

Intermediate Sanctions for Female Offenders Policy Group. 1995. *Oregon intermediate sanctions for women offenders.* Salem, OR: Oregon Department of Corrections.

Kohlberg, L. 1981. *The philosophy of moral development.* San Francisco: Harper & Row.

Macy, J. 1991. *Mutual causality in Buddhism and general systems theory.* Albany, NY: State University of New York Press.

McGarry, P. 1993. The intermediate sanctions process: Rethinking your criminal justice system. In *The intermediate sanctions handbook: Experiences and tools for policymakers,* eds. McGarry, P. and Carter, M. M., 11–14. Washington, D.C.: U.S. Department of Justice, National Institute of Corrections.

National Criminal Justice Association 1997. Disparity in sentences between men and women. *Justice Bulletin* 17: 1–3.

National Task Force on Correctional Substance Abuse Strategies 1991. *Intervening with substance-abusing offenders: A framework for action.* Washington, D.C.: U.S. Department of Justice, National Institute of Corrections.

Sampson, R. J., and Laub, J. H. 1993. *Crime in the making.* Cambridge, MA: Harvard University Press.

Senge, P.M., et al. 1990. *The fifth discipline fieldbook.* New York: Doubleday.

Von Bertalanffy, L. 1968. *General systems theory: Foundations, development, applications.* New York: G. Braziller.

Zaplin, R.T. 1998. A systems approach to the design and implementation of a day program for women offenders. In *Complex challenges, collaborative solutions: Programming for adult and juvenile female offenders* ed. Morton, J.B., 129–140. Lanham, MD: American Correctional Association.

CHAPTER 4

Social Treatment: A Multiphased Event

Frank B.W. Hawkinshire

Editor's Notes

Chapter Three stressed the need for adopting a systems perspective in order to construct a coherent description of the female offender herself and her interrelationship with the key components of the criminal justice and other human service systems that she necessarily encounters, in order to learn how she is transformed by these encounters, as a single process. Chapter Three also stressed the need for tolerance in the system for relapse and relearning as part and parcel of the rehabilitative process. Hawkinshire, in Chapter Four, greatly elucidates on both of these notions, particularly recidivism, within a conceptual model for planned change. The author contends that an understanding of this model is critical to what program designers and treatment staff must learn in order to change permanently and positively behavioral repertoires of female offenders. The conceptual model of change is inclusive of the work done by systems theorists discussed here in the context of the model presented and introduced in Chapter Three. It also builds on a number of so-

cial treatment theories described, particularly the work of Kurt Lewin (1890–1949), one of the leading social scientists of that day and the first, according to Hawkinshire, to resolve the debate over the structure of the behavioral change process. In doing so, Lewin looked at the complex interplay of cultural, historical, sociological, psychological, and physical forces when attempting to explain criminality. Hawkinshire extends the Lewinian model, making it possible to understand the long history of failure in rehabilitation attempts with offenders that gave rise to the widely, and currently held belief that "nothing works."

In order to understand the planned change model presented, Hawkinshire contends that an understanding of the context, past practices, and the change process is required. The chapter begins with an overview of the context and past policies so that those who do not know what was tried during previous eras can be informed. This information delineates what problems emerged as planned change in the behaviors of criminals was attempted and provides a useful perspective from which to view current practices to rehabilitate female offenders. Next, the origins of the long-standing argument "lock them up" vs. rehabilitation are reviewed. This discussion sheds much light on why this debate continues unabated today. Finally, and most importantly for those interested in changing the behavioral repertoire of female offenders, the model of planned change is presented. This model, although not female-specific, is essential—and, Hawkinshire argues, is currently lacking—in current designs of rehabilitative programs for female offenders.

It is important to emphasize here that the discussion of the issues presented is intentionally unabbreviated because mastering the details of how to induce transformations in the behavioral repertoire of offenders is still central to what many criminologists and treatment providers must learn. This overview also provides broad details of how contextual social forces induce criminality. This is important information that relates directly to all of the chapters in this book. For example, because, according to Hawkinshire, many of the promising efforts of the early pioneers in social treatment programs for offenders were not elaborated, refined, improved, or even maintained, a consensus still does not exist as to the necessary elements of standard models of effective intramural and extramural social treatment. Rigorous assessment therefore continues to presume that the treatment model is valid and that the specified outcomes can be produced by the particular interventions employed. Not only does this prolong the debate of "lock them up" vs. rehabilitation, but without these models, according to the author, "whatever was offered in the past that was thought to induce reformation will continue to be borrowed by persons starting programs [for female offenders]." Further, as dis-

cussed in Chapter Seventeen, most formal evaluations of social treatment programs continue to rely on evidence of recidivism. Hawkinshire calls this perspective a "common sense" view of planned change because, according to the author, "evidence was not sought by researchers to support the claims of criminologists that some changes were occurring in a nonlinear fashion, across time, in the behavioral repertoire of criminals." One of Hawkinshire's core arguments, based on these claims, is that any program designed to induce planned change must be prepared to provide "hurdle help" to deal with the potentially negative contextual forces in the larger environment. In other words, these contextual forces have a continuous impact on program participants before, during, and after completing the program in ways that could minimize the effectiveness of treatment, thereby contributing to regression during treatment and recidivism after treatment.

It is important to emphasize here that if we do not take the time to examine the record of over two hundred years of past practices (the first American penitentiary was authorized by the Pennsylvania state legislature in 1790) and what mistakes were actually made, rather than merely relying on misleading reports to determine what was learned over time, we are doomed to repeating the same mistakes over and over again. For example, the preponderance of rehabilitative programs for female offenders continue to be based on an "all and then none" treatment approach that fails to provide what Hawkinshire calls "the needed hurdle help" to offenders when they return to the environments from whence they came. As a result, upon successful completion of a treatment program, spontaneous remission of what was learned in treatment often takes place. This results in girls and women deciding to revert to old patterns to adapt to the standards set by those around them as a way to succeed. That is to say, they assume that their new ways of thinking and doing cannot be tolerated by old friends.

The cost of not learning from the mistakes made in the past is not only high in terms of dollars but, more importantly, it is high in terms of wasted human poten-

tial, a cost that this, or any society, can ill afford to bear. Alternatively, by using the knowledge provided by the planned change model, program designers will have the details they require to create more efficacious programs for female offenders, and program evaluators will have a more appropriate way of measuring success.

INTRODUCTION

"Lock them up" is the call of pessimistic criminologists, while optimists plead for more "effective social treatment" in the future.[1] Long-term confinement is supported by pessimists, because, in their view, no form of social treatment works. Acknowledging that "curing" the criminoses (rehabilitation) is impossible is the policy pessimists want adopted.[2] It logically follows to them, that locking criminals up and giving them long sentences should be the future course of action. Optimists reject the pessimistic position, and hold to the notion of rehabilitation as a valid future direction. Moreover, they lobby for even more efficacious intramural and extramural programs to deal with the complexities of rehabilitation.

These policy debates are neither new, purely philosophical, nor simply an expression of humanitarian concerns. Despite the antiquity of the controversy, there are at least two urgent reasons to reach resolution, and end the colloquy between these highly partisan camps. First, the need for bed space and the resulting building boom in prison construction is allowing a *de facto* policy of "warehousing" to emerge. Facilities are being designed and built that may prove totally inadequate to house programs dissimilar from current ones over the next 100 years. Second, unresolved controversies over major policy matters become a disincentive for initiative-taking by correctional staff. This makes it less likely that newly created treatment programs will be more effective in suppressing criminality.

Resolution of this debate can occur if a different approach is taken to formulating correctional policy because both sides are advancing faulty arguments. Pessimists are wrong when they charge "nothing works," and optimists are wrong if their programs lack appropriate treatment elements. For a more informed correctional policy to evolve, better understanding of the context, past practices, and the change process is required.

Plan of This Chapter

To make this information available to criminologists holding either position, three themes are covered in this chapter. First, the context and past policies and practices are reviewed so that those who do not know what was attempted in previous eras can be informed. This will clarify what difficulties were encountered by earlier criminologists, who employed various methods with some degree of success to suppress criminality. This information should alert current criminologists to the need to employ more comprehensive concepts, which already exist, in their designs to rehabilitate criminals. Second, the origins of these alternative conceptual perspectives are presented, so that criminologists will understand why these notions were not previously employed when treatment programs were designed. (3) A model that addresses the details of the change process is presented, because this information is lacking in designs of current correctional treatment programs. Without this knowledge, correctional designers will continue to propose treatment models that are not robust enough to cure the criminoses. The first theme covered is the context and past practices to be learned so that criminologists can obtain a better grasp of the issues in this debate.

Historical Context

Vengeance, retaliation, penance, confinement, reformation, and rehabilitation are concepts that can be found in legal writings dating back to the ancient Sumarian Code (2474–2398 BC). The Hammurabi (2133–2081 BC), Roman (400 BC), and Justinian (528–537 AD) codes were replete with ways to obtain vengeance and retaliation. Restriction of freedom, which ranged from forms of house arrest to the stocks, became central in subsequent policy formulations that were implemented through legal processes. This development started with the rise of Feudal law (600 AD), the rule of Charlemagne (800–814), and the spread of the Cluniac Monastic System (1100).

Confinement, as a policy, was formally introduced with the revival of Roman Law by Irnerius (c. 1150). It was further confirmed with the adoption of the Magna Carta (1215), enactments of the Fourth Lateran Council (1215), and authorizing of English and French inquisitions by Pope Gregory IX (1233). The Council, for example, explicitly endorsed the policy of imprisonment as slaves, for those confined on galley ships. Those who were assigned to dungeons of castles, churches, and monasteries were confined as penitents.

The suppression of monasteries by Henry VIII (1535–1540) eliminated spaces for confinement. This shift in policy eventually resulted in Elizabeth I's authorizing transportation of children, women, and men to colonies (1597–1890). Imprisonment, for purposes other than detention for trial, became more widespread as transportation became more difficult with the loss of colonies.

A theme running through these historic policy formulations was the search to "cure" criminality. These policies were all designed to induce changes in the entire behavioral repertoire, not just stopping criminals from enacting a few illegal behaviors. Consequently, the concern with mastering techniques of planned change became the *sine qua non* early on in attempts to suppress criminality.[3] Once the centrality of planned change was accepted in policy and in law, during the twelfth century, then those charged with implementation in the criminal justice system were faced with the responsibility for accomplishing three things. They had to design efficient social treatment programs, identify both costs and benefits of every element, and assess the efficacy of the output of the model.

As imprisonment for children, women, and men became more widely employed over the next 600 years, criminologists faced a series of questions. These troublesome focusing questions included:

- Question 1: Can old patterns of criminality be unlearned and new ones mastered?
- Question 2: Is there a structure to this change process?
- Question 3: Is it possible to gather creditable evidence that desired transformations in patterns of criminality are occurring?
- Question 4: If new behavioral patterns can be learned in one setting, will they be used in a different one?
- Question 5: Should these planned change efforts take place within prisons or within the community?

During this developmental period, the last question dominated the debate over the efficacy of extramural or intramural treatment. Frequently, what was done in either setting was unknown or unclear to many criminologists trained in recent years, resulting in a faulty reading of this record. Consequently, clarifying past policies and practices is the next step.

PAST POLICIES AND PRACTICES

Once rehabilitation was accepted as the societal mandate in the twelfth century, how best to alter the behavioral repertoire of criminals became the issue at controversy. Authors in this book have accepted one position in this colloquy that split corrections for years. They adopted the ancient position that extramural social treatment for women and delinquent girls was an efficacious way to rehabilitate these offenders. It was widely assumed by those who advocated this point of view that community treatment was a more humane and far less expensive way to suppress female criminality.

Those holding the opposing position postulated that humane administration of intramural social treatment for women and girls could be accomplished. Adopting this seventeenth century position allowed two important conditions to be met. They were isolation of inmates from prior criminogenic mileux in which they had lived, and supervision of their social interactions to minimize continued relationships with more hardened criminals. These reformers acknowledged higher direct costs of operating prisons, but they pointed to lower indirect societal costs, due to victimization, resulting from the criminality of freed convicts. Furthermore, they would probably argue that it was not humane to promote discouragement and loss of self-esteem due to repeated failures resulting from constant community temptations. This is a complex debate that needs to be unfolded in order to understand the issues.

Originally it was only issues of humanity, efficacy, efficiency, and costs that were central to this controversy dating back to 1664.[4,5] Then the policy of imprisonment was proposed as a humane form of social treatment in place of hanging, pillorying, whipping, and branding. During the next 125 years, while these policy issues were discussed here and abroad, little resolution was possible, because penitentiaries had not yet been created. The first American penitentiary was authorized by the Pennsylvania state legislature in 1790, and the Philadelphia Quakers submitted a design. They proposed that the Walnut Street Jail, built in the 1770s, be remodeled and opened as a penitentiary for children, women, and men. When opened, with Mr. and Mrs. Weed as wardens, it contained separate facilities for women and children and supervision of their social interactions.[6]

Once prisons were operational, the debate moved to a different level. It now was possible to assess differential outcomes of intramural and extramural treatment. In the next 200 years, proponents made their own observations of their successes and failures, but these views did not alter opponents' opinions. Everybody had to await improved empirical research methods to document successful outcomes for extramural and intramural treatments in terms of efficacy, efficiency, and costs.

When empirical research evidence was at hand as to the efficacy of treatment, it was disappointing.[7] Gibbons made the point in 1968 that: "The student of criminality quickly learns, that criminal statistics must be treated gingerly and with a good deal of skepticism...."[8] By 1979 it was evident that it was impossible to say if either extramural or intramural social treatment was efficacious in light of the evaluation techniques applied.[9]

Several things contributed to this inability of criminologists to resolve the controversy. As early as 1956, Bloch and Flynn identified technical problems related to the research methods employed when conducting these studies.[10] More serious were problems inherent in the structure and elements of the treatment design, even though these flaws were not clearly identified by these authors. Despite these studies, data were not readily available to answer the following focusing questions: [11]

- Question 6: How treatment was actually administered?
- Question 7: Whether appropriate subjects were given the treatment?
- Question 8: How the measurement of planned change efforts were conceived?

These questions still arise, because no standard extramural or intramural treatment models exist, which consist of specified elements with previously demonstrated efficacies. Therefore, it was premature to base treatment designs on existing practices, and then subject these programs to evaluation. Rigorous assessment presumes that the treatment model is valid and that the specified outcomes can be produced by the particular interventions employed. Unless this presumption is valid, evaluation reveals little that will permit sound policies to be formulated. Therefore, it is necessary to examine the record, rather than merely relying on misleading reports to determine what was learned over time.

Extramural Position

Social treatment outside of prisons goes back to 1841 when John Augustus (1785–1859) began obtaining parole for convicts in Boston. This work began informally with *no* clearly specified design. Humane reasons drove Augustus to employ impromptu, but minimal efforts, because of the desperate conditions experienced by over 2,000 female and male inmates. He did what he thought would encourage over 700 girls and women to avoid the unpleasantness of prisons. This exposure to confinement and release was an early form of rehabilitation now being called "scared straight."[12] It was his expectation that once in jail, convicts would promptly "change their minds" about engaging in crime, if given a "second chance." For a small number his policy worked, but for the majority it did not.

Objectives for a formal method of parole were described in 1846 by the Frenchman, Bonneville de Marsangy. Not much happened with his policy statement, because no one undertook further specification of the necessary and sufficient elements of demonstrated efficacy for this form of social treatment.[13] Even so, the practice and discussion of the conceptual basis of parole became more frequent after the Society of Friends proposed their design for imprisonment in 1790. It was the failure to implement fully the Quakers' design that increased discussions and heightened opposition to imprisonment.

This nineteenth century opposition to confinement on humanitarian grounds continued over the years. Greater specification of the necessary and sufficient treatment elements of an efficacious extramural model were neither established, nor employed. Despite lack of progress in this arena, influential criminologists like Harry E. Barnes (1889–1968) and Negley Teeters (1896–1971) voiced support for the policy of extramural treatment. They wrote that "...rehabilitation of delinquents outside of institutions...should be a major objective of the field."[14] The authors made a strong case, back in 1951, that kept alive the push for social treatment to be conducted outside of correctional facilities.[15] What was problematic about their stance was that their strong endorsement included no standard model of an effective extramural treatment program that could be employed.

During this period, a central policy concern can be identified in the writings of many criminologists supporting the extramural position. What seemed to drive this concern was the belief that noninstitutional treatment avoided many unintended, even if predictable, side effects of imprisonment. Most of these negative experiences that prisoners encountered within penal systems were continuously documented for over two centuries by criminologists with anecdotal and historical records. It was these reports of negative experiences, not lack of efficacy, in dealing with the complexities of intramural treatment that drove the continued support for the extramural position.

Intramural Position

The current formal intramural position in corrections dates from *the Declaration of Principles* issued by the 1870 Cincinnati Congress of Corrections. Delegates, under the leadership of Enoch Wines (1806–1879), took the position that an enlightened and humane form of social treatment could be conducted within prisons. When adopting this perspective, the membership used the 1790 design prepared by the Quakers, and elements of reported exemplary programs operated by criminologists.

The Philadelphia Quakers advocated specific elements of social treatment in their pioneering design for the Walnut Street Jail. Moreover, European advocates, such as the French penologist J. M. Charles Lucas, argued for the replacement of the poorly implemented penitentiary system with one aimed at rehabilitation.[16] Other progressive penologists included George Obermaier (1789–1885), warden of the Kaiserslautern Prison in Bavaria, and Manuel Montesinos (1794–1862), administrator of the Valencia Prison in Spain. These reformers made use of effective elements including indeterminate sentences, vocational training, and humane conditions in their programs of intramural social treatment.

In 1840 Naval Captain Alexander Maconachie (1787–1860) assumed control of the Norfolk Island Prison community in Australasia. For the nine years that he was in charge, he introduced the basic elements of a treatment program that became known as the Irish mark system. This system gained wide support in prison circles both here and abroad. It was described by Barnes and Teeters as:

> …the determination of the time to be served by conduct while in prison, promotion to release through graded stages of increasing freedom and responsibility, stress on the importance of teaching industrious habits to achieve rehabilitation, and the use of a rudimentary parole system.[17]

This promising form of treatment was fully implemented as the mark system in the 1850s by Walter Crofton (1815–1897) at the Mountjoy prison in Ireland and by Joshua Jebb (1793–1863) in England. It was these components of social treatment programs that delegates subsequently incorporated into the 1870 Declaration of Principles. The specified details of the Principles made them appear to be a valid standard model for social treatment. Now the possibility was available to criminologists to measure the efficacy of each element, and the ability of the total program to produce desired outcomes.

After formalization of the Principles, a version of the design was implemented by Zebulon Brockway (1827–1920) at the Elmira Reformatory in New York in 1876. As Barnes and Teeters noted, "Other states followed the example of New York in building reformatories, and glowing reports from the superintendents and observers filled the penal journals for many years."[18] This initial wave of enthusiasm for this form of social treatment was followed by other innovations. Thomas M. Osborne (1859–1926) introduced his ideas of the Mutual Welfare League into the Auburn, New York, prison in 1913, where it received public support. When Osborne became warden of the Sing Sing, New York, prison in 1914, he took his plan with him. In 1917, he initiated the program at the Portsmouth Naval Prison in New Hampshire when appointed warden. Howard B. Gill (1890–1989) continued this effort when he opened the Norfolk Penal Colony and started his experiment in social treatment in Massachusetts in 1927.

The promising, but limited, efforts of these pioneers were not elaborated, refined, improved, or even maintained. As reported in *The Survey of Release Procedures*, commissioned by Attorney General Homer Cummings:

> The reformatory program could not be maintained with the ever-changing political personnel or the starvation diet given it by the legislatures. As far as the majority of the prisoners were concerned, except for changes in housing, imprisonment in 1900–1935 was *substantially what it had been one hundred years earlier*: custody, punishment, and hard labor. By the end of the period in many prisons it reverted to just custody and punishment.[19]

The political climate, lack of trained personnel, and inadequate funding to keep up with the growing prison population proved critical. The serious financial problems created by the Great Depression doomed the Reformatory movement. At this point the answer to focusing question 1 appears to be: "No, patterns of criminality cannot be altered by the methods tried." This answer needs to be examined more closely.

What Was Learned from 200 Years of Experimentation?

The common belief of these pioneers, from both sides of the policy controversy, was the ideal of less reliance on traditional forms of imprisonment. Criminologists differed as to which form of social treatment was best, but the controversy was never resolved by programs that were efficacious, efficient, and reduced costs. On the basis of this record, the answer to focusing question 5 is: "It is unclear whether intramural or extramural treatment is most efficacious." Neither side had sustained their claims through empirical research.

This controversy will not be settled, if those in corrections continue current practices. A high level of consensus still does not exist as to the necessary elements of standard models of effective intramural and extramural social treatment.[20] Without these models, whatever was offered in the past that was thought to induce reformation will continue to be borrowed by persons starting programs. This situation will continue to exist even though better designs, long forgotten, were proposed by the Quakers, Lucas, Marsangy, and members of the Cincinnati Congress of Corrections. Barnes and Teeters made this point when they considered the quality of the Cincinnati Congressional design. In 1951 they stated that this design had:

> ...never been put into complete operation anywhere, and only incompletely in the federal prison system and in the systems of some of the more enlightened states. Therefore, it is not inaccurate to state that even the most enlightened penal practices of our day has not even yet fully caught up with the theory expounded by the more progressive of the veteran penologists.[21]

Because the Delegates' design was never fully implemented, the efficacy of their model is still unknown despite the contention of pessimists that "nothing works."

Even if the 1870 design for social treatment was fully accepted, there were major problems with their statement. What the members proposed in their design statement did not adequately answer the focusing questions. For example, they did not specify how various intervention techniques were expected to contribute to alterations in the behavioral repertoire. Morever, they did not assert the power of each technique—used separately and in combination—to induce desired transformations. Furthermore, they failed to delineate the characteristics of tasks and the physical setting in which they were enacted, which were likely to facilitate change. Finally, they did not set forth how the internal personal characteristics of inmates contributed to their succeeding in the reformatory program.

The problem for the Congress was that so little was known about what techniques do, when, on whom, and how. Thus, the design that they proposed was not particularly efficacious when subjected to empirical research. Despite these limitations, both sides were able to demonstrate some change for some offenders, but they could not rule out alternative interpretations for these convicts' apparent rehabilitation.[22] It could have been that they were "scared straight," experienced "spontaneous remission of their criminoses," or they "matured and changed their minds" about participating in crime.[23] Since 1870, however, major developments have taken place in theory that can enhance social treatment designs. Now the challenge to correctional workers is to incorporate this theoretical knowledge into their designs by doing the time consuming design work to produce robust treatments. This kind of work requires learning to use appropriate theories of planned change, rather than continued reliance on common sense notions.

WHAT IS THE NATURE OF PLANNED CHANGE?

The limitations of a common sense approach can be illustrated by the efforts of Brockway at Elmira. He offered statistical data as evidence of successful outcomes of the experiment based on common sense. Nevertheless, his claims of successful rehabilitation of offenders were questioned by members at the *International Penal and Penitentiary Congress*, meeting in Brussels in 1900. Critics of this program made instructive and still relevant comments:

> One objected to the large population at Elmira [1500], stating that it militated against "personal influence" of the superintendent; it was also felt that the average duration of the sentence was too short for effective trade training [12 to 18 months]....There was also some skepticism of Brockway's statistics that 75 to 80 percent of the discharged youth were reformed. Still another admitted the system was ingenious but contended that its results had not been sufficiently verified.[24, 25]

These criticisms of the Reformatory model were heard but no actions were taken. Nevertheless, by 1900 social theorists began to create more complex models designed to alter the behavioral repertoire of individuals. This work, which moved beyond common sense, was done outside of criminology. What the common sense notions are that underlie social treatment are identified first, and then the work of social theorists on planned change are presented.

Common Sense View of Planned Change

The common sense view is to think of change as a bipolar event—women convicts either have or have not been reformed. For many who hold this view, change is a linear process in which either success (change), or failure (no change) is the outcome. Most formal evaluations of the process that relied on evidence of "recidivism" followed this common sense view. Accordingly, evidence was not sought by researchers to support the claims of criminologists that some changes were occurring in a nonlinear fashion, across time, in the behavioral repertoire of criminals. Therefore, a better conceptual view that provides details about the transfiguring of repertoires is necessary, in order to have a more appropriate way of measuring success.[26]

There were social theorists who set out to specify the details of the change process.[27] It is from this body of work that descriptors of planned change were derived, which can now be used by criminologists to identify elements for an efficacious standard treatment model.

Conceptual Views of Planned Change

Contemporaneous with the work of Augustus, Marsangy, Lucas, Obermaier, Montesinos, and Maconachie was that of Auguste Comte (1798–1857). The focus of Comte's work was on the relatively smooth transformations that take place within societies as they are altered. His thinking became seminal to writers in his tradition, called organismic theorists.[28]

Organismic Change Theorists

For those holding the organismic point of view, change must be smooth and implemented in a gradual way over a long period of time. Failure to induce transformations slowly, and in small amounts, would result in dysfunctioning of the system and collapse—not change. Consequently, measurement of successful change would show no disruptions.

When a planned change effort is viewed this way, it means the repertoire is altered by adding new behaviors alongside old. Thus, persons will display new actions, but at times will also return to old ones. For this reason theorists postulated two critical notions to add to any understanding of planned change. It was not always progressive and linear, but sometimes regressive and wavelike, or sinusoidal.

Conflict Change Theorists

Simultaneously, there was a different strand of thinkers, initiated by Karl Marx (1818–1883), who also addressed societal change. Those in the Marx tradition, known as conflict theorists, proposed descriptors of change as necessarily a disruptive process. These theorists offered a direct challenge to the organismic perspective by emphasizing the rapid, discontinuous, and disruptive aspects. They took the position "...that change is endemic to all social organisms,...[but they also considered] conditions tending towards stability...."[29] By shifting attention to forces that produced disequilibrium, these theorists gave a different perspective to change. As they spelled out the process, signs of disruption were not indications of failure, but inherent in any successful effort to transfigure systems.

Resolution of the Theoretical Controversy

These competing views of change were not resolved until a new perspective began to influence the social sciences. In the 1910s, social theorists in Germany began to alter their views of social processes from unitary to multiple factors producing change.[30] They considered the social field as consisting of multiple competing and cooperating forces, differing in size, acting on societies, groups, and individuals. In this way, they incorporated into one position competing views of the process. As they saw it, molar events (the largest forces such as social, economic, and culture events) established the field. Macro events (middle size forces of social relationships such as families, social groups, and neighborhoods) shaped what happened within the field. Micro events (smallest forces such as values, social perceptions, and personality attributes) were precursors of specific human actions.

Kurt Lewin (1890–1949), one of the leading social scientists of that day, contributed to this paradigm shift in Germany. He left Germany and settled in the United States, and became one of the leading exponents of this theoretical perspective. In 1939, he described the new direction social theorists had to take to deal with complex social events, such as criminality. What Lewin urged American social scientists to do was a radical departure from their tradition. When dealing with social events, such as criminality, they had to enlarge greatly the boundary conditions of their inquiry. Then they had to direct their efforts toward multiple targets that included molar, macro, and micro forces as their scope conditions. He said it this way when he wrote that the task for social scientists such as criminologists was the

> ...integrating of vast areas of very divergent facts and aspects: The development of a scientific language (concepts) which is able to treat cultural, historical, sociological, psychological, and physical facts on a common ground." [31]

Lewin called attention to the unified nature of science, a position that was already breaking down disciplinary walls in Europe. As a result of launching this intellectual endeavor, much more attention was given to describing how a coherent set of multiple forces transformed behavioral repertoires. This alteration in perspective by his colleagues made it easier for them to produce a more detailed field theory model of the complex change process. This perspective made the theoretical work of social scientists more relevant to criminologists, and a positive answer could be given to focusing question 2. "Now it appeared that there was a structure to the change process."

To propose a field theory model from findings in this extensive literature required dealing with two prior focusing questions. "Was it possible to use the various theoretical traditions to understand how individuals, such as criminals, change?" "Were field theorists correct when they claimed that there were common properties of systems, regardless of the units of analysis?"

Lewin answered "Yes" to both questions and postulated a general theory of planned change that incorporated the ideas of both organismic and conflict theorists. These ideas could be applied by criminologists to suppress criminality as illustrated in Figure 4–1.

Ronald Lippitt, Jeanne Watson, and Bruce Westley followed up on this initial effort and considered Lewin's work as being:

> ...a general theory of change...[that could be]...used to assist understanding such diverse situations of planned change as are met in psychotherapy, child rearing, industrial management, race relations, and community development.[32]

By taking this intellectual stance, these authors were pointing to characteristics of change theories that would be useful to criminologists. What was central in Lewin's theoretical work was that he used generic principles to explain diverse intervention strategies and techniques. These principles could be used to direct the design of a wide range of treatment interventions to alter the behavioral repertoire of criminals.

To see if this derivation of general principles was warranted, Lippitt, Watson, and Westley reviewed other "... descriptions of change—in persons, groups, organizations, and communities—in terms of this sequence of phases."[33] This qualitative literature review helped them to see Lewin's ideas as fitting (isomorphic) with descriptors of varied efforts to induce planned change in social treatment.

William Liggett conducted a quantitative review of 29 authors and confirmed the postulated isomorphism between Lewin's principles and concepts from other traditions.[34] He agreed with Lippitt, Watson, and Westley that central Lewinian postulates were reflected in the work of others. For example, the notion that change takes place typically over a relatively long period of time as criminologists reported in 1900. Change is disruptive of the status quo, yet there are equilibrating mechanisms that create smoother phases, and at

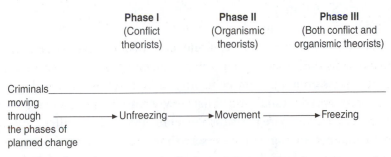

Figure 4–1 Representation of Lewin's phases of change showing a way to incorporate divergent views of the process.

times, reduction in tensions. Lewin was explicit about the need for various theories to be combined in order to explain multiple internal and external change forces when he stated that:

> Psychology cannot try to explain everything with a single construct, such as association, instinct, or gestalt. A variety of constructs has to be used. These should be interrelated, however, in a logically precise manner.[35]

Following this line of thinking, effective rehabilitation must be induced by organizing the forces emerging from tasks, social situations, and physical settings in which they were embedded.[36] All of these contextual forces belong to the field, according to Lewin, "…on the basis of their interdependence…." and therefore have to be employed when designing treatment.[37] These notions, now called field theory, were in line with the work of general systems theorists in Europe and later in America.[38]

General Systems Perspective

Contemporaneous theorists, such as Henderson, Whitehead, and James G. Miller, had similar ideas to Lewin's approach when dealing with complex social events.[39] System theorists considered it necessary to operate conceptually from the perspective of what might be called a theoretical net when dealing with social systems. The complexity of these systems required a net to be constructed consisting of a series of "…micro theories which could ultimately be combined [with macro theories] toward the goal of [adding a molar theory to create a complex] integrative general theory."[40] Systems theorists took this position, because they thought that social processes, such as criminality, could only be understood if "…the interrelationships among coacting components [micro and macro units were viewed as parts] of an organized whole…."[41] Adopting this perspective for correctional treatment designs meant that tasks, properties of groups, and characteristics of individuals and milieu had to be utilized as change forces.

General systems theorists, as described in Chapter Three, thought of single micro theories as necessary but *not* sufficient building blocks. These coacting components were studied to determine what they revealed about relevant personal characteristics of individual actors and tasks. Once inspected for the details that they contained, theorists then placed them where they belonged within macro theories that described aspects of social interactions. With the details of macro units identified, they then placed these units within the molar unit that described contextual forces creating an integrated general theory.

George Miller justified the necessity of employing this entire sequence by calling attention to the fact that theorists often ignored the totality of forces. He illustrated this point by commenting that scientists used journals to publish newly emerging knowledge "as if" they were catalogs in which to list "…spare parts for a machine they never buil[t]."[42] Worse still, authors in the 1950s and continuing to the present time acted as if there was no need to assemble these "parts" into a whole. Royce gave justification for this radically different, and prodigious, theory-building effort when he went on to note that "The big contribution which [a] theory [net] makes is that it brings order out of chaos; it provides meaning where it has previously not existed...."[43] A systems theorist would also argue that a theory net is required if criminologists are to grasp the totality of the field of forces that induce criminality. It is this very different perspective that optimistic criminologists must learn, if they are going to develop programs that are efficacious.

This was the strategy adopted by twentieth-century general systems theorists when they placed multiple theories into a single model. In doing so, they demonstrated the point, contrary to practices followed by criminologists of that day, that theories did not have to be used as competing notions. Therefore, the issue here is to construct a coherent theory net of use to contemporary criminologists dealing with extramural and intramural treatment of girls and women.

Theoretical Net

Because it is possible to select from a variety of theories, it is necessary to avoid an *ad hoc* approach. Many would question the legitimacy of what might seem to be arbitrary choices of theories. If a macro theory does not address, in sufficient detail, patterns of criminality, then some fail to see how to combine it with a micro theory that does.

F. H. George addressed this point when he described the potential relationship between two theories. If two theories are aimed at different levels of analysis, then they can be employed, according to George, if they are nested.[44] This means that the molar theory provides broad details of how contextual social forces induce criminality. Next, a logical relationship is established if the macro theory provides specific details about how these social forces operate within a given context for criminality to emerge.

Once this requisite degree of isomorphism is established between theories, then they are nested. When nesting is accomplished, then the initial steps have been taken to create a theory net. When a net is constructed, then criminologists can use it as a template to derive a standard model and evaluate the potential efficacy of the treatment.

Analytic Schemes Describing Change Process

The task of drafting a template useful to clinicians requires setting boundary conditions as to what theories to include. Therefore, various theories need to be examined in terms of what they can be used for in creating a theory net. In this chapter, theories of both planned and unplanned change are employed, because these notions were not always differentiated.

When theorists established the focus of their inquiries, various scope conditions (targets) were employed. Thus, it is necessary to determine what units and levels of analysis were taken as the target of their inquiry. Because molar theorists set as their scope condition the largest social unit, relevant general forces of societies were identified.[45] The level of analyses of these writers was focused on forces emerging from social structures, political functioning, mass communication, and economic factors. Less attention was given to examining data at the level of actions of individuals undergoing transformations generated by these contextual forces.

Criminologists, such as Thorsten Sellin, in the 1930s described the importance of understanding molar forces as an aspect of the crime picture. Sellin was interested in how contextual cultural forces shaped the way societies functioned to facilitate the emergence of different patterns of criminality among various ethnic groups.[46] Accordingly, any program designed to induce planned change must deal with these contextual molar forces as potentially negative pressures operating in the field. They have a continuous impact on participants before, during, and after completing the program in ways that could minimize the effectiveness of the treatment.

It is these molar forces that sometimes contribute to the regression that occurs during treatment that are usually considered management problems.[47] If these same signs of regression appear after treatment, then they are often considered signs of recidivism. George Homans is a particularly useful molar theorist who illustrated the operations of these contextual forces in the field.[48]

Criminologists, such as Frederic Thrasher and Albert Cohen, took as their scope condition medium size (macro) units.[49] The level of their analyses was aimed at the functioning of small groups, but neither the actions of societies nor individuals were stressed. The theoretical work of Robert Bales can be used to illustrate macro notions that criminologists such as Thrasher and Cohen employed in their work on delinquent gangs.[50] Bales studied how groups functioned when engaged in tasks and interpersonal encounters. His ideas apply equally to what happens within prosocial families, support groups, or criminal syndicates. As practitioners learned long ago, what the social relationships are inside any treatment project is critical.[51] The peer culture in which participants are immersed within the program, can facilitate or block the change effort.[52]

Still other criminologists, such as Fritz Redl and David Wineman, selected as their scope condition the smallest size (micro) unit of children.[53] Those concerned with describing patterns of an individual's criminality, followed in this tradition and provided important details about the criminoses. The level of the analyses of many of these theorists was directed toward internal personal characteristics of actors. Those who directed their attention in this way, focused on such things as perceptions, cognitive structures, and emotional states. Others attended to elements within the behavioral repertoire, and still others examined patterns of social interactions. Kurt Lewin fixed his attention on descriptions of individuals, and thus his work can be supplemented with Redl and Wineman's micro ideas. These criminologists attempted to detail what happens when behavioral repertoires of delinquent girls and boys are transfigured. In this chapter the details of the micro unit are examined as part of the construction of the theory net.

Micro Unit of the Theoretical Model

With an understanding of where Lewin's ideas fit into twentieth century developments in social science, the details of his model may be considered. The first phase can be described as follows.

Unfreezing. For successful change to come about, it is necessary for an offender to stop acting one way. This means deciding to alter the status quo by eliminating, minimizing the use of, or substituting one item for another in the behavioral repertoire. In deciding what to give up, alter, or add, some tension, or emotional "stir-up," as conflict theorists maintained, is associated with this decision. This tension can be expressed in mild or very exaggerated terms, depending on at least four things that are related to the behavioral repertoire of the offender.

1. Establishing how central in the repertoire is the original behavior. More central behaviors require greater force because they are more difficult to change, whereas more peripheral behaviors need less force and are easier to alter. Thus, the structure of the repertoire contributes important internal forces that help shape offenders' vulnerability to external change forces.
2. Tasks in which criminals engage, as part of the process, are a source of external forces. These task forces have demand characteristics that build up and release internal tensions that are associated with the transformation process. In this way, demand characteristics of tasks are important forces that contribute to facilitating or inhibiting the transfiguring of the repertoire.
3. There are stimulating or repressing external forces inherent in the surrounding social situation and physical setting. These contextual forces aid in dampening down and/or exacerbating the level of tension associated with behavioral change. Thus, demand characteristics of the context must be considered in terms of whether they enhance or depress desired alterations of the repertoire.
4. The field, consisting of multiple internal and external forces, is either stable or labile. Accordingly, these multiple forces may not exert constant pressure across time, and thus alterations in performance of certain actions may be very uneven.

If these issues are considered, then it should be apparent that transforming the behavioral repertoire of offenders is complicated. Moreover, when offenders enter into the unfreezing phase, the change process is likely to appear somewhat different across persons, because of these variable forces. Consequently, a simple descriptor of what is to be expected during unfreezing is inadequate when designing a treatment program.[54]

Movement. Once offenders resolve to alter their repertoires, then there is the effort required to formulate, try out, and master new behaviors. As these three events take place in the movement phase, there should be evidence that new, along with old actions, are appearing in the way offenders respond. Lewin referred to this condition as *statu nascendi*. Whether new or old actions are displayed depends on the person perceiving tasks, other persons, and context as same, similar, or different from before. If any combination of these three elements is considered same, then there is a greater tendency to "act the same" (perseveration) than if things are seen as different. As offenders learn to differentiate between similar or different fields of forces, their ability to act in new ways increases.

How frequently offenders encounter new forces from the three elements can determine how quickly they learn to select alternative behaviors. It is not enough, however, that ap-

propriate behaviors are selected, they must also be enacted in a way that meets some criterion. Seldom enacted behaviors are not likely to meet either the person's, or others', notions
of a minimally acceptable level of performance (MALP). More frequently enacted behaviors are more likely to reach MALP.

It takes time for these modifications in perception, selection, and enactment from the
behavioral repertoire to occur. Thus, movement must be measured across time, and involve
various tasks enacted in varying contexts. Close observation of offenders in this phase will
not show linear development in which new behaviors are simply added continuously to
replace old ones. Moreover, what appears in their actions can be represented as a branching
tree, as individuals encounter shifting conditions in this phase. Furthermore, it is likely that
offenders will return to old ways (recidivism), even as successful alterations are occurring
in their behavioral repertoires. This return to prior patterns is likely to occur when pressure
is released due to alterations in the forces in the field.

While all of the above is taking place, a certain level of frustration should be expressed
with this phase. The level of frustration should vary along with changes in tension, and it
may be displayed in several ways. Even so, this phase should appear less tension-filled,
unfold more smoothly, and offenders express a greater range of thoughts, feelings, and
actions than during unfreezing.

Freezing. As a certain level of proficiency is gained in learning to act in new ways, there
should be two outcomes. First, an accompanying sense of satisfaction at what was achieved
during the movement phase. Second, some anxiety over enacting new behaviors in the
future that are in the repertoire. Offenders must now display these new actions consistently,
in varying situations at MALP, at the appropriate time, and without support. This is a relatively complex task, even though the new behaviors are incorporated into the repertoire.

What creates the difficulty for offenders is the requirement to enact this sequence correctly
facing variously configured forces within different fields. Under these varied conditions, the
potential for misperceiving forces, selecting the wrong behaviors, and/or not performing at
MALP are real. This is likely to be the case, even though there is an increased sensitivity to
the demand characteristics of tasks and context that shape responses. This higher level of
sensitivity to the field of forces makes it easier to respond quickly to familiar events, but
slows responses to unfamiliar forces. Now, the tendency to perseverate in the face of familiar
cues facilitates making appropriate choices, whereas novelty inhibits the process.

The issues that have to be dealt with in this phase make it clear that the process of change
is not over. There are still issues that offenders undergoing transfiguring of the role repertoire are involved in that need to be described.

Hawkinshire's Extension of Lewin's Model

Ideas about these issues were described by Lewin when he dealt with the way learning
occurs within a field of forces.[55] These ideas were not incorporated by Lewin into his
model, so Hawkinshire addressed these issues in his work.[56]

As a result of rethinking the process, it became apparent that there was a need to differentiate conditions at the beginning and end of the transformation. Thus, a readiness phase was added at the start of the sequence as a way to incorporate Lewin's point about how alterations of repertoires occur. The ending was extended by two phases, termination and nonsupport, in view of what Lewin said about the importance of regression, retrogression, and development.[57] The product of this re-analysis of Lewin's work resulted in six phases: readiness, unfreezing, movement, freezing, termination, and nonsupport.

Before the six phases could be considered a generic model of the process, the ideas had to be tested against others' work. Readiness and nonsupport were seldom discussed, but termination was; therefore the degree of isomorphism between usage in the field and the formulation could be established.[58]

Alexander undertook this task in a quantitative review of 69 authors in which she examined their descriptions of termination.[59] As a result of her analysis, she found that the degree of isomorphism with Hawkinshire's 11 propositions (listed in note 61), ranged from 30 percent to 80 percent. Only two of the propositions were supported by less than 55 percent of the authors (note 11, 30 percent and note 12, 45 percent). She concluded that adequate support existed for Hawkinshire's contention that these were generic descriptions of termination. These added phases are described in the following manner.

Readiness. Lewin specified that the degree of readiness persons brought to the process was an important precondition that influenced what followed. Therefore, it is necessary to keep in mind at least four things about the readiness phase.

1. Ascertaining readiness is not done just for the purpose of determining if offenders are currently capable of undergoing change. It is also done so as to know what the various manifestations of readiness are as criminals enter treatment. This means learning offenders' levels of willingness to alter aspects of their repertoire. Gathering this information makes it possible to ascertain what are the presenting issues with which offenders think they should or should not deal.

2. It is important to ascertain the *veridicality* (sameness) of perceptions of offenders and staff about what is to be transformed. Women may arrive at the treatment facility ready to participate in altering their behavioral repertoire. However, their perceptions about what aspects of self are in need of alteration may differ from those of the staff. When these varying perceptions are clarified, then these offenders' level of willingness to deal with these new issues may be radically altered. Level of willingness to change is only an abstraction until there is *veridicality* between the offenders' and staff's perceptions about the targets of change.

3. What is the manifest level of awareness of offenders as to what it takes to alter their behaviors? Unfortunately, the answer is that most of the dimensions of this issue are likely to be out of the awareness of many offenders. They have few clues to tell them what to expect, so they are relatively blind to the details of the process. In particular, they lack knowledge about ways transformations occur, the amount of effort re-

quired, the length of time, and the speed it will take. Furthermore, they have little understanding of the extent of what needs altering, how central the targeted behaviors are to their functioning, and how related these behaviors are to other aspects of themselves. They seldom think about how their changes will influence their interactions with others. Until they learn what these things mean for them, they will have little information to decide how ready and willing they are to reform.

4. Prior knowledge about change can work against preparing offenders for the process. Women who have had previous experiences altering their behavioral repertoire may assume that the prior process is similar, or identical with the impending one. However, the intensity, level of expectations to be met, or speed of change may be very different. Thus, what was initially considered a familiar experience may become thought of as strange. In this way, prior experiences serve to generate insecurity over what will happen in the future.

These issues illustrate the complexity of what is encountered in the readiness phase. Increased awareness of them makes it possible for staff to be better prepared to cope with offenders' unfreezing.

Termination. Lewin discussed termination, but he did not include this phase in his model. The importance of this point in the process, for criminologists working with offenders, prompted Hawkinshire to specify details of this phase in his extensions. How best to describe this phase, as was the case with the others, was an issue, because the notion was at controversy for some time.[60] When the literature was examined, it was clear that some authors stressed the fact that termination, like unfreezing, was an anxious and turbulent period. Others considered this phase to be a smooth one for offenders.

This controversy was resolved by consolidating and elaborating both positions and creating a generic description. It had to include the notion that termination was both anxiety and pleasure producing, which he described it in 11 propositions.[61] These multiple notions, first described by Redl and Wineman, were employed because people reacted to termination in different ways.

For the staff working with offenders, the process of termination from a program produces expected and unexpected events. The mere mention of the approaching end, the termination point, can increase anxiety and decrease performance. If termination is understood and planned for during this interval, the termination episode, then the experience, can be shaped so that offenders are better prepared for what will happen. With time, offenders gain confidence and their performance returns to an already successful pattern at the end, the point of separation. Despite the fact that offenders successfully adapt to the termination phase, there are two latent behavioral patterns likely to emerge. At the termination point, the first emergent pattern is likely to be a retrospective examination of their performance history. In doing so, offenders reflect on how they performed before, or while in the early or latter days of involvement in the program. In either case, they may overemphasize on past failures and mistakes, and ignore successes. This could mean thinking about how badly they performed, how many missed opportunities for success occurred, and their failure to do what they knew. Others overemphasize by attending to their successes and ignoring any past failures and mistakes. Either way, girls and women are not examining the entire record in ways that will help them to be successful in the future.

The second pattern, a triggering of the "what if" syndrome, can occur during the termination episode. Here women and girls focus on potential scenarios and attend less to actual events. This has the potential of narrowing their ability to assess the field of forces currently being experienced and responding appropriately. In this case, perseveration works against them as they are attending to clues, but not responding appropriately to them.

Spotting these reactions and providing tailored assistance to help girls and women over these hurdles can recover their sense of competence to cope. However, without an accurate diagnosis, the increased tension and subsequent regression in performance is often mistaken as a sign that they are not ready to terminate. In fact, this is exactly the opposite conclusion to come to, in view of the transformation taking place during the termination episode. Girls and women are dealing with termination, and, if it is appropriately handled, these signs should quickly subside, and efforts toward leaving should be continued.

If appropriate intervention does not reverse the pattern, then this is evidence that offenders are not at the termination point. Further treatment efforts are required. The decision to leave the program should be held until evidence accumulates that girls and women are prepared for transition to the next phase.

Non-Support. One of the vexing parts of the change process is the situation encountered *after* the point of separation. With some effort, ex-offenders have mastered what they were expected to learn, and by this definition they have succeeded. With pride they are separated from the program, and expectations of success are generated in their heads and/or projected onto them by others. Within a short period of time, evidence rapidly accumulates that things are not going as planned. Women find out that the nonsupport phase is a difficult one in which they encounter new and old challenges with which they must cope. Failure, considered recidivism, is likely, unless careful preparation is made, so that they can acquire critical "hurdle help" over barriers, often of their own creation.

The two barriers that are likely to emerge are (1) spontaneous remission of their knowledge and skill base, and (2) retraumatization by toxic contexts. The first is an apparent loss of knowledge and skills that they had learned in the program. The second occurs after leaving the safe haven of the program that was devoid of very toxic social situations and/or physical settings. The remission in knowledge and skills can come from several tendencies, some less pathological than others. The most problematic is a deliberate strategy ex-offenders pursue of returning to old patterns to succeed. This is done because they think these old patterns are "easier" to enact and/or "more appropriate to old social settings." It is a choice that is made as a way to cope when reestablishing former relationships.

These old interactions are thought to be constrained by certain norms and action patterns. At first it is difficult for ex-offenders to know if these prior relationships can be maintained while adhering to new norms and displaying new actions. Too often the assumption is made that they cannot, and spontaneous remission of what was learned in treatment takes place. This results in girls and women deciding to revert to old patterns to adapt to the standards set by those around them as a way to succeed. They assume that their new ways of thinking and doing cannot be tolerated by old friends. Immediate assistance is called for in rebuilding old relationships, where appropriate. This means helping them apply new norms and action patterns relevant to these old interactions that are in keeping with their treatment.

A less problematic form of spontaneous remission is an "accidental return to old patterns without thinking." What this reveals is a side effect of an increased level of sensitivity to contextual forces. When exposed to powerful old forces, which were neutralized or reduced in potency in the program, they regress when re-exposed to them in their original strength. The strategy to deal with this issue is to have girls and women learn to focus on planned ignoring. Ex-offenders must come to recognize that their new sensitivity to contextual forces does not require an active response to everything that is perceived. They must learn that they can decide whether or not to respond, and, if they do, how to act so as to minimize spontaneous remission.

The second cause in the decline in performance during the nonsupport stage can come from a highly toxic context. Here a large and varied number of negative forces are ranged against ex-convicts who are trying to continue to enact newly mastered patterns. They suffer retraumatization if they are confronted with this toxic context, because it is worse than anything previously experienced. Under these circumstances, girls and women may be sufficiently traumatized that they can perceive no clear contextual clues as to what skills they should employ. Now, they can neither disengage, nor counter the negative contextual forces, because they are in trauma and suffering from faulty signal detection. This then results in their inability to call up correct skills to respond to the toxic context. It is a paralysis of both their assessment and response mechanisms that immobilizes them, rather than their unwillingness to do what they were taught. Hurdle help in this situation requires a quick diagnosis and laying out short, correct, and concrete actions. Getting ex-convicts to take these small steps until their trauma subsides, permits them to take hold of their life once they are ready to do so. When this point is reached, then they have been restored to the *status quo anti*.

A secondary gain from experiencing this toxic condition can be helpful. Women and girls learn that it is possible to cope with an extremely toxic context and survive based on what they already know. Furthermore, they frequently learn that solutions to difficulties they experienced are relatively simple, if quickly diagnosed and remedies systematically proposed and followed. These are difficult circumstances under which to learn, but they are important in assisting ex-offenders to determine what they can do on their own.

These reactions during nonsupport are also important for staff to face, and with which they must learn to deal. It is not good enough for staff to say that these "things happen," and therefore nothing can be done. What is taking place at this point is an important part of the change process. Ex-offenders are faced with making better assessments of altered and/or novel social situations, and they must develop strategies to adopt more functional responses.

What is described above are different ways to think about events that happen in the nonsupport phase that are usually classified as failures. What these examples illustrate is the necessity of building into the treatment process, mechanisms that make it possible to offer intermittent hurdle help when required.

Manifest and Latent Events. This view of the added phases makes it clear that manifest and latent events must be considered in treating the criminoses. Lewin discussed some of these notions associated with these phases and indicated the importance of thinking of events taking place on manifest and latent levels. This kind of clarity is necessary, because specific types of thoughts, feelings, behaviors, and actions are associated with these phases. In order to describe the process of change in a way that is useful to criminologists, it is necessary for them to know what manifest (visible) actions are likely to appear along with expressed thoughts and feelings. It is also important that the latent (invisible) unexpressed thoughts, feelings, and considered behaviors that contribute to what is enacted be described. Despite discussing manifest and latent events taking place during restructuring of the behavioral repertoire, Lewin did not make these notions explicit. Consequently, Hawkinshire attempted to clarify these details in his extension of the model. In attempting to do so, examples were searched for in the literature that could be associated with each phase. Many of these notions were already described by Redl and Wineman, who worked with highly aggressive delinquent girls and boys. These criminologists studied transformations in the behavioral repertoire of children rather than adults, because youth have fewer ways to disguise their reactions to what takes place during the transfiguring process.

It is possible to assume that these reactions Redl and Wineman observed were related to existing pathologies of these delinquents. This specific point was investigated, and what these boys demonstrated about change was not related to their levels of aggressiveness. Both Liggett and Alexander gathered data on this question and found similar responses by adults who had similar difficulties handling alterations of their behavioral repertoires.[62] When the details of manifest and latent events were displayed across phases, overlap was apparent. Thus, these events could be clustered into four zones in order to make the model more descriptive of the continuous process. The four zones were designated as follows in Figure 4–2.

By providing detailed descriptions of the thoughts, feelings, behaviors, and actions for each zone, it was possible to know what to expect as change took place. The numerous behavioral patterns are ways individuals conceive of acting, but they are not descriptors, *per se*, of the actions they always display. The multiple listings give examples of various things that are likely to be said and done by most people, but not all of them are spoken or enacted by every convict. The details of the full model are presented in Figure 4–3.

These listings make it possible to conceptualize what offenders going through the change process are likely to experience and/or express. This provides two different kinds of information. The first is what convicts are dealing with at the moment, and the second, some indication of where they are in the change cycle. Thus, it is possible to shape the design and

| Initial | Critical | Termination | Non-support |

Figure 4–2 Zones of change.

treatment process by what offenders can be expected to say and do. Knowing what may be encountered makes it possible to assess the progress that is being made as girls and women go through treatment.

IMPLICATIONS DRAWN FROM THE MODEL ABOUT PAST PRACTICES

With this elaboration of the micro details of the change model, it is now useful to reflect on the historic controversy. The shift in policy across time from vengeance to altering the behavioral repertoire of offenders was a notable event. In making this transition in policy, it was not possible to determine the efficacy of extramural or intramural treatment.

Intramural policy advocates, like the Quakers, Lucas, Maconachie, Crofton, Jebb, Wines, and Brockway, concluded that their designs altered the behavioral repertoire of some prisoners. Evidence was offered of these successes, but it was not possible for criminologists, like the Gluecks, to provide satisfactory evidence of consistent results in reforming offenders. Nobody was able to avoid the serious problem of "recidivism" for most prisoners upon release. Skeptical criminologists, like Barnes and Teeters, repeatedly pointed to the unacceptable side effects of high costs and inhumane conditions associated with intramural social treatment. These negative factors, along with inadequate evidence of consistent rehabilitation, reinforced their belief that intramural treatment was not efficacious.

Augustus and Marsangy offered models of social treatment in extramural settings that eliminated problems encountered with intramural treatment. They maintained that these extramural designs transfigured the behavioral repertoire and obtained secondary gains of having offenders living free within their communities. These were powerful arguments.

Despite claimed successes, these advocates were continually plagued with the side effects of their designs. Only minimal isolation was possible from prior criminogenic milieux, and no supervision was effectuated for their social interactions. Enrolled offenders were continuously involved in criminality that produced higher recidivism rates and victimization costs. The conclusion that pessimistic criminologists came to was that neither method transformed the behavioral repertoire of offenders, and talk of the "futility of rehabilitation" became widespread.

This extended Lewinian model makes it possible to understand this long history of failure and criminologists' pessimism over the feasibility of rehabilitating criminals. The limited number of intervention techniques proposed by both groups could not deal with the range of reactions encountered in offenders. Therefore, it is possible to see why these extramural and intramural reforms proved to be ineffective for the majority of offenders.

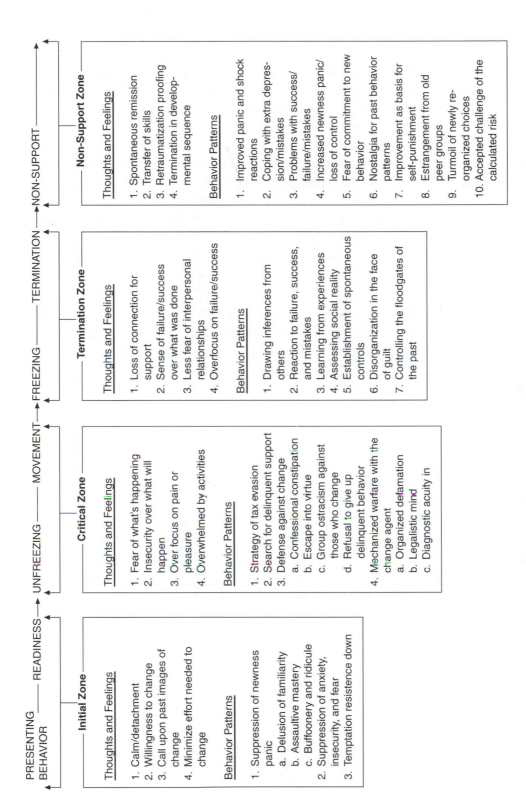

Figure 4–3 Hawkinshire's extended model of change showing both individual phases and zones of change. The thoughts, feelings, and behaviors that are symptomatic of each zone are listed. Note Hawkinshire's extension of Lewin's original phases.

What neither side knew was that certain elements were essential to produce desired outcomes. Whether an intramural or extramural treatment design is employed, it must include a comprehensive long-term strategy with multiple techniques. Moreover, any form of "all and then none" treatment is not sufficiently extensive enough to cope with the last phase of change. Without intermittent interventions during nonsupport, as part of the design, neither extramural nor intramural treatment is likely to prove successful.

Extensive assessments are required to determine the level of readiness of girls and women to enter treatment, and how they are changing across time.[63] This later information can be ascertained by continuous data collection from all settings in which girls and women interact with staff and other offenders. This setting should include work sites, residence areas, academic and vocational schools, and therapeutic groups. Staff members must be trained to deal with the complexities of offender moving through the change process.

With hindsight it is possible to see what contributed to the faulty designs. Criminologists undertook the task of specifying details of social treatment without making use of evolving conceptual work on the change process. The resulting formulations that they employed were too narrowly focused and devoid of necessary elements. They neither addressed the field of multiple forces exerting continuous influences on offenders, nor did they explicate the dynamics of how behavioral repertoires were transformed. Both issues had to be addressed in their designs, if their interventions were to be powerful enough, and continue long enough, to produce desired outcomes.

At this point in history, future options facing the field should be clear if a more rigorous model of social treatment is rejected. Pessimists support incapacitation and "doing your time" in clean and less overcrowded facilities. "Doing your time" will also mean indoctrination by other inmates into patterns of criminality, and intimidation of staff and inmates into corrupting the system. It will also include evading social and financial responsibilities to offenders' families, victims, and society. Rampant idleness, rapid deterioration of self-esteem, and widespread loss of opportunities for self-improvement will become the norm.

The future scenario can be very different if criminologists support the optimistic position of a comprehensive model designed to bring effective social treatment to offenders. This will mean that criminologists will have to accept the difficult, demanding, and protracted tasks of creating and maintaining a therapeutic milieu while abolishing idleness, illiteracy, and destruction of self-esteem. All of this is imperative to accomplish, while providing continuous pro-social socialization experiences to transform behavioral repertoires. If optimists are supported, it should be possible to specify what happens when offenders participate in "effective social treatment."

NOTES AND REFERENCES

1. The term "social treatment," or variants of it, is used here instead of "curative program" advocated by J. M. Charles Lucas in his book, *The Theory of Imprisonment*, 3 volumes, Paris: E. Legrand et J. Bergonuioux, 1836–1838. It does not mean that the activities offered were necessarily appropriate and/or likely to achieve the stated objective and/or endstate of the designer.

2. When the word "criminoses" is used here, it is a general descriptor of the psychological, social, and behavioral components of criminal actions.

3. The definition of planned change used here is taken from the book by Ronald Lippitt, Jeanne Watson, and Bruce Westley, *The Dynamics of Planned Change* (New York: Harcourt, Brace & Company, 1958), 10, in which they indicate that "the planned change that originates in a decision to make a deliberate effort to improve the system and to obtain the help of an outside agent in making this improvement. We call this outside agent a change agent. The decision to make a change may be made by the system itself, after experiencing pain (malfunctioning) or discovering the possibility of improvement, or by an outside change agent who observes the need for change in a particular system and takes the initiative in establishing a helping relationship with that system."

4. A recent discussion about costs is presented by Isaac Ehrlich in the article, "The Economic Approach to Crime: A Preliminary Assessment," published in *Criminology Review, Yearbook,* eds., Sheldon L. Messinger and Egon Bittner, Vol. 1. (Newbury Park, CA: Sage Publications, 1979), 39–42. Historic discussions were undertaken by writers in the eighteenth and nineteenth century who belonged to the Classical School of Criminology. These were serious attempts to describe social costs that were initiated in the writings of Cesare Beccaria (1730–1794), followed by Adam Smith (1723–1790), William Paley (1743–1805), Thomas Malthus (1766–1834), James Mill (1773–1836), Jeremy Bentham (1784–1830), Edwin Chadwick (1801–1890), and John Stuart Mill (1806–1873). Current cost estimates per bed are $87,000 to build and $30,000 per annum to operate a prison in 1997 dollars.

5. Harry Elmer Barnes and Negley Teeters, *New Horizons in Criminology*, 2nd ed. (New York: Prentice-Hall, 1951), 377, wrote about the formal framing of this controversy in what was called the Hempstead Code: "They were first promulgated on March 1, 1664, at Hempstead, Long Island, although they were taken from codes of earlier dates enacted for the New Haven Colony."

6. Mr. Elijah Weed died of yellow fever in 1793, but Mrs. Mary Weed stayed on as the Warden from 1793 until 1800.

7. For extensive evaluations of extramural treatment programs, see Helen L. Witmer and Edith Tufts, *The Effectiveness of Delinquency Prevention Programs*, U.S. Children's Bureau Publication (Washington, D.C.: Government Printing Office, 1954), 350; Richard J. Lundman, P. T. McFarlane, and Frank R. Scarpitti, "Delinquency Prevention: A Description and Assessment of Projects Reported in the Professional Literature," *Crime & Delinquency.* July 1976, 297–308.

8. Don C. Gibbons, *Society, Crime, and Criminal Careers: An Introduction to Criminology* (Englewood Cliffs, New Jersey: Prentice-Hall, 1968), Preface, v.

9. Some of the most noted works included the series of studies by Sheldon and Eleanor Gluecks: *Five Hundred Criminal Careers* (1930); *Five Hundred Delinquent Women* (1934); *One Thousand Juvenile Delinquents* (1934); *Criminal Careers in Retrospect* (1943); *Unraveling Juvenile Delinquency* (1950). Another example was the extensive series of studies conducted on the Cambridge-Somerville Youth Study project that included the work of: Edward Powers and Helen Witmer, *An Experiment in the Prevention of Delinquency* (1951); Joan and William McCord, "A Follow-up Report on the Somerville Youth Study," *Annals of the American Academy of Political and Social Science*, March 1959, 322, 89–96; and Joan McCord, "A Thirty-Year Follow-Up of Treatment Effects," in Messinger and Bittner, eds., *Criminology Review Yearbook,* 688–693. A third example is the long-term follow up study done by Solomon Kobrin, "The Chicago Area

Project—A 25-Year Assessment," *Annals,* 19–29.

10. Herbert A. Bloch and Frank T. Flynn, *Delinquency: The Juvenile Offender in America Today* (New York: Random House, 1956), provided a critique of research studies done up to that time. Subsequently, Donald Campbell and Julian Stanley wrote a classic on the subject of research designs that provides an excellent critique of strong and weak points of each type. Even though 30 years old, their book. *Experimental and Quasi-Experimental Designs for Research* (Chicago: Rand McNally College Publishing Company, 10th ed., 1966), is still definitive. A more general discussion of issues to be considered when reviewing research methods is contained in Earl Babbie, *The Practice of Social Research*, 7th ed. (Belmont, CA: Wadsworth, 1995).

11. Marguerite Q. Grant addressed some of these issues in the article "Interaction Between Kinds of Treatments and Kinds of Delinquents, A Current Trend in Correctional Research," in *Inquiries Concerning Kinds of Treatments for Kinds of Delinquents*, California Board of Corrections Monograph No. 2 (Sacramento, CA: Documents Section, 1961), 5–14, as did Michael Argyle, "A New Approach to the Classification of Delinquents with Implications for Treatment," *ibid.*, 15–26. A trenchant discussion of some of these issues was presented by Richard Lundman and Frank R. Scarpitti, in "Delinquency Prevention: Recommendations for Future Projects," *Crime and Delinquency*, April 1978, 24: 2, 207–220.

12. This is a prevention strategy in which persons identified as potential delinquents are taken to prisons to hear inmates talk about life behind bars. The graphic details convicts use to describe the experience are thought to be effective in convincing some persons that a life of crime is not what they want for themselves.

13. Many people have provided ideas, but the two conditions of, necessary and sufficient, were not met in these discussions. Examples of some of those writing on the subject across the years included William Healy, *The Individual Delinquent: A Textbook of Diagnosis and Prognosis for All Concerned in Understanding Offenders* (Boston: Little, Brown, 1915); Helen D. Pigeon, *Probation and Parole in Theory and in*

Practice (New York: National Probation Association, 1942); Helen H. Perlman, *Social Casework: A Problem-Solving Process* (Chicago: University of Chicago Press, 1957); Pauline V. Young, *Social Treatment in Probation and Delinquency*, 2nd ed. (1969); and Robert W. Roberts and Robert H. Nee, *Theories of Social Casework* (Chicago: University of Chicago Press, 1970); Herbert Quay and Craig Love, "Behavioral classification for female offenders" (Longmont, CO: U.S. Department of Justice, National Institute of Correctional Information Center, 1989); Paul Gendreau, Claire Goggin, and Mario Paparozzi, "Principles of Effective Assessment for Community Corrections," *Federal Probation* 60 (1996): 64–70.

14. Barnes and Teeters, *New Horizons in Criminology*, v.

15. *Ibid.*, 459–481, Chapter XXII, "The Cruelty and Futility of the Modern Prison."

16. Lucas put forth ideas for a standard model of social treatment in his book *The Theory of Imprisonment* (1836).

17. Barnes and Teeters, *New Horizons in Criminology*, 522–523.

18. *Ibid.,* 526.

19. *Prisons* (Washington, D.C: Government Printing Office, 1940), Vol. V, 29. This report was initiated in 1935 with the first director of the study being Justin Miller. Wayne Morse completed the study and published the results in five volumes between 1939 and 1940. Emphasis added.

20. Lundman and Scarpitti's *Crime and Delinquency, op. cit.* (1940) provided thoughtful comments about the necessary elements to be included in social treatment programs. Nevertheless, they did not address the issue of how to produce a valid standard model for treatment specialists to work from in creating their intervention programs.

21. Barnes and Teeters, *New Horizons in Criminology,* 524.

22. Much attention was given to this problem in the book by Alexander B. Smith and Louis Berlin, *Treatment of the Criminal Offender* (Englewood Cliffs, NJ: Prentice-Hall, 1981), 2nd ed.

23. The Gluecks took this "maturation" position as a result of their empirical research findings that

as criminals got older they tended to engage in less criminality.

24. Quoted in Barnes and Teeters, *New Horizons in Criminology*, 528, and taken from the digest of Section II, Question 2, by Negley K. Teeters, *Deliberations of the International Penal and Penitentiary Congress, 1872–1950* (Philadelphia: Temple University Book Store, 1950), 109. Emphasis added.

25. An example of figures that sharply contradicted those of Brockway about the value of reformatory treatment were gathered by Sheldon and Eleanor Glueck in *Five Hundred Criminal Careers* (1930). Their study was of 510 men who had been released on parole from the Massachusetts Reformatory at West Concord. Barnes and Teeters, *New Horizons in Criminology*, 538, summarized this study as follows: "Of the 510, the criminal records of 422 were traceable. It was found that of this total 89, or 21.1 percent had made a reasonably adequate adjustment; 307, or 72.7 percent committed recorded crimes during the post-institutional period; and 26, or 6.2 percent had committed crimes for which they were not arrested. In short, 80 percent of the cases were failures for the Reformatory." This work should be compared with the study done by Daniel Glaser, reported in *The Effectiveness of a Prison and Parole Program* (Indianapolis, IN: Bobbs-Merrill, 1964). Walter C. Reckless, American Criminology: New Directions (New York: Appleton-Century-Crofts, 1973) quoted from this work in which Glaser found in a four-year follow-up study of 1,015 inmates that only "…31 percent had been re-imprisoned at some point during the four-year time span," roughly a 69 percent success rate (p. 397).

26. Many clinicians tend to be dismissive of theory, as they think it provides little in the way of specifics necessary to create effective treatment programs. For a better understanding of how theory can be of use in clinical practice, as it was done in Germany in the 1920s, it is important to start with the work of Chris Argyris and Donald Schon. In their book *Theory In Practice: Increasing Professional Effectiveness* (San Francisco: Jossey-Bass Publishers, 1974), they indicate that there are different types of theories that clinicians can employ. Their ideas about theories-of-action, theories-

of-practice, and theories-in-use are examples. These notions were then extended by Howard M. Weiss in "Role Theory in Practice and Training: A Unified Paradigm for Family Therapy," unpublished PhD dissertation (New York: New York University, 1982). Here he attempted to show how a theory-of-practice is used. This work is recommended for those who want more details about how to guide the construction of clinical intervention strategies based on theory. What is being advocated is how to put theories-of-practice into operation so as to guide the use of interventions. A theory-of-practice-in-use is the term used to here to described this type of theory.

27. Richard P. Appelbaum, in his book, *Theories of Social Change* (Chicago: Markham Publishing Company, 3rd printing, 1971), 117–137, subsumes the work of various theorists under the work of Comte. William A. Liggett, Jr., followed up on this work and provided illustrations of how to order these works in "Unfreezing Behavior During Social Change: An empirical Test of Selected Theoretical Propositions," unpublished PhD dissertation (New York: New York University, 1980).

28. Richard Appelbaum, *Theories of Social Change*, 117–137.

29. *Ibid.*

30. James Grier Miller*, Living Systems* (New York: Macmillan, 1983), XIV, made the point that "The twentieth century characteristically has drawn its metaphors from Einstein's relativistic field theory, which clearly influences the philosophy of organism of Whitehead, the Gestalt psychology of Wertheimer, Kohler, and Koffka, and general systems theory."

31. Kurt Lewin, "Field Theory and Experiment in Social Psychology," (1939), in Dorwin Cartwright, ed., *Field Theory in Social Science: Selected Theoretical Papers* (Chicago: Midway reprint, University of Chicago Press, 1976), 132.

32. Lippitt, Watson, and Westley, *The Dynamics of Planned Change*, vii.

33. *Ibid.*, 5.

34. Liggett, *op. cit.* The elements of Lewin's notions included the following:

    1. all social systems, persons, groups, and societies, are in a quasistationary equilibrium

between opposing change and resistance forces.

2. emergence of conflict forces can be seen in all social systems such as individuals and groups.

3. changes in these opposing forces occur whenever the point of equilibrium moves.

4. resistant forces to change that exist within the system are associated with the maintenance of old habits.

5. change requires breaking habits that results in the phenomenon of unfreezing.

6. change in the structure of systems results in what might be described as emotional stir-up, catharsis, or reaction.

7. changes in social structure occur in several phases.

According to Liggett, when these seven major points of Lewin's model were examined in the writing of these authors, the degree of isomorphism ranged from 72 percent to 100 percent. There were only two points, 2 (72 percent) and 5 (79 percent), which were below 90 percent in terms of authors who were in agreement with Lewin.

35. Kurt Lewin, "Formalization and Progress in Psychology" (1940), in *Field Theory in Social Science*, 7. Gordon Allport warns of the problems associated with "simple and sovereign theories" that for too long dominated theoretical work in the social sciences in "The Historical Background of Modern Social Psychology," in *The Handbook of Social Psychology,* Gardner Lindzey and Elliot Aronson, eds. (Reading, MA: Addison-Wesley Publishing Co., 1968, 5 volumes), 2nd ed., Vol. I, 10–40.

36. Lewin described these interactions in much more detail in "Behavior and Development as a Function of the Total Situation," (1946), *Field Theory in Social Science*, 273–297.

37. Lewin, in "Field Theory and Experiment in Social Psychology," (1939), *Field Theory in Social Science,* 132.

38. Otto Neurath was an early advocate of a more unified view of science that moved away from disciplinary divisions. He indicated the origin of this work in a letter written in 1935 that "he was at work on the project at least as early as 1920. He wrote that he first talked it over with Einstein and Hans Hahn and had early discussions about it with Carnap and Philipp Frank. In the 1930s Neurath was with the Mundaneum Institute of the Hague. He had set up the Unity of Science Institute in 1936 as a department of the Mundaneum Institute, and in 1937 this department was renamed the International Institute for the Unity of Science with Neurath, Frank, and Morris forming the executive committee." Charles Morris, "On the History of the International Encyclopedia of Unified Science," in *Foundations of the Unity of Science: Toward an International Encyclopedia of Unified Science*, Otto Neurath, Rudolf Carnap, and Charles Morris, eds. (Chicago: The University of Chicago Press, 1969, 2 volumes), ix.

39. These ideas were expressed in L. J. Henderson, *The Order of Nature* (Cambridge, MA: Harvard University Press, 1917), and Alfred N. Whitehead, *Science and the Modern World* (New York: Macmillan USA Publishing, 1925).

40. James Grier Miller, *Living Systems,* XIV.

41. *Ibid.*

42. George A. Miller, "Psychology's Block of Marble," *Contemporary Psychology*, 1956, 1: 252.

43. J. R. Royce, "Toward the Advancement of Theoretical Psychology," *Psychological Review*, 1957, 3: 4.

44. F. H. George, "Formalization of Language Systems for Behavior Theory," *Psychological Review*, 1953, 60, 238–240.

45. *Ibid.*, 238–240. F. H. George discussed the concept of molar units in "Formalization of Language Systems for Behavior Theory." Richard Appelbaum discussed units and levels of analysis in his *Theories of Social Change,* 2–11.

46. An explanation of Thorsten Sellin's work appears in *Culture, Conflict, and Crime* (New York: Social Science Research Council, Bulletin 41, 1938).

47. The term "regression," as used here, follows Lewin's definition instead of the classic psychoanalytic formulation of S. Freud. Lewin defines the terms in his article "Regression, Retrogression, and Development," (1941) in *Field Theory in Social Science,* 113, as "...a change in a direction opposite to the changes characteristic of development."

48. George C. Homans, *The Human Group* (New York: Harcourt & Brace, 1950).

49. Frederic M. Thrasher, *The Gang* (Chicago: University of Chicago Press, 1927) and Albert Cohen, *Delinquent Boys* (Glencoe, IL: Free Press, 1955).

50. Robert F. Bales, *Interaction Process Analysis: A Method for the Study of Small Groups* (Cambridge, MA: Addison-Wesley Publishing Co., 1950). The methodological work of Bales is central to developing useful notions about groups at work. A more recent compilation of where thinking stands in the field can be found in a two-volume collection edited by Erich Witte and James Davis, *Understanding Group Behavior* (Mahwah, NJ: Lawrence Erlbaum Associates, 1996).

51. Roger Uhlich, in "Social Influence as a Factor in Behavior Change," unpublished PhD dissertation (New York: New York University, 1981), provides details about social influence processes that must be considered when designing efficacious treatment programs.

52. Maxwell Jones dealt with this matter in some detail in *The Therapeutic Community* (New York: Basic Books, 1953). Henry Brill traces the "Historical Background of the Therapeutic Community," in Herman C. B. Denber, ed., *Research Conference on the Therapeutic Community* (Springfield, IL: Charles C Thomas Publisher, 1960), 3–12. A more contemporaneous view is presented by Lemar T. Empey and M. L. Ericson, *The Provo Experiment: Evaluating Community Control of Delinquency* (Lexington, MA: Lexington Books, 1972).

53. Fritz Redl and David Wineman, *The Aggressive Child* (Glencoe, IL: The Free Press, 1957). This book represents a one-volume edition of their previously published books, *Children Who Hate: The Disorganization and Breakdown of Behavior Controls* (1951), and *Controls from Within: Techniques for the Treatment of the Aggressive Child* (1952).

54. Lewin discussed various aspects of the change process in "Field Theory and Learning" (1942), 60–86, and "Regression, Retrogression, and Development" (1944), 87–129, in *Field Theory in Social Science.*

55. Kurt Lewin, "Field Theory and Learning" (1942), *Field Theory in Social Science*, 60–86.

56. This material was first covered in a series of lectures delivered for the course, "Advanced Strategies and Techniques of Planned Change, II," New York University, offered for the first time in Spring, 1972.

57. Kurt Lewin, "Regression, Retrogression, and Development" (1944), *Field Theory in Social Science,* 87–129.

58. A listing of these propositions appears in endnote 61.

59. Alexander, M. Termination behaviors during social change: empirical tests of selected theoretical propositions. PhD dissertation (New York: New York University, 1983).

60. *Ibid.*, 10–27, reviewed the controversy in the literature on the termination phase. The first problem encountered was that no standard definition existed describing this phase. Therefore, the following three notions were clarified in Alexander's work. They were termination point, termination episode, and point of separation. "The termination point was set as, "…that point in time when the SU (social unit) makes the decision to end the change or when the person realizes that the end is approaching."' "The termination episode was defined as…that period of time from the termination point until the final point of time from the termination point until the final point when the supports are removed."' "The point of separation occurred when the ongoing process changed and the supports were actually removed."

61. An abbreviated form of the 11 termination reactions as described by Redl and Wineman are as follows:

    1. sense of loss of connection for support,

    2. sense of accomplishment/failure,

    3. less fear of interpersonal engagement,

    4. overfocus on success and/or mistakes,

    5. drawing inferences from what happens to others, to self, correctly,

    6. reactions to failure, success, and mistakes,

    7. learning from experience—what is relevant to the person,

    8. assessment of social reality,

    9. spontaneous establishment of substitute controls,

    10. disorganization in the face of guilt, and

11. control of floodgates of the past—joy, sorrow, and experience.

62. Liggett, *op. cit.*, and Alexander, *Termination Behaviors.*

63. A model designed to measure planned change of delinquent boys in a community-based treatment program is described by Frank B. W. Hawkinshire, V, in "Social Assessment: A Model for the Assessment of Planned Change," unpublished PhD dissertation (Ann Arbor: University of Michigan, 1967).

CHAPTER 5

The Relational Theory of Women's Psychological Development: Implications for the Criminal Justice System

Stephanie S. Covington

Editor's Notes

In Chapter Three, Zaplin stated that it is "increasingly urgent" to consider female and male offenders separately when developing and implementing rehabilitative programs and the policy that guides them. In Chapter Four, Hawkinshire stated that it is urgent to reconsider our ideas about recidivism, usually considered failure when it occurs among offender populations. That is, recidivism as it is generally used, is an "all or none" concept—either the person stopped criminal behavior or she did not. A recidivist would be a woman who failed completely in her efforts to stop criminal behavior. In Chapter Four, Hawkinshire demonstrated that persons will conscientiously return to old ways as a survival mechanism, i.e., they will recidivate even as successful alterations are occurring in their behavioral repertoire. The reason for this being the case is linked to how women and girls develop psychologically and learn.

The relational theory of development described in Chapter Five is a theory of women's psychological development based on women's experience. This theory sheds much light on how women and girls learn. The theory focuses on the movement of mutual initiative and responsiveness, mutual empathy, and empowerment as the core organizing dynamics in women's lives. This concept is particularly useful as a theoretical basis for program and policy development related to female offenders.

Chapter Five applies relational theory to the criminal justice system specifically addressing the following questions: What are gender-specific services? What does relational theory tell us about the childhood and adult experiences of female offenders? What does relational theory tell us about corrections on a systemic level? In addressing these questions, Chapter Five emphasizes the need for the application of relational theory on a systems-wide basis. Additionally, because many female offenders have histories of addiction and trauma, Chapter Five also looks at two other theories that incorporate a systems perspective: a holistic theory of addiction and a theory of trauma. These theories are examined through a relational theory lens to aid program designers further in designing gender-specific services for the majority of female offenders who have addiction and trauma issues. Specifically, the holistic model of addiction, according to Covington, the author of Chapter Five, requires that "we look at the complete woman and try to understand the connection of addiction to every aspect of the self—physical, emotional, and spiritual. We understand that the addicted woman is not using alcohol or drugs in isolation, and we take into account her relationships to family, loved ones, her local community, and society."

Covington argues that the environment of most correctional facilities does not facilitate growth and development in women's lives. With an understanding of women's psychological development, it is possible to discover the kind of environment that does facilitate growth. Relational theory can help those who work with female offenders to create the kinds of programs and environment in the criminal justice system that will be most effective for women and girls.

INTRODUCTION

Some of the most neglected and misunderstood women in our society are those in our jails, prisons, and community correctional facilities. While women's rate of incarceration has increased dramatically, tripling in the last decade, prisons have not kept pace with the growth of the number of women in prison (Bloom et al. 1994). Nor has the criminal justice system been redesigned to meet women's needs, which are often quite different from the needs of men.

The relational theory of women's psychological development helps us understand what women need from our criminal justice system. The purpose of this chapter is to explain what relational theory is and how it applies to correctional settings. First, we will review who female offenders are—race, class, age, offenses, and experiences of trauma and addiction. It's important to remember the population we are serving in order to determine what will make a difference in their lives. Second, we will discuss what relational theory is, and what a "growth-fostering relationship" is. Third, we will then begin to apply relational theory to the criminal justice system, asking: What are gender-specific services? What does relational theory tell us about the childhood and adult experiences of female offenders? And, what does relational theory tell us about corrections on a systemic level? Fourth, because many female offenders have histories of addiction and trauma, we will look at theories of addiction and trauma in light of relational theory to see how best to treat women and girls with these issues.

Sources: Reprinted with permission from *Gender and Alcohol: Individual and Social Perspectives,* edited by Richard W. Wislnack and Sharon C. Wislnack. Copyright 1997, Alcohol Research Documentation, Inc., Rutgers Center of Alcohol Studies, Piscataway, NJ 08854 and J. Dougherty, *Women and Criminal Justice,* Vol. 4, No. 2, pp. 91–114, © 1993. The Haworth Press, Inc.

WOMEN AND GIRLS IN THE CRIMINAL JUSTICE SYSTEM: WHO ARE THEY?

This section is a brief review of some of the more detailed information found in Chapters One and Two. The rate of women's incarceration tripled in the 1980s and continues to grow at a faster rate than men's, despite a decrease in violent crime committed by women. Tougher sentencing for women's drug offenses, the building of new facilities for women, and an increase in women's non-violent property crimes during two economic recessions seem to account for the increased rate of imprisonment.

Female prison populations differ from their male counterparts in several significant ways. First of all, they are less likely to have committed a violent offense and more likely to have been convicted of a crime involving alcohol, other drugs, or property. Many property crimes are economically driven, often motivated by poverty and/or the abuse of alcohol and other drugs. A 1994 study of California inmates showed that 71.9 percent of women had been convicted on a drug or property charge, versus 49.7 percent of men. Men also commit nearly twice the violent crimes that women do (Bloom et al. 1994). These statistics are consistent with national trends (see Chapter One by Steffensmeier and Allan). Women are significantly less violent than their male counterparts and show more responsiveness to prison programs, although they have less opportunity to participate in them than male prisoners do. While men often deal with their anxiety by working their bodies constantly, women tend to fear the central yard, working out their anxieties with too much sleep, food, and prescription pills (LeBlanc 1996).

Juvenile offenders also reflect this contrast in type of crime. Rates for less serious crimes, such as smoking marijuana and shoplifting, are similar for boys and girls. But rates of serious and violent crime are far lower among girls. Girls are more likely than boys to be arrested and detained for status offenses—acts that would not be offenses if committed by an adult, such as promiscuity, truancy, or running away (Belknap et al. 1997, p. 13). The system seems to believe that boys will be boys, but girls should behave like ladies.

Most female prisoners are poor, undereducated, unskilled, single mothers, and a disproportionate number of them are women of color. In a study of California prisons, over half of the women were African American (35 percent) and Hispanic (16.6 percent). One-third of the people were Caucasian and the remaining 13 percent were made up of other minorities. Of those who had been employed before incarceration, many were on the lower rungs of the economic ladder, with only 37 percent working at a legitimate job. Twenty-two percent were on some kind of public support, 16 percent made money from drug dealing, and 15 percent were involved in prostitution, shoplifting, or other illegal activities (Bloom et al. 1994).

These statistics show that issues of race and class permeate the criminal justice system (Chesney-Lind and Bloom 1997). For example, a Minnesota law (recently held unconstitutional) dictated that first-time users of crack cocaine would receive mandatory four-year sentences, but first-time users of cocaine in its powdered form receive only probation. Because 92 percent of those arrested on charges for possession of crack in 1988 were African Americans and 85 percent of those arrested for possession of powdered cocaine were Caucasian, the law was clearly racist (Raspberry 1991).

Two-thirds of incarcerated women have children under the age of 18 (Bureau of Prison Statistics, 1991). Many feel enormous guilt about being absent from their children's lives and worry about whether they will still have custody of their children when they get out (Bloom and Steinhart 1993; Watterson 1996). These and other concerns, including unresolved issues of physical and sexual abuse, lead female inmates to make requests for psychological counseling that far exceed those made by men. Criminal justice experts agree that women would benefit from additional services (Salholz and Wright 1990).

Many incarcerated women either abuse or are addicted to alcohol and/or other drugs. Nationwide, "up to 80 percent of the women offenders in some State prison systems now have severe, long-standing substance abuse problems" (Center for Substance Abuse Treatment 1997, p. 2). Drug violators make up 61 percent of women in federal prisons (up from 38 percent in 1986), 21 percent of the women in state facilities (up from 9 percent), and 23 percent of those in local jails (up from 9 percent) (Snell 1994).

Along with their history of alcohol and other drug use, many women in prison also have a history of physical and sexual abuse. In California prisons, nearly 80 percent have experienced some form of abuse. Twenty-nine percent report being physically abused as children and 60 percent as adults, usually by their partners. Thirty-one percent experienced sexual abuse as a child and 23 percent as adults; 40 percent reported emotional abuse as a child and 48 percent as an adult (Bloom et al. 1994).

Research on adolescent girl offenders reveals abuse histories that parallel those of adult women. For example, a study of girls involved in violent street crime in New York City found that almost all came from homes characterized by poverty, domestic violence, and substance abuse. Those who became delinquent as younger adolescents, as opposed to later in their teens, were more likely to come from neighborhoods with "high concentrations of poverty," to have been sexually or physically abused by a stranger, and to have friends involved in violent crime (Sommers and Baskin 1994, p. 477).

A national study found that institutionalized girls are far more likely to think about and attempt suicide than are boys (Wells 1994). One explanation for this self-destructiveness is that, like their adult counterparts, girls in the criminal justice system have high rates of physical and sexual abuse. (Abuse survivors in general attempt suicide more often than do persons without abuse histories.) Also, many girls enter the system pregnant; some become pregnant while incarcerated (Belknap et al. 1997).

In short, the females flooding our criminal justice system are mostly young, poor, undereducated, women and girls of color with complex histories of trauma and addiction. Most are nonviolent and not threats to the community. Survival (of abuse and poverty) and addiction are the most common pathways to crime for women. Their greatest needs are multifaceted treatment for addiction and trauma recovery, and education for job and parenting skills. They need the opportunity to grow, to learn, to make changes in their lives.

As Mary Leftridge Byrd, Superintendent of the Muncy Women's Prison in Pennsylvania, says in her message to new inmates, "This period of incarceration…can be a 'time out' for reflection, collecting yourself and honestly confronting the reason you find yourself in this place….Do not simply serve time, let the time serve you. Do not just let things happen, make things happen" (Byrd 1998).

However, the current focus and goal of our criminal justice system is control, not change. The environment of most correctional facilities does not facilitate growth and development in women's lives. But what kind of environment would help women change? When we understand women's psychological development, we discover the kind of environment that facilitates growth. Relational theory can help us create the kinds of programs and environment in the criminal justice system that will be most effective for women and girls.

RELATIONAL THEORY: WHAT IS IT?

Over the past two decades, we have begun to recognize and acknowledge the differences between men and women. One difference is the way in which men and women develop psychologically. Jean Baker Miller posed the question of how women develop in her 1976 book, *Toward a New Psychology of Women*. Until then, traditional theories of psychology described development as a climb from childlike dependence to mature independence. A person's goal, according to these theories, was to become a self-sufficient, clearly differentiated, autonomous self. A person would spend his or her life separating and individuating until he or she reached maturity, at which point the person was equipped for intimacy.

Miller challenged the assumption that separation was the route to maturity. She suggested that those theories might be describing men's experience, while a woman's path to maturity was different. A woman's primary motivation, said Miller, is to build a sense of connection with others. Women develop a sense of self and self-worth when their actions arise out of, and lead back into, connections with others. Connection, not separation, is the guiding principle of growth for women.

Previously, theoreticians had treated women's emphasis on connection as a sign of deficiency. In her book, *In a Different Voice: Psychological Theory and Women's Development*, Carol Gilligan observed, "The disparity between women's experience and the representation of human development, noted throughout the psychological literature, has generally been seen to signify a problem in women's development. Instead, the failure of women to fit existing models of human growth may point to a problem in the representation, a limitation in the conception of the human condition, an omission of certain truths about life" (Gilligan 1982, pp. 1–2).

Miller's work led a group of researchers and practitioners to create the Stone Center at Wellesley College for the purpose of thinking through the qualities of relationships that foster healthy growth in women (Jordan 1984, 1985; Jordan and Surrey 1986; Kaplan 1984; Surrey 1985; see also Chapter Eleven by Swift). The basic assumption of the Stone Center model is that "connection" is a basic human need, and that this need is especially strong in women (Jordan et al. 1991). All people need both connection with others and differentiation from others, but females are more attuned to connection while males are more attuned to differentiation. Bylington (1997) explained this connection as follows:

> Theoretically, girls perceive themselves to be more similar than different to their earliest maternal caretakers, so they do not have to differentiate from their mothers in order to continue to develop their identities. This is in contrast to boys, who must develop an identity that is different from the mother's in order to continue their development. Thus, women's psychological growth and development occur through adding to rather than separating from relationships. Consequently, defining themselves as similar to others through relationships is fundamental to women's identities. (p. 35).

A *connection* in the Stone Center relational model is "an interaction that engenders a sense of being in tune with self and others, of being understood and valued" (Bylington 1997, p. 35). True connections are mutual, empathic, creative, energy-releasing, and empowering for all participants (Miller 1986). Such connections are so crucial for women that women's psychological problems can be traced to disconnections or violations within relationships—whether in families, with personal acquaintances, or in society at large.

Mutuality means that each person in a relationship can represent her feelings, thoughts, and perceptions, and both can move with and be moved by the feelings, thoughts, and perceptions of the other person. Each person, as well as the relationship, can change and move forward because there is mutual influence and mutual responsiveness.

Empathy is a complex, highly developed ability to join with another at a cognitive and affective level without losing connection with one's own experience. An empathic person both feels personally authentic in the relationship and feels she can "see" and "know" the other person. A growth-fostering relationship requires mutual empathy, which in turn requires that both parties have the capacity to connect empathically.

Mutuality and empathy empower women not with power *over* others, but rather power *with* others. In traditional relationships, one person or group of persons is often dominant and the other subordinate, or one person or group is assigned the task of fostering the psychological development of others. Historically, women have been assigned the task of fostering the psychological development of others, including men and children. By contrast, in mutually empowering relationships, each person grows in psychological strength or power. Women become more able to share power for constructive, creative ends.

Mutual, empathic, and empowering relationships produce five psychological outcomes. All participants gain: (1) increased zest and vitality, (2) empowerment to act, (3) knowledge of self and others, (4) self-worth, and (5) a desire for more connection (Miller 1986). These outcomes constitute psychological growth for women. Mutuality, empathy, and power with others are essential qualities of an environment that will foster growth in women.

By contrast, Miller (1990) has described the outcomes of disconnections—nonmutual or abusive relationships—which she terms a "depressive spiral." These are: (1) diminished zest or vitality, (2) disempowerment, (3) unclarity or confusion, (4) diminished self-worth, and (5) a turning away from relationships. All relationships involve disconnections, times when people feel their separateness and distance. However, growth-fostering relationships are able to allow disconnections that, with effort on each person's part, can be turned into connections. In nonmutual and/or abusive relationships, disconnections are not turned into true connections.

RELATIONAL THEORY AND THE CRIMINAL JUSTICE SYSTEM

Gender-Specific Services

An understanding of relational theory is important for those who work in the criminal justice system for several reasons. First, most current programs have been designed by men for men. In order to develop effective services for women, we need to create programs for women based on the reality of their lives and on what we know about women's growth and development. In a 1997 report on gender-specific services for adolescent girls to the Governor from the Office of Criminal Justice Services for the State of Ohio, Belknap et al. (1997) wrote,

> When examining gender-specific programming, it is important to recognize *equality does not mean "sameness."* Equality is not about providing the same programs, treatment and opportunities for girls and boys....Equality is about providing opportunities that mean the same to each gender. This new definition legitimizes the differences between boys and girls. Programs for boys are more successful when they focus on rules and offer ways to advance within a structured environment, while *programs for girls are more successful when they focus on relationships* with other people and offer ways to master their lives while keeping these relationships intact. (p. 23, emphasis added)

That report went on to list the following criteria for gender-specific programming and service delivery systems (Belknap et al. 1997, p. 23):

- meet the unique needs of females
- acknowledge the female perspective
- support the female experience through positive female role models
- listen to the needs and experiences of adolescent females
- recognize the contributions of girls and women
- respect female development
- empower girls and young women to reach their full potential
- work to change established attitudes that prevent or discourage young women from recognizing their potential

At a meeting of the National Institute of Corrections, Barbara Bloom defined gender-specific programs for women and girls in similar terms. She added other guiding principles, such as (Bloom 1997, pp. 4–5):

- Whenever possible, women and girls should be treated in the least restrictive programming environment available. The level of security should depend on both treatment needs and concerns for public safety.
- Cultural awareness and sensitivity should be promoted and the cultural resources and strengths in various communities should be utilized.
- Educational and vocational training opportunities should be commensurate with girls' and women's interests and abilities so as to garner their potential (including both traditional and nontraditional career options).
- Program staff should reflect the diversity of the population and be representative in terms of gender, race/ethnicity, and sexual orientation.
- Women and girls can benefit from positive role models; mentors from their particular communities who exemplify survival and growth, as well as resistance and change.

Stressing the importance of relational issues for girls, the Ohio report recommended providing "the safety and comfort of same-gender environments," offering learning experiences once trusting relationships have been established, and helping girls to understand "that they can be professionally and emotionally successful in life and still have strong relationships (Belknap et al. 1997, p. 24).

Issues of women's and girls' lives that gender-specific programs would address include, but are not limited to (Bloom 1997, p. 6; Belknap et al. 1997, p. 24):

- development of a sense of self and self-esteem
- establishment of trusting, growth-fostering relationships
- physical health
- sobriety—clean and sober living
- sexuality
- mental health
- physical fitness and athletics
- pregnancy and parenting skills
- decision-making skills
- trauma from physical, emotional, and sexual abuse—treatment and prevention
- cultural awareness and sensitivity
- spirituality

The Relational Experiences of Women

The second reason why we need to understand relational theory is to avoid recreating in correctional settings the same kinds of growth-hindering and/or violating relationships that women and girls experience in the free world. It is also important to consider how women's life experiences may affect how they will function in the criminal justice system.

Disconnection and violation characterize the childhood experience of most women and girls in the system. According to a recent sampling of women in a Massachusetts prison (Coll and Duff 1995), 38 percent of the women had lost parents in childhood, 69 percent had been abused as children, and 70 percent had left home before age 17. They lacked experience of mutual and empathic relationships. Although Gilligan et al. (1990) report that girls are socialized to be empathic more than boys, incarcerated women and girls have been exposed repeatedly to non-empathic relationships and so either lack empathy for both self and others, or are highly empathic toward others but lack empathy for self. In order to change, women need to experience relationships that do not re-enact their histories of loss, neglect, and abuse.

Likewise, disconnection and violation have characterized most of the adult relationships of women in the system. Seventy percent of women in the Massachusetts study had been repeatedly abused verbally, physically, and/or sexually as adults (Coll and Duff 1995). Another study, this one of drug-abusing pregnant women (Amaro and Hardy-Fanta 1995), found that:

> Men who go to jail, men who do not take care of them or their children, and men who disappoint them fill the lives of these women. Even more striking is the extent to which the women suffered physical abuse from their male partners....Half of the women in this study reported abuse from the men in their lives; occasionally from "tricks," although more typically from their partners.(p. 333).

Robbery, beatings, and rape by men on the street were commonly reported. Women were often first introduced to drugs by partners, and partners often continued to be their suppliers. Attempts to get off drugs and failure to supply partners with drugs through prostitution often elicited violence from partners. However, women remain attached despite the neglect and abuse. (For more on the effects of violence on women, see Swift, Chapter Eleven.)

Women at high risk for drug abuse are frequently socially isolated—single parents, unemployed, or recently separated, divorced, or widowed (Finkelstein 1993; Finkelstein and Derman 1991; Wilsnack et al. 1986). Psychological isolation also occurs when the people in a woman's world fail to validate and respond to her experience or her attempts at connection. Miller (1990) has described the state of "condemned isolation" where a woman feels isolated in her important relationships and feels that she is the problem; that she is condemned to be isolated, with no possibility of changing this situation. This state of shame and condemned isolation is highly correlated with drug use, as drugs become a way of coping with intense feelings and a sense of hopelessness.

Jordan et al. (1991) have described the tremendous cultural shaming around women's yearnings for connection, sexuality, and emotionality. Women are prone to feel personally deficient—"something is wrong with me"—to take responsibility for problematic relationships, and thus to seek all kinds of ways to alter themselves. In nonmutual relationships, women often carry the disavowed feelings of pain, anger, or fear of those with whom they are connected. Women and girls in the criminal justice system endure even heavier shame, as society stigmatizes them as female offenders.

Together, abuse, isolation, and shame can send women into the previously mentioned "depressive spiral" that is the opposite of growth: (1) diminished zest or vitality, (2) disempowerment, (3) unclarity or confusion, (4) diminished self-worth, and (5) a turning away from relationships. This depressive spiral characterizes too well the females in our criminal justice system.

Relational Theory: A Systems View

Tragically, current correctional settings often re-enact these relationships of disconnection and violation on a systemic level. Our criminal justice system, which is based on power and control, reflects the dominant/subordinate model of our patriarchal society (see Dougherty in Chapter Six). It is a microcosm of the larger social system. Relationships in correctional settings are based on ranking people, with women and girls at the lowest rung of the ladder. This ranking is even reflected in the classification and pay scale of correctional employees. Those who work with females often earn less and are seen as having less important jobs.

In addition, the women who work in correctional settings often feel neglected and abused by the sexist culture. When relationships among staff are nonmutual and disrespectful, there is an increased risk that staff will treat offenders in the same way.

"Condemned isolation" describes what women and girls often experience in this system. Although their life experiences have much in common, they are not encouraged to bond and connect with one another. In their isolation from families and children, they often try to create "pseudo-families" on the inside. These families and relationships are discouraged.

Furthermore, drugs are often available in jails and prisons, sometimes brought in and sold or bartered by correctional officers (Salholz and Wright 1990). Staff members can form the same kinds of destructive relationships with women that women have had with their supplier-partners on the outside.

Women are also at risk for abuse within the prison system. An ongoing investigation by the Human Rights Watch Women's Rights Project documented custodial misconduct in many forms, including verbal degradation, rape, sexual assault, unwarranted visual supervision, denying goods and privileges, and use or threat of force. "Male correctional officers and staff contribute to a custodial environment in state prisons for women that is often highly sexualized and excessively hostile" (Human Rights Watch Women's Rights Project 1996, p. 2). Chesney-Lind and Rodriguez (1983) found a significant risk of male staff and other inmates sexually assaulting incarcerated girls. Yet the girls, not the males, are stigmatized: "there is considerable documentation of incarcerated pregnant females being encouraged or even forced to give their babies up for adoption…even if the girl became pregnant while incarcerated" (Belknap et al. 1997, p. 15).

What women need instead is an application of relational theory on a system-wide basis. As Carolyn Swift explains (see Chapter Eleven), a pilot project in a Massachusetts prison found women benefiting from a group in which women both received information and had the opportunity to practice mutually empathic relationships with each other. Women also need relationships with correctional staff that are respectful, mutual, and compassionate. Respect was one of the main things girls in the Ohio study said they needed from staff (Belknap et al. 1997, pp. 25–26). Finally, women will benefit if relationships among staff members, and between staff and administration, are mutual, empathic, and aimed at power-with-others rather than power-over-others. The culture of corrections (the environment created by the criminal justice system) can be altered by the application of relational theory.

OTHER RELEVANT THEORIES

We have seen how relational theory can help us develop an approach to programs in correctional settings that is gender sensitive, addressing itself to the realities of women's and girls' lives. Two other theories—a holistic theory of addiction and a theory of trauma—can further aid us in designing gender-specific services. Because addiction and trauma dominate the lives of many female offenders, it makes sense to understand how these experiences affect women and how women recover from such experiences. We will examine both theories through a relational lens.

Addiction Theory

Drug violators typically return to criminal patterns of behavior after release unless their drug addiction is addressed while they are incarcerated or immediately upon release (Moon et al. 1993). Because 61 percent of women in federal prisons are there for drug offenses, and because up to 80 percent of women in state prisons are long-standing substance abusers, we need to understand how addiction and recovery work among women. Recovery is possible, and we have the opportunity to assist women and girls in beginning the recovery process.

Addiction can be viewed as a kind of relationship. The addicted woman/girl is in a relationship with alcohol or other drugs, "a relationship characterized by obsession, compulsion, nonmutuality, and an imbalance of power. It is a kind of love relationship in which the object of addiction becomes the focus of a woman's life" (Covington and Surrey 1997, p. 338). Addicted women frequently use relational imagery to describe their drug use, such as "My most passionate affair was with cocaine." At first the drug is her best friend, but as women describe the progress of their addiction, they say things like, "I turned to Valium, but then Valium turned on me." We can speak of addiction as a contraction of connection. Recovery, then, is an expansion of connection (Covington and Beckett 1988).

Moreover, women frequently begin to use substances in ways that initially seem to make or maintain connections, in an attempt to feel connected, energized, loved, or loving when that is not the whole truth of their experience (Surrey 1991). Women often turn to drugs in the context of relationships with drug-abusing partners—to feel connected through the use of drugs. Male friends and partners often introduce women to alcohol and drugs, partners are often their suppliers, and partners often resist their efforts to stop using drugs.

Women may begin to use substances to alter themselves to fit the relationships available. Miller (1990) has described this basic relational paradox—when a woman cannot move a relationship toward mutuality, she begins to change herself to maintain the relationship. Stiver (1990) has written about children of "dysfunctional" families who frequently turn to substances to alter themselves to adapt to the disconnections within the family, thus giving the illusion of being in relationship when one is not or is only partially in relationship.

Women often use substances to numb the pain of nonmutual, nonempathic, even violent relationships. Addicted women's lives are full of men who disappoint them, don't provide for their children, and go to jail. These women long for the fathers of their children to provide emotional and financial support, but such longings often lead to disappointment and solace in drug use. Worse, many women report violence from the men in their lives. Nonmutual or abusive relationships produce the "depressive spiral" described above, and women may then turn to substances to provide what relationships are not providing, such as energy, a sense of power, or relief from confusion. These behaviors are characteristic of chemically dependent women in general, yet it is magnified for those in the criminal justice system.

Traditionally, addiction treatment has been based on a medical model, which views addiction as a disease. The most commonly used analogy is that addiction is like diabetes, a physical disease that carries no moral or social stigma. This analogy is often useful because neither diabetes nor addiction can be managed by will power. They both require adherence to a lifestyle regimen for physical and emotional stability.

However, this analogy sees the disease/disorder rooted solely in the individual. As we move into the twenty-first century, health professionals in many disciplines are revising their concept of disease in general. Based on a holistic health model, we are now acknowledging not only the physical aspects of disease, but also the emotional, psychological, and spiritual aspects (Northrup 1994).

We will better understand addiction as a disease/disorder if we see it holistically and include cancer as an analogy. The diabetes model is useful, but too individualistic and simplistic to adequately explain addiction.

"Like cancer, addiction has a physical component as well as emotional, psychological, and spiritual dimensions….[T]wo other components of disease must also be added to a fully holistic model: the environmental and the sociopolitical dimensions" (Covington 1998, p.147). It is interesting that few people question that cancer is a disease, while many question that addiction is a disease, even though up to 80 percent of doctors link cancer to lifestyle choices (diet and exercise) and the environment (pesticides, emissions, nuclear waste, etc.) (personal communication, Siegel 1996). There are also sociopolitical aspects of both cancer and addiction: both carcinogenic products and addictive substances (legal and illegal) make huge profits for powerful business interests. In addition, medical doctors prescribe 80 percent of the amphetamines, 60 percent of the psychoactive drugs, and 71 percent of the antidepressants to women (Galbraith 1991). Companies that produce and sell alcohol are indirectly responsible for over 23,000 deaths and 750,000 injuries each year—and these are only the figures reported to insurance companies (Zawistowski 1991). Even though some women may have a strong genetic predisposition to addiction, an important treatment issue is acknowledging that many of them have grown up in an environment where drug dealing and addiction are a way of life.

A holistic model of addiction is essentially a systems perspective. We look at the complete woman and try to understand the connection of addiction to every aspect of the self—physical, emotional, and spiritual. We understand that the addicted woman is not using alcohol or other drugs in isolation, and we take into account her relationships to family, loved ones, her local community, and society.

The Center for Substance Abuse Treatment (CSAT) funds ongoing studies of women's addiction and treatment, establishes minimum standards for treatment, and provides demonstration models for treatment in programs around the country. It operates within the U.S. Public Health Service, an agency of the Department of Health and Human Services. CSAT (1994, p. 178) recognizes the need for gender-specific treatment for women, and has stated the following issues essential to a comprehensive treatment program:

- The process of addiction, especially gender-specific issues related to addiction (including social, physiological, and psychological consequences of addiction, and factors related to the onset of addiction)
- Low self-esteem
- Race, ethnicity and cultural issues
- Gender discrimination and harassment
- Disability-related issues, where relevant
- Relationships with family and significant others
- Attachments to unhealthy interpersonal relationships
- Interpersonal violence, including incest, rape, battering, and other abuse
- Eating disorders
- Sexuality, including sexual functioning and sexual orientation
- Parenting
- Grief related to the loss of alcohol or other drugs, children, family members, or partners
- Work
- Appearance and overall health and hygiene
- Isolation related to a lack of support systems (which may or may not include family members and/or partners) and other resources
- Life plan development
- Child care and custody

Notice presented the holistic approach takes into account physical, psychological, emotional, spiritual, and sociopolitical issues. Notice also how similar this list is to the list of issues proposed at the National Institute of Corrections and the Ohio study (Bloom 1997, p. 6; Belknap et al. 1997, p. 24).

When a diverse group of recovering women were interviewed, they identified four issues that changed the most for them in recovery and that most contribute to relapse: self, relationships, sexuality, and spirituality (Covington 1994). These four issues parallel the items in the CSAT list above. The first two of these issues—self and relationships—are briefly discussed here.

Addiction can be understood as a self-disorder. A generic definition of addiction is, "the chronic neglect of self in favor of something or someone else." One of the first questions women in recovery need to begin to address is, "Who am I?" Women in our culture are taught to identify themselves according to role: mother, professional, wife, partner, daughter. Women in the criminal justice system also identify themselves—as does society—as offenders, and they become stigmatized. Many women also enter the system with a poor self-image and a history of trauma and abuse. Creating the kinds of programs that help women to develop a strong sense of self, an identification that goes beyond who they are in the criminal justice system, is vital to their reentering society. Recovery is about the expansion and growth of the self.

Relationship issues are also paramount in early recovery. Some women use addictive substances to maintain relationships with using partners, to fill up the void of what is missing in a relationship, or to deal with the pain of being abused. Women in the criminal justice system often have unhealthy, illusory or unequal relationships with spouses, partners, friends, and family members. For that reason, it is important for programs to model healthy relationships, among both staff and participants, providing a safe place and a container for healing (Covington and Beckett 1988). One of the greatest challenges is to overcome the alienation fostered within prison walls, and replace it with a greater sense of relationship in community. Being in community—that is, having a sense of connection with others—is essential for continuous, long-term recovery.

Trauma Theory

An understanding of trauma is also essential. Trauma is not limited to suffering violence, but includes witnessing violence, as well as the trauma of stigmatization because of poverty, racism, incarceration, or sexual orientation. We have seen that the vast majority of female offenders have been physically and/or sexually abused both as children and adults. Thus, most female offenders are trauma survivors when they enter the system, and then they are at risk for retraumatization by the system. Incarceration can be traumatizing in itself, and the racism and classism that characterize the criminal justice system can be further traumatizing. Many women use drugs or alcohol in order to medicate the pain of trauma. Trauma skews a woman's relational experience and hinders her psychological development.

Psychiatrist Judith Herman (1992) writes that trauma is a disease of disconnection and that there are three stages in the process of healing from trauma: (1) safety, (2) remembrance and mourning, and (3) reconnection. "Survivors feel unsafe in their bodies. Their emotions and their thinking feel out of control. They also feel unsafe in relation to other people" (Herman 1992, p. 160). Stage One (safety) addresses the woman's safety concerns in all of these domains. In Stage Two of recovery (remembrance and mourning), the survivor tells the story of the trauma and mourns the old self that the trauma destroyed. In Stage Three (reconnection), the survivor faces the task of creating a future; now she develops a new self.

Safety, the Stage One recovery from trauma, is the appropriate first level of intervention for a criminal justice setting. If we want to assist women in changing their lives, we must create a safe environment in which the healing process can begin to take place. We can help a woman feel safe in her external world by keeping facilities free of physical and sexual harassment and abuse. We can also help women feel safe internally by teaching them self-soothing mechanisms. Many chemically dependent trauma survivors use drugs to medicate their depression or anxiety because they know no better ways to comfort themselves.

It is also important to acknowledge that for some women and girls, their first experience of safety is in a correctional setting. Violence and abuse have been their experience at home and on the street. It is a harsh social reality when a female needs to be incarcerated to feel safe.

For other women and girls, their experience in the criminal justice system is traumatizing and triggers memories of earlier instances of abuse. It can be retraumatizing when a sexual abuse survivor has a body search or must shower with male guards nearby. It can be retraumatizing when a battered woman is yelled or cursed at by a staff person. Survivors of trauma often experience symptoms of post-traumatic stress disorder (PTSD). *The Diagnostic and Statistical Manual of Mental Disorders,* fourth edition, lists these symptoms of PTSD:

- Reexperiencing the event through nightmares and flashbacks
- Avoidance of stimuli associated with the event (for example, if a woman was assaulted by a blond man, she may fear and want to avoid men with blond hair)
- Estrangement (the inability to be emotionally close to anyone)
- Numbing of general responsiveness (feeling nothing most of the time)
- Hypervigilance (constantly scanning one's environment for danger, whether physical or emotional)
- Exaggerated startle response (a tendency to jump at loud noises or unexpected touch) (American Psychiatric Association, 1994, pp. 427–429)

Because PTSD can affect the way a woman or girl relates to staff, peers, and the environment of a correctional setting, it will be helpful to ask, "Is this person's behavior linked to PTSD?"

"Women recovering from childhood molestation, rape, or battering are teaching us about the impact of such trauma on relational development. When early parental relationships are abusive, violating, and dangerous, all future relationships are impacted. The very high rate of substance abuse and addiction among survivors of abuse and violence suggests the likelihood of turning to substance abuse when healthy relationships are unavailable and when faith or trust in the possibility of growth in human connection is impaired. The use of alcohol and other drugs has become a way for women to deal with the emotional pain resulting from earlier abuse by someone close to them, someone they trusted" (Covington and Surrey 1997, p. 342).

Finally, personal violence toward women must be understood in the larger societal context of systemic violence and oppression, including racism, classism, heterosexism, and ageism (see Dougherty, Chapter Six).

In summary, women begin to heal from addiction and trauma in a relational context. Recovery happens in connection, not in isolation. Nonmutual, nonempathic, disempowering, and unsafe settings make change and healing extremely difficult. The more we understand and apply relational theory, the more able we will be to help women who suffer from trauma and addiction. The theoretical approach in this chapter has been developed into a treatment and training program (Covington in press).

CONCLUSION

Many women and men who work in criminal justice settings struggle with daily contradictions. One contradiction is that a system based on power and control is antithetical to what helps women to change, grow, and heal. Hence, creating a new gender-specific program or changing an existing program is a partial solution to meeting women's needs. Systemic change is essential.

One of the primary goals of our criminal justice system must be to help women and girls reintegrate into society and lead productive lives. What can we do? We can intervene in the status quo on many different levels.

1. Try to change mandatory sentencing laws. Addicted women and girls need treatment, not prisons. Drugs are a public health problem, not a criminal justice problem. Treatment is both cheaper and more effective than prison at reducing recidivism (Gerstein et al. 1994, Finigan 1996). CSAT (1997) writes, "Addicted women who are incarcerated because of our tightened drug laws will keep recycling through the criminal justice system unless they receive treatment….Most women do not need to be incarcerated to protect the community. The treatment they need can be provided in the community, with their families intact and with the chance to become sober and drug-free under real-life conditions" (p. 2.).

2. Staff our jails, prisons, and community correctional facilities with more female wardens and correctional officers. Female staff can serve as role models and help to

reduce the risk of retraumatization by providing women and girls with a sense of safety. Only women and men who can do the above have the right to work with females.

3. Give supplementary training to correctional officers. Training academies often teach information and skills that apply only to men's facilities. Officers in women's facilities need to understand the realities of women's lives and the value of mutually empathic relationships, not just the kinds of rules and structure that are effective with men. They need to understand how disconnection, addiction, and trauma affect women.

4. Teach women to value life, especially their own. It is hard for women to do so in a misogynist society where women get messages that their lives are trivial.

5. Help women keep contact with their children. Currently, women's facilities are often set at great distances from where women's children live, so that visitation is difficult. But it is often their connections with their children that keep women alive and motivate them to change. It is equally essential that children's need for connection with their mothers is supported and facilitated.. Maintaining these relationships is one form of prevention for families in the criminal justice system.

6. Become aware of our own attitudes about women and girls. Commit to changing our personal social system away from a system of power and control, and toward a system of mutually empowering relationships. Work to create an environment for change and healing in our own lives.

Women need a criminal justice system that takes into account their realities and their need for connection in their lives and their experience of damaging disconnection. They need a system in which relational theory provides the underlying philosophy, shapes the dynamics of staff and offender relationships, and affects the ways staff interact and make decisions. Women and girls need to experience an environment of growth-fostering relationships based on respect, mutuality, and empowerment.

As we move into the twenty-first century, it is time to move beyond the culture of punishment and retribution that characterizes our criminal justice system and create a culture of community and healing. It is time for transformation.

REFERENCES

Amaro, H., and Hardy-Fanta, C. 1995. Gender relations in addiction and recovery. *Journal of Psychiatric Drugs* 27: 325–337.

American Psychiatric Association 1994. *The diagnostic and statistical manual of mental disorders*, 4th ed. Washington, D.C.

Belknap, J., et al. 1997. *Moving toward juvenile justice and youth-serving systems that address the distinct experience of the adolescent female.* A Report to the Governor. Office of Criminal Justice Services, Columbus, OH.

Bloom, B. 1997. Defining "gender-specific": What does it mean and why is it important? Presentation at the National Institute of Corrections Intermediate Sanctions for Women Offenders National Project Meeting. Longmont, CO, September.

Bloom, B., et al. 1994. *Women in California prisons: Hidden victims of the war on drugs.* San Francisco: Center on Juvenile and Criminal Justice.

Bloom, B., and Steinhart, D. 1993. *Why punish the children? A reappraisal of incarcerated mothers in America.* San Francisco: National Council on Crime and Delinquency.

Bureau of Prison Statistics 1991. *Women in prison.* Special Report. Washington, D.C.: U.S. Department of Justice, Bureau of Prison Statistics.

Bylington, D. 1997. Applying relational theory to addiction treatment. *Gender and addictions: Men and women in treatment,* eds. Straussner, S.L.A., and Zelvin, E., 33–45. Northvale, NJ: Jason Aronson.

Byrd, M. 1998. *Inmate handbook supplement,* rev. ed. Muncy, PA: State Correctional Institution.

Center for Substance Abuse Treatment 1994. *Practical approaches in the treatment of women who abuse alcohol and other drugs.* Rockville, MD: Department of Health and Human Services, Public Health Service.

Center for Substance Abuse Treatment 1997. *Substance abuse treatment for incarcerated women offenders: Guide to promising practices*, draft. Rockville, MD: Department of Health and Human Services, Public Health Service.

Chesney-Lind, M., and Bloom, B. 1997. Feminist criminology: Thinking about women and crime. In *Thinking critically about crime,* eds. MacLean, B., and Milovanovic, D., 54–65. Vancouver, BC, Canada: Collective Press.

Chesney-Lind, M., and Rodriguez, N. 1983. Women under lock and key. *Prison Journal* 63: 47–65.

Coll, C., and Duff, K. 1995. Reframing the needs of women in prison: A relational and diversity perspective. *Final report, women in prison pilot project.* Wellesley, MA: Stone Center.

Covington, S. 1994. *A woman's way through the twelve steps.* Center City, MN: Hazelden Educational Materials.

Covington, S. 1998. Women in prison: Approaches in the treatment of our most invisible population. In *Breaking the rules*, eds. Harden, J., and Hill, M., 141–155. Binghamton, NY: Haworth Press.

Covington, S. In press. *Helping women to change in correctional settings: A program for treating substance abuse.* San Francisco: Jossey-Bass Publishers.

Covington, S., and Beckett, L. 1988. *Leaving the enchanted forest: The path from relationship addiction to intimacy.* San Francisco: HarperCollins Publishers.

Covington, S., and Surrey, J. 1997. The relational model of women's psychological development: Implications for substance abuse. In *Gender and alcohol: Individual and social perspectives,* eds. Wilsnack, S., and Wilsnack, R., 335–351. New Brunswick, NJ: Rutgers University Press.

Finigan, M. 1996. *Societal outcomes and cost savings of drug and alcohol treatment in the State of Oregon.* Prepared for the Office of Alcohol and Drug Abuse Programs, Oregon Department of Human Resources.

Finkelstein, N. 1993, July. The relational model. In *Pregnancy and exposure to alcohol and other drug use,* eds. Kronstadt, D., et al. Washington, D.C.: U.S. Department of Health and Human Services, Substance Abuse and Mental Health Services Administration, Center for Substance Abuse Prevention, pp. 126–163.

Finkelstein, N., and Derman, L. 1991. Single-parent women: What a mother can do. In *Alcohol and drugs are women's issues,* ed. Roth, P., 78–84. New York: Scarecrow Press.

Galbraith, S. 1991. Women and legal drugs. In *Alcohol and drugs are women's issues,* ed. Roth, P., 150–154. New York: Scarecrow Press.

Gerstein, D., et al. 1994 *Evaluating recovery services: The California drug and alcohol treatment assessment.*

Gilligan, C. 1982. *In a different voice: Psychological theory and women's development.* Cambridge, MA: Harvard University Press.

Gilligan, C., et al. 1990. *Making connections.* Cambridge, MA: Harvard University Press.

Herman, J. 1992. *Trauma and recovery.* New York: Basic Books.

Human Rights Watch Women's Rights Project 1996. *All too familiar: Sexual abuse of women in U.S. state prisons.* New York: Human Rights Watch.

Jordan, J. 1984. *Empathy and self boundaries.* Work in Progress No. 16. Wellesley, MA: Stone Center, Working Paper Series.

Jordan, J. 1985. *The meaning of mutuality*. Work in Progress No. 23. Wellesley, MA: Stone Center, Working Paper Series.

Jordan, J., and Surrey, J. 1986. The self-in-relation: empathy and the mother-daughter relationship. In *The psychology of today's woman: New psychoanalytic visions*, eds. Bernay, T., and Cantor, D. New York: Analytic.

Jordan, J.V., et al. 1991. *Women's growth in connection: Writings from the Stone Center*. New York: Guilford Press.

Kaplan, A. 1984. *The self-in-relation: Implications for depression in women*. Work in Progress No. 14. Wellesley, MA: Stone Center, Working Paper Series.

LeBlanc, A. N. 1996. A woman behind bars is not a dangerous man. *The New York Times Magazine* June 2, 1996: 35–40.

Miller, J. B. 1976. *Toward a new psychology of women*. Boston: Beacon Press.

Miller, J. B. 1986. *What do we mean by relationships?* Work in Progress No. 22. Wellesley, MA: Stone Center, Working Paper Series.

Miller, J. B. 1990. *Connections, disconnections, and violations*. Work in Progress No. 33. Wellesley, MA: Stone Center, Working Paper Series.

Moon, D. et al. 1993. Patterns of substance abuse among women in prison. In *Women prisoners: A forgotten population,* eds. Fletcher, B., et al. 45–54. Westport, CT: Praeger Publishers/Greenwood Publishing Group.

Northrup, C. 1994. *Women's bodies, women's wisdom*. New York: Bantam Books.

Raspberry, W. 1991. Why are so many people in prison? *Washington Post* June 2: 57.

Salholz, E., and Wright, L. 1990. Women in jail: Unequal justice. *Newsweek* June 7: 37–38, 51.

Snell, T. 1994. *Women in prison: Survey of state prison inmates, 1991*. Washington, D.C.: U.S. Department of Justice, Bureau of Statistics.

Sommers, I., and Baskin, D. 1994. Factors related to female adolescent initiation into violent crime. *Youth and Society* 24: 468–489.

Steffensmeier, D., and Allan, E. 1998. The nature of female offending: Patterns and explanation. In *Female Offenders: Critical perspectives and effective interventions,* ed. Zaplin, R. Gaithersburg, MD: Aspen Publishers, Inc.

Stiver, I. 1990. *Dysfunctional families and wounded relationships*. Work in Progress No. 38. Wellesley, MA: Stone Center, Working Paper Series.

Surrey, J. 1985. *Self-in-relation: A theory of women's development*. Work in Progress No. 13. Wellesley, MA: Stone Center, Working Paper Series.

Surrey, J. 1991. *Women and addiction: A relational perspective*. Colloquium presented. Wellesley, MA: Stone Center.

Swift, C. 1998. Surviving violence: Women's strength through connection. In *Female Offenders: Critical perspectives and effective interventions,* ed. Zaplin, R. Gaithersburg, MD: Aspen Publishers, Inc.

Watterson, K. 1996. *Women in prison: Inside the concrete womb* rev. ed. Boston: Northeastern University Press.

Wells, R. 1994. America's delinquent daughters have nowhere to turn for help. *Corrections Compendium* 19: 4–6.

Wilsnack, S., et al. 1986. Epidemiological research on women's drinking, 1978–1984. In *Women and alcohol: Health-related issues,* 1–68. National Institute on Alcohol Abuse and Alcoholism Research Monograph No. 16; DHHS Publication No. ADM 86–1139. Washington, D.C.: Government Printing Office.

Zawistowski, T. 1991. Criminal addiction/illegal disease. *The Counselor* March/April: 8–11.

CHAPTER 6

Power-Belief Theory: Female Criminality and the Dynamics of Oppression

Joyce Dougherty

Editor's Notes

In Chapter Five, Covington emphasized how our criminal justice system, which is based on power and control, reflects the dominant/subordinate model of our patriarchal society. She stated: "It is a microcosm of the larger social system." It is also a major reason why the task of reintegrating female offenders into a society that is misogynist is so daunting a challenge. Power-belief theory presented in Chapter Six by Dougherty, provides an additional theoretical framework on which issues related to the patriarchal order of society can be systematically examined. The theory also serves as a foundation on which innovative ways to rehabilitate female offenders can be grounded.

The fundamental assertion of power-belief theory presented is that female criminality can best be understood within the context of the dynamics of oppression in patriarchal societies in which both sex and age are key organizing principles of the hierarchical order of power.

Dougherty contends that it is within this structural and ideological context of oppression that women and girls develop a matrix of beliefs about themselves, about their own power, and about the legitimacy of the patriarchal order. She further contends that the development of these beliefs represents the essence of the dynamics of oppression from which the rule violating (criminal, and/or delinquent) behavior of females manifests itself. The author suggests that exploring the variability of these dynamics is what holds the key to understanding and effectively treating female offenders. Finally, the author suggests that breaking the cycle of intergenerational criminality by reintegrating female offenders successfully into society is only possible if the rehabilitative needs of female offenders become the driving force in the criminal justice and juvenile justice systems, *not* the organizational demands of correctional institutions that traditionally have ignored those needs.

INTRODUCTION

For decades, those interested in the study of female offenders have focused attention on the inadequacies of traditional criminological theories. In 1987, Frances Heidensohn noted:

> A whole litany of writers (Heidensohn 1968; Klein 1976; Smart 1976; Shacklady Smith 1978; Leonard 1982; Millman 1982) have shown the fundamental flaws in traditional criminological writing on women, focusing particularly on the way in which folk myths about the inherent "nature" of women were taken over by criminologists and used as the basis of pseudo-scientific psycho-biological theories (Lombroso and Ferrero 1895; Thomas 1923; Pollak 1950). (p. 17)

The challenge confronting contemporary criminologists centers on the development of strategies to rectify these inadequacies. As Daly and Chesney-Lind (1988) point out, "some scholars…assume that previous theory can be corrected by including women" (p. 504), and thus efforts to determine how already established theories can be adapted to explain the law-violating behavior of females. While such efforts mark a critical step in the evolution of criminological theory, power-belief theory marks yet another. It introduces an innovative perspective on female criminality, providing important insights into the unique experiences and treatment needs of female offenders.

Power-belief theory asserts criminality can best be understood within the context of oppression in patriarchal societies. It is *not* a "female-specific" theory. It does, however, suggest the appropriateness of a gendered theoretical approach, and the focus of this chapter is on female offenders. It also is important to emphasize power-belief theory remains, up to this point, untested. At this stage of its development, the theory does not answer the question: "Why do some females engage in this kind of rule-violating behavior, while so many others do not?" Certainly explanatory factors are suggested, some of which clearly have their roots in the socio-historical evolution of the statuses of women and children in patriarchal societies. However, answering the "why" question will require systematic, empirical testing of power-belief theory.

When assessing the "liberated" world of modern women and the "protected" world of modern girls, the tendency seems to be to trivialize or even dismiss evidence of their oppression. The first section of this chapter presents evidence that the traditional targets of oppression in patriarchal societies—women and children—occupy uniquely powerless places in the social order. What also is established in this section is the degree to which culturally dominant social constructions of gender and childhood function to support and sustain these persistent and pervasive patterns of subordination. Central to power-belief theory is the contention that within this structural and ideological context of oppression, as women and girls struggle to cope and in some instances simply survive, they develop a matrix of beliefs about themselves, about their own power, and about the legitimacy of the patriarchal order. The development of these beliefs represents the essence of the dynamics of oppression from which rule-violating (criminal, and/or delinquent) behavior manifests itself. The next section of this chapter begins with an overview of these beliefs, along with an outline of some fundamental propositions of the dynamics of oppression. According to power-belief theory, exploring the variability of these dynamics is what holds the key to understanding and effectively treating female offenders. This section ends with a presentation of the matrices of beliefs it is being suggested are most likely to be found among populations of female offenders.* The conclusion of this chapter consists of a brief look at some theoretical and empirical implications of the power-belief theory and a discussion of some of its practical ramifications in regard to criminal justice policy, and the organization and implementation of treatment for females involved in the adult criminal and juvenile justice systems.

The explanatory value of power-belief theory holds great promise for contemporary criminologists. However, the hope is power-belief theory also will provide a viable theoretical foundation for policy-makers and practitioners who have come to recognize they need to find innovative ways to overcome the traditional barriers and forces that facilitate the consistent failure of efforts to rehabilitate female offenders.

THE STRUCTURAL AND IDEOLOGICAL CONTEXT OF OPPRESSION

The Structural Realm of Oppression

According to power-belief theory, the interactive effects between two realms of patriarchal societies—the structural realm and the ideological realm—create a context of oppression. The structural realm of patriarchal societies consists, in part, of networks of interactive social relationships that form basic economic, political, legal, religious, educational, and familial institutions. A pivotal assumption underlying power-belief theory is that within this realm, sex *and* age are the key organizing principles of the hierarchical order of power. The suggestion that sex and age are the key organizing principles of the hierarchical order of power in patriarchal societies is not meant to imply other factors, such as class, race, ethnicity, or national origin are irrelevant; it simply is meant to assert the primacy of sex and age. In other words, public and private patriarchal institutions consistently place *adult males* in positions of power, privilege, and leadership, and women and children in subordinate and/or subservient positions.

Historically the family, as a private social institution, has played a central part in the structural maintenance of patriarchal societies. This was not accomplished, of course, without the support of a multitude of public institutions. For centuries, women and children were completely denied access to major economic, political, legal, religious, and educational institutions. While their status gradually evolved from that of property to practical investments, children, in particular girls, were consistently relegated to the very bottom of

---

*This section represents the evolution and expansion of work originally published in "Women's Violence Against Their Children: A Feminist Perspective" (Dougherty 1993).

the social scale. This placed them at even greater risk of maltreatment than their male counterparts, especially female infants who were too young to work. Interpretations of old census data and period writings from seventeenth century France suggest female babies were far more likely to be the targets of infanticide or some other form of lethal abandonment than were male babies, who were looked upon as "the social security and pension plans" of the preindustrial world (Empey and Stafford 1991, p. 22 and 41).

Most scholars agree historically what had the greatest impact on the statuses of women and girls (and men and boys for that matter) was industrialization. During the last half of the eighteenth and early nineteenth centuries, the production of commodities gradually shifted from rural homes to urban factories, and survival no longer centered around family life. This and other dramatic changes that took place as a direct result of industrialization held the promise of ushering in an era of unprecedented challenges to the structural organization of Western patriarchal societies. By 1840 in the United States, women and children made up approximately 40 percent of the industrial work force (Reskin and Padavic 1994, p. 20). One might think the sheer number of women and children in the paid labor force would have been sufficient enough to present a major challenge to persistent patterns of adult male domination. However, as the number of people looking for work began to exceed the number of available jobs, it was the women and children who came to be viewed as threats to the employment and wages of men. Early unions, controlled by men, worked to eliminate the competition by driving women and children out of the paid labor force. They did so with the support of middle-class reformers who sought to enact laws to protect women and children, particularly girls, from the "dangerous or immoral working conditions" in factories and mines (Reskin and Padavic 1994, p. 20; Messerschmidt 1993, p. 66).

It was the institutionalization of the doctrine of separate spheres that eventually helped to drive all but the poorest women and children out of the paid labor force. Within the structural realm of Western patriarchal societies, the doctrine of separate spheres, which originated among the English upper-middle classes, called for the separation of work into the public sphere and family into the private sphere (Reskin and Padavic 1994, p. 21). Ultimately it would come to serve as both the structural and ideological key to the perpetuation of the subordination of all classes of females in the United States. The doctrine assigned men to paid work and women to unpaid work. This made life very difficult for working- and lower-class married (and especially unmarried) women, many of whom were immigrants and African Americans whose families depended on their earnings. As employers embraced the notion that a woman's place was in the home, they refused to hire women for "respectable" higher paying jobs, reserving them instead for their male counterparts. Some firms actually enforced rules against hiring women altogether (Reskin and Padavic 1994, p. 21).

Restricted to the private sphere of the family with their labor in the home going unpaid, the economic activity of women was effectively marginalized, figuratively and literally devalued. This forced upon women an economically subordinate status that manifested itself in a variety of ways. For middle-class married women, economic survival came to mean becoming completely dependent on a single-family wage earned by men (Messerschmidt 1993, p. 68). For the poorest women, married and unmarried, it meant struggling to survive in an increasingly hostile economic environment that provided them with fewer and fewer opportunities to earn a decent living because of their sex.

While the doctrine of separate spheres had a profound impact on the economic status of women in the United States, it also set the stage for major changes in their status as mothers within the private sphere of the family. This involved the institutionalization of the status of women as full-time, unpaid, expert mothers. Mothers—middle-class mothers in particular—were entrusted with both the care and education of their children. (Hawes 1991). It was now considered a mother's responsibility to impart civic virtues into the hearts of her children. Zelizer (1985) suggests the institutionalization of this status spread to the working-class as the ideal of the "cult of true womanhood" (p. 9).

Among the working-class and urban poor, these middle-class ideals of domesticity and motherhood carried with them especially heavy burdens in reality. These were the women who still had to find whatever work they could out of economic necessity, and so the tasks of this new motherhood were profoundly difficult for them. Having embraced the ideal, they believed child rearing was their job, and as mothers they saw themselves as primarily responsible for the well-being of their children. Unfortunately for them, the urban environment within which they were forced to raise their children posed unique dangers that did not threaten upper- and middle-class children. So while their children needed even greater protection than the children of the privileged classes, they had limited time and resources to provide that protection. As society made increasing demands on mothers to stay at home to meet the needs of their children, it is not surprising poor urban women had great difficulty conforming to these middle-class ideals, and as a result, the quality of their mothering, in particular, was called into question (Kasinsky 1994, p. 102).

Finding the appropriately subordinate place for children, especially girls, in the world according to the doctrine of separate spheres posed a formidable challenge to middle-class reformers who were influenced by multiple and often contradictory views of children's nature. Gordon (1988) suggests it was under the auspices of an emergent protective ideology that these reformers managed to unify their apparently irreconcilable charitable and controlling impulses (p. 29), and eventually completely transform the status of children. Having once occupied a place in preindustrial patriarchal families as economic resources— for hundreds of years they had been prized as "practical investments," "objects of utility"— under the doctrine of separate spheres, children were transformed into objects of sentiment, "prized emotionally and for the symbolic value of their present and future achievements" (Skolnick 1975, p. 48; Zelizer 1985, p. 7). Zelizer (1985) describes what happened to the status of children from the 1870s to the 1930s as a process of "sacralization" (p. 11).

This newly guarded, but nonetheless distinctly subordinate place to be occupied by children was, however, still a place where a male child held a position superior to his female counterpart. Robert Wiebe's (1967) description of how Progressives in the United States at the turn of the century viewed the status of children articulates the degree to which it was a profoundly patriarchal vision:

> The child was the carrier of tomorrow's hope whose innocence and freedom made him singularly receptive to education in rational, human behavior. Protect him, nurture him, and in his manhood he would create that bright new world of the Progressives' vision….Instead of molding youth in a slightly improved pattern of their fathers…the new reformers thought in terms of fluid progress, a process of growth that demanded constant vigilance. (p. 169)*

Some have suggested (Degler 1980) children's transformed status within the separate spheres of the industrialized Western world fell perfectly into place with the new status of women as full-time, unpaid, expert mothers, and together they raised the already idealized private sphere of domesticity to a new and higher level of respectability (Zelizer 1985, p. 9). However, the implications of leaving the care of children *exclusively* in the hands of mothers within the private sphere must have haunted middle-class reformers in the United States who struggled to reconcile their competing charitable and controlling impulses: Could *all* mothers really be entrusted to provide the constant vigilance their children's growth process demanded? What about the "dangerous" children of working- and lower-class immigrant and African American mothers? What about all of those "unfit" mothers? By the turn of the century, Progressives turned to experts for advice on how to resolve the questions that must have troubled them. Psychologists, social workers, and physicians became the ones who determined what children's needs were and how they should be met. While experts agreed the care of full-time, expert mothers was a necessary part of how those needs should be met, maternal care was not considered sufficient enough to cope with the "newly discovered psychic complexity of childhood" (Zelizer 1985, p. 28). A variety of new public institutions had to be created. As Wiebe describes it, once uncomplicated demands for the abolition of child labor in the United States turned into complex social movements that transferred much of the power to control the lives of children, especially female children, from the private to the public sphere, a trend that Hawes (1991) contends has been expanding ever since:

> What would become of the…children? The urban progressives advocated nurseries and kindergartens, better schools and tighter attendance laws, recreational facilities and social clubs. Was the child any safer outside the factory? They spread the gospel of personal hygiene and public sanitation, proper diet and prompt inoculation. And what of the child's home environment? Many others supported adult labor laws [placing limits on women's participation in the labor

---

*It should be noted Wiebe does not make the point that the status of male children was considered superior to that of female children by the Progressives. His language, however, and his emphasis on manhood and the patterning children after their fathers, effectively communicates this.

market] and adult education, trade unions and family courts….they transformed the sin of child labor into the sin of the unprotected child. (Wiebe 1967, p. 171)

Not surprisingly, the protection afforded female children came to mean something quite different than the protection afforded their male counterparts:

Girls were often the clear losers in [the] reform effort. Studies of early family courts reveal that virtually all the girls who appeared in these courts were charged for waywardness or immorality (which usually meant evidence of sexual intercourse)….Typically, gynecological examinations were routinely ordered for the girls….More to the point, the sanctions for such misbehavior were extremely severe. For example, in Chicago (where family court was founded), half of the girl delinquents, but only one-fifth of the boy delinquents were sent to reformatories between 1899–1901. (Chesney-Lind 1995, p. 77)

At one level, the transformed status of female children appeared to exalt them to a place safe from the evils of an industrialized world that was more than willing to exploit them as cheap economic resources. At another level, however, the institutionalization of the doctrine of separate spheres ensured children of all ages would remain at the bottom of the social scale, with female children still securely located at the very bottom of the scale. Their new status may have held the promise of protection, but it also effectively perpetuated their subordination by giving an ever-expanding number of adults in the public sphere the power to structure and control their development.

In recent years, a great deal of attention has been focused on the apparent liberation of women, in particular, from the confines of their traditionally subordinate status in post-industrial Western patriarchal societies. Linda Gordon (1988) suggests the civil rights, antiwar, student and women's movements in the United States combined to raise critical questions that posed a direct challenge to the hierarchical order of power institutionalized under the doctrine of separate spheres (p. 25). Some have even theorized the women's movement triggered an increase in the rate of female offending (Adler 1975; Simon 1975). Power-belief theory, however, maintains female criminality can best be understood within a context of oppression, not liberation.

While it may appear as if the structural support for the doctrine of separate spheres in the United States today has waned, and people may seem to be more willing to acknowledge adult females *ought* to have the opportunity to participate on an equal basis with adult males for positions of power in both the public and private spheres, appearances can be deceiving. Evidence that the hierarchical organization of social relations within the public sphere is still based on sex is not difficult to find. Any apparent improvement in the economic status of women is tempered by the following findings:

Women are concentrated at low levels in the organizations that employ them and in the lower ranks in their occupations and professions. Even in predominantly female lines of work, such as nursing, the higher the position, the more likely the job holder is to be male....Women supervise fewer subordinates than men and are less likely to control financial resources. Even women managers...are less likely than men to make decisions, especially decisions that are vital for their employer. (Reskin and Padavic 1994, p. 32)

In spite of rising expectations of change, the vast majority of women still must struggle within the confines of a labor market that limits their opportunities because of their sex. Scarpitti et al. (1997) maintain the wage structure in the United States today still is based on the family wage system; the same system institutionalized under the doctrine of separate spheres at the turn of the century. It is a system grounded in the assumption men are primarily responsible for the family income and, therefore, should be paid more for their labor than women. It is this family wage system that has contributed directly to the persistence of patterns of wage discrimination and workplace segregation based on sex.

It also has been suggested the vast majority of women who do work outside the home find themselves confined to persistent "female ghettos" (O'Kelly and Carney 1986, p. 165). While there has been a significant shift out of private household work since the 1960s, especially among African American women (Currie and Skolnick 1997, p. 154), in 1990, women still worked in what have come to be considered primarily "female occupations." They were secretaries, typists, clerks, stenographers. According to Reskin and Padavic (1994), "the most common occupations for women in 1990 [were] almost identical to those that employed the most women in 1940" (p. 54). What inspired use of the term "ghetto" to describe this sex segregation of the workplace is the money women are likely to earn in these "female occupations." Estimates are, in general, women in the United States who work full-time, year-round earn just under 70 percent of what men who work full-time, year-round earn (Reskin and Padavic 1994, p. 32). According to Scarpitti et al. (1997), "the worst paid jobs are those where African American women, Latinas, and Native American women are most concentrated...[and] those jobs where White men are most concentrated are the best paid" (p. 226).

Beyond persistent patterns of wage discrimination (the earnings gap) and workplace segregation (the female ghettos) based on sex, another disturbing legacy of the institutionalization of the family wage system under the doctrine of separate spheres has been the so-called feminization of poverty. In general, over the past 15 years in the United States, there has been a dramatic increase in the number of people who work full-time but still cannot raise their family income above the poverty line (Scarpitti et al. 1997, p. 145). However, the vast majority of people living below the poverty line are women and their children: "More than half of poor families are headed by women. The poverty rate for female-headed households is five times that for married-couple families, and the fastest growing poverty is found among single mothers with children" (Scarpitti et al. 1997, p. 147).

As part of a broad-based dialogue on democratic principles, equality may have become an important sociopolitical issue, and expectations of change may have risen. However, the reality for women who have ventured out into the public sphere over the last 50 years in the

United States is that wage discrimination and sex segregation in the labor market, along with a multitude of other structural barriers have effectively sustained their subordinate status. Given the persistence of these patterns of subordination in the public sphere, it is not surprising to find there is evidence of their persistence in the private sphere as well. The legacy of the idealization of domesticity and motherhood under the doctrine of separate spheres looms large in the lives of contemporary women of *all* classes in the United States. As Reskin and Padavic (1994) describe it:

> Today, the typical married woman works for pay in the labor force in addition to working at home as a homemaker. . . .In the early industrial period, the doctrine of separate spheres kept middle- and upper-class women out of the work force, and the task of combining paid work and family responsibilities fell largely on working-class and poor women. But today, a family's economic level no longer determines whether a woman works outside the home. Thus work/family conflict spans the entire economic spectrum. (p. 143)

More precisely, family/work conflict spans the entire economic spectrum of *women*. Men have been slow to the plate in regard to the sharing of domestic responsibilities in the private sphere. In her book, *The Second Shift*, Hochschild (1989) pulls no punches in her characterization of the role American men play in today's family: "…men do not share the raising of their children and the care of their homes. Men think and feel within structures of work which presume they don't do these things" (pp. x–xi). Interestingly, most men still *say* they believe working couples should share household responsibilities (Schor 1991, p. 104). However, as is often the case, actions speak louder than words. The burdens of domestic responsibilities are still shouldered primarily by women, even those who work full-time in the paid labor market:

> Data from the University of Michigan's Panel Study of Income Dynamics show that men average just 7 hours of housework per week, vs. women's 20. In families where both husband and wife are employed, the proportions change, but not by much: men's hours stay the same, while women's decrease to 17. (Currie and Skolnick 1997, p. 197)

Whatever the expectations of change within the structural realm of private social relations may be, the idealization of domesticity and motherhood remains an imposing force in the lives of modern women, inasmuch as it continues to impact directly on how many women define their statuses as wives and mothers. The unfortunate reality is that the women who embrace these ideals are the very women who will find themselves vulnerable to one of the most insidious aspects of the subordination of modern women: physical, sexual and/or emotional victimization and the threat of such victimization at the hands of their intimate partners and ex-partners. The reason the women who embrace these ideals are especially vulnerable to this kind of victimization is based on the fact that a common thread found among violent families, one that is often ignored or at least trivialized by researchers, is their patriarchal organization (Dougherty 1993, p. 105). Swift also discusses this phenomenon in Chapter Eleven. Each year at least one million women in the United States become victims of some form of violence at the hands of their husbands, ex-husbands, boyfriends, or ex-boyfriends (Castro 1996, p. 1). In the United States women are in nine times more danger of being victimized in their own homes than they are on the streets, and over 50 percent of the women killed are killed by their intimate male partners or ex-partners (Strassler 1994, p. 5).*

Even when they are *not* at home, women still face the risk of violent attack by men they know. According to a 1996 report by the Women's Bureau of the U.S. Department of Labor:

> At *work* [emphasis added], women are more likely than men to be attacked by an intimate, whereas men are more likely to be attacked by a stranger….During the period 1987–1992, five percent of women victimized at work were attacked by a husband, ex-husband, boyfriend, or ex-boyfriend compared to one percent of men who were victimized by an intimate….Homicide is by far the most frequent manner in which women workers are fatally injured at work….during the period 1992–1994, 17 percent of their alleged attackers were current or former husbands or boyfriends. For Black women, the figure was 28 percent, for Hispanic women, 20 percent. (Castro 1996, p. 1)

It is not just that this kind of victimization functions to decrease women's power in the private sphere, it also serves to decrease their power in the public sphere by directly contributing to the persistence of their subordinate economic status. According to the same Labor Department report:

> …96 percent of [the battered women] who were employed had some type of problem in the workplace as a direct result of their abuse or abuser. These included being late (more than 60 percent), missing work (more than 50 percent), having difficulty performing one's job (70 percent), being reprimanded for problems associated with the abuse (60 percent), or losing a job (30 percent). (Castro 1996, p. 1)

While it is true battered women come from all walks of life, and there are those who argue social class, and ethnic or racial backgrounds make no difference (Dwyer et al. 1996, p. 69), some women apparently are more vulnerable than others. There is evidence, once again, that working-class and poor women of color and immigrants shoulder an especially heavy burden when it comes to this kind of victimization in the United States today. Belknap (1996) notes women of color "appear to have disproportionately high victimiza-

---

*Strassler's material is from the study and resource guide that accompanied the videotape version of the 1993 Academy Award winning documentary, *Defending Our Lives*. The statistics cited were adapted by Strassler from *Domestic Violence: The Facts* distributed by Battered Women Fighting Back! Inc., a human rights agency based in Boston that focuses on domestic violence against women.

tion rates, yet they are much less likely to have their victimization acknowledged" (p. 133). While Bonilla-Santiago (1996) recognizes woman battering occurs among all cultural and ethnic groups, she argues the situation for battered Latinas is different from that of White or African American women:

> Latinas [in general] face barriers of gender, national origin or race, and language that also affect the experiences of battered Latina women. Feelings of vulnerability and helplessness because of the lack of resources available to Latinas, the dearth of bilingual or bicultural services from social services, hospitals, and shelters, as well as cultural isolation experienced by Latinas who do not speak English or whose cultural norms differ from those prevailing in the United States, converge and set boundaries on battered Latina women. (p. 230)

Whatever their nationality, battered immigrants are uniquely vulnerable, according to Paisner and Knight (1996). They argue immigrant women, particularly those who marry American citizens (native-born or naturalized) hoping to become citizens themselves automatically and who subsequently find themselves victimized by their partners, are at the greatest risk. Once they learn marriage to a citizen only makes automatic the first step toward acquiring citizenship, that is, the right to apply for permanent residency, these women realize they are completely dependent on the "good graces" of their violent spouses if they ever hope to become citizens. Paisner and Knight (1996) describe the following as typical of the kinds of threats and coercive actions that commonly occur in these types of marriages:

> The citizen-spouse in violent relationships frequently uses residency status as a figurative club to go with the often literal one. A [citizen] spouse may threaten to report his partner to INS [Immigration and Naturalization Service] and have her deported, withhold filing immigration papers altogether or withdraw the petition he filed. He may tell her he will have someone harm her family members in her home country. He may force her to work illegally when she does not have a work permit, then threaten to report her to INS for doing just that. He may force her to sign English-written court papers or IRS [Internal Revenue Service] forms that she doesn't understand. He may intimidate her by hiding or destroying such important papers as her passport, her children's passports and health care cards. (p. 3)

There seems to be little doubt, as Susan Schreiber of the Midwest Immigrants Rights Center in Chicago notes, "all of the issues of domestic violence have their special twist in immigration" (Paisner and Knight 1996, p. 6). With no immediate family members in the country to turn to for support, the isolation of battered immigrants often is magnified. Language barriers make dealing with authorities like police, court personnel, social workers, etc., difficult—if not impossible—in communities without bilingual staffs. Battered immigrant women commonly are misinformed. They do not realize what is happening to them is against the law in the United States and they have legal options to stop it. They do not know they can call the police, obtain custody of their children, or get a restraining order even if they are undocumented (Paisner and Knight 1996, p. 6).

While a great deal of attention has been focused on the liberation of women today and expectations of change in regard to their status within the structural realm have risen, it is clear the hierarchical order of power institutionalized under the doctrine of separate spheres has endured. If female criminality is in any way related to the status of women within the structural realm of patriarchal societies, then it must be recognized as a status that leaves many women marginalized, particularly economically, and victimized interpersonally, struggling to find ways to cope or in some cases simply survive. But the question remains, what about the status of girls? If, as power-belief theory asserts, the interactive effects between structural barriers and ideological forces create a context of oppression that directly impacts on the lives of female offenders of *all* ages—that both sex *and* age are key organizing principles of the hierarchical order of power in patriarchal societies—then what remains to be established is evidence that patterns of subordination based on age also have persisted. Indeed, a great deal less attention has been focused on "girls' liberation" from the confines of their traditionally subordinate status. If anything, more attention has been focused on whether or not it is even appropriate to talk about "liberation" within the context of the protected world of modern girls.

When turn-of-the-century reformers transformed the status of children from objects of economic utility to objects of sentiment, many looked on the transformation as a vital part of what was needed to protect children, especially girls, from the evils of industrialization. According to those same reformers, this protection also necessitated handing complete control of children's lives over to adults, not just to their parents in the private sphere, but to an ever-expanding number of adults in the public sphere as well. They assumed children would benefit from all of this control because they believed it would protect them from the negative trappings of the adult world. What this means is evidence of the persistence of patterns of subordination based on age in the United States today is not very difficult at all to find. Despite the emergence of a full-fledged children's rights movement in the 1960s, legislative action has played a key role in formally establishing adult control over the lives of modern girls, and thus in perpetuating their subordinate status in both the private and public spheres. As Humm et al. (1994) note in the introduction to their reader, *Child, Parent and State*, "the law permeates the lives of all children at every turn" in the United States today (p. xv). What remains to be seen is whether or not all of this paternalistic control over the lives of modern girls has been mitigated by the kind of specialized care and protection promised to them by reformers so many decades ago.

Within the specific context of legal proceedings, children are supposed to be protected by the fact that when they act, they do not act alone. A child is just "one part of a triangle that also includes parents and the state" (Humm et al. 1994, p. xvi). Whatever is done in court is *supposed* to be done in "the best interests of the child." In other words, in any case involving a child, the court is supposed to strike a balance between furthering justice (doing the right thing) on the one hand, and promoting the well-being of the child, on the other. But are children's interests *really* being protected in these legal proceedings? Critics suggest they are not. Théry (1986) contends legal standards like "the best interest of the child" have nothing to do with the person of the child. She argues such standards are an "alibi: an alibi for dominant ideology, an alibi for individual arbitrariness, an alibi for family and more general social policies for which the law serves as an instrument" (p. 344). More recently, Martin Guggenheim (1994) outlined what he maintains are the many defects of the "best interest" standard:

> It gives judges unbounded discretion, yet provides them with no guidance on matters such as burden of proof and presumptions. It encourages costly litigation that often is detrimental to children and their parents. Finally, because the "best interest" concept is so elusive, it invites judges to engage in open-ended inquiry and to rely on their own value-laden preferences. As a result, one simply cannot be confident that a court's final conclusion about a child's best interests is anything other than a reflection of the judge's personal values. (p. 27)

Beyond the domain of the law, there is even more striking evidence that the subordinate status of modern girls has not been mitigated effectively by any kind of special care or protection. While the place created for children under the doctrine of separate sphere may be better in some ways than it was some 130 years ago, for many children, especially female children, life at the very bottom of the social scale continues to be profoundly unpleasant, and in many instances simply unsafe. Experts estimate between 20 and 25 percent of all American children are currently living below the poverty line. The fastest growing poverty in the United States today is found among families made up of single women with children (Scarpitti et al. 1997, p. 147). Living in poverty takes a toll on America's children. A 1992 North Carolina study found poor children are seven times as likely to die by fire, six times as likely to die by poisoning, five times as likely to die by pneumonia, influenza, or by homicide, and four times as likely to die of heart disease than their non-poor counterparts (Currie and Skolnick 1997, p. 258). Many of those "single women with children" who live in poverty are children themselves. In the United States today, it is estimated four in ten females will become pregnant before the age of 20 (Vobejda and Havemann 1997, p. A24). According to Scarpitti et al. (1997), teens account for 10.9 percent of the births among White females and 23.1 percent of the births among African American females. Typically a single teen who has a baby ends her formal education, leaving her to face chronic unemployment or trapped in low paying, low status jobs (pp. 149, 386).

For centuries, girls' status at the very bottom of the social scale ensured they would be subjected to horrific violence within the context of Western patriarchal families. It was not until their status was transformed under the doctrine of separate spheres that "cruelty to children," what is now referred to as child abuse and neglect—or, more generally, childhood maltreatment—was even defined as a social problem. Formally defining cruelty to children as a problem seemed to suggest that a systematic effort to provide all children with special protection from this kind of victimization was finally underway. From the outset, however, the promise of protection against child abuse and neglect provided by social service agencies was a conditional one. Feeling compelled to uphold the practice of corporal punishment as an acceptable part of family life in America, Henry Bergh, the founder of the Society for the Prevention of Cruelty to Children, once proclaimed, "'A good wholesome flogging,'…would be appropriate for 'disobedient children'" (Hawes 1991, p. 21). There are those who even go so far as to argue early anti-cruelty organizations operated primarily as agencies of social control rather than agencies of child protection (Kasinsky 1994). But what about today's agencies?

Evidence indicates modern child protective service laws and the agencies created to enforce those laws continue to fail to protect children, especially female children, from all forms of abuse in a disturbingly systematic fashion. One study of girls adjudicated as delinquent in Arkansas found 53 percent had been sexually abused, 25 percent reported scars from beatings, and 38 percent told researchers they had experienced bleeding from abuse (Chesney-Lind 1997a, p. 3). Of the 61.2 percent of the girls involved in the juvenile justice system who said they experienced physical abuse in their homes in 1990, many said they *did* report the abuse to authorities, but the majority of those girls said, "either nothing changed (29.9 percent) or that reporting it just made things worse (25.3 percent)" (Chesney-Lind 1997b, p. 26). When it comes to the handling of sexual abuse cases by officials, victims, most of whom are girls, are not provided with any more effective protection. In fact, these types of cases routinely are looked on as notoriously difficult to prosecute. Sagatun and Edwards (1995) outline the following as typical of the obstacles in such cases:

> …inability to establish the crime, insufficient evidence, unwillingness to expose the [abused] child to additional trauma, and the belief that child victims are incompetent, unreliable, and not credible as witnesses. The decision not to prosecute may be related to the age of the child, the child's willingness to testify, support from family members, the existence of corroborative evidence, and other factors….Prosecutors may not want to do the extra work necessary to prosecute these cases. (pp. 114–115)

Finding evidence of the persistence of patterns of subordination based on age in the United States today is not very difficult. However, there also is overwhelming evidence that the absolute power adults in both the public and private spheres exert over children has not been mitigated by any systematically effective means of providing them with special care or protection. What this means is just as sex is, age is a key organizing principle of the hierarchical order of power within the structural realm of patriarchal societies, and like that of their adult female counterparts, the status of modern girls leaves them marginalized and victimized, struggling to cope and often simply survive.

The Ideological Realm of Oppression

According to power-belief theory, the interactive effects between structural barriers *and* ideological forces are what create a context of oppression in patriarchal societies. It is within the ideological realm that the hierarchical order of power subordinating women and girls within the structural realm is rationalized and legitimated. As Dobash and Dobash (1979) describe it:

> The ideology is supportive of the principle of a hierarchical order, as opposed to an egalitarian one, and of the hierarchy currently in power. It…serves as a means of creating acceptance of subordination by those destined to such positions. (p. 44)

The ideology of patriarchal societies is grounded in social constructions of gender and childhood that define women and girls as deserving of their subordination because of their innately inferior natures. In their treatise on the social construction of reality, Berger and Luckmann (1967) argue "humanness," human nature, is a variable sociocultural construct, a human production, that is subject to power in the social order. They suggest, "power in society includes the power…to *produce* reality" (Berger and Luckmann 1967, p. 119). For centuries, the reality produced in patriarchal societies defined adult males as worthy of power, privilege, and leadership. Once produced, what came with this reality was a vested interest in the structural maintenance and ideological justification of the status quo. In the United States and many other Western industrialized patriarchal societies, it was the doctrine of separate spheres that eventually came to serve as both the structural and ideological key to the subordination of all classes of women and girls. It facilitated the perpetuation of the patriarchal status quo by popularizing what would become the culturally dominant social constructions of gender and childhood.

Under the doctrine of separate spheres, hegemonic masculinity, along with its complementary emphasized femininity, emerged as the dominant social construction of gender. In the United States, both constructs were closely associated with White, middle- and upper-class adult men and women. Hegemonic masculinity also was associated with the following characteristics:

> …work in the paid-labor market, the subordination of women, heterosexism, and the driven and uncontrollable sexuality of men. . .practices toward authority, control, competitive individualism, independence, aggressiveness, and the capacity for violence. (Messerschmidt 1993, p. 82)

Hegemonic masculinity became the "culturally honored, glorified, and extolled" image of masculinity, the ideological exaltation of manhood that would serve to stabilize the structural dominance of men in the public and private spheres (Messerschmidt 1993, p. 82). Its complement, emphasized femininity, came to be characterized, first and foremost, by sociability. It also was associated with "fragility, compliance with men's desire for ego stroking, sexual receptivity, marriage, housework, and child care" (Martin and Jurik 1996, p. 38). So as men were to strive aggressively toward independence and control over others in the public and private spheres, women were to strive gently toward the building and nurturing of social relationships primarily in the private sphere. It was emphasized femininity that provided the ideological justification for the idealization of domesticity and motherhood under the doctrine of separate spheres.

Just as power in society includes the power to produce reality, it also "includes the power to determine decisive socialization processes" (Berger and Luckmann 1967, p. 119). Within the ideological realm of modern patriarchal societies, gendered socialization processes teach people to believe that the culturally dominant constructs are a part of the "rightful nature" of the social order (Dobash and Dobash 1979, p. 44). If successful, these processes allow the subordination of females to go unquestioned, or, as was the case in the past, to make challenges seem "unnatural or immoral" (Dobash and Dobash 1979, p. 44).

Further, there is substantial evidence gendered socialization processes have been and continue to be quite successful, especially when it comes to the socialization of girls. As Chesney-Lind (1997b) notes, "Despite expectations to the contrary, gender-specific socialization patterns have not changed very much, and this is especially true for parents' relationships with their daughters" (p. 24). Gendered socialization processes are what teach girls to become women according to the tenets of emphasized femininity and boys to become men according to the tenets of hegemonic masculinity. According to Jordon (1993), girls today are socialized toward a love/empathy mode of self, and boys today are socialized toward a power/dominance mode of self. Thus girls learn to feel most comfortable when they are relating to, or "in connection with" others, and boys learn to feel most comfortable when they are in control of others, or "in separation." Boys, then, learn to look on relationships as a means to an end, while girls learn to look upon relationships as an end in and of themselves. The identities girls internalize are, then, defined by their sociability. As Striegel-Moore (1995) observes, "a woman's failed effort in finding mutuality and understanding in a relationship is experienced as a fundamental challenge to her identity and invokes feelings of shame, self-doubt, and low self-esteem" (p. 227).

Ultimately, it is *what* gendered socialization processes teach that facilitates the internalization of the culturally dominant social constructions of gender, both hegemonic masculinity and emphasized femininity. It is *how* the lessons of gendered socialization are taught that facilitates the internalization of the culturally dominant social construction of children as inferior and incompetent. Alice Miller (1983) points out the ideology of traditional child rearing reached its peak at the turn of the century during the heyday of the doctrine of separate spheres. The fundamental principles underlying this ideology, what Miller identifies as the "poisonous pedagogy," however, have persisted. Those principles include: adults are the masters of the dependent child; adults determine what is right and what is wrong; children are responsible for the anger of adults; what children feel is a threat to the autocratic authority of adults; and the will of children must be broken as soon as possible (Miller 1983, p. 59). According to the precepts of hegemonic masculinity, fathers hold a position of authority over their children greater than that of mothers, despite the fact that mothers are expected to carry the burden of child care. When putting these traditional child-rearing principles into practice, today's fathers (and mothers when they discipline) are encouraged to lie, manipulate, use scare tactics ("you just wait until your father gets home!"), and even withdraw love. When they see fit, parents also may isolate, humiliate, scorn, ridicule, and coerce their children (Miller 1983, p. 59). As the overwhelming numbers of parents who report utilizing some form of corporal punishment to discipline their children indicates, this coercion routinely involves physical violence. These traditional principles and practices of child rearing appear to contribute directly not just to children's vulnerability to physical abuse, but to sexual abuse as well. In her assessment of the cultural factors that facilitate child sexual abuse, Kathleen Coulborn Faller (1990) concludes the following:

> First, norms that sanction the right of adults to control and impose their will on children may be used to justify the imposition of the adult sexual desires on children. Second, norms that support male dominance can play a contributing role in sexual maltreatment. Third, similar cultural supports for paternal control over what occurs within the family may contribute to sexual victimization. And, fourth, male sexual socialization may be important. Norms related to male sexuality include the assumption that males should enjoy sex and seek it out and that they should prefer smaller and younger sexual objects. (p. 59)

Faller (1990) suggests these norms, clearly reflective of the precepts of hegemonic masculinity, help to explain why there is such a high proportion of male perpetrators and a preponderance of female victims of child sexual abuse (p. 59). The lessons children learn about themselves and about their relationships to adults when their parents rely on traditional child-rearing principles and practices also facilitate this and other kinds of abuse. Some of these lessons include: parents deserve respect because they are parents and children are undeserving of respect simply because they are children; obedience makes a child strong and good; the way you behave is more important than who you really are and what you really feel; parents are free of drives and guilt; and parents are always right (Miller 1983, pp. 59–60). Many also take with them from childhood a particularly pernicious lesson—people who love you may also hurt you, sometimes severely.

Gendered socialization processes (as explained by Covington in Chapter Five) ensure girls and boys will internalize these lessons differently. While *all* children may come to see themselves as inferior, incompetent, when they compare themselves to the adults that control their lives, it is apparent "the socialization of girls, particularly during adolescence, is very different" from that of boys (Chesney-Lind 1997b, p. 30). Evidence indicates girls commonly experience "dramatic and negative changes in their self-perception" (Chesney-Lind 1997b, p. 30) during adolescence, and are likely to emerge from it feeling "somehow not quite as good, not quite as able, not quite as bright, not quite as valuable" as their male counterparts (Rivers et al. 1979, p. 25).

When gendered socialization processes and traditional child-rearing practices are successful, they promote the general acceptance of the culturally dominant social constructions of gender and childhood. This acceptance means those who challenge the "rightfulness" of the dominant constructs will be pressured to conform. These processes and practices, however, are never absolutely successful. The fact is there always has been some degree of resistance to them. This resistance speaks to the fact that among those who have *not* internalized the culturally dominant social constructions of gender and childhood as "rightful," competing images of masculinity, femininity, and childhood flourish. Nonetheless, evidence that the structural and ideological context of oppression within which modern women and girls struggle is persistent and pervasive is overwhelming. This struggle is especially poignant for female offenders. Most of them are young, uneducated, and unemployed mothers (Simon and Landis 1991, pp. 78–88) with long histories of childhood maltreatment. (Details on the relationship between childhood maltreatment and female offending can be found in Chapter Ten of this text.)

They are, in fact, among the most extremely marginalized and victimized women and girls in modern patriarchal societies. While power-belief theory asserts criminality can best be deciphered within this context of oppression, its basic premise is that exploring the variability of the *dynamics* of oppression is what actually holds the key to understanding female offenders and effectively assessing their treatment needs.

FEMALE CRIMINALITY AND THE DYNAMICS OF OPPRESSION: AN INTRODUCTION TO POWER-BELIEF THEORY

The dynamics of oppression suggest it is within a context of structural and ideological oppression in patriarchal societies that females of all ages struggle to cope and—in some instances—survive. In the midst of their struggles they develop a specific matrix of beliefs themselves, about their own power, and about the legitimacy of the patriarchal order. The development of these beliefs represents the essence of the dynamics of oppression from which rule-violating behavior manifests itself. According to power-belief theory, determining precisely how an individual female defines herself and her situation—how she subjectively experiences this context of oppression and her struggle within it—will lead the way toward answering the most vital question in regard to female criminality: why do some women and girls become female offenders while so many others do not? Power-belief theory suggests the matrices of beliefs that women and girls develop are comprised of the following:

- *Beliefs about oneself as powerful or powerless.* To what degree has a female internalized a sense of herself as powerless or powerful? Does she believe she is a person who has the *ability* to make a difference? Does she believe she is a person whose feelings and opinions matter? Does she believe she is a person with good judgment who has the *ability* to make the right decisions?

- *Beliefs about one's power in relation to the hierarchical order of power*. While a female may define herself as powerful, as having the *ability* to make a difference, does she believe she *can* make a difference in her own life and/or in the lives of others? To what degree does she believe she actually *has* power? This is *not* about whether a female actually occupies a position of power. It asks, regardless of her objective position of power, does she *believe* she has any power? While this may be expressed in terms of feelings of control over one's life and/or the lives of others, it really reflects subjective interpretations of objective power or powerlessness.
- *Beliefs in the legitimacy of the patriarchal ideology*. To what degree has a female internalized a belief in the legitimacy, in the "rightful" nature, of the culturally dominant social constructions of gender and childhood? Does she believe in the appropriateness of her subordination?
- *Beliefs in the legitimacy of the hierarchical order of power*. To what degree does a female express a belief in the legitimacy of the status quo, i.e., in the legitimacy of the authority of those in positions of power?

What follows in the remainder of this section is an outline of the seven fundamental propositions of the dynamics of oppression, and a presentation of the belief matrices it is being hypothesized are likely to be found most often among female offenders. There are, however, two caveats. First, the beliefs coming together in the matrices have been dichotomized (i.e., powerful/powerless; has power/ does not have power, etc.) for illustrative purposes—in reality they are likely to be reported by women and girls in varying degrees of intensity. Thus, there probably will be a considerable degree of variation among the females who fall within the same general belief matrix. Further, a specific woman or girl may not seem to fit neatly into one specific matrix; the boundaries between matrices probably will be quite blurred in reality. Second, this is an *introduction* to power-belief theory. All of the propositions and matrices hypothesized here need to be empirically tested. Some later may be proven to be valid, others may not, and it is very likely new propositions and matrices will need to be included.

Some Fundamental Propositions of the Dynamics of Oppression

- *Proposition One:* Criminality is more likely to manifest itself when a female has internalized a belief in herself as powerless; when she believes she is a person who does not have the *ability* to make a difference. Not all females who have internalized this belief, however, will exhibit criminal or delinquent behaviors.
- *Proposition Two:* A female who has internalized a belief in her own powerlessness, that is, who believes she does not have the *ability* to make a difference, also will believe she is a person who *cannot* make a difference.
- *Proposition Three:* A female's objective position of power within the structural realm of either the public or private sphere should not be equated with her subjective belief

she is a person who actually has power. For example, a woman who is a mother, a position of relative power in regard to her children, may *not* believe she has power or can make a difference in her life or the lives of her children.

- *Proposition Four:* Girls, as children, will come to believe they do not have power—they cannot make a difference.
- *Proposition Five:* A female's location within a specific belief matrix may not remain static throughout her lifetime. Once developed, any or all of her beliefs may change. Those changes may be brought about by salient life experiences and/or by professional intervention (for example, counseling). Adolescence will be a particularly important time of change in the lives of females.
- *Proposition Six:* Because evidence indicates poor females of color consistently have carried the heaviest burdens of oppression in patriarchal societies, class, race, ethnicity, and national origin will impact directly on the degree to which a female will report she believes herself to be a person who has power. These factors also may impact on her belief in the legitimacy of the traditional hierarchical order of power.
- *Proposition Seven:* Physical, sexual and emotional abuse—childhood maltreatment—will increase the likelihood a belief in her own powerlessness will be internalized by a female, and she will come to believe she is *not* a person who has power. The degree of powerlessness reported by victims of abuse will be greater than that reported by females who have not been victimized. Witnessing interpersonal violence, for instance, being the daughter of a battered woman, may similarly affect the beliefs a female is likely to develop.

The Belief Matrices of Female Offenders

According to power-belief theory, even a slight variation in the dynamics of oppression may prove critical when it comes to understanding the unique experiences of female offenders and assessing their treatment needs. Given the fundamental propositions outlined in the previous section, it can be hypothesized that the belief matrices illustrated in Table 6–1 will most likely be found among female offenders.

These matrices reflect the variability of the dynamics of oppression experienced by the women and girls who fall within them. As a population of especially marginalized and victimized women and girls, all of the female offenders who fall within these matrices will share two fundamental beliefs. First, they all will have internalized a belief in themselves as powerless. They will not believe their feelings or opinions matter, or that they have the *ability* to make a difference. Second, none of them will believe they actually *have* power, that they *can* make a difference in their own lives or in the lives of anyone else.

Accepting the legitimacy of the patriarchal ideology, embracing the basic tenets of traditional gendered socialization, including the legitimacy of their own subordination, the women and girls who fall into the first matrix will exhibit signs of gender role entrapment as characterized by Steffensmeier and Allan in Chapter One. As such, they will direct any

Table 6–1 The Belief Matrices of Female Offenders

Belief about oneself as powerful/power-less	Belief about one's own power in relation to the hierarchical order of power	Belief in the legitimacy of the patriarchal ideology	Belief in the legitimacy of the hierarchical order of power
1. Powerless	Does not have power	Legitimate	Legitimate
2. Powerless	Does not have power	Legitimate	Illegitimate
3. Powerless	Does not have power	Illegitimate	Illegitimate

negative feelings they experience (i.e., anger, frustration, etc.) inward toward themselves. They probably will blame themselves for much of what is wrong in their lives and in the lives of their immediate family members, particularly their children if they have any. For many of these women and girls, the interpersonal violence they have experienced and/or witnessed will have become so much a part of their routine lives for so long they will have "normalized" it. (Chapter Ten discusses the problem of the "normalization" of abuse in regard to its being a critical consideration during treatment in more detail.) These females will have difficulty naming what they have experienced or witnessed as abusive. Even those who are able to identify themselves as having been abused probably will remain trapped in violent relationships because they will blame themselves for their own victimization.

Females who fall into this belief matrix will exhibit a general pattern of self-destructive behavior that may include a history of drug and/or alcohol abuse, self-mutilation, eating disorders, and attempted suicide. They will express quite openly a great deal of guilt about those behaviors, as well as a great deal of guilt and remorse about their adult criminal and/or juvenile delinquent behaviors. Those behaviors will consist primarily of nonviolent offenses: status offenses, minor property crimes, prostitution, etc. If they do become involved in serious, perhaps violent crime, they probably will have been initiated into it by males to whom they will have served primarily as accomplices. Their offending can be seen as the way these females have come to cope with the pressures they feel in regard to their obligations to protect relationships and/or emotional commitments. Their acceptance of the legitimacy of the hierarchical order of power, combined with their open expressions of guilt and remorse, will make them appear to be quite amenable to treatment. From the outset, they will be relatively cooperative with treatment providers. Their rehabilitative needs, however, will be enormous, requiring much more than conventional empowerment strategies. Among other things, they literally will need to "relearn" how to think and feel about interpersonal relationships and violence in their lives.

The women and girls who fall into the second matrix will share many of the same characteristics and behavioral patterns, the same signs of gender role entrapment, as the females who fall into the first matrix because they too believe in the legitimacy of the patriarchal ideology. The difference is these females do not believe in the legitimacy of the hierarchical order of power. They will have negative attitudes toward people in positions of authority. Those attitudes may be traced to the racial and ethnic backgrounds of the offenders. As women and girls of color, they may have developed a generalized belief that those in positions of power are prejudiced and not to be trusted. Those same beliefs, however, also may be rooted in the salient life experiences of females who have endured extreme marginalization and victimization within the structural and ideological context of oppression. For example, a girl who runs away from an abusive environment may find no one believes her stories of abuse; that is, of course, if she is capable of naming the violence. In either case, there is a high probability officials will do nothing about the abuse. She may be returned home, only to have the abuse get worse, or she may find officials seem more interested in criminalizing her status offense behavior—punishing her for running away—than they are in helping her. As a result of this kind of life experience, a girl will be more apt to develop a belief that the authority of those in positions of power—police, probation officers, judges, etc.—is illegitimate. The patterns of self-destructive behavior and criminality among the females who fall into this matrix probably will be very similar to those who fall into the first matrix. However, in spite of their belief in the legitimacy of the patriarchal ideology, their negative attitudes toward authority figures may mean at least some of the negative feelings they experience (i.e., anger, frustration, etc.) will be directed outward not inward. The expression of these negative feelings, however, probably will not be overt. They will present themselves to treatment providers as being emotionally shut off from the rest of the world. However, what they really are is simply reluctant to reveal their feelings to individuals whom they will have come to see as occupying positions of power in their lives, individuals they generally will have come to distrust. Thus, while they actually do have feelings of guilt and remorse about their behaviors, they probably will not be willing to express them openly. Although they will be amenable to treatment, they will appear to be quite resistant to it because they will have come to believe treatment providers are a part of "the system" that has failed them. Establishing a trusting relationship will prove to be the biggest challenge for treatment providers working with females who fall into this matrix, but, like the females who fall into the first matrix, their rehabilitative needs will be enormous, particularly in regard to their need to "relearn" how to think and feel about interpersonal relationships and violence in their lives.

Rejecting the legitimacy of the patriarchal ideology, the females who fall into the third matrix will be far from "liberated." They will, however, be more likely to direct any negative feelings they experience outward toward others, and not inward toward themselves, in very overt ways. Their use of drugs and/or alcohol probably will be self-reported as a means of escape and may not fall into a general pattern of other types of self-destructive behaviors. Despite the fact that they will have internalized a sense of themselves as powerless, they probably will define themselves as "tough," as doing whatever it takes to survive; that frequently will include committing crimes and/or acts of delinquency. Their criminality will include the conventional status offenses, minor property offenses, prostitution, etc., but it also may include serious— even violent—crimes committed on their own or with others. As they direct their negative feelings outward, they will express little or no guilt or remorse. They probably will come across to treatment providers as being extraordinarily cold, unfeeling, and generally untouched by whatever has happened to them and/or by whatever they have done. While they may be quite capable of naming the interpersonal violence they have suffered and/or observed, they probably will minimize or even deny its significance.

Having developed a belief that the authority of those in positions of power is illegitimate, the attitude of the females who fall into this third matrix toward treatment providers will go far beyond the generalized lack of trust exhibited by the females who fall into the second belief matrix. These women and girls will freely express intense feelings of disdain toward anyone they perceive occupies a position of power over them. They will have come to believe these are the people who do things *to* you and not *for* you. By design, the emotional wall that surrounds them will seem impenetrable to treatment providers. They will be overtly resistant to all attempts to help them. As a result, many of these females may be labeled "beyond help" or "lost causes." While they will, no doubt, present treatment providers with their toughest challenges, even these women and girls are amenable to treatment despite their apparent resistance to it. Those who struggle to work with these female offenders must recognize that the maladaptive strategies that these females have relied on for so long have been subjectively defined as the key to their survival. Any alternative rehabilitative strategies proposed by treatment providers will be seen at best as frightening and at worst as threatening. Thus it will take more than just developing a trusting relationship to help them. These women and girls will have to be convinced they can abandon their maladaptive strategies and still survive before any meaningful treatment can begin.

CONCLUSION

Some Theoretical and Empirical Implications of Power-Belief Theory

It is important to reiterate power-belief theory remains untested. At this stage in its evolution, while it suggests a context within which female criminality can best be understood, it does not answer the question: "Why do some females engage in this kind of rule-violating behavior and others do not?" Comparative studies that identify what distinguishes offending and non-offending females who share the same matrix of beliefs, for instance, may prove to be very enlightening when it comes to providing an answer to the "why" question. It also is important to reiterate power-belief theory is not a "female-specific" theory. Beyond expanding on its applicability to women and girls, particularly in regard to adolescent girls who become involved in delinquency, more work needs to be done to see if the theory also provides a context within which the criminality of men and boys can best be understood.

The major methodological challenge facing those who set out to test power-belief theory will be the development of accurate measures of the beliefs that comprise the essence of the dynamics of oppression. Established techniques for the quantification of these kinds of subjective beliefs may prove useful and should be explored. However, qualitative techniques also will have to be employed if one hopes to flesh out what really distinguishes offending and non-offending females who share the same belief matrix. The inductive nature of qualitative research also may prove vital to the ultimate accurate determination of just which beliefs should be included among those contributing to the dynamics of oppression.

Some Practical Ramifications of Power-Belief Theory

The potential practical implications of power-belief theory are enormous. At the level of policy making, power-belief theory suggests a context within which the "difference/equality" debate may be more effectively addressed than it has been in the past. The problem plaguing criminal justice and other policy makers for decades has been that while policies acknowledging gender differences tend to create disparate treatments that disfavor females, so do policies that stress the importance of equal treatment. Chesney-Lind and Pollock (1995) note, "With the emphasis on parity and with a male model of imprisonment, women are clearly short-changed" (p. 168). Rafter (1993) also suggests there are problems with insisting on equal treatment: "Outwardly even-handed treatment produces inferior treatment for incarcerated women because the norm is still set by male administrators, working with male needs uppermost in mind" (p. 10). Such models also may resurrect a "separate but equal" mentality that then may be used to justify the inferior treatment of females.

Power-belief theory suggests conventional approaches to this problem must be transcended by policy makers. Power-belief theory puts the affirmation of differences between women and men, *and* between girls and boys, into a unique context. Traditionally, equality in patriarchal societies has been measured against an adult male standard that mismeasures women and girls. The alternative standards that have been proposed to remedy this problem, norms like the "universal care-giver" or Eisenstein's (1988) "pregnant woman," may be more inclusive, but they still exclude and, therefore, necessarily mismeasure children, especially girls. Power-belief theory suggests policy makers need to strive toward a standard against which the needs of *all* people of *all ages* can be fairly measured if they hope to achieve some semblance of social justice in their treatment of female offenders. Clearly there are significant differences between women and men that cannot be dismissed. As Chesney-Lind and Pollock (1995) point out, "In order for women offenders to receive justice, it must be recognized that men and women inhabit different social realities and that women are not necessarily best served if they are treated in ways that their needs are identical to their male counterparts" (p. 170). However, according to power-belief theory, it is just as important to acknowledge that girls and boys (as children), not just women and men (as adults), inhabit different social realities.

Traditional approaches to difference by policy-makers has helped to institutionalize and legitimate the dominance of the needs of male offenders over the needs of female offenders in criminal and juvenile justice systems. Power-belief theory provides policy-makers with a context within which the different needs of women *and* girls can be understood and appreciated in a non-traditional way that clearly challenges rather than legitimates their subordination. It is a theoretical context that also should prove useful to a wide range of practitioners who seek to develop integrated, holistic approaches to treatment because it advances the notion that the rehabilitative needs of offenders must become the driving force in criminal and juvenile justice systems, *not* the organizational demands of those systems. What this means is new ways of thinking about how these systems work will need to be developed. It also is a theoretical context that suggests conventional risk-assessment approaches to classification need to be replaced by an integrated needs assessment approach. As treatment providers embrace this approach, power-belief theory would suggest they should be careful not to assess a female's needs by focusing exclusively on the overt behaviors she exhibits. Females who share the same offense patterns may be experiencing a very different dynamic of oppression and, therefore, have very different treatment needs. Power-belief theory provides a foundation on which all of these important macro-organizational and micro-level innovations designed to help women and girls in trouble with the law can be grounded.

Power-belief theory does hold great promise in regard to its practical ramifications; however, much work, both empirical and theoretical, remains to be done. Until power-belief theory is thoroughly tested and proven to be valid, its practical potential will remain unfulfilled.

REFERENCES

Adler, F. 1975. *Sisters in crime*. New York: McGraw-Hill.

Belknap, J. 1996. *The invisible woman: Gender, crime and justice*. Belmont, CA: Wadsworth.

Berger, P. L., and Luckmann, T. 1967. *The social construction of reality: A treatise in the sociology of knowledge*. Garden City, NY: Anchor Books.

Bonilla-Santiago, G. 1996. Latina battered women: Barriers to service delivery and cultural considerations. In *Helping battered women: New perspectives and remedies*, ed., Roberts, A.R., 229–234. New York: Oxford University Press.

Brownell, K. D., and Fairburn, C. G., eds. 1995. *Eating disorders and obesity: A comprehensive handbook*. New York: Guilford Press.

Carlen, P., and Worral, A., eds. 1987. *Gender, crime and justice*. Philadelphia: Open University.

Castro, I. L. 1996. *Domestic violence: A work place issue*. DOL Publication No. 96–3. Washington, D.C.: U. S. Department of Labor Women's Bureau.

Chesney-Lind, M. 1995. Girls, delinquency, and juvenile justice: Toward a feminist theory of young women's crime. In *The criminal justice system and women: Offenders, victims and workers*, eds. Price, R.P., and Sokoloff, N.J., 71–88. New York: McGraw-Hill.

Chesney-Lind, M. 1997a. What about girls? Hidden victims of congressional juvenile crime control. Paper presented at the meeting of the American Society of Criminology in San Diego, November.

Chesney-Lind, M. 1997b. *The female offender: Girls, women, and crime*. Thousand Oaks, CA: Sage Publications.

Chesney-Lind, M., and Pollock, J. M. 1995. Women's prisons: Equality with a vengeance. In *Women, law and social control,* eds. Merlo, A.V., and Pollock, J.M., 155–175. Boston: Allyn & Bacon.

Costanzo, M., and Oskamp S., eds. 1994. *Violence and the law.* Thousand Oaks, CA: Sage Publications.

Crites, L., ed. 1976. *The female offender.* Lexington, MA: Lexington Books.

Currie, E., and Skolnick, J. H. 1997. *America's problems: Social issues and public policy.* New York: Longman.

Daly, K., and Chesney-Lind, M. 1988. Feminism and criminology. *Justice Quarterly 5,* 497–535.

Degler, C. 1980. *At odds: Women and the family in America from the revolution to the present.* New York: Oxford University Press.

Dobash, R. E., and Dobash, R. 1979. *Violence against wives.* New York: Free Press.

Dougherty, J. 1993. Women's violence against their children: A feminist perspective. *Women and Criminal Justice* 4: 91–114.

Dwyer, D. C., et al. 1996. Domestic violence and woman battering: Theories and practice implications. In *Helping battering women: New perspectives and remedies,* ed. Roberts, A.R., 67–82. New York: Oxford University Press.

Eisenstein, Z. 1988. *The female body and the law.* Berkeley, CA: University of California Press.

Empey, L. T., and Stafford, M.C. 1991. *American delinquency: Its meaning and construction.* Belmont, CA: Wadsworth.

Evans, M., ed. 1982. *The woman question.* London: Fontana.

Faller, K. C. 1990. *Understanding child sexual maltreatment.* Newbury Park, CA: Sage Publications.

Gordon, L. 1988. *Heroes of their own lives: The politics and history of family violence.* New York: Penguin USA.

Guggenheim, M. 1994. The best interests of the child: Much ado about nothing? In *Child, parent and state: Law and policy reader,* eds. Humm, S.R., et al., 27–35. Philadelphia: Temple University Press.

Hawes, J. M. 1991. *The children's rights movement: A history of advocacy and protection.* Boston: Twayne.

Heidensohn, F. M. 1968. The deviance of women: A critique and an enquiry. *British Journal of Sociology* 19: 160–173.

Heidensohn, F. M. 1987. Women and crime: Questions for criminology. In *Gender, crime and justice,* eds. Carlen, P., and Worrall, A., 16–28. Philadelphia: Open University.

Hochschild, A. 1989. *The second shift: Working parents and the revolution at home.* New York: Viking.

Humm, S. R., et al., eds. 1994. *Child, parent, and state: Law and policy reader.* Philadelphia: Temple University Press.

Jordon, J. V. 1993. The relational self: Implications for adolescent development. In *Adolescent psychiatry,* eds. Jordon, J.V., et al., Vol. 19, 228–239. Chicago: University of Chicago Press.

Kasinsky, R. G. 1994. Child neglect and "unfit" mothers: Child savers in the progressive era and today. *Women and Criminal Justice* 6: 97–129.

Klein, D. 1976. The aetiology of female crime: A review of the literature. In *The female offender,* ed. Crites, L., Lexington, MA: Lexington Books.

Leonard, E. 1982. *A critique of criminological theory: Women, crime and society.* New York: Longman.

Lombroso, C., and Ferrero, W. 1895. *The female offender.* London: T. Fisher Unwin.

Martin, S. E., and Jurik, N. C. 1996. *Doing justice, doing gender: Women in law and criminal justice occupations.* Thousand Oaks, CA: Sage Publications.

Messerschmidt, J. W. 1993. *Masculinities and crime: Critique and reconceptualiztion of theory.* Lanham, MD: Rowman & Littlefield.

Miller, A. 1983. *For your own good: Hidden cruelty in child-rearing and the roots of violence.* New York: Noonday Press.

Millman, M. 1982. Images of deviant men and women. In *The woman question,* ed. Evans, M., London: Fontana.

O'Kelly, C. G., and Carney, L. S. 1986. *Women and men in society.* Belmont, CA: Wadsworth.

Paisner, S. R., and Knight, D. 1996. Domestic violence victims and new laws: Do these changes go far enough? *National Bulletin on Domestic Violence Prevention* 2: 3–7.

Pollak, O. 1950. *The criminality of women.* Philadelphia: University of Pennsylvania Press.

Rafter, N. H. 1993. Equality or difference? In *Female offenders: Meeting the needs of a neglected population,* 7–11. Laurel, MD: American Correctional Association.

Regoli, R. M., and Hewitt, J. D. 1997. Delinquency in society. New York: McGraw-Hill.

Reskin, B., and Padavic, I. 1994. *Women and men at work.* Thousand Oaks, CA: Pine Forge Press.

Rivers, C., et al. 1979. *Beyond sugar and spice: How women grow, learn and thrive.* New York: G. P. Putnam's Sons.

Sagatun, I. J., and Edwards, L. P., eds. 1995. *Child abuse and the legal system.* Chicago: Nelson-Hall.

Scarpitti, F. R., et al. 1997. *Social problems.* New York: Longman.

Schor, J. B. 1991. *The overworked American: The unexpected decline of leisure.* New York: Basic Books.

Shacklady Smith, L. 1978. Sexist assumptions and female delinquency. In *Women, sexuality and social control,* eds. Smart, C., and Smart, B., London: Routledge and Kegan Paul.

Simon, R. 1975. *Women and crime.* Lexington, MA: Lexington Books.

Simon, R., and Landis, J. 1991. *The crimes that women commit: The punishments they receive.* Lexington, MA: Lexington Books.

Skolnick, A. 1975. The limits of childhood: Conceptions of child development and social context. *Law and Contemporary Problems* 39: 38–77.

Smart, C. 1976. *Women, crime and criminology: A feminist critique.* London: Routledge and Kegan Paul.

Strassler, K., ed. 1994. *Defending our lives: A film about domestic violence—study and resource guide.* [Brochure] Cambridge Documentary Films, Boston.

Striegel-Moore, R. H. 1995. A feminist perspective on the etiology of eating disorders. In *Eating disorders and obesity: A comprehensive handbook,* eds. Brownell and Fairburn, 224–229. New York: Guilford Press.

Théry, I. 1986. "The interest of the child" and the regulation of the post-divorce family. *International Journal of the Sociology of Law,* 14, 341–358.

Thomas, W. I. 1923. *The unadjusted girl.* Boston: Little, Brown.

Vobejda, B. and Havemann, J. 1997, May 2. Teen sexual activity shows first decline. *The Philadelphia Inquirer,* A1, A24.

Wiebe, R. H. 1967. *The search for order: 1877–1920.* New York: Hill and Wang.

Zelizer, V. A. 1985. *Pricing the priceless child: The changing social value of children.* New York: Basic Books.

PART II

Treatment Considerations and Strategies

In Part I, The Theoretical Perspective, the multiple rehabilitative needs of female offenders were described. It was evident from the descriptions that the prototypical female offender who interfaces with correctional agencies often lacks basic education, vocational skills, successful work or school experience, stable family, or social support systems. However, a treatment response that consists of more education, better work skills, cognition and social skills development, values clarification, and other pragmatic and social functioning skills development *alone* cannot rehabilitate her. She usually presents with years of substance abuse and offending behavior. For this reason, she must be provided a comprehensive, long-term, treatment response in order to address the highly complex and multifaceted problems underlying their risk behaviors. Issues relevant to this treatment response are the focus of Part II. It is recommended that the following guidelines also be considered in treatment decision-making.

- While treatment involves providing a safe environment and empowering the woman or girl to establish a sense of control in her life, treatment in correctional settings, whether in institutions or in the community, does not preclude the use of supervision and monitoring. Supervision, interventions, and sanctions can be melded in a way that are efficient and effective for rehabilitative purposes.
- To be effective, treatment must ensure accountability and responsibility on the part of the female offender. This accountability and responsibility is best achieved when the treatment is voluntary and the woman or girl is receptive and ready to try an alternative lifestyle. When the female offender is not receptive to treatment, it is appropriate to help her find good reason to work on her problems, if only to work towards release from institutionalization or avoidance of future institutionalization.
- The effectiveness of treatment in a community-based correctional setting is often dependent on the availability of ancillary support such as child care, and transportation to available community resources to treatment and health care.
- Relapse must be seen on the part of both the service provider and the female offender as part of the treatment process and as a learning tool. As discussed in detail in Chapter Four of this book, social treatment is a multiphased event inclusive of relapse events.

- Relationships are central to women's and girls' lives as discussed in detail in Chapter Five on relational theory. Treatment interventions that build upon this reality by encouraging the development of trusting and supportive relationships with other women and girls can help female offenders develop healthy connections. Further, as will be described in Chapter Eight, group therapy can be particularly effective as group members with similar experiences are able to understand and support each other. According to Baugh, Bull, and Cohen, the authors of Chapter Eight, group therapy also helps to reduce shame, increase self-esteem, and decrease isolation. Finally, the relationship afforded by a caring person such as a mentor, able to make a long term commitment, can make a significant difference in the life of a female offender.
- Prevention and early intervention responses are vital. Ideally, a continuum of sanctions and interventions should be available to respond to female offenders at every age and stage of their involvement with the justice system.
- A continuum of rehabilitative interventions with female offenders requires an integrated systems approach to implementation and service delivery. Such an approach is the opposite of the single focus approach that tends to reduce a person to the sum of her separate problems. It is important that treatment interventions avoid the single focus approach that, as will be described in detail in Chapter Thirteen, contributes to female offenders' failures.
- Treatment providers must identify those indicators on which to develop a treatment plan when there is no official report. This guideline is discussed in detail in Chapter Ten.
- Treatment providers must learn to recognize and respond to female offenders who have normalized maladaptive behaviors. This guideline is discussed in detail in Chapter Ten.
- Treatment providers need to be culturally sensitive. There are pressing reasons to do so (see Chapter Fourteen). On average, the female jail population has grown 10.2 percent annually since 1985. In 1996, the female prison population growth rate was nearly twice that of males. Yet, between 1985 and 1995, the total number of incarcerated African American females increased by 204 percent. During the same ten-year period, the number of Hispanics in prison rose by 219 percent, with an average 12.3 percent increase each year (Murnola and Beck 1997, p. 4–6, 9).

The sequence of chapters in this section range from the most theoretical to the most "nitty-gritty" treatment considerations and strategies. The first chapter in this section, Chapter Seven, serves as a logical theoretical "bridge" from Part I, "The Theoretical Perspective." In this chapter, entitled," The Treatment of Female Offenders: Individual Psychotherapy in Systems-Theory Perspective, "Weitzman applies the lens of systems theory to an understanding of individual psychotherapy. The author offers the view that the treatment relationship, the interaction of therapist and client, forms a system within which the conflicting emotions of the client can move towards resolution. This understanding of the relationship as a system facilitates such resolution, ultimately breaking the intergenerational cycle of criminality.

In Chapter Eight, "Institutional Classification of Females: Problems and Some Proposals for Reform," Brennan examines female classification, its strengths and weaknesses, and certain key issues regarding the appropriateness of current systems for female offenders as well as issues such as fairness, validity, and legal issues. Specifically, the author examines the current gender-neutral classification systems usually employed that are not well-aligned with either the goal of risk assessment for female offenders or the goals of needs assessment and rehabilitation. Potential options for addressing these issues are presented.

In Chapter Nine, "Mental Health Issues Related to Treatment," Baugh, Bull, and Cohen focus on transitional counseling issues and diagnosis and treatment of mental health disorders most frequently seen in the women offender population.

In Chapter Ten, "Female Offenders and Childhood Treatment: Understanding the Connections," Dougherty unravels some of the complexities of the link between childhood maltreatment and female offending, introduced in Chapter 2. The author clarifies the challenges treatment providers who work with these women and girls must confront.

In Chapter Eleven, "Surviving Violence: Women's Strength through Connections," Swift explores the connection between women and male violence to outline treatment approaches for battered women based on relational theory presented in Chapter Five. The author considers the implications of relational theory for the education and treatment of women offenders who have a history of victimization through violence. The benefits in providing group support are compared with the potential for group support in women's prisons.

In Chapter Twelve, "Needs Assessment and Treatment Goal Planning," Bradley provides clinical considerations for choosing and training an effective assessor, suggestions for developing individualized assessment protocols and strategies for facilitating treatment goal planning with female offenders. This chapter provides important insights into dealing with female offenders who have normalized maladaptive behaviors.

As stated, the chapters in this section have important implications for treatment providers. They also have important implications for correctional policy researchers and administrators who are interested in ensuring that the treatment strategies they use are appropriate for female offenders.

REFERENCE

Murnola, C. J., and Beck, A. J. 1997. *Prisoners in 1996*, NCJ 164619. Washington, D.C.: U.S. Department of Justice, Office of Justice Programs.

CHAPTER 7

The Treatment of Female Offenders: Individual Psychotherapy in Systems-Theory Perspective

Bernard Weitzman

Editor's Notes

In Chapter Seven, Weitzman describes a therapeutic response from a Rogerian perspective. A core belief of this perspective is that self-rejection is based on the experience of emotional rejection, on the withdrawal of emotional contact by significant people in one's developmental histories. In Carl Roger's (1959) view, this self-rejection is the cause of all neurotic suffering and dysfunction. Self-rejection is also the hallmark of the psychological histories of the majority of female offenders. As discussed in previous chapters, most have had multiple trauma histories where they continually experienced emotional rejection such as loss of parents in childhood and child abuse. As adults, the experience of emotional rejection continues in the form of repeated verbal, sexual, and physical abuse usually both in and out of their homes. According to Weitzman, these considerations are particularly relevant in the present because a female offender is likely to be very troubled in her self-regard. In addition, Weitzman says, "She is often a member of a minority, and typically comes from a background of low (socioeconomic status) SES. As a woman she suffers the threats to self-respect that have been so ably delineated in the past decade by the feminist movement and suffers the threats to self-respect of minorities and individuals of low SES."

Weitzman emphasizes that it is the self-rejection or self-denigration experienced by the female offender that typically undermines impulses to plan and to look for ways of positively transforming her lifestyle. From this perspective, the female offender's self-acceptance and positive self-regard is a first treatment priority, a major therapeutic goal. The basic ground for this therapeutic goal is that the intelligence of the woman or girl be respected. Weitzman states, "Feigned respect offered by a therapist will not hit the mark—it will be felt as a confirmation of self-denigration." Considering female offenders from this perspective may seem a lofty concept to some. Yet, treatment experience has demonstrated that female offenders must be afforded the opportunities to make uplifted choices about their lives if they are to successfully reintegrate into society.

It should be emphasized here that the therapeutic goal elaborated upon in this chapter is best achieved in a community-based correctional setting for the simple reason that the broader prison context *does* remove autonomy and control. This reality exacerbates the female offender's already low self-esteem, lack of basic confidence, and willingness to self-denigrate.

From a systems perspective, this therapeutic goal involves treatment staff developing new competencies and working collectively to provide what Weitzman calls "a team-based program of systemic treatment." It also requires examining what therapist characteristics affect a client's self-acceptance and positive self-regard. Ideas designed "to inspire, to enable, and to empower a client, in her capacity to use the services being offered by other team members" and the treatment considerations and strategies for transforming negative self-regard on the part of the female offender are presented.

INTRODUCTION

The project of applying the lens of systems-theory to an understanding of individual psychotherapy is very gradually taking place. Studies of this kind (Hoffman 1990) have been long delayed because one of the early influences of the family therapy movement was to de-emphasize or reject individual psychotherapy as a relevant intervention (Haley 1978 or Minuchin 1974)—to regard the problems presented by individuals seeking therapy in purely systemic terms and to seek change in the system as the means to alleviation of the suffering of the individual. Systems-theory as a horizontal metaphor, the individual viewed in his or her social world, and depth psychology as a vertical metaphor, the search for understanding the impact of conflicting emotions within the person, can be regarded as antagonistic, mutually exclusive alternatives, or as mutually enriching perspectives on the same human reality—the axes of a gyroscope. This chapter adopts the second alternative—it applies the lens of systems-theory from a depth psychological perspective. It offers the view that the treatment relationship, the interaction of therapist and client, form a system within which the conflicting emotions of the client can move towards resolution. It is argued that applying this understanding of the relationship as a system, facilitates such resolution.

In the early rush of enthusiasm for the application of the insights of systems-theoretical insights to the psychological problems of families, the orientation of those traditional psychotherapies that seek alleviation of unhappiness by studying the causal structure of the mental life of individuals, was rejected. It was, instead, argued that the system and the individual embedded in it are co-creators of the dysfunctional patterns that are the origins of misery.

These arguments were important and appropriate—it is true that the dysfunctional characteristics of an individual are always interdependently determined by a network of systemic factors—familial, cultural and societal dynamics. On the other hand, it is a mistake to imagine that practitioners of individual psychotherapy were, or are, blind to systemic considerations. It is important for systems-oriented therapists to appreciate the intelligence of traditional psychotherapies and to harness the usefulness of their approaches. Individuals, for example, who are embedded in social networks that cannot be brought into a family therapy environment, can often change those networks by their own initiatives. Individuals can change systems just as surely as systems affect individuals.

It is in understanding the emotional factors that determine how individuals deal with dysfunctional aspects of their environments, that the usefulness of the depth psychologies is most acute. Some individuals submit to social abuse, some remove themselves and declare war on the institutions that have abused them. Some individuals work to produce constructive change that serves both their own needs and, simultaneously, corrects faults of the system that damage others. A fully competent therapeutic agenda aspires to freeing clients to pursue this third alternative. In the service of this agenda, the broad range of psychoanalytically oriented therapies, as well as approaches such as the Rogerian or Existential, with their traditional focus on intra-individual conditions of function and dysfunction, are relevant and useful.

At the same time it is helpful to see how, in traditional depth-psychological perspectives, intra-individual considerations can have systemic consequences. Freud (1917), for example, framed the notion of "secondary gains." A neurotic symptom comes into being as an attempt to deal with a problem located within the dynamic system of the individual. However, it frequently also has social consequences. The secondary gains are typically to be found in the relationship of the individual with the social system. Some of the social consequences of the symptom may make it precious to the individual. So, for example, a person who develops agoraphobic difficulties and who cannot leave home without a companion, may be able to enlist caretaking attention from his children. If such a person has, in the past, felt lonely and neglected by his children, his desire for the attention his symptom brings him from them might lead him to cling to his agoraphobia. Such gains make a neurotic symptom difficult to relinquish. Freud believed that, in general, the secondary gains of neurotic symptoms, such as those provided by a receptive and accommodating environment—the sympathy, special allowances, and so forth that suffering elicits from social others—perpetuate the dysfunctional condition.

Freud (1933) hoped that the creation of psychoanalysis would serve as a corrective, within the social framework, of such individual neurotic difficulties. He thought that the psychoanalytic education of the general public, leading to a growing awareness of the deceptions involved in maintaining neurotic symptom patterns, would create an atmosphere hostile to neurosis. He thought that, in the absence of accommodation by the social system, neurotic symptoms would not flourish so robustly.

In these ways, Freud's analysis of the dynamics of secondary gains had, and has, systemic consequences—it provides a therapist with an important tool of understanding, in helping an individual to free herself of the web of entanglement that perpetuates her symptoms. There are many such instances of systemic thinking in the main body of psychoanalytic thought.

Probably most revealing of the systems-oriented perspective of individual psychotherapy, is that it has long been understood that the therapeutic dyad, the relationship of therapist and client, is itself a system. Traditional therapeutic topics are the dynamics of the family of origin, SES, and other factors in the background of the client. Jung (1954), for example, argued that a neurosis is always a pattern of neurotic, interpersonal relationships. He said that what each person experiences in an interaction is the meeting with the other person—the way they "rub up" against one another. If either person were to bring something different to the interaction, Jung argued, each would experience something different. Ignoring the mutuality of this process—denying that the experience of being together is a joint creation—either claiming responsibility for characteristics of the experience, or holding the other person responsible for such characteristics—was his definition of "projection." In his view, such projections are the source of the distortions that are the basis of all neurotic relationships. Equally, in discussions of countertransference, the technical term for those dynamics that lead a therapist to distort the meanings being conveyed by the client, environmental influences in the background of the therapist are carefully examined.

Because, in a system, individuals are rubbing up against one another and creating a texture, setting up an atmosphere, by changing what he or she brings to the system—by changing herself or himself—an individual can change the system. This view of the relationship of individuals in a dyad is systemic and empowering. It offers a potent vehicle of understanding, for systemic interventions in individual as well as in family therapy contexts.

Every therapist knows that clients bring their relationships with them into the consulting room. Clients develop patterns of projection in the cradle of the family. These patterns are further developed and modified in later relationships. The patterns of projection become part of the client's contribution to the dynamics of the therapeutic dyad—Harry Stack Sullivan (1953) argued that it is impossible to leave them outside—even a hermit in a mountain cave carries his projections with him. What is too often ignored, however, is that this is true of the therapist as well—she brings her own historically evolved projective patterns into the therapeutic situation.

Much of the ongoing flow of the literature in which the therapeutic discourse of the profession is conducted, deals with issues of transference and countertransference. Transference and countertransference are the concepts that Freud and others framed in trying to understand how relationships are pathologized within the therapeutic dyad.

Discussions of transference and countertransference deal with psychotherapy as a particular form of human relationship. There is obvious justification for this perspective. There is, however, a widely evident tendency to speak of the therapeutic dyad as if it were somehow free of the ordinary obstacles that relationships encounter in everyday life. There is a vision, in the profession, of an ideal therapeutic relationship that is fundamentally different from ordinary relationships. In such an ideal relationship, the therapist is a realized master of his or her own mind. The motivations, needs, and conflicts that lead to distortions and misunderstandings in other relationships do not occur in this ideal therapeutic relationship.

There is a tendency among psychotherapists to speak as if such an ideal situation is being approximated. This is not the case. It is undoubtedly true that unbiased listening by therapists sometimes takes place. Does it take place more frequently than in conversations between, e.g., friends, or between lovers, or between teacher and student, etc.? We simply don't know—we merely hope. Beyond question, and by the testimony of the professional literature, it is unlikely that such listening is more than a momentary event in the therapeutic relationship. It is likely that distortions and falsifications take place frequently.

To a very great extent, the discourse of the profession is devoted to a search for ways of dealing with these self-evident facts—the truth that therapists are as vulnerable to interpersonal difficulties as are their clients. In this literature there is a more modest ideal delineated. An ideally managed countertransference would be one in which a therapist would be competent to track the distortions that her own projections introduce into the interaction, and, in this way, be able to constantly reconstruct the "true" meaning being communicated by her client. It is unlikely that even this more modest aspiration is more than approximated—and then, only some of the time.

More reasonably, there are theorists who deny that therapists have any reason to claim superiority in their ability to manage their projections. There is an argument appearing with increasing frequency in the psychotherapeutic literature urging therapists to acknowledge the fact that the therapeutic relationship is just that—another relationship (see Hoffman 1992).

What is at issue in this discussion is the *nature* of systems, which involve human interaction. Systems-oriented thinkers would do well to see that within the heartland of individual psychotherapeutic thinking, systemic questions are being asked. Are there experts in human affairs? If so, who are they? How can we identify them? Are people who hold MDs or PhDs and who practice as psychotherapists any more happy, sane, or well-functioning than lawyers, doctors, bricklayers, or janitors? The argument of this chapter is that one becomes an expert only by accepting the fact that one is not an expert—by identifying oneself and one's own projective patterns as *the therapeutic problem*. The therapeutic system, the therapeutic dyad, can function as a healing environment only to the extent to which the therapist takes responsibility for her own projective dynamics.

Although in some sense this view is commonplace in the world of depth psychology—e.g., therapists are typically urged to undergo intensive, long-term psychotherapy as part of their training—the language of psychoanalytic discourse makes access to this realization structurally difficult. The term "countertransference" conceives the pathologized reaction of the analyst as a response to the patient's projections. Thinking in this linguistic framework, one might then assume that the analyst is merely reactive. One might think that if the client didn't contaminate the relationship with transference projections, the analyst would be able to remain clear. This is the perspective Freud introduced—of the analyst as an expert—ideally standing above the human situation—, e.g., "In a disagreement with the patient whether he said some particular thing, or how he said it, the physician is usually right" (Freud 1912, p. 110)—cultivating a coldness and distance that Freud compares with that of a surgeon. The perspective of systems-theory presents a radical challenge to this posture. It is entirely possible, even likely, that the therapist's projections spring into action together with those of the client—interaction is a system.

Perhaps the most radical challenge to the traditional view of therapy arises from post-modern theorists who argue that knowledge is a social phenomenon. In their view therapy is a conversation between two people—whatever reality is claimed for it depends on consensus—on agreement between the participants (Hoffman 1990). The conception of knowledge as a social phenomenon, if understood properly, becomes a powerful tool for examining and regulating the therapeutic process. For example, a consensus between therapist and client that good progress is being made in treatment is a crucially important positive criterion. Such a judgment must be respected by those outside the dyad. A client who feels she is being helped should be encouraged to continue even by relatives who do not see evidence of the changes the client claims are taking place. Equally, a client who claims she is not being helped by her therapist should be supported in her wish for change.

Still, despite the danger that one might undermine the therapeutic relationship, there are common sense grounds on which a therapist-client consensus can legitimately be challenged—the system extends far beyond the walls of the consulting room. This topic is thin ice. The treatment situation is, in its essence, private, and the relationship on which it depends is often fragile and filled with anxiety and uncertainty. Still, the common sense views of friends, relatives, and others are not irrelevant. Seeing the legitimacy of "the social phenomenon" view of knowledge brings into focus the fact that the therapeutic dyad is a power-relationship and that influence-processes are its nature. The therapist is "robed," invested by society with the mantle of a physician, a healer, an expert, and so on. The "patient" is needy and vulnerable—a supplicant seeking help. Viewed in this way, it becomes obvious that the therapeutic relationship is easily liable to misuse. Vigilance about such dangers is appropriate for those concerned with the welfare of the client.

When the therapeutic relationship is seen from the perspective of power-systems, it is apparent that influence processes, e.g., "word games," have enormous impact. The ways in which we think and how we view our worlds is decisively influenced by our use of language. Obviously, the worlds of advertising, of political rhetoric, and, in general, persuasion processes depend upon such influences. Often, however, the influences of language are more subtle—it is often difficult to discern how they wield their power. It has been argued, for example, that we try to see our world in terms of the reality that science delineates for us. Thus we "know" that plants do not have intentional mental processes. We know that they are biochemical response systems that are reactive to temperature, moisture, and so forth. Even though we think that way about plants, deeper levels of belief may remain active in us. A person, for example, who is so unfortunate as to be lost in the wilderness, who panics and begins to run, is likely to feel that the undergrowth is tearing at her skin and clothing, tripping, and otherwise intentionally impeding her progress. The scientific "knowledge" of plant life evaporates.

The opinions of experts—those who wear the mantle of power—are not a court of last resort. From a systems-theory point of view, common sense is often our most reliable "good-sense." Common sense identifies a level of practical reality where the "final" or "objective" nature of things—the subject of scientific or philosophical discourses—is less critical than the way we use these things. Experts are expected to promulgate "objective" knowledge. Of course, there is a sense in which claims to such knowledge are valid. Because they identify a consensus that is based on certain methodological and linguistic conventions, the knowledge they offer is often useful. But when an expert's opinion doesn't make sense to us, we need to be very careful. Common sense is based on another consensus—one that is often superior—it might even be called wisdom.

In the case of psychoanalytic theory, the term "countertransference" is the carrier of an attitude, a professional posture—one that was specified in considerable detail by Freud and has been developed and elaborated by his school. Although the languages we speak may not easily change the deepest levels of our responsiveness to the world—remember the person who is lost and running through the woods—still they have enormous influence. "Countertransference" is such a power term. It conveys a view in which the client is the origin of the distortions that enter the therapeutic relationship. The view of systems-theory invites the intelligence of the client. It points out the obvious—therapeutic interaction relies on verbal interactions, on conversations between people. It urges that the client bring his or her common sense into a domain that had long been ruled by authority. Where expert opinion and common sense conflict, common sense may well be the best bet.

Of course Freud's view of the expert therapist was challenged in his own time and within his own circle. Jung described the nature of the therapeutic relationship as a chemical reaction (Jung 1946). If anything therapeutic happens, he said, the participants are both transformed. Jung applied this view to outcome criteria. He thought it was quite out of the question for the therapist to know what has actually happened to the client. All he or she can know is what has happened to him or herself. Thus, if the analyst is changed by the relationship, then there is some chance that the client was also changed. This is an authentically systemic way of understanding what happens in a healing relationship. Healing takes place interactively—if it happens, each of the participants is healed.

In short, a systems-theory approach to psychotherapy must give equal attention to the characteristics of the client and to the characteristics of the therapist. Applied to the question of the setting of therapeutic goals, this means that goal conceptions needs to be formulated for each of the participants in the therapeutic dyad.

SELF REGARD—THE CLIENT

The most effective and useful role that individual psychotherapy can play in a team-based program of systemic treatment is to inspire, to enable, and to empower a client in her capacity to use the services being offered by other team members. The issue here, as briefly drawn above, is the possibility of an individual changing a system—how can an individual be counseled in a way that is most empowering to her, in her task of changing her relationship with the systems through which she moves? The theoretical framework for setting out to serve a client in this way is precisely what psychotherapeutic thinking has to offer the systems-oriented team.

There are many possible theoretical languages that might be used here. One that is particularly helpful is offered by Carl Rogers and his "client-centered" approach to psychotherapy. Rogers (1959) believed that people develop "conditions of worth"—they come to regard themselves as being worthy people only under certain conditions—when they behave in certain ways or feel certain ways—and they come to regard themselves as unworthy people under certain other conditions. In Rogers' view, such conditions of worth are the source of psychopathology and human misery—they obstruct development in directions needed by a person, in favor of development dictated by significant others. Conditions of worth are not naturally occurring phenomena—they come about when parents or other caretakers withhold warmth and affection, or turn anger, scorn, and other denigrating emotional forces, as socializing punishments, toward the developing child. The child comes to introject these emotional reactions and to turn them against herself.

It is likely that a child whose socialization was largely accomplished in this way, will be sensitized to rejection by the " fathers" and "mothers" of society. A female offender who has been marginalized for reasons of SES, color, or ethnicity, will feel scorned, rejected, and denigrated by society. Agents of society will bear the projection of the pain she experienced and the anger she harbors in relation to her parents—authorities will be another generation of oppressive parents. Just as the wounding happens through social rejection of the child's naturally occurring feelings, healing takes place in the encounter with a person who is willing to know how she really feels about things and whose reactions do not withhold contact and intimacy.

Feeling like a worthwhile person means feeling like a person worthy of respect by others, like a person who has a right to live—to exist in this world. Feeling like a worthy person is the fundamental condition for being able to engage a dysfunctional system and bring it into balance. The client who needs to find a new relationship to her social world, to the institutional and structural system in which she is embedded, is most likely to have some success if she feels positively about herself. By contrast, feeling negatively about herself, she is likely to constantly generate further trouble for herself.

The Client: A Female Offender

These considerations are particularly relevant in the present context because a female offender is likely to be very troubled in her self-regard—her dynamics are likely to be pervasively structured by conditions of worth. She is often a member of a minority, and typically comes from a background of low SES. As a woman she suffers the threats to self-respect that have been so ably delineated in the past decade by the feminist movement and suffers the threats to self-respect of minorities and individuals of low SES. She is thus particularly liable to develop a self-regard that is painfully self-condemning and self-denigrating.

Working with Negative Self-Regard

Working with difficulties that center on conditions of worth, it is often helpful to make self-denigration an explicit topic. It is important that the client know that the therapist is aware of her problems in this area and notices them as they occur. The willingness of the therapist to hear a client's attacks on herself for what they are—to recognize them and to display a willingness to talk about them—can be very helpful in this regard.

There is a point that must be understood clearly in order for such an approach to be effective. It is urgent that the intelligence of the client be respected. Feigned respect offered by a therapist will not hit the mark—it will be felt as a confirmation of self-denigration. The danger in using the approach being recommended is to imagine that it is an invitation to be wooly-minded. It is not. Clear and explicit recognition of faults is necessary. Such recognition supports self-respect. What is at issue here is a client's negative judgment, self-disparagement, self-revulsion, and so on. What is not at issue is her objective self-appraisal and self-criticism. On the contrary. Her self-critical perception is her intelligence. Realism is a critically important aspect of her developing self-confidence and improved functioning—it should be supported.

Negative judgments that undermine a client's sense of her worthiness, on the other hand, wound confidence and should be identified as expressions of low self-regard and as active forms of inflicting self-injury. For example, the client who says, "I was such a jerk to do that," probably did something dysfunctional, but that doesn't make her a jerk. Calling herself "a jerk," in fact, probably lessens the chances that she will learn from her mistake and not repeat it. Labeling oneself is always self-denigrating. "Jerk" is a label that summarizes a whole person. Rogers (1959) correctly points out that any attack on a part of the self is received, in experience, as an attack on the whole self. In family and other kinship systems, when these systems are functioning in a wholesome and healthy way, people are not labeled (compare Shweder 1991). Where kinship is intact, someone might say, "Oh yes, Jane lies when she's scared and sometimes when she gets real frustrated." No one would say, "Jane is a liar."

Simply pointing out to a client that she injures herself by labeling herself "a jerk" can be helpful. If she responds, "But I was a jerk," the therapist's wisdom is challenged. If the respect of the client for the therapeutic situation is to be protected, the therapist must see and acknowledge the "jerkiness" of what the client did. At the same time there must be a shared understanding that mistakes are made by the most intelligent people and that significant learning generally takes place by examining mistakes without the blinders of judgment. A client can be encouraged to acknowledge what she already knows—people do become jerky when they are in a lot of pain or frightened. That doesn't make them jerks. There aren't any "jerks." There are people who make mistakes. A client who is in pain or frightened is helped by sympathy and not by scorn and is healed by respect and not by insincere and saccharine reassurance.

A therapist who helps a client to see that sympathy with herself is more helpful than calling herself a "jerk" is realistically supportive. It might be appropriate to suggest to her that she talk about her pain and her fear—that she try to think about and to understand the difficulties that led her to behaving in the way she did. A client who engages such a process of self-exploration may find herself in a position to think about how she might help herself. She will learn that sympathy leads to fewer mistakes and that negative judgments and putting oneself down keeps the mistakes happening.

In working with conditions of worth and the dynamic of self-denigration, a therapist needs to train her capacity to read subtle messages in a client's behavior in order to understand her own reactions. Self-denigration is expressed in subtle ways as well as in the gross ways of the above example—i.e., calling oneself a "jerk." Choice of words or grammatical construction may both be vehicles for sarcasm or self-ridicule. Equally, tone of voice can be self-disparaging—for example, the resonance of speech pressed into the nasal cavities and sounding like a sneer or a whine can be profoundly self-denigrating. Posture, gesture, and indeed the entire range of expressive behavior can serve as a means of inflicting self-injury. Noticing these—encouraging a client to pay attention to herself and to take responsibility for how she treats herself can be a supportive direction for interventions.

The idea of paying attention to oneself opens a field of exploration that goes far beyond the immediate situation of the female offender. It points to one of our oldest and most venerated values—the importance of self-knowledge based upon intimate, immediate, and direct experience. At the same time, it is important and applicable in the context of a systemic team effort.

Every human being, at some point in her life, aspires to a heroic ideal. It is this aspiration that we try to satisfy when we identify with superheroes, with athletes, or with famous people whose lives seem to us filled with adventure and vitality. At its best, this aspiration inspires bravery and compassionate encounters with life. At its worst, the feeling that the action is always someplace else, in the lives of the people we see on TV or read about in the papers, reflects a sense of one's own life as drab, colorless, and hardly worth living. The self-regard that lurks in the background of this experience can be painful when brought into consciousness.

Encouraging a client to approach her own life with a sense of interest and, if possible, a spirit of adventure, can be a strong communication of confidence from the therapist. Working with conditions of worth, refusing to accept them as correct and unchangeable, is a crucial message. Self-denigration typically undermines impulses to plan and to look for ways of positively transforming a person's lifestyle. It is at the root of what will make a client able or not able to effectively deal with the system. The confidence that needs to be supported is the client's belief in her own intelligence and in her capacity to learn from mistakes. This is the birthright of every human being. Encouraging a client to turn this intelligence towards the possibilities of a self-supporting, autonomous and independent life, offers her an empowerment to assume a healthy sense of pride that will make taking help and advice from others possible, without loss of self-esteem.

Obviously, however, no cookbook set of things to say is fundamentally to the point. What is necessary is that the therapist deal with her own self-denigrating patterns and find sympathy with herself. She will then know what to say to help a client.

THE THERAPIST

We turn now to the question of the therapeutic goals to be set for the therapist. To follow up the logic of the therapeutic goals we have suggested for the client—the question of what interactive variables, what therapist characteristics affect a client's self-acceptance and positive self-regard, is a first priority. Carl Rogers (1959) identified the single most salient and significant feature of the healing process: he argued that emotional contact, unconditional willingness on the part of the therapist to stay in contact, to be fully there in the presence of the client's pain, is the condition of therapeutic effect. It was his experience that this willingness will be directly experienced by the client.

For those of you who might prefer a psychoanalytic terminology, you could say that when a therapist is able to maintain "evenly hovering attention" (Freud 1912), to be transparent, to continue to listen in a way that is open to every reaction but that always remains present without bias, the client will feel understood at the most basic level—unconscious to unconscious communication will take place.

As described above, Rogers argued that self-rejection is based on the experience of emotional rejection, on the withdrawal of emotional contact by significant people in our developmental histories. As has already been stated above, in Rogers' view, this self-rejection is the cause of all neurotic suffering and dysfunction. In response to such rejection, we learn to withhold our feelings, our spontaneous reactivity from ourselves and from others—we turn instead to living conceptual versions of ourselves. Of course our native and spontaneous ways of reacting do not disappear simply because they have been rejected by other people. They do, however, go into hiding. While we are all familiar with the ways in which we learn to hide our anger from ourselves because of the denigrating reactions of others, we may be less aware of how easily soft, caring, and loving feelings can be driven into hiding. A principle way these wounds can be healed and a resumption of the life path most appropriate for the individual can be found is in a therapeutic meeting with a person who has the courage and the training to stay in emotional contact with a client who is struggling with such feelings and who is hiding from them.

To stay present with another person's pain is not easy. Our reactions to the pain of others are very subtle and complex. When, for example, someone is angry at you, there may be a tendency to brace yourself against what feels like an attack, to tighten yourself, grit your teeth, and be angry in return. Or, there may be a reaction of fearful shrinking away from the anger. There are many possibilities of this kind. In all of these cases, there is the danger that you may withdraw into yourself, pull away from the other person, and, in this way, prevent a therapeutic moment from unfolding. This same analysis is applicable to a wide range of the feeling states we encounter in other people—they hurt us, they frighten us, they disgust us, and they make us opaque.

The critical issue is the therapist's willingness to be explicitly aware, articulately conscious of the reactions she is experiencing. Rogers (1959) believed that the therapist withdraws by hiding aspects of her reactions from herself. This hiding is accomplished by avoiding explicit cognitive identification of what she is feeling. Because the therapist also has conditions of worth and has learned to avoid knowing her own feelings, her ability to be present for the client will be based upon her capacity to work with her own experience. She may be afraid that the client will be hurt or frightened by her reaction, or she may feel that she is a bad person for having such a reaction, and so forth. Rogers argued that the therapist who is willing to stay conscious will be felt by the client to be offering "unconditional positive regard"—even if the therapist's reaction is negative, the client will feel supported. The important message here is—"I'm willing to be in intimate contact with you even when I'm angry with you—even when I don't like something you've done, and even when the way you're feeling is repugnant to me."

When a client does or says something self-denigrating, it is likely that the therapist will feel the negativity the client is expressing—it might be recognized as a subtle sense of revulsion—it is what the client is feeling in that moment—self-revulsion. There may also be, as Winnicott (1947) has described it, a flash of hatred and a wish to eradicate the client—to extinguish the source of the irritation. This also is a compassionate sharing of what the client is feeling. The point here is, that whatever the reaction, whatever the therapist might feel, whether or not she understands its origin, the fate of the therapeutic project depends upon her willingness to remain genuine—to remain conscious of her own reactivity. This is the heart of the therapeutic process.

Finally, a danger that is growing daily more acute in our culture, is the application of diagnostic labels to a client. The professionalism of the therapist who wields DSM IV labels is directly parallel to the example of the client who calls herself a "jerk," or a "liar." When diagnostic labels are applied, it is very difficult for the person to be seen. The application of a label may be a signal that kinship has been ruptured—that the client has ceased to be seen as an individual, as a peer with a set of problems, and has become, instead, a member of a class. The systems-theoretical approach is, not unreasonably, closed to the indiscriminate use of such diagnostic labels—they have particular uses in very circumscribed areas. In the therapy consulting room they are an enormous obstacle—one that few therapists can leap over. The danger of the use of labels points to a whole set of innerpersonal challenges a therapist must face. In presenting the Rogerian perspective, we have emphasized the critical importance of the therapist's emotional openness. With the danger of the use of diagnostic labels, we take Freud (1917) as our teacher. He argued that evenly hovering attention, the listening attitude I have compared with Rogers' unconditional positive regard, will be disrupted by any beliefs, expectations, or inclinations in the mind of the therapist. Such disruptions of the appropriate listening attitude will lead to falsifications by the therapist—misunderstandings of the emotional meaning of what a client is communicating. Obviously, then, the therapist's cognitive functioning is as important as her emotional openness. Thinking in languages that contextualize a client in predefined groups, be they dynamically or symptomatically conceived, creates barriers to open and undistorted communication.

These considerations delimit a set of therapeutic goals for the therapist. The possibility of accomplishing these goals requires continual growth in self-awareness on the part of the therapist. It is necessary that she become increasingly able to remain articulately aware, as Rogers put it, "to symbolize in awareness"—to know, in semantic terms, her reactions to her client. Using the information provided by this self-awareness, the therapist needs to guide her observational capacities towards ever finer and keener discernment of gross and subtle forms of self-denigration in the speech and in the demeanor of her client. In this way, a healing process serving the potential for growth in positive self-regard that a client brings into the therapeutic relationship can be initiated and carried forward.

CONCLUSION

We have argued that in the context of a systems-oriented team effort to restore female offenders to normal, productive lives, the best contribution of psychotherapy is a correction of the client's negative self-regard. The conditions of worth a client brings into the therapeutic dyad will play themselves out in the relationship, offering the therapist opportunities to support a healing and corrective emotional experience. This is accomplished by the work of a therapist in clearing out her own preconceptions, working on her own self-denigrating habitual patterns, and cultivating an attitude of open, attentive and genuine presence in the face of every expression of emotional pain and turmoil presented by her clients.

REFERENCES

Freud, S. [1912] 1955. *Recommendations to physicians practicing psychoanalysis*. Standard edition, 109–120. London: Hogarth Press.

Freud, S. [1917] 1966. *Introductory lectures on psychoanalysis,* 475–478. New York: W.W. Norton & Company.

Freud, S. [1933] 1965. *New introductory lectures on psychoanalysis*. New York: W.W. Norton & Company.

Haley, J. 1978. *Problem solving therapy: New strategies for effective family therapy*. New York: Harper-Calophon.

Hoffman, I. Z. 1992. Some practical implications of a social-constructivist view of the psychoanalytic situation. *Psychoanalytic Dialogues* 2: 287–304.

Hoffman, L. 1990. Constructing realities: an art of lenses. *Family Process* 29: 1–12.

Jung, C. G. [1946] 1954. Psychology of the transference, In *The practice of psychotherapy, Vol. 16. The collected works of C. G. Jung*, eds. Read, H. et al., New York: Pantheon Books, 1954.

Jung, C. G. 1954. *The practice of psychotherapy, Vol. 16. The collected works of C. G. Jung*. New York: Pantheon Books.

Shweder, R.A. 1991. *Thinking through cultures: Expeditions in cultural psychology*. Cambridge, MA: Harvard University Press.

Sullivan, H.S. 1953. *The interpersonal theory of psychiatry*. New York: W.W. Norton & Company.

Minuchin, S. 1974. *Families and family therapy.* Cambridge, MA: Harvard University Press.

Rogers, C. 1959, A theory of therapy, personality and interpersonal relations. In *Psychology: A study of a science*, ed. Koch, S., Vol. 3. New York: McGraw Hill, 84–253.

Winnicott, D. W. 1947. Hate in the countertransference. *International Journal of Psycho-Analysis* 30: 69–74.

CHAPTER 8

Institutional Classification of Females: Problems and Some Proposals for Reform

Tim Brennan

Editor's Notes

Dougherty, in Chapter Six states that power-belief theory is a theoretical context that suggests that women are not necessarily best served if they are treated in ways that their needs are identical to their male counterparts. The theoretical context also suggests that conventional risk-assessment approaches to classification need to be replaced by an integrated needs assessment approach. Brennan, in Chapter Eight, like Dougherty, argues that rehabilitation needs should replace risk as the central purpose of classification for women offenders and reviews studies that support this same conclusion. The reality is that most of the current gender-neutral systems are not well aligned with either the goal of risk assessment for female detainees or the goal of needs assessment and rehabilitation purposes. The author explores these issues and other important issues, related to classification of women offenders in depth, including equity, parity issues, and other legal issues, and presents guidelines for designing objective classification systems for fe-

male inmates. Potential options for solving problems with current classification systems are also presented.

The importance of classification cannot be overstated. According to Brennan, "Both male and female inmates have enormous stakes in valid and equitable classification because it governs decisions regarding: eligibility and access to programs, housing assignments, selection of cell-mates, safety, access to worker status, and the fairness, equity and appropriateness of virtually all inmate processing decisions while incarcerated." The author also emphasizes that classification labels profoundly influence how an inmate is informally "perceived" by both jail staff and other prisoners. With more women being incarcerated, increased litigation, and the ongoing weaknesses of current classification systems for women inmates, the need to improve classification systems for women is becoming a critical issue for criminal justice policy makers, legal advocates, and administration.

Interestingly, the current status of institutional classification for female inmates remains poorly developed and continues to be neglected by both researchers and practitioners. The result of continued reliance on gender-neutral classification systems, which are based on security and custody risk considerations, is that they may incorrectly label and house women inmates at higher levels than needed, even though women offenders pose far lower institutional risks than males. The fact is, however, that most correctional staff and administrators appear to prefer a single system for both sexes. The gender-neutral, risk-based approach, even if somewhat adjusted for females, has, according to Brennan, low predictive validity. Yet it influences treatment of female offenders significantly.

With respect to treatment, current classification systems are cursory. They often underestimate the real treatment and rehabilitation needs of female detainees. The information provided in this chapter is intended as a guide for treatment providers who are interested in ensuring that the classification systems used by their institutions are appropriate for female inmates.

INTRODUCTION

Institutional classifications embody the policies of the institutions in which they are implemented. They function as decision-making tools, and directly impact the processing, treatment, and overall welfare of persons who fall under the control of these institutions. Yet, classification procedures for women in both prisons and jails have been largely ignored for decades. This contrasts to a rather steady stream of studies on male prisoners (Nesbitt and Angelo 1984; Fowler 1993). With more women being incarcerated, increased litigation, and the on-going weaknesses of current classifications for female inmates, the need to improve classification systems for women is becoming a critical issue for criminal justice policy makers, legal advocates, and administrators. An increasing number of correctional agencies are starting to re-examine their current policies and procedures for female classification (Forcier 1995; Austin et al. 1993; Jackson and Stearns 1995). Unfortunately, only a handful of research studies are available to guide correctional administrators on how best to design and implement such systems (Clements 1984; Brennan 1987a, 1987b). Classification for female inmates remains poorly developed and continues to be neglected by both researchers and practitioners (Fowler 1993; Gendreau et al. 1996). Classification systems explicitly designed for female inmates remain rare. Most correctional institutions classify their female inmates with procedures designed primarily for males, incorporating behaviors and risk factors with primary relevance for males. This chapter examines classification procedures for women detainees, it's strengths and weaknesses, and certain key issues regarding the appropriateness of current systems for female prisoners, as well as issues such as fairness, validity, legal issues, and so on. The chapter is aimed at correctional policy researchers, administrators, treatment providers, and others who are interested, or who are required by litigation, to ensure that the classification systems used by their institutions are appropriate for female inmates.

Dissatisfaction Regarding Current Classification Systems for Female Inmates

There appears to be substantial dissatisfaction with current classification methods for women among correctional practitioners (Burke and Adams 1991). This dissatisfaction arises from the fact that most current offender classification systems were designed to meet a set of purposes and policies of primary relevance to male prisoners, and then tested and evaluated on samples overwhelmingly composed of male inmates. Such systems are commonly referred to as "gender-neutral" classifications, and are seen by many administrators as being quite fitting for female offenders. They are the norm in both jails and prisons (Burke and Adams 1991; Austin, et al. 1993). They make the assumption that the same classification factors, weighting and scoring formats are equally salient, and equally effective, for both males and females. Such assumptions would be appropriate if the classification factors and decision thresholds were equally predictively valid and relevant for both males and females. However, these assumptions are highly questionable. Evidence has been accumulating that women prisoners present different profiles—of both needs and risks—when compared to male inmates, as well as differing in various social, medical, and psychological needs (Nesbitt and Angelo 1984). A common feeling of practitioners is that current systems overclassify females, and may incorrectly label and house female inmates at higher levels than needed (Austin et al. 1993; Nesbitt 1994; Chesney-Lind 1992). In a broad review of these issues, Burke and Adams (1991) have bluntly asserted that current "gender-neutral" classifications place women in higher custody levels than required.

Why Has Classification Become such an Important Issue?

The need for improved female classification systems has been intensified by the enormous surge in female incarcerations in the United States. Although women still make up a relatively small share of the prison and jail populations, the past two decades have witnessed a substantial increase in their absolute numbers, and a growth rate that far exceeds that of males.

Taking jails as an example, recent national data, through 1996, shows that while the nation's jail populations more than doubled since 1985, from 265,615 to 518,492, the number of incarcerated females has nearly tripled from 19,077 to 55,700 (see Table 8–1). Although female inmates represent only 11 percent of today's jail population, their numbers have dramatically increased. In addition, the critical roles of offender classification decisions in governing many aspects of jail operations and offender welfare, became strikingly clear. This occurred during the 1980s as a result of litigation against jails and prisons (Belbot and Del Carmen 1993; Tonry 1987). Both male and female inmates have enormous stakes in valid and equitable classification because it governs decisions regarding: eligibility and access to programs, housing assignments, selection of cell-mates, safety, access to worker status, and the fairness, equity, and appropriateness of virtually all inmate process-

Table 8–1 U.S. jail populations by sex 1985–1996

Jail population category	1985		1996		% Change 1986–1996
	Number	%	Number	%	
Total inmates	256,615	100	518,492	100	102
Adults	254,986	99	510,400	98	100
Adult males	235,909	92	454,700	89	93
Adult females	19,077	8	55,700	11	192

Source: Reprinted from *Bureau of Justice Statistics Bulletin*, Prison and Jail Inmates at Midyear 1996, January 1997, U.S. Department of Justice.

ing decisions while incarcerated. Classification labels also appear to profoundly influence how an inmate is informally "perceived" by both jail staff and other prisoners.

Although litigation was the primary impetus in explicating many of these classification purposes and roles, some correctional administrators had already noted the multifaceted importance of classification as a fundamental management tool for correctional administrators (Fowler and Rans 1982; Brennan 1987b).

Key Questions

In this chapter, several key questions facing correctional administrators are discussed. The aim is to provide correctional administrators with some guidance in deciding whether their current classification is effective, valid, and equitable for their female populations. Currently, from a legal standpoint, a correctional agency may not have separate classification systems for men and women. However, there is a long, unresolved, and controversial history on this topic. By addressing the questions listed below, this document can serve as a guide for jail administrators on whether to modify their current classification practices and procedures.

- Do female prisoners have unique attributes, risk factors, or needs, when compared to males?
- To what extent is a "gender-neutral" classification system inappropriate for the special needs of female inmates?
- Should a correctional institution have a totally different classification system for females?
- Can current "gender-neutral classifications" be adjusted for female inmates?
- What implementation strategies may best guide a correctional institution in designing, validating, and institutionalizing new methods for female classification?

CURRENT CLASSIFICATION PRACTICES IN DETENTION FACILITIES

Detailed technical descriptions of current classification methods in correctional facilities are not given in this chapter because these are available in several other publications (National Institute of Corrections 1994, 1995, 1996; Clear 1988; Brennan 1993). Two basic approaches to objective classification have been dominant in the last decade, i.e., additive points scale and logical decision trees. These approaches are designed to classify both male and female inmates, and in this sense are "gender-neutral." The classification factors incorporated in these approaches consist of simple behavioral and legal factors. These factors are primarily aimed at security and custody risk considerations, and can be easily verified by justice practitioners, e.g., number of prior assaultive felonies, prior escapes or escape attempts, seriousness of current charges, and so on. Several reviews of the predictive validity of these classification factors are available (Clear 1988; Brennan 1987b; Jones 1993). However, almost all of this validation work has been carried out using male-only samples, or samples in which females are dramatically under-represented. In addition to such numerically based classification techniques, the "clinical" approach to classification judgment remains widespread in correctional practice.

Using a Single Classification for both Male and Female Inmates

Most criminal justice detention institutions rely on a single classification system for both male and female detainees. These systems mainly focus on security risk and use identical classification factors for both sexes. Identical needs assessment forms are also used with no modification for female detainees. Some evidence suggests that most correctional staff and administrators appear to prefer a single system for both sexes rather than two separate systems (Nesbitt and Angelo 1984). However, this was based on a single survey, and virtually no recent work has been published to support this preference. From an organizational perspective, a preference for a single system may emerge from several considerations. First, two different systems may create additional work for staff, as well as additional training needs. Second, research efforts to design and validate these systems would be doubled. Third, legal concerns over "disparate treatment" may dissuade administrators from adopting a separate classification system optimized for female detainees.

A widespread problem is that many detention facilities adopt single gender-neutral systems somewhat expediently, without conducting the needed research to examine the validity and "fit" of these systems to their female detainees. Nesbitt (1994) challenges such expediency, arguing that many unvalidated classifications are arbitrarily imposed on women. This expediency clearly violates the standards of practice laid out by the American Correctional Association and the National Institute of Corrections, as well as relying on the arguable assumption that what works for male detainees always generalizes to female detainees. Although there is a serious lack of validation work to establish the saliency and relevance of these security and "risk-based" classification systems for female detainees, the use of a single system for both sexes is the predominant practice nationally.

Introducing Adjustments to Gender-neutral Classifications to Increase their Fit for Female Detainees

Another strategy—mainly found in prisons—is to "adjust" such gender-neutral systems so that they achieve a better "fit" for female detainees (Clements 1984). This is often prompted by a concern that female detainees are overclassified by the single system. In effect, minor changes are made to the scoring or weighting of factors, or the cutting points on the additive scale. The goal is to achieve comparable "disciplinary problem rates" in comparable security levels for males and females. Thus, women detainees classified as medium security should have similar infraction rates as males classified as medium, and so on.

This approach is illustrated by Austin et al. (1993), who adjusted an additive point system used in a state prison system that was suspected of overclassifying females. However, the very low base rate of females for disciplinary behaviors used as outcome criteria were found to be an almost insurmountable problem. Very large percentages of female detainees were found to have no formal disciplinary behaviors (between 80 percent to 90 percent) across all security levels. Such low base rates, coupled with the weak predictive validity of the risk factors used in the gender-neutral system, seriously undermine the attempt to adjust such factors or the cutting points. Because base rates for disciplinary behaviors among female prisoners are much lower than males, the basic problem is the extremely weak predictive validity of these classifications for female detainees. Thus, "adjusting" a nonpredictive system makes little difference—the system is ineffective whether adjusted or not! Austin et al. were aware of this problem, acknowledging that "…changing the instrument…is not likely to gain a marked difference in the outcome." More generally, any risk classification characterized by low predictive validity and low base rates faces this dilemma. The current "gender-neutral classifications" used for risk classification in jails and prisons clearly fall in this category—particularly for female prisoners. Mounting evidence suggests that these systems have very low predictive validity when applied to female prisoners.

Making adjustments to reclassification procedures (which have stronger statistical correlations to disciplinary outcomes) was found to be more successful (Austin et al. 1993). Adjustments to the weights and cutting points actually brought female infraction rates for each security class "…into parity with male prisoners" (Austin et al. 1993, p. 30). This resulted in about 10 percent of female detainees being shifted downwards into minimum or low medium levels when compared to the gender-neutral classification system. The authors concluded that there had been a small amount of over-classification. The final breakdowns for female detainees in this reclassification phase were 56 percent of females in minimum security, 23 percent in medium, 15 percent in high medium, and about 6 percent in maximum.

In conclusion, introducing minor "adjustments" to such gender-neutral classifications seems both unsatisfactory and, perhaps, technically impossible. The weakness of predictive validity for initial classification is a serious problem, because overclassification at this point has a high influence on initial processing, housing, and treatment of female detainees. Poor validity at initial classification—whether adjusted or not—is likely to produce more over-classification than at reclassification (which has slightly higher predictive validity).

PROBLEMS IN CLASSIFYING FEMALE OFFENDERS

Several problems confront an agency when dealing with the classification of female offenders. Administrators must be aware of the implications of each of these issues when deciding which approach to adopt.

Inadequate Research Base on Female Classification

Correctional administrators have very little reliable information to guide their decisions regarding methods for classifying female detainees. A huge gap exists between research on male classification compared to that on female detainees (Burke and Adams 1991). The knowledge gap on female classification is so severe that Nesbitt and Angelo's 1984 conclusion that "…we don't know with accuracy how our classifications are working" applies with almost equal force today. Gendreau et al. (1996) in a recent review noted the regrettable lack of prediction studies of female offenders. Available studies often fail to include females, or do not disaggregate samples to examine the results for females. An additional problem is that the few studies that have examined prediction in female adult offenders (Bonta et al. 1995; Coulson et al. 1996) have not consistently established that the same predictors are found for male recidivisms (see Gendreau et al. 1996). Thus, at least among adult offenders, any generalizations from male to female offenders may be hazardous. In this vein, Jackson and Stearns (1995) comment on the danger of inappropriate generalizations regarding female detainees and ironically refer to the "myth of the universal inmate."

The research gap regarding female classification in correctional agencies is likely to continue for several reasons: inadequate support for research, administrative complacency, inadequate sampling, and so on. Legal action is often the only factor that motivates correctional agencies to undertake research on female samples. Research on classification is also often undermined by a failure to meet appropriate scientific, statistical, and measurement standards. Much available research on classification of female detainees violates design standards for predictive risk assessment research (e.g., sample size, disaggregation of results for females, unreliable instruments, etc.). Reliable findings emerge only when adequate scientific designs and measurement standards are present.

Misplaced Policy Priorities for Classification: The Problems of Male Detainees Remain Dominant

Risk prediction and security concerns remain the central "driving policies" that govern the design of most institutional classifications (Austin et al. 1993). Risk prediction obviously deserves a high priority for male prisoners given their higher violence and risk levels.

However, to extend this same priority to female classification has been criticized as a thoughtless generalization, or a sexist imposition of male priorities (Burke and Adams 1991; Nesbitt and Angelo 1984).

A major concern is that current gender-neutral classifications—which prioritize "risk" and provide only a cursory assessment of needs—are fundamentally misaligned with more basic concerns, purposes, and policies of concern for women inmates. For example, all available statistical evidence suggests that female detainees present much lower levels of risk behaviors while incarcerated, and lower levels of serious and violent offenses when released to the community. Fairness (to female detainees) would seem to require that a classification for women should be designed around policy goals relevant to the concerns, needs, and risk levels of women. If the current policy priorities that drive current classification practices (i.e., risk prediction and security) are not as relevant for women, then a reorientation of institutional policies and purposes that drive classification is urgently needed. A fundamental policy shift that appears to be required for women would reduce the central role of security and risk, and upgrade the priority of needs assessment, treatment, and rehabilitation. For classification to be "equally relevant" for females, it should be driven by policy priorities that more truly reflect the nature and correctional needs of female offenders, as well as addressing the institutional needs for safety, orderliness, and public accountability. If risk prediction and security concerns are less central for females, then current classification systems are arguably focused on inappropriate goals.

The design of any classification system fundamentally depends on its purposes and policy goals. Several alternative goals could replace "risk assessment" as the organizing principle of inmate classification, e.g., safety, treatment, consistency, fairness, least restrictive custody, rehabilitation, reintegration needs, etc. (see Brennan 1987b) A reorientation of purposes or policies would change classification for females to meet different performance criteria and policy goals (e.g., to minimize recidivism, to properly assess acuity demands for cost accounting purposes, and so on). Medical and hospital classification systems provide an alternative model that is focused on acuity and service needs, while at the same time being highly concerned with the overall "safety" of the patient. The current emphasis on a policy goal (i.e., risk) that is arguably less relevant for females, would appear to be unfair and perhaps even legally indefensible. Replacing "risk" as the central purpose of classification for women offenders seems to be supported by four major arguments. First, the weakness of current classification methods to reach even minimal validity in predicting female disciplinary risk underlines the need for an alternative principle for classification, and for risk assessment instruments to cover a broader range of criminogenic and treatment needs. Several studies have reached this conclusion. Alexander and Humphrey (1988), in examining classifications to predict female institutional misconduct, concluded that such prediction is a "formidable barrier" for gender-neutral systems and perhaps a "mission impossible" (see also Clear 1988). Second, current institutional risk classifications have simply failed to find effective risk factors. Third, most of the current risk assessment approaches have downgraded the priority of "needs assessment" to such a degree that these assessments are quite cursory and do not provide a sufficient basis for effective reha-bilitation planning. Fowler (1993), for example, argues that current risk classifications do "nothing positive" to prepare women to return to their community, to be adequate parents, or to develop critical survival skills. The recent emphasis on alternative sanctions, treat-ment, prevention, and post-release support, is consistent with a reorientation of classifica-tion policy toward rehabilitation. Fourth, the absence of systematic research is such that the research community is basically unable to recommend any effective risk factors for risk classifications for women.

Adopting different central principles or policies for classification is fundamentally a po-litical and administrative decision and would require explicit policy directions and new organizational policy goals to be promulgated by senior policy makers. Burke and Adams (1991) and Fowler (1993) have clearly challenged correctional policy makers by suggest-ing that improved classification for women in correctional agencies will not result from advances in "risk" assessment, but by adopting "habilitation" as a new central principle. This would require a dramatically altered design of classification systems to address these habilitation needs.

Lack of Standardization in Approaches to Offender Classification

A problem that plagues classification for both sexes is that, to date, corrections has failed to reach consensus on any standardized procedures for classification. Different cor-rectional organizations are free to choose from widely disparate classification approaches. The result is a patchwork of different systems across regions and institutions. Sometimes, even within a local jurisdiction, different agencies use quite different approaches. This causes tremendous confusion of language, predictions, communication breakdowns, and often an erosion of trust between local agencies. The current situation in corrections is akin to mental health diagnosis about 100 years ago, when a patient's diagnosis mainly depended on which hospital she entered. The resulting chaos became intolerable to the medical profession, and over a hundred years of research eventually culminated in a de-gree of standardization and generalization for diagnosis and classification across different hospitals and regions.

While ongoing litigation and court decisions have resulted in some general legal stand-ards and due process procedures, local correctional administrators have wide latitude in choosing from a diverse array of classification methods, risk factors, goals, validation pro-cedures, and so on. Local culture, politics, values, and the training background of local decision makers basically determine the selection of classification models and practices. There is no consistency of meanings, definitions, procedures, goals, or even of basic terms (e.g., maximum, close, medium, and minimum security) across different correctional orga-nizations and across jurisdictions. It would appear absurd that an offender's classification (and thus housing, treatment, security levels, etc.) may depend more on the agency she enters than on objective features of her behavior, social background, or situation. The cost 'to female (and male) detainees is the inconsistency and poor validity of the classifications imposed by local institutions.

It seems unlikely that in the foreseeable future, the field of corrections will achieve standardized institutional classifications. The implementation and political challenges of achieving standardization across regions or nationally would become even more difficult if separate classifications were mandated for female and male offenders. Thus, unfortunately, criminal justice and correctional agencies, as well the offenders being processed within these institutions, must live with the consequences of nonstandardized classifications (*vis à vis* inconsistent definitions, disparate procedures, communication difficulties, and so on).

Invalid Risk Factors in Current Risk-Based Classifications for Women

Risk-based classifications depend heavily on the predictive validity of the risk factors included in the system. A key deficiency of current risk-based classifications is the very poor predictive validity of their risk factors. This applies to both sexes, but is even more serious in the case of women detainees (Austin et al. 1993; Brennan 1987). Low validity implies high error rates. Current statistical validities are so poor in predicting institutional misconduct that the available risk-based classifications are arguably inapplicable to female detainees in the sense that they fail in their most fundamental task (Austin et al. 1993). Of the various factors used in current security and custody classifications, age alone reaches a modest correlation to disciplinary adjustment, such that younger female inmates have somewhat higher misconduct problems (Alexander and Humphrey 1988). Burke and Adams (1991) and Rans (1984), and others, have claimed that risk prediction simply does not work for females and have called for different approaches (e.g., classification goals, methods, risk factors, etc.). Yet, the lack of research support is such that few new classification models or risk factors have emerged, and very little research is supported or published in this area.

Over-classification: The Problem of False Positive Errors

A serious and recurrent criticism of gender-neutral classifications is that they over-classify female inmates (Nesbitt and Angelo 1984, Chesney-Lind 1992; Burke and Adams 1991). However, only a handful of studies have examined this issue. The available data suggest that a modest amount of overclassification may occur, particularly into medium security levels (Austin et al. 1993). This report concluded that "it is obvious" that some female inmates were being overclassified. They recommended that a larger percentage of women detainees enter into minimum security. A methodological problem, however, is that it is almost impossible to avoid overclassification errors when "risk prediction" is the main goal of classification and when the behavior being predicted has a low base rate (Clear 1988; Brennan 1993). The conjunction of low base rates, poor validity, and predictive intent virtually assures numerous false positive errors (see also Jones 1993).

In the case of female detainees, two additional sources of over-classification may be noted. First, when women are charged with serious violent offenses, they are often accessories and clearly do not have the role of leaders or instigators. Second, female violence often occurs in the context of long-term domestic or romantic relationships. This kind of violence is unlikely to generalize to other situations. Yet, in both of these situations, current gender-neutral systems do not make adjustments to the basic criminal charges or scoring weights, and arguably assign inappropriately high-risk scores to women in such situations. The joint effect of these two factors is that many female detainees receive higher scores than warranted. These two factors appear responsible for practitioners, feelings that many women are over-classified by current risk methods (Burke and Adams 1991).

Excessive Use of Discretionary Overrides when Classifying Females

A related problem stemming directly from low predictive validity is the excessive use of discretionary overrides by classification staff. Discretionary overrides reflect staff disagreement with a risk assessment procedure, and their use of it when they view the formal classification as inappropriate. In effect, staff replace the objective risk method with their own intuitive judgment (Nesbitt 1993; Austin et al. 1993). The high override rates for female inmates when gender-neutral classifications are used reinforces the conclusion that these systems are misaligned with female inmates (Clements 1984; Austin et al. 1993). For example, in Austin's study, the override rate for females was over 40 percent. This is far higher than for males and about double the conventionally acceptable upper level of 20 percent. This imposition of staff judgment, and the concomitant rejection of the gender-neutral risk assessment, underlines the conclusion that these risk systems do not address the key classification issues essential for female inmates and thus misclassify women detainees.

Inadequate Housing and Its Impact on Classification

Moving away from methodological problems, it has often been noted that for an offender classification to be effective, appropriate housing and treatment options must exist in the institution (Fowler and Rans 1982, p.40). Yet, housing and programming options for women detainees are frequently inadequate—particularly in jails that are often designed mainly for males. Housing for women is often given "lower priority" and has been described as a creative afterthought in mixed gender jails. The fundamental problem is that inadequate housing has consequences that progressively undermine the ability of the classification system for women to achieve several of its key goals. Some of these are listed below:

Chaotic and Inappropriate Comingling

A first casualty of inadequate housing for women is that many needed separations become impossible. The comingling that may result from crowded conditions or insufficient housing can undermine most traditional correctional goals, e.g., safety, order, least restrictive custody, and so on. Fowler (1993) has charged that needed separations for violent female detainees, or those with special needs, too often fail to be accommodated, and they are simply comingled with less serious offenders. Nesbitt (1994) similarly has pointed out that the commingling of lifers, mentally retarded, and minor female offenders is "...all too common."

Inappropriate and Excessive Security Provisions for Many Women Offenders

Given the exceedingly low risks of violence, escape, or serious disciplinary infractions when compared to male detainees, the strong physical security arrangements imposed on many women inmates has been challenged as inappropriately excessive and clearly violates the principle of least restrictive custody. Much statistical data suggests that women detainees do not warrant these physically "hard" security arrangements (Austin et al. 1993). Additionally, it appears that psychological damage and needless stigmatization may occur, because high security arrangements send a—not so implicit—message to anyone (e.g., family and friends or other visitors) who interacts with or visits women held in these conditions. Additionally, many have argued that such high security physical arrangements are inappropriate for family visitations. A more valid classification system that rigorously avoids over-classification, coupled with more appropriate physical arrangements, may partially address this problem. Yet, strong security arrangements are the traditional norm in most jails and prisons and continue to be imposed nationwide.

The Breakdown of Institutional Classification: Inconsistency and Space Available Placements

When crowding and inadequate housing coexist, a common occurrence is that institutional classification procedures break down completely, and staff revert to the expediency of "space available" classification, i.e., a new detainee is simply held in whatever cell is available, irrespective of security and custody factors. This situation also typically occurs in institutions that have not yet adopted objective techniques, and who must rely on subjective classification decisions (officer judgment). This approach to classification typically produces highly inconsistent decisions. When coupled with the pressure of crowding, it also degenerates into the chaos of "space available" assignments. Chesney-Lind (1992) similarly comments that much current female classification is chaotic.

Inadequate Program Resources: Access to Treatment, Work, Vocational, and Other Programs

Classification may also be rendered ineffectual if needed programs are unavailable, or where demand exceeds supply. Access to appropriate programs in correctional agencies can be limited by crowding, insufficient program resources, or by a general lack of emphasis on programming (for both sexes). Considerable evidence exists that program participation—for both male and female detainees—often falls far below the level of need, and not all detainees who need a particular program or service have access to the needed programs (Forcier 1995; Austin and Lipsky 1980).

Programs that are particularly needed, or are unique to females, have often been found inadequate to meet the demands. Such program resources include: medical services, substance abuse programs, vocational training, child care, child visitation arrangements, preparation of reentry into the community, access to law libraries, and social survival skills (Morash 1992). Complacency among administrators may be a factor. Morash (1992) suggests that the persistence of such deficits may recur because administrators exert less pressure to meet female needs compared to that of males.

Access to programs can also be restricted by the tendency of risk systems to over-classify women detainees. Being classified into a higher security than warranted often serves limit or deny access to desired programs. Thus, when placed into a higher security placement, a woman detainee may become ineligible, or have severely restricted access to certain programs (e.g., certain work assignments, vocational and educational programs, etc.). Also, access may be limited or denied when the classification underestimates, or fails to record, the real treatment and rehabilitation needs of the women detainees. Fowler (1993) notes that in many instances females are assigned disproportionately into low-level, low-paying, or sexually stereotyped jobs (e.g., food services, cosmetology, cleaning, etc.). Such assignments may be inconsistent with the real rehabilitative and social needs of women detainees and may simply reflect sexist notions. Such practices may be vulnerable to a charge of disparate treatment.

Inadequacy of Current Assessment Systems for Community Placement and Rehabilitation Guidance

As jails and other correctional institutions become more crowded, the need for more informative, broad-based classifications to guide decisionmaking regarding alternatives to incarceration has emerged with a vengeance (Morash 1992). Yet, a glaring weakness of most current institutional classifications—particularly in jails—is the low priority and weak assessment of the social and habilitation needs of both male and female detainees. Most current classifications have little ability to distinguish between females needing secure confinement, and those who are appropriate for various levels of community programs (Chesney-Lind 1992). The inability to provide decision support for placement into community programs, and for the transition from detention to the community, is particularly tragic because reintegration and rehabilitation, as emphasized throughout this book, are especially salient for women offenders. This claim stems directly from their lower threats to public safety and the severity of their needs for social, educational, vocational, and family supports.

A few multiple-factor risk and needs assessments have been developed recently that provide a broader assessment of rehabilitative needs related to treatment planning, rehabilitation, and reintegration (Gendreau et al. 1996; Brennan 1996). Such instruments assess multiple risk and needs factors, they are more complex, and thus require a more in-depth interview than current risk-based classifications. However, they provide a more complete profile of the various social, vocational, family, and other key needs factors that enter the concept of "habilitation."

A Brief Review of Legal Issues

Legal challenges to classification have naturally emerged as a result of the above weaknesses and dissatisfaction with gender-neutral classifications, as well as the resource problems related to classification in general. Additionally, the heightened visibility of the role of classification in driving decisions that govern the welfare and rights of female offenders has also raised legal challenges. Several legal principles are invoked in this litigation, e.g., unequal access, parity concerns, failure to protect, and so on. A major issue is the constitutional right of female inmates to equal protection and equality of access to opportunities. This applies to housing, as well as to all programs including education, vocational, rehabilitation, equal wages, and other privileges. According to federal statutes on equal protection and equal rights, equivalently placed male and female detainees should be given equal opportunity and equivalent programs—in both form and substance. Any procedure or policy that violates this equivalency of access is suspect. Achieving this equality has been an on-going struggle, and Fowler (1993) has noted that years of "arduous litigation" have sought to improve the access of female prisoners to many programs.

A classification system may be vulnerable to legal challenge if it produces decisions that result in women being treated unequally relative to males. A valid and consistent classification system will help ensure equivalency of treatment, consistency, and fair access to services. The validity and reliability of a classification constitute the scientific basis for fairness, equity, and least restrictive custody. However, the validity of any single classification system may be differentially achieved, i.e., a particular classification system may be more valid for males and less valid for females. In this case, women detainees may be poorly served by a particular classification if the decisions based on it are less relevant, less accurate, or less valid for females as compared to males.

Another potential source of inequity, when a correctional agency uses the same classification for both sexes, occurs if differential resources are provided to support the needs of either sex (e.g., the relative adequacy of housing, programs, medical care, and so on). If the services and resources for female classification levels are unequal, then disparate treatment of females may occur relative to males. If an agency fails to assign sufficient resources to meet the legitimate needs of each female classification level, legal vulnerabilities will exist. Unequal treatment of women relative to males will violate constitutional rights to equal protection under the Fourteenth Amendment (Belbot and Del Carmen 1993). Classification that incorporates ethnicity, national origin, sex, and so on, are also currently viewed as legally suspect. Thus, including gender in a correctional classification procedure would make the process vulnerable to legal challenge. The use of an identical classification for both sexes may be legally required to avoid a charge of disparate treatment. However, a conundrum emerges from this requirement. A classification policy that explicitly uses gender may clearly result in "disparate treatment." Yet, equality (for each gender) may actually demand classifications to be "equally" relevant to the specific needs and concerns of each gender. This may require gender-specific classifications that make use of classificatory factors that are "equally relevant" to the needs of each gender. Thus, different selections of classification factors, or weighting of classification factors, may be required to achieve the desired equality of relevance for each sex.

The key question is whether current gender-neutral classifications can achieve the legal requirement of equality if different needs and weightings are required for each sex? The question cannot be answered with confidence because of the lack of research on the issue. The meager research evidence to date suggests that current gender-neutral risk systems are focused on a set of goals that are far less relevant to women offenders, and that they over-classify a modest number of truly lower-risk women inmates into higher levels (Austin et al. 1993). The revision of gender-neutral systems can involve two approaches. First, cutting points can be changed to place more women inmates into minimum custody. Second, scoring formats for violence (for both sexes) may be adjusted by adding categories for being an accessory, or for situational violence in the context of family or other long-term relationships. However, the progressive effect of such adjustments may change a system so much that men and women are eventually being classified by different set of standards and rules. Thus, an "adjusted" risk classification, by systematically placing more females in lower security, may then be vulnerable to accusations of unfair and disparate treatment of males and provoke anti-discrimination statutes.

Basically, if a valid gender-neutral classification for risk assessment cannot be designed to meet statistical and legal requirements, parity and equity may only be reached by separate classification systems that reach "equivalence of relevance" for each gender. This line of argument is consistent with the many calls made for separate classification systems designed explicitly for females (Rans 1984; Burke and Adams 1991). An interesting twist is that some large prison systems have become concerned that *not* having a separate female classification system may expose them to litigation (Austin et al. 1993).

The design of legally defensible classification procedures must also take account of due process rules (Belbot and Del Carmen 1993). Due process rules and procedures apply to male and female inmates equally. This includes requirements that classification methods cannot be arbitrary or capricious that methods be objective, standardized, and validated; that they use relevant classification factors, and satisfy reasonable demands that they be explainable, rational, and coherent. The subjectivity and discretion of traditional approaches to classification have been criticized for inconsistency and a vulnerability to bias and prejudice. In the routine operation of correctional facilities, a number of basic procedural issues have been mandated that would apply equally to classification procedures for both male and female detainees (e.g., written notices, adversarial hearings for certain decisions, rights to appeal classification decisions, etc.). Legal scrutiny has also focused on inadequate implementation of classification, e.g., sloppy and weak supervision, poor training, inadequate review of overrides.

A key requirement is that classification systems be validated and that they use valid (and reliable) risk factors. We assume that this requirement implies that the classification should be equally valid for both sexes. Unfortunately, as noted earlier, many current approaches to classification have never been validated for female detainees, and have been developed and tested only on male samples. Additionally, many of the risk factors used in current systems appear to have very poor predictive validity regarding the institutional behavior of females. In addition to these methodological failings, the implementation of classification for females, as noted earlier, is typically compromised—relative to male classification—by serious resource deficiencies (e.g., inadequacies of housing, programming, and other services). The resulting vulnerability to litigation should motivate correctional agency administrators to pay attention to the integrity of classification procedures for female detainees, as well as implementation deficiencies.

GUIDELINES FOR DESIGNING OBJECTIVE CLASSIFICATION SYSTEMS FOR FEMALE INMATES

The above review has several implications for correctional administrators, treatment providers, or researchers who are involved in designing institutional classification systems for female detainees. The sequence of tasks to design and validate a classification system for female offenders is identical to that required for males. Detailed descriptions of these implementation guidelines are available in several other publications and will not be fully reviewed here (see Burke and Adams 1991; Brennan and Wells 1993; Nesbitt and Argento 1984). In brief, the task sequence is as follows:

Step 1: Obtain Institutional Support and Commitment (Fighting Complacency)

The initiative to build an adequate classification system for women offenders faces an enormous wall of complacency. In prior years, the relatively small numbers of women offenders held in institutions and their relatively low risk were such that many correctional agency managers had no sense of urgency about this issue. With the recent rapid increases in populations of women detainees, the support, buy-in, and commitment from agency management for the development and implementation of upgraded classification systems for women offenders is now critically needed. The design, validation, and implementation of improved classification for women will require resources of time, staff, and management inputs. Complacency, half-hearted commitment, or failure to understand the importance of this project will be fatal. Whether the jail or prison selects a single, gender-neutral system, or a dual system of risk and needs, or two separate systems for males and females, the active commitment and support of top management is essential.

Step 2: Establish a Sufficiently Powerful Implementation Team to Guide the Project

Overcoming the tradition, inertia, and entrenched attitudes of correctional agencies will require that a supportive coalition extends beyond the top manager. In most correctional agencies, a successful transformation of classification techniques—particularly where traditional approaches are being challenged—requires a strong coalition of stakeholders. This often varies between 5 to 15 unit managers of various levels of seniority, as well as line classification staff, treatment providers, and technical support experts. Success in overcoming resistance, and securing needed resources, can be enhanced if a strong committee of change agents and key stakeholders assume leadership for the project. Resistance, skepticism, and inertia are endemic in corrections, and difficult obstacles and roadblocks are bound to emerge. A powerful implementation team is almost a mandatory requirement for success.

Step 3: Clarify and Communicate the Vision, Goals, Purposes, and Performance Requirements of New Classifications for Women

Successful transformation always requires a clear vision of the reasons for making a change, as well as technical performance requirements (Brennan 1987b). The expected benefits of an improved and salient classification for women detainees must be clarified and widely communicated. Also, the deficiencies and vulnerabilities of current classification approaches must also be clearly articulated. Clarifying the performance deficits of current classification methods for female detainees—with input from all the main stakeholders—will help staff and management appreciate the urgency of improving classification for women inmates. Additionally, the legal requirements for valid classification pertinent to women must be communicated. In finalizing the technical design of a new classification for female offenders, the classification purposes, correctional and legal goals, and technical performance requirements represent an important early challenge (Brennan 1993; Brennan and Wells 1992). This design phase must not exclude line classification staff, treatment providers, legal advocates for women offenders, or other key stakeholders. The practical perspective of the "end users" is critical in discovering and clarifying any design flaws or practical constraints during this design process.

Step 4: Finalizing the Technical Design of the New Classification

Three tasks make up the basic technical design of a new classification. These are as follows:

1. *Finalize the correctional goals and central organizing principles or policies of classification for females.* This is a decision for a higher-level policy team and key stakeholders. The implementation team in conjunction with agency leadership must decide whether "risk" will be the central priority of the classification, or whether other organizing principles (e.g., habilitation, acuity, criminal behaviors, reintegration, etc.) should be prioritized. Persuasive arguments have been offered that risk

prediction (for behavioral and disciplinary misconduct) is perhaps an impossible goal for women offenders—at least when using most of the current instruments. Furthermore, if risk is to remain the central "driving" principle of classification, the classification design must comply with conventional technical standards for predictive instruments and reach acceptable levels of predictive validity, reliability. It must also be based on standardized and objective risk factors, appropriate samples, relevant and accurate behavioral outcomes, and sufficient outcome intervals.

2. *Specifying risk and needs factors: Innumerable risk factors may be selected for a new classification approach to women offenders.* The selection depends on the purposes, goals, and the "driving principle" of the classification. Different policy priorities—e.g., public safety risk, institutional risk, rehabilitation—will determine the selection of classification factors in designing a new classification. If the classification is to be reoriented towards needs and rehabilitation, a more diverse selection of risk and needs factors will be required than has traditionally been used in correctional classification (see Clear 1988; Clements 1984; Brennan 1987b; Andrews and Bonta 1994, among others).

3. *Selecting a classification algorithm and scoring format*: A logical or statistical procedure is required to integrate the selected risk factors into a classification decision. This procedure is chosen during the design phase. This technical question is independent of the organizing policy, the goal, or the risk factors. Various statistical or logical methods can be applied to any set of classification factors. In current practice, the choice is usually made between additive point scoring, matrix procedures, or decision trees (Clear 1988; Gottfredson 1987; Brennan 1993). No marked statistical performance differences have been established between linear additive points, regression methods, decision tree methods, and some of the newer methods, such as neural networks. These objective numerical methods are generally consistent with legal requirements of logical coherence, rationality, consistency and reliability, and so on. More advanced statistical techniques have not yet been found to outperform simple additive scales, although an array of innovative statistical and advanced mathematical methods are being developed (Brennan 1993).

Step 5: Pilot Testing and Validation Study

A pilot test is typically conducted on the new "prototype" classification to identify and address any pre-implementation problems not discovered during the design phase, e.g., initial statistical validation, user acceptance, testing the new classification in "natural" conditions, and data problems. A preliminary pilot test will help identify problems in administering new classification forms, data availability problems, and other practical problems. It will also give preliminary data on the statistical percentages of female detainees falling into different custody and needs levels. The new classification can also be evaluated for practical feasibility, ease of use, and its likely acceptance by end users.

A pilot test is thus an integral component of implementation of a new classification and should occur before the classification is promulgated as formal agency policy. Adequate samples of female detainees are required to conduct the statistical validation tests on outcomes and group differences in a defensible and valid manner (Alexander and Austin 1992). Appropriate "behavioral outcomes" must be collected on each detainee to examine the predictive validity of each risk factor and of the overall classification. Outcomes may include the number and kind of disciplinary convictions and charges, program performance, various rehabilitative outcomes, counselor ratings, days in administrative or disciplinary segregation, etc. The "time at risk" must be carefully recorded for all sample members. Acuity measures are currently not typically used in correctional classification outcome studies (i.e., the time, staff, and resources needed by each detainee) but may be useful for correctional planning and resource acquisition studies. It is worthwhile noting that acuity is a "central principle" in many patient classifications developed in the health care system, yet acuity is rarely acknowledged or used in criminal justice as a policy basis for classifying offenders (of either sex).

Step 6: Finalize the Classification System to be Implemented

After the pilot test, the examination of validity data, the management team must accept, reject, or further revise the new classification system. In this task, staff involvement remains critical, and their participation may help consolidate their "buy-in" and acceptance of the new classification.

Step 7: Implementation into Routine Agency Procedures

In this phase, the new classification is implemented into routine agency operations. Implementation into standard operations typically follows the pilot study, the analysis of practical feasibility in "live conditions," and the consideration of feedback from line staff. The preliminary percentages of detainees falling into different custody and needs levels are required to guide any redesign of the housing plans of a detention facility, or assessing planning and resource needs for overall service providers. Preliminary training of all end users of the classification is mandatory before the formal adoption of the new classification.

Step 8: On-Going Evaluation, Monitoring, and Revisions

Managers, end-users, and basically all stakeholders, should undertake continuous performance evaluation, process analysis and revision of a new system. This is particularly important when resistance or complacency is present in an agency, or when a completely new classification is being implemented. A new classification is basically a new "policy experiment," and it is obviously prudent to evaluate whether it is achieving the desired goals.

Sabotage, or the reversion to "business-as-usual," are constant dangers. As an agency gains experience with innovative female classifications, suggestions for further revisions and improvements may emerge from the various users. Periodic evaluations and on-going process monitoring may also suggest revisions to improve a new system. Management, treatment providers, and supervisors must pay attention to the on-going performance of the new classification. Classification systems can progressively evolve over time, as new data, problems, and conditions emerge, and users must be alert to needed changes.

CONCLUSION AND RECOMMENDATIONS

This chapter aims to help managers of correctional agencies, classification directors, treatment providers, and researchers in designing or considering new approaches to classifying female detainees. Various research problems, legal conundrums, and policy issues must be faced. Some of these issues remain unresolved. However, local jails, prisons, and other correctional agencies are faced with the need to conduct classification, make housing decisions, and offer services to female offenders, on a daily, continuous basis. They must classify the offenders who enter their agencies and cannot wait for the above conundrums to be resolved.

A primary general conclusion of this chapter is that most of the current gender-neutral systems are not well aligned with either a policy goal of risk assessment for female detainees, or with the policy goals of needs assessment, treatment, and rehabilitation. In addition to their extremely low predictive validity in regard to security and disciplinary risks, they have a propensity to overclassify some women offenders. The resources needed to properly implement classification for women detainees (housing, programs, visitation, etc.) are often inadequate—particularly in male-dominated jails. We now examine several potential options for solving the above problems.

Option 1: Separate Classification Systems for Male and Female Inmates

This option has the advantage in that it allows the assessment of both risk and needs factors to be optimized for female inmates and to take account of their unique needs. Risk and habilitation factors could be chosen that are more "relevant" for female populations, and there would be less danger of the specific concerns and salient classification factors for women being submerged or dropped when they are combined into much larger male prisoner samples. The use of separate classification systems for females is strongly advocated in several papers (Rans 1984; Burke and Adams 1991). The fundamental position of these reports is that if correctional agencies are serious about adequately addressing the needs and legal rights of female detainees, their classification systems must be as valid for females as they are for males. Achieving equal validity may require the use of additional or different risk factors that are objectively and statistically demonstrated to be salient for females. Additionally, if "risk prediction" is technically impossible, given the very low base rates for women offenders, then we may conclude that this approach may be simply less relevant for females (than males). It thus may be arguably misguided to impose this unworkable goal as the central purpose when classifying female offenders. Other central classification purposes may then be used in designing and testing of new classification systems for women.

The disadvantage of separate classifications for women offenders is that they may be vulnerable to charges of disparate treatment, and of being regarded as a "suspect classification" from a legal viewpoint (Starr 1992). However, if the aim of the separate classification system is to reach "equal relevance" for each sex, then this challenge might be neutralized. In effect, the single, gender-neutral classification itself then becomes a target for charges of "disparate treatment" because these approaches are differentially less "relevant" in addressing the risks or correctional needs of women detainees.

Option 2: Implement a Behaviorally Based Classification

This simple option has the merit of being free of charges of disparate treatment and of having high face validity to correctional practitioners. In this approach, risk prediction is abandoned as the central classification principle, and current behavior is used as the basis for classification. A single classification approach (behavioral rating and observation) is used for both sexes. The detainee's current behavior drives all reclassification and movements across classification levels. Staff observation and reclassification procedures assume a dominant role. In this approach all female detainees would initially enter a medium or minimum level, and systematic and periodic reclassification is used to control subsequent movement across custody levels (Austin et al. 1993). A major disadvantage of this approach is that there may be inappropriate "comingling" of high- and low-risk detainees during the initial period preceding reclassification. In essence, the approach simply waits for those female detainees who are violent, poorly behaved, or highly manipulative to show their true colors. There is no attempt to initially separate according to criminal propensity or seriousness. Thus, a hardened or sophisticated criminal may be mingled freely with first-time arrestees. A further challenge is that this approach places a strong burden on the ability of correctional staff to accurately observe the behavioral patterns of detainees during the period preceding reclassification. Such observational skills are not always present among correctional staff—particularly in overcrowded institutions.

Option 3: Adjusting the Scoring and Weighting Procedures of Gender-Neutral Systems to "Fine-Tune" Them for Female Detainees

This option aims to "adjust or fine-tune" the gender-neutral risk methods that most correctional organizations currently use. This is an expedient option, and it assumes that minor fine-tuning can render such classification instruments equally appropriate for female detainees. The typical aim is to minimize any over-classification of women inmates and ensure equality of base rates of disciplinary problems across the two sexes at each classification level. Thus, women classified as maximum would have about the same base rate for institutional infractions as males similarly classified. As noted earlier, Austin et al. (1993) found that this option is technically difficult for initial classification, but perhaps more feasible at reclassification.

Some basic changes to current gender-neutral systems appear to have merit. First, the scoring format for assaultive offenses could be modified depending on whether the person was an accessory, and whether the violence occurred in the context of a long-term relationship. Each of these forms of violence would be given a lower point score. This change could be equally applicable to both men and women offenders. Second, as attempted by Austin et al. 1993, the decision threshold on a linear additive scale could be adjusted upwards specifically for females, thus placing fewer of them into higher-risk custody levels. The goal of this adjustment is to equalize the base rates for disciplinary problems across the two sexes, because it is well established that females have lower base rates for disciplinary problems in each custody level. A disadvantage of this latter change is whether such adjusted classifications would survive legal challenge because they arguably may produce disparate treatment of male and female detainees.

Option 4: The Use of Criminal Involvement and Sophistication as the Central Organizing Basis (Instead of Risk)

In this option, risk prediction is abandoned as the driving principle of classification and is replaced by a purely descriptive classification that uses history of criminal involvement, antisocial behavior, and perhaps other social history factors, as the basis for classification. This is not a predictive classification, but is purely descriptive and thus less vulnerable to charges that it has no predictive validity. Detainees of both sexes would be classified according to the range, pattern, and seriousness of their criminal behaviors, criminal sophistication, and so on. The use of a descriptive classification has several advantages. It avoids all of the problems associated with risk prediction, i.e., low base rates, weak predictive factors, low predictive validity, false positive errors, and so on. It has the ability to separate violent, hardened, and habitual criminals from first-time offenders and minor offenders. It would minimize the commingling of offenders at different levels of criminal history and sophistication. Initial classification could use this approach and be followed by a "behaviorally based" model of reclassification as described above.

Option 5: Implement a Predictive Classification Using Public Risk (Recidivism) as the Organizing Basis

A variation of the risk approach is to base classification on the prediction of "street recidivism" rather than disciplinary behaviors. Risk remains the organizing principle, but the emphasis is on public risk (recidivism) rather than institutional risk (disciplinary and behavioral problems). This risk of recidivism has a higher base rate and thus generally higher predictive validities than that of institutional risk. Another possible advantage of this approach is that it appears that the risk factors for recidivism are common between males and females (e.g., age at first offense, prior record in the past five years, prior probation past five years, frequent residence changes, unstable job, drug problems, criminal attitudes, family problems) (see Forcier 1995; Alexander and Humphrey 1988; and others). Thus, an identical classification may be feasible for both males and females if public risk is the organizing principle of the classification. However, the findings on the commonality of risk factors may require more research.

However, a major disadvantage of this approach is that the managers and administrators of correctional institutions are generally anxious to implement "internal" classification systems that are explicitly geared to their immediate task of managing detainees while incarcerated in their institutions. This motivation among practitioners is unlikely to diminish, and for this reason the acceptance of public risk as the central principle for correctional institutions appears to be unlikely.

Option 6: Expanded Research to Discover More Powerful Risk Factors for Classifying Female Detainees

Given the dearth of research on female offender classification and the relative lack of knowledge regarding effective risk and classification factors, another longer-term strategy is to support a more aggressive research program to discover effective and valid risk and classification factors for female offenders. This strategy could retain "institutional risk" as the central driving principle of classification or could experiment with other central policies for classification. The use of valid classification factors is a foundation of sound classification for women offenders (Burke and Adams 1991; Rans 1984; Clements 1984). A very large array of potentially useful risk factors could be explored. Yet, the dearth of research on female institutional classification is such that most of these potential risk factors have not been thoroughly studied for female detention populations (e.g., psychological factors, behavioral factors, relationship and social factors, and so on) (see Rans 1984; Andrews and Bonta 1994; Jones 1993). Additionally, theory-driven classification, and complex interaction-based classifications using configuration-seeking statistical methods (Brennan 1993, 1987a) have hardly been examined with female offenders. Thus, several new avenues of research are available. However, systematic research programs on female detainees remain generally unsupported by the major funding agencies. Correctional practitioners thus continue to receive virtually no guidance on this problem. Large correctional facilities, however, may be well placed to conduct such research. They have steadily larger numbers of female detainees, adequate data resources, and appropriate management information systems to support such research. These resources would have to be complemented by the will and commitment of the senior administrators of these institutions to support such research.

Option 7: Prioritize Habilitation and Treatment as the "Central Driving Principle" of Classification and Then Strengthen Implementation

An obvious policy is to reorient classification design so that rehabilitation and needs assessment are given a central role. The problem of disparate or unequal treatment could be avoided by adopting the same strategy for males. The following may be considered:

- *Intensify and broaden classification for rehabilitation.* The rehabilitation and needs assessment components of classification could be strengthened by incorporating a broader coverage of key needs and treatment factors. The historical policy emphasis on risk assessment in many correctional agencies could be complemented by a stronger approach to diagnostic needs and assessment to support treatment, case management, and rehabilitation.

- *Complement the internal classification with new classifications geared to Intermediate sanctions and community corrections.* Female offenders in many instances do not require secure detention. This claim is justified by their low risk of violence, misconduct and escape, and their lower rates of serious and violent crimes. The well-demonstrated needs of female offenders for independent living skills, vocational and educational training, and so on, requires supportive programs to help them survive in their communities. Classification systems geared to decisions for placement in alternative sanctions and rehabilitative programs could be more explicitly designed.

- *Stronger support for medical and mental health care.* The intensity of the needs for medical, mental health, and reproductive problems (pregnancy, prenatal care, etc.) appears to require more specialized and intensive responses. Yet, many correctional agencies—particularly jails—have serious resource deficiencies in these areas. These intense, and possibly unique, needs of female detainees may warrant special attention and resources.

- *Visiting rights and visitation expansion.* The maintenance of ties with children and family cannot be overlooked. Classification decisions may restrict or enhance the provision of visitation privileges. Needless restrictions on visitation—often resulting from overclassification errors—must be minimized. The current risk-based systems are not well aligned with this need of female detainees. An additional recommendation is that detention facilities expand their visitation programs. This would allow the mother and her children more opportunity to maintain their relationship (see Chapter Fifteen for further discussion). Such expansion, and a review of visitation arrangements, is important in detention facilities where inappropriately high physical security, limited housing space for women, and geographical inaccessibility all conspire to undermine the visitation process.

- *A wider range of community options.* A well-designed classification for community placements should ideally be matched by an expanded range of community sanctions (Harlan 1995). These may vary in control and security arrangements, thus representing a "continuum of sanctions."

Option 8: Changes to Facility Design

Correctional institutions that are planning expansion or building new facilities, have the chance to rethink the design of their new facilities. Much new construction occurs without sufficient foresight, particularly to the housing, programming, and visitation needs of female inmates. Thus, architects and planners could be given more specific guidelines on the needs of female detainees. Visitation needs, housing needs, privacy, and special housing must all be incorporated into the design of new facilities.

Option 9: Improved Assessment of Abuse and Victimization

Physical and sexual abuse, and other kinds of victimization, are widespread among female offenders. Thus, the assessment of these problems must be improved for female classification. The psychological consequences of abuse appear to be related to the adjustment of female detainees to incarceration (Quay and Love 1989). Different forms of abuse have been associated with aggression, passive dependent behaviors, and so on. Risk-based classification systems virtually ignore the assessment of such issues. New approaches to female classification could re-examine these issues and explore their relevance for both the internal management of females while incarcerated, as well as for their support and rehabilitation when given community sanctions.

REFERENCES

Alexander, J., and Austin, J. 1992. *Handbook for evaluating objective prison classification systems.* Washington, D.C.: National Institute of Corrections.

Alexander, J., and Humphrey, E. 1988. *Initial security classification guidelines for females.* New York State Department of Correctional Services. Longmont, CO: National Institute of Corrections Information Center.

Andrews, D., and Bonta, J. 1994. *The psychology of criminal conduct.* Cincinnati: Anderson.

Austin, J., et al. 1993. *Women classification study—Indiana Department of Corrections.* San Francisco: National Council on Crime and Delinquency.

Austin, J., and Lipsky, P. 1980. Multi-jail classification study. Washington, D.C.: National Institute of Corrections.

Belbot B., and Del Carmen, R. 1993. Legal issues in classification. In *Classification: A tool for managing today's offenders.* Laurel, MD: American Correctional Association.

Bonta, J., et al. 1995. Predictors of recidivism among incarcerated female offenders. *The Prison Journal* 75: 277—294.

Brennan, T. 1987a. Classification: An overview of selected issues. In *Prediction and classification: Criminal justice decision making,* eds. Gottfredson, D. M., and Tonry, M., 201–248. Chicago: University of Chicago Press.

Brennan, T. 1987b. Classification for control in prisons and jails. In *Prediction and classification: Criminal justice decision making,* eds. Gottfredson, D. M., and Tonry, M., 323–366. Chicago: University of Chicago Press.

Brennan, T. 1993. Risk assessment: An evaluation of statistical classification methods. In *Classification: A tool for managing today's offenders,* 46–70. Laurel, MD: American Correctional Association.

Brennan, T., and Wells, D. 1992. The importance of inmate classification in small jails. *American Jails* May/June: 49–52.

Brennan, T. and Wells, D. 1993. *Guidelines for implementing objective classification systems in jails*. Traverse City, MI: Northpointe Institute for Public Management.

Burke, P., and Adams, L. 1991. *Classification for women offenders in state correctional facilities: A handbook for practitioners*. Washington, D.C.: National Institute of Corrections.

Chesney-Lind, M. 1992. Rethinking women's imprisonment: A critical examination of trends in female incarceration. Unpublished paper. National Institute of Corrections Information Center, Longmont, CO.

Clear, T. 1988. Statistical prediction in corrections. *Research in Corrections*: 1–39.

Clements, C. 1984. *Offender needs assessment: Models and approaches*. Longmont, CO: U.S. Department of Justice, National Institute of Corrections.

Coulson, G., et al. 1996. Predictive utility of the LSI for incarcerated female offenders. *Criminal Justice and Behavior* 23: 95–115.

Forcier, M. 1995. *Massachusetts Department of Correction female offender objective classification: Technical assistance project*. Washington D.C.: National Institute of Corrections.

Fowler, L. T. 1993. What classification for women? In *Classification: A tool for managing today's offenders*. Laurel, MD: American Correctional Association.

Fowler, L. and Rans, L. 1982. Classification design implementation: Technologies and values. In *Classification as a management tool: Theories and models for decision makers*, ed. Fowler, L. College Park, MD: American Correctional Association.

Gendreau, P., et al. 1996. Principles of effective assessment for community corrections. *Federal Probation* 60: 64–70.

Gottfredson, S. 1987. Prediction: An overview of selected methodological issues. In *Prediction and Classification: Criminal justice decision making*, eds., Gottfredson, D. M. and Tonry, M. Chicago: University of Chicago Press.

Harlan, A., ed. 1995. *Choosing correctional options that work: Defining the demand and evaluating the supply*. Newbury Park, CA: Sage Publications

Jackson, P., and Stearns, C. 1995. The myth of the universal inmate: Gender and jails. *American Jails* 33–39.

Jones, P. 1993. Risk prediction in criminal justice. Paper presented at annual conference of the International Association of Residential and Community Alternatives. November, Philadelphia.

Morash, M. 1992. *Identifying effective strategies for managing female offenders*. U.S. Department of Justice. Longmont, CO: National Institute of Corrections Information Center.

National Institute of Corrections, 1994, 1995, 1996. Workbooks for seminars in objective jail classification. Longmont, CO.

Nesbitt, C. 1994. The female offender in the 1990's is getting an overdose of parity. Unpublished paper. National Institute of Corrections Information Center, Longmont CO.

Nesbitt, C., and Angelo, A. 1984. Female classification: An examination of the issues. College Park, MD: American Correctional Association.

Quay, H., and Love, C. 1989. *Behavioral classification for female offenders*. U.S. Department of Justice. Longmont, CO: National Institute of Corrections Information Center.

Rans, L. 1984. Designing an objective classification system for female offenders. In *Female classification: An examination of the issues*, eds. Nesbitt, C., and Argento, A., 54–71. College Park, MD: American Correctional Association.

Starr, P. 1992. Social categories and claims in the liberal state. In *How classification works*, ed. Douglas, M., 154–179. Edinburgh, Scotland: Edinburgh University Press.

Tonry, M. 1987. Prediction and classification: Legal and ethical issues. In *Prediction and classification: Criminal justice decision making*, eds. Gottfredson. D. M., and Tonry, M., 367–413. Chicago: University of Chicago Press.

CHAPTER 9

Mental Health Issues, Treatment, and the Female Offender

Susan Baugh, Susan Bull, and Kathy Cohen

Editor's Notes

The need for improved classification systems for female offenders so that rehabilitation and needs assessment is given a more central role was emphasized in Chapter Eight. Chapter Nine focuses on transitional counseling issues and diagnosis and treatment of the mental health disorders most frequently seen in women offenders. The authors, Baugh, Bull, and Cohen, base their discussion of these mental health issues as they are classified in the revised third edition of the *Diagnostic and Statistical Manual of Mental Disorders* (DSM-III-R 1987), and on their work with women offenders at Atkins House, a residential and out-patient treatment community corrections center in central Pennsylvania. It is important to note here that in Chapter Seven, Weitzman cautions the reader about the indiscriminate use of "diagnostic labels." Specifically, Weitzman refers to the use of such labels as an enormous obstacle in the therapy consulting room. The author does not argue their utility in prescribed circumstances, however. In Chapter Nine, diagnostic labels are particularly useful for

the purpose of delineating the mental health disorders most frequently seen in the women offender population.

Baugh, Bull, and Cohen first discuss substance use disorders, or drug abuse and dependence and alcohol abuse and dependence. These are the most prevalent mental disorders diagnosed among women offenders in recent research studies. Then they discuss personality disorders, specifically borderline personality disorder and antisocial personality disorder, the second most frequently seen mental health disorders diagnosed in women offenders. Next, they discuss the anxiety disorder, post-traumatic stress disorder, the third most prevalent mental health disorder diagnosed in women offenders. Depressive disorder and bipolar disorder, two mood disorders, are also often found in women offenders. Interestingly, they have diagnosed at least 60 percent of the women in the Atkins House program with attention deficit/hyperactivity disorder (ADHD). These disorders and ADHD are also discussed.

From a treatment perspective, women offenders often present with two

205

or more disorders and are labeled dually diagnosed. These dually diagnosed individuals create a dilemma to both correctional personnel and treatment providers alike because they often fall through the human service network, largely because there are no facilities specifically targeted to meet their multiple needs.

The chapter describes both treatment and programming implications related to mental health disorders. It is included in this section of the book rather than the next section, "The Program Perspective," because of the in-depth overview of mental health issues, and emphasis on treatment strategies and considerations. For example, the authors describe the need for a debriefing period for those women offenders not sentenced directly to a community-based setting; women who enter this setting from prison. They contend that the effects of the prison setting are so strong that the prison mentality must be overcome during an intense debriefing period, regardless of the incidence or severity of any substance use disorder, mental health disorder, or ADHD. This debriefing period lasts for at least the first month of programming and is combined with treatment for substance abuse and mental health issues.

Because an important aspect of treatment and rehabilitation of the female offender is the identification and diagnosis of psychiatric disorders that may adversely impact successful adjustment to community living, needs assessment and treatment goal planning are discussed briefly here (Chapter Twelve discusses needs assessment and treatment goal planning in more detail) in the context of the treatment program at Atkins House. The authors also make the case, initially introduced in Chapter Three, that the community-based correctional setting is more effective than institutionalization for treatment and counseling for mental health issues. Specifically, they suggest that community-based programs can offer cooperation between caseworkers and counselors within the agency in determining the individual rehabilitative needs of the woman offender. In addition, cooperation between agency personnel and community resources personnel can offer a wide range of services that the woman offender needs to access in her effort to become a self-supporting, contributing member of the community.

INTRODUCTION

As a group, women offenders have high rates of substance abuse or dependence and have higher rates of mood disorders than women in the general population. Studies of women in prison confirm that treatment for substance use disorders, personality disorders, anxiety disorders, and mood disorders is necessary to reduce recidivism rates (Jordan et al. 1996). A less researched disorder among the criminal population, attention deficit disorder (ADD), may be prevalent among the incarcerated female population (Hodgins 1992). Each of these disorders, substance related, personality, anxiety, mood, and attention deficit disorders, are considered mental health issues in the American Psychiatric Association's *Diagnostic and Statistical Manual of Mental Disorders*, fourth edition (DSM-IV) (1994).

This chapter will focus on transitional counseling issues and diagnosis and treatment of the mental health disorders most frequently seen in the women offender population. Substance use disorders, or drug abuse and dependence and alcohol abuse and dependence, as they are classified in the revised third edition of the *Diagnostic and Statistical Manual of Mental Disorders* (DSM-IIIR 1987), are the most prevalent mental disorders diagnosed among women offenders in recent research studies. Personality disorders, specifically borderline personality disorder and antisocial personality disorder, are the next most frequently seen mental disorders in the woman offender population. The third most prevalent mental health disorder diagnosed in the woman offender is the anxiety disorder, post-traumatic stress disorder. Mood disorders, specifically depressive disorder and bipolar disorders, are often found in women offenders. From a treatment perspective, women offenders often present two or more disorders, and are labeled dually diagnosed (with two concurrent disorders) or comorbid (with more than two concurrent disorders). Research on the prevalence of attention deficit/hyperactivity disorder (ADHD) among the woman offender population has only recently begun. In our work with women offenders at Atkins House, a residential and outpatient treatment community corrections center, we have diagnosed at least 60 percent of the women in our programs with ADHD.

Research in the area of psychiatric disorders has consistently demonstrated that psychiatric disorders are over-represented in the offender population (Scott et al. 1982; Washington and Diamond 1985; Teplin et al. 1996). These studies have shown higher rates of at least some specific psychiatric disorders than are found in the general population, with lifetime rates often reported to be 50 percent or more (Jordan et al. 1982).

Recently, research on psychiatric disorders and the female offender has begun to emerge, providing some insight as to the scope of psychiatric disorders found in the female offender population. In an attempt to gather accurate epidemiological data on psychiatric disorders of incarcerated women, Teplin et al. (1996) conducted a study on 1,272 female arrestees awaiting trial at the Cook County Department of Corrections in Chicago. Over 80 percent of the women studied were found to have had a lifetime psychiatric disorder. The most common lifetime psychiatric disorders were drug abuse or dependence (63.6 percent), alcohol abuse or dependence (32.3 percent) and post-traumatic stress disorder (33.5 percent). Of the personality disorders, only antisocial personality disorder was evaluated in the Teplin et al. (1996) study and was identified in 13.8 percent of the women. In other studies, borderline personality disorder has been reported with the highest frequency in the female offender population (Jordan et al. 1996; Washington and Diamond 1985). Teplin et al. (1996) do not address the reason for not including borderline personality disorder and other personality disorders; however, it appears to be a limitation of the diagnostic interview tool used in the study.

Similar findings of psychiatric disorders among female offenders are reported by Jordon et al. (1996) in their study of 805 women felons entering prison in North Carolina. The study found that about two-thirds (64 percent) of the sample met DSM-IIIR criteria for at least one of the eight disorders assessed. Drug abuse and dependence (44.2 percent), alcohol abuse and dependence (38.6 percent), and borderline personality disorder (28 percent) were the most prevalent lifetime disorders. Lifetime prevalence of other psychiatric disorders includes major depression (13 percent), antisocial personality disorder (11.9 percent), dysthymia (7.1 percent), panic disorder (5.8 percent), and generalized anxiety disorder (2.7 percent).

It is interesting to note that of these two major research papers on psychiatric disorders of the woman offender, Teplin et al. (1996) found post-traumatic stress disorder to be the third most frequent psychiatric disorder among the sample (33.5 percent) and Jordan et al. (1996) found borderline personality disorder to be the third most common psychiatric disorder among the sample (28 percent). In each of the studies, the most common disorders were first, drug abuse and second, alcohol abuse. When comparing the ranking and prevalence of posttraumatic stress disorder and borderline personality disorder in these respective studies, it is also interesting to note that the Teplin et al. (1996) study did not include borderline personality disorder among the disorders evaluated in the sample, and the Jordan et al. (1996) study did not include post-traumatic stress disorder among the disorders evaluated in their sample.

According to the American Psychiatric Association DSMIV (1994), diagnosis of post-traumatic stress disorder requires the person to have been exposed to a traumatic event, while borderline personality disorder has been associated with a childhood history of physical and sexual abuse, neglect, hostile conflict, and early parental loss or separation. It is well documented that physical and sexual abuse are disproportionately common among female offenders (Gilfus 1988; Miller 1986; Bunch et al. 1983). It appears reasonable to assume that if either of these studies had included both posttraumatic stress disorder and borderline personality disorder, a higher proportion of women would have been diagnosed with a psychiatric disorder. It also seems reasonable to assume that given the high incidence of sexual and physical abuse among women offenders, the prison system, with its inherent structure of limiting personal freedom and privacy, would exacerbate the symptomatology and concomitant effects of abuse.

In the general population it has been found that those with an alcoholic disorder are 21 times more likely to have an antisocial personality disorder, 3.9 times more likely to have a drug abuse disorder, 6.2 times more likely to have manic depressive disorder, and 4 times more likely to have schizophrenia than subjects without an alcoholic disorder (Helzer and Pryzbeck 1988). Research examining dually-diagnosed clients in noncorrectional settings suggests that drug abusers have lifetime prevalence rates of depression exceeding 70 percent (Mirin et al. 1988). Regier et al. (1990) report that 64 percent of drug users seeking treatment have a concurrent disorder. In a study of cocaine abusers seeking treatment, 35 percent met the DSM-IIIR criteria for childhood ADHD, and 47 percent met the criteria for antisocial personality disorder (Jordan et al. 1996).

In a study of 100 women admitted to a Pennsylvania forensic center, Strick (1989) suggests "that a large segment of the women in the study suffered with severe and debilitating mental illness, yet, upon discharge, few provisions existed for their proper care and maintenance in jails or within the community" (p. 447). The study also suggests that prevention and other counseling services need to be available to women offenders after their release from prison. Furthermore, a number of women in the study had no knowledge of resources in the communities they were returning to and no available support system to turn to for help in discovering and accessing resources.

Community corrections halfway-house programs can provide women offenders with housing for the transition between prison and independent living. The historical development of halfway houses supports the theoretical assumption that gradual reintegration in the realistic setting of the community is more effective in reducing recidivism than in the prison/rehabilitation ideology (Seiter and Carlson 1977). In addition, these programs can offer support in a job search for the woman and treatment and counseling for mental health issues, or, at the very least, help the woman offender to access community treatment services.

TRANSITIONAL COUNSELING FROM PRISON TO THE COMMUNITY

In our treatment program at Atkins House for women making the transition from prison to the community, we have found that we must deal with the inmate mentality before effective treatment can begin. In prison, women have been treated as if they were children. As Smith and Fried (1974) point out, there is very little personal decision-making allowed in a prison setting. Arbitrary rules and regulations, which may or may not be enforced equitably, determine any activity. Women coming out of prison have been in a socially isolated setting and have been separated from their families and community. Social control, deemed necessary for the smooth operation of a prison, requires that women report any infraction of the rules by other prisoners. Favors and special privileges are earned by women who cooperate with correctional officers. Treatment programs are seen as a method of earning "good time," a means of reducing the time in prison (Allen and Simonsen 1989). In such a counselor-client relationship, little real work on mental health issues can occur. Empowerment is antithetical to the prison setting. The longer the incarceration period, the more difficult it is to empower women and help them develop a sense of self-efficacy and control. When women lack these traits, treatment is less effective (Parsons 1991).

OVERCOMING THE PRISON MENTALITY

Regardless of the incidence or severity of any substance use disorder, personality, anxiety, mood, or ADHD, because of the effects of the prison system, a debriefing period is necessary for all women offenders coming out of prison. Community corrections centers can offer an opportunity for this debriefing period by providing a transition between the prison lifestyle, which allows few chances for decision-making, to a less structured lifestyle, which allows gradual levels of independent decision-making. For all women during the debriefing period, staff members need to stress that rules and regulations are guidelines for living in a community, rather than a means of social control of prisoners in an institution. Counselors can help the woman offender develop good decision-making skills and stress consequences as a reasonable outcome of decisions, rather than as a punishment for rule infractions.

During the debriefing period in some community corrections centers, women are allowed to vent their feelings about their incarceration and separation from families and children. For example, Carmelita,* a woman in her mid-forties came to Atkins House community corrections center directly from a state prison, where she was serving 4 to 10 years for killing her husband. She had suffered 15 years of severe physical abuse from him and had not retaliated until he began physically abusing their three-year-old daughter. She shot him after he beat their daughter while he was drunk.

When Carmelita entered the center, she was diagnosed with dysthymia (i.e., mild depression) as a presenting problem. She had a history of alcohol abuse and joined an area Alcoholics Anonymous group. In addition, she received individual drug and alcohol counseling at the center. In counseling sessions, Carmelita was able to verbalize her anger at a system that she felt had not protected her from her husband's abuse, and that had instead punished her for protecting her child. She was angry at a system that had incarcerated her in an institution that was six hours driving distance away from her daughter and teenage son, who had rejected a college scholarship in order to support himself and his sister while their mother was in jail. In expressing her rage during her counseling sessions— a counseling technique to deal with depression—rather than suppressing it, as she had done in the prison counseling programs, she and her counselor were able to alleviate her depression.

One of the activities most community corrections centers insist on during the debriefing period is the job search. Most women offenders were unemployed or underemployed at the time of incarceration. Employment is usually a condition of release from most community corrections centers and offers not only income, but is a means of enhancing the woman offender's self-esteem and self-efficacy. The work schedule itself becomes a means of structuring and containing daily living activities for women who, in most cases, have never had a healthy life structure.

For women who have substance abuse histories, local support group meetings should be a requirement of the programming and an integral part of the debriefing period. In this way, the woman offender can begin to develop healthy peer group relationships with others in recovery from substance abuse and find emotional support for her own recovery. All women coming into a community corrections center must develop healthy relationships with people in the community if they are to become productive members of society.

In every case, women offenders could benefit from a month-long debriefing period where the focus is on treatment and developing decision-making skills and healthy self-

---

*Names of female offenders have been changed in all examples. Case histories reflect, in most instances, a composite of clients from Atkins House, a community corrections center.

esteem. The emphasis of the debriefing period is usually on finding employment and working at a job. While this adds structure and helps to build self-esteem, the treatment focus becomes secondary to the need for employment. The reality is that most women offenders cannot afford to be without employment and therefore, debriefing activities, including counseling, medical help, and alcohol or drug recovery support group attendance, must coincide with job duties. Often, this means the debriefing period becomes extended from what would normally take one month of intensive counseling to achieve, to three, and, sometimes even four, months.

TREATMENT

Therapeutic treatment, which should begin during the debriefing period, involves a series of interactions between the trained counselor and the woman offender. A voluntary, cooperative relationship between the two participants must be established in order for any healing to take place. With the woman offender, this relationship can take time to develop, but counselors who work with this population understand the necessity of devoting time to the process. "Clients who are forced into treatment likely will view it as a mere exercise in compliance, or a punishment. Unless time and effort are taken to convince them otherwise, treatment will fail" (Rosenhan and Seligman 1989, p. 639).

Connie , a woman in her late twenties, was sentenced to two-and-one-half years to five years in prison for killing her infant son. She was "slow" in school and had been in special education classes. She saw herself as having no importance as a person outside of her ability to have children. At the age of 28, she had given birth to five children. During her trial, there was strong evidence presented that indicated that her youngest son may have been a victim of Sudden Infant Death Syndrome. The jury, though it convicted her of manslaughter, asked for "leniency and treatment" for Connie. Connie maintained that she had not killed her son, even after her conviction.

During her stay in a state prison, her counselors focused on getting her to admit she had murdered her son, rather than dealing with her feelings of loss and grief at the death of her son, who she believed would be given back to her by God, if she was "just good enough." All of her children were placed in adoptive homes during her incarceration, and she did not know where they were.

Connie's prison counselor told her she would not be paroled until she admitted she had killed her son. She served two-and-one-half years in prison before she finally agreed to admit guilt. Four years after she had completed serving her sentence, she was still receiving treatment in the Atkins House counseling program to help her adjust to the reality that she would never see her children again and that her youngest son was no longer alive. Prison counseling programs are often exercises in compliance for many women, and some women, like Connie, see the treatment program as a part of their punishment. Counselors many times must overcome the perception of treatment as punishment before they can establish therapeutic relationships with women who have been incarcerated.

Because of these attitudes of women leaving prison, one of the first steps in community corrections treatment programs for women offenders is to define the expectations of both the counselor and the client. The counselor is responsible for making it clear that the purpose of therapy is to help the client deal with problems and that it takes time and practice to implement what the client learns in therapy. The client needs to understand that the counselor is there to listen and understand the problems and to offer guidance, rather than to issue orders (Hoehn-Saric et al.1964). This approach is in direct opposition to most prison treatment program approaches that focus on adjustment to incarceration (Allen and Simonsen 1989), and therefore, the formerly incarcerated client needs time and assurance to overcome her distrust of the therapeutic situation.

ASSESSMENT AND DIAGNOSIS

An important aspect of treatment and rehabilitation of the female offender is the identification and diagnosis of psychiatric disorders that may adversely impact successful adjustment to community living. Effective treatment begins with effective diagnosis. Needs assessment and treatment goal planning are covered in Chapter Twelve, and will therefore not be covered in this chapter. However, in our treatment program at Atkins House, the assessment may or may not be done by the counselor who is assigned to the woman. In our treatment team meetings, all intake assessments are discussed, and the clinical supervisor determines the counselor who is best suited to work with the client. It is the counselor who completes the psychosocial history with the client and then works with the client to complete a treatment plan. These treatment plans are reviewed by the clinical supervisor, who is also responsible for assuring that the plan is being followed in the counseling sessions. In addition, for clients who are treated through the State Medical Assistance program, the treatment plan must be reviewed and signed by the Atkins House physician.

The counselor and clinical supervisor must determine if treatment involves primarily substance use, personality, anxiety, mood, or ADD issues or two or more of these disorders. All too often, clinicians have been trained either in the mental health field or addiction field. Hence, client evaluation and subsequent treatment planning reflects the training of the clinician, rather than appropriate treatment based on accurate diagnosis of client pathology. With the regular treatment team meetings, we avoid this dilemma at Atkins House.

For example, Ruby, a drug-addicted offender, who began experimental drug usage at 14 years of age, was in and out of juvenile detention centers during her adolescence. During those years she progressed to a cocaine/crack addiction and sold drugs to support her addiction. The courts referred her to a drug and alcohol program for treatment. This began a cycle of drug and alcohol treatments. Ruby had varying lengths of abstinence and several relapses, and was finally incarcerated for selling drugs.

As a condition of her release, Ruby was placed in a community corrections center, Atkins House, which has an in-house counseling program. Ruby's counselor at the center conducted a more in-depth evaluation and diagnosed coexisting conditions of ADHD and a related depression disorder. The treatment goals expanded to include not only drug and alcohol counseling, but education about ADHD issues and help with developing coping skills. In addition, Ruby was referred for a psychiatric evaluation; the physician prescribed psychotropic treatment for ADHD and depression. Ruby successfully completed the center's program and was able to remain abstinent. She could cope with the ADHD and depression with continued medication. Without evaluation of mental health, substance abuse, and learning disorder issues, female offenders like Ruby will not be able to receive appropriate treatment.

Comorbidity (dual diagnosis) of psychiatric disorders—the presence of two or more illnesses in the same person—is an important aspect of diagnosis and treatment. Because research on comorbidity rates of psychiatric disorders among female offenders is severely limited, it is necessary to generalize conclusions from studies of comorbidity rates of psychiatric disorders among the general population. A University of Michigan national comorbidity survey (Noorani 1994), the first of its kind, revealed that 79 percent of lifetime disorders occurred among persons reporting two or more conditions. Therefore, although mental and addictive disorders are easier to study and treat as a unidimensional concept, and all too frequently are treated as such, in reality they often exist together and impact each other. A vast majority of female offenders are likely to have two or more psychiatric disorders. This is an idea suggested by current research findings, which conclude that possibly 80 percent of female offenders have a lifetime psychiatric disorder, and the national comorbidity finding that concludes 79 percent of those with a lifetime disorder will have comorbid disorders.

In examining comorbidity from the mental health perspective, depression has been found to be elevated in people with antisocial personality disorder when they are confined, and their comorbidity of depression and borderline personality disorder is substantial in the incarcerated population (Widiger and Hyler 1989). Consequently, treatment of women in transition from incarceration to the community must focus on depression, as well as treatment for the personality disorders. In addition to mental disorders, many inmates have characteristics indicative of ADD or ADHD that are evidenced through learning disorders (Bell et al. 1983). When assessing mental health, it is important to address current symptoms and the history of symptoms, as well as whether symptoms occurred before, after, or during substance usage. This information is invaluable to the evaluator in diagnosing a comorbid mental illness, attentional disorders, and drug abuse/addiction.

SUBSTANCE USE TREATMENT

Treatment of drug and alcohol abuse, the most common disorder among female offenders, requires a series of steps. The first step is detoxification, which may occur in a medical or nonmedical setting. Often the first time the female offender goes through detoxification is in jail.

For example, Carolyn, a 42-year-old woman, was arrested and convicted of drunken driving. After her second conviction, she was sentenced to a community corrections center for six months. She had detoxed while she was in jail and during that time, a counselor from the center interviewed her. The counselor explained that Carolyn had to make a conscious decision to recover or not recover. Carolyn listed the pros and cons of recovery as opposed to continued alcohol usage, as the counselor asked her to do, and then made a declaration that she had decided to choose recovery.

When Carolyn entered the center, she began intensive counseling, which involved education on the disease concept of addiction and tools for recovery. She was taught and aided in implementing recovery skills, such as developing a support system, utilizing a 12-Step program, identifying, acknowledging, and handling feelings, and cognitive restructuring techniques. During this stage, Carolyn learned to change her thought processes from "I need a drink" to "I need to talk to my sponsor," and she developed the ability to mentally picture herself as functioning clean and sober, rather than as an addict. During the next phase of her recovery, Carolyn learned relapse prevention skills, such as handling a "slip" in recovery, recognizing relapse warning signs, and developing her abstinence plan. Her continuing treatment involved the implementation of her recovery program with the guidance of the counselor.

BORDERLINE PERSONALITY DISORDER

Among female offenders, borderline personality disorder is the second most common disorder. The borderline personality disorder is experienced in the individual most often by her emotions overwhelming her cognitive functioning (thinking). Intense emotional fluctuations are usually present and frequently manifest as extreme anger or depression. Impulsivity is seen in areas such as drug and alcohol usage, sex, eating, and thrill-seeking behavior. Suicide attempts and self-mutilation are common among women with this disorder. Women with borderline personality disorder have extreme difficulty in interpersonal relationships and can be needy and demanding in their interactions with others. Their relationships with others may be characterized by a pattern of vacillating between closeness and distance, idolization and anger, often with an underlying fear of abandonment. Women with this disorder see others in terms of "all or nothing."

A case in point is Denise, a 32-year-old woman offender, who came to Atkins House from the county prison, where she had been sentenced to one year for selling drugs. During her counseling sessions, her counselor diagnosed borderline personality disorder. Her moods vacillated between extreme anger and deep depression. She was constantly demanding that staff members give her hugs, talk with her late into the night, and would call many times during the day from work to talk with her caseworker and counselor. If they were not available, she would ask to talk with other staff members and complain angrily because the caseworker and counselor were not available. She often verbally attacked staff who were unable to be present when she wanted them there. She felt she was not able to function without constant contact with the center's staff, and often expressed extreme anger when her needs were not met immediately, assuming that the staff member hated her.

A psychiatric evaluation confirmed the borderline personality disorder, and Prozac was prescribed to help stabilize Denise's behavior and mood swings. The counselor worked with Denise to help her understand and establish appropriate boundaries and to maintain those boundaries, not only with the counselor, but with the staff. The clinical supervisor gave all of the residential staff a training session on establishing and maintaining appropriate behavioral boundaries with Denise. Less and less structure and more chances for positive decision-making, rather than indulging in impulsive behaviors, gradually helped Denise to overcome the behaviors of her disorder.

A number of researchers feel that the borderline client can best be treated in a long-term, intensive, and highly structured environment, where women can gradually develop independent decision-making skills (Long 1995a, 1995b). Long-term treatment programs in community corrections centers offer such an environment and can help women expand their independence. Long (1995a) identifies the goals of treatment as "decreasing acting out, clearly identifying and working with inappropriate behaviors and feelings, accepting with the patient the magnitude of the therapeutic task, fostering more effective interpersonal relationships, and working with both real and transference relationships." (p. 3)

The most successful and effective psychotherapeutic approach to date has been cognitive behavior therapy, specifically dialectical behavior therapy. Research indicates that Linehan et al.'s (1994) dialectical behavior therapy, which seeks to teach the client how to better take control of his or her life, emotions, and self through self-knowledge, emotion regulation, and cognitive restructuring, is particularly successful. Borderline personality disorder clients have consistently been found to have higher rates of neuropsychological abnormalities than the general population, with preliminary studies indicating a problem with the neurotransmitter, serotonin (Gabbard 1995). Low levels of serotonin appear related to more impulsive and destructive behaviors. Gabbard (1995) states that with further research, selective serotonin reuptake inhibitors like Prozac may produce less impulsivity, less anger, and more stable moods. Both Long (1995a) and Gabbard (1995) indicate that medication should not be used without therapeutic counseling that involves increasing levels of independent decision-making.

ANTISOCIAL PERSONALITY DISORDER

Another common personality disorder among female offenders is antisocial personality disorder. The salient feature of antisocial personality disorder is a pattern of behavior in which the basic rights of others, and/or societal norms or rules, are violated. The pattern is evident in childhood and adolescence with symptoms of conduct disorder, and this pattern continues into adulthood. Women with this disorder may repeatedly engage in illegal activity; disregard the wishes, rights, and feelings of others; are frequently manipulative, conning, and deceitful in order to gain personal profit or pleasure; demonstrate impulsivity manifested by failure to plan ahead, or by making decisions without considering the consequences; tend to be irritable and aggressive and may commit acts of physical assault (e.g., child beating). A characteristic feature of this disorder is a pervasive lack of remorse or guilt for behaviors that have victimized others (American Psychiatric Association, 1994).

Effective treatment for antisocial personality disorder is unsatisfactory, with many researchers indicating that this is a pattern of behavior that seems to limit itself after age 40, and is for the most part unresponsive to treatment (Long 1995b; Longabaugh et al. 1994; Tennet et al. 1993). Women with antisocial personality disorder rarely seek treatment on their own. Court referrals for assessment and treatment are the most common referral source. The antisocial client is not likely to be intrinsically motivated for treatment; however, a counselor may be able to encourage the client to see the benefits that may come to her through making changes in behavior. Threats, which are never a good motivator for change, are particularly harmful in treatment of antisocial personality disorder. It is appropriate to help the client find good reason to work on her problems, if only to work towards release from incarceration or avoidance of future incarceration.

Research indicates that a structured, hierarchical setting may offer the best hope for treatment of antisocial personality disorder (Long, 1995b). While the treatment setting should be structured, the individual with antisocial personality disorder must also be given opportunities to develop healthy decision-making processes. Prisons, with arbitrary rules and little chance for personal decision-making, often exacerbate antisocial behaviors. Community correction centers can offer a structured setting in which every aspect of the woman's life affects, and is affected by, her progress through the program.

Margarita, a 38-year-old woman, was sentenced to one year, eight months to four years in state prison for retail theft. She had 10 prior adult arrests for retail theft, prostitution, and credit card fraud. She had a background of sexual and emotional abuse and had attempted suicide at the age of 16. She was also a heavy crack/cocaine user. Margarita exhibited many of the behaviors associated with antisocial personality disorder, including failure to conform to social norms, repeatedly failing to honor her financial obligations, repeated lying, use of aliases, and conning money out of a large number of people. She was totally without remorse for her behaviors and felt that she, not the people she had stolen from, was the victim.

Margarita's program at Atkins House began with very few privileges and moved through a hierarchy of privileges, with increasing levels of responsibility for personal decision-making. As Margarita moved through the residential and individual counseling program, she acquired self-esteem and awareness of her emotions, and began to develop social, and interpersonal competency. Counseling sessions became times during which she became emotional without exposing herself completely to others. Sharing her feelings in group settings was necessary in the later stages of her treatment, so she was encouraged to join an Atkins House counseling group that focused on spending behaviors and recognition of her victimization of others through her criminal lifestyle.

Long (1995b) suggests that the counselor treating someone with an antisocial personality disorder "faces the challenge of separating control from punishment and separating help and confrontation from social isolation and retribution" (p. 2). A focal point of treatment of the antisocial client is supporting the client in discovering and identifying her feelings and emotions. Unlike treatment with the borderline client, where cognitive restructuring is targeted to dampen emotional lability or instability, work with the antisocial personality woman focuses on connecting feelings, or lack of feelings, with behaviors. As the woman learns to experience various emotions, one of the first emotions she experiences may be depression. The counselor should be supportive and empathetic during this time and reinforce any emotions other than anger. Experiencing intense affect is usually a sign of progress (Long 1995a, 1995b).

The woman with antisocial personality disorder has most probably experienced difficulties with authority figures. The counselor must take care to remain neutral and not engage in arguments and debates about morality or authority. In working with this client, the counselor should avoid telling the client what to do and support the client in exploring alternatives and choices.

Group therapy and self-help groups can be beneficial to the woman with antisocial personality disorder. This therapy has the potential to provide caring, support, and a sense of belonging that these women have most likely not experienced.

POST-TRAUMATIC STRESS DISORDER

According to Teplin et al. (1996), one in three female offenders is likely to suffer from post-traumatic stress disorder. Post-traumatic stress disorder symptoms may be categorized as intrusive symptoms, avoidant symptoms, or symptoms of hyperarousal. Intrusive symptoms may involve flashbacks (sudden emotionally painful memories about the traumatic event), nightmares, and sudden onslaught of emotion such as crying, fear, or anger, with seemingly no cause. Symptoms of avoidance behavior include emotional numbing, avoidance of close emotional ties, avoidance of situations that remind the individual of the traumatic event, and diminished interest in activities. Symptoms of hyperarousal are primarily related to anxiety and include an exaggerated startled reaction, panic attacks, hypervigilance, irritability, and insomnia.

Tieisha, a woman in her late twenties, was paroled to the Atkins House residential program after spending three years in a state prison on drug charges. She had been heavily medicated with antidepressants during her prison term. On admission to the center, which also has an outpatient drug and alcohol treatment center, Tieisha agreed to address her dependence on the prescription drugs she had been taking for over 10 years. She was admitted to a detoxification center and returned to the community corrections center, where she received intensive drug counseling and joined the local Narcotics Anonymous support group. Within two months of her return from the detoxification center, Tieisha experienced panic attacks. She soon began to have flashbacks to her childhood, when her mother brought men into the house who paid the mother for sex with Tieisha. Drugs had served as a means of avoiding the painful memories of her childhood, and without them Tieisha was diagnosed as suffering from post-traumatic stress disorder.

Tieisha began intensive individual counseling at Atkins House to help her cope with the intense emotions, crying, fear, and anger that she experienced after the flashbacks began. The night desk staff often spent hours talking with her when she was unable to sleep. Tieisha's counselor helped her to find ways that she could feel she was gaining control of her life. Her caseworker in the residential program encouraged her to recognize the amount of control she was taking in her employment, her personal relationships, and in her reunification with her two children. She was able to purchase a small house after she graduated from the residential program and regain custody of her two children. She continued her individual counseling sessions to help her deal with the trauma of the sexual abuse, and also began counseling to help her reunite with her sons. As soon as a group for women who have been sexually abused was formed at Atkins House, she joined the group.

Treatment of post-traumatic stress disorder involves providing a safe environment and empowering the woman to re-establish a sense of control in her life. It is important to aid the sufferer to accept the trauma that occurred, while helping her not to be overwhelmed by the recollection. Group therapy can be particularly effective, as group members with similar experiences are able to understand and support each other. Group therapy helps to reduce shame, increase self-esteem, and decrease isolation.

ATTENTION DEFICIT DISORDER

Antisocial personality disorder is often associated with ADD, and this condition, which begins in childhood, can continue through adolescence and into adulthood. There is a link between violence and learning disabilities, and the associated impulsivity can lead to juvenile delinquency (Gordon 1991). Some of the behavioral characteristics exhibited by the learning disabled are hyperactivity, attentional deficits, poor impulse control, low frustration levels, a tendency to be excessively aggressive, and the inability to show empathy (Sikorski 1991).

There are physiological factors that may impede cognitive information processing in the learning disabled, resulting in scholastic underachievement. These factors, together with accompanying social-emotional malfunctioning, form a solid scientific foundation upon which to begin to understand the etiology of deviance and some of the factors that may lead the learning disabled into the criminal justice system.

In our educational system, a dichotomy of attitudes and knowledge exists concerning the learning disabled population. Learning disabled students may have a growing sense of incompetence in an unaccommodating system. Academic underachievement serves to enhance over-arousal characteristics—defensive tendencies emerge and frustrations are externalized through antisocial and aggressive behavior. Deficits in information processing not only impair academic success but also inhibit the ability to properly access verbal and nonverbal communication, as well as other social cues. As the perception of inadequacy deteriorates educational and social functioning in the adolescent, self-esteem also diminishes (Sikorski 1991).

At least 42 percent of adults who are incarcerated have learning disabilities, with 82 percent of this population displaying characteristics associated with specific learning disabilities. In a study of inmates at nine penal institutions, three maximum-security prisons, three medium-security prisons, and three female prisons in the states of Louisiana, Washington, and Pennsylvania, it was discovered that the levels of education are substantially lower among the inmate population than among the general population. The study also documented higher illiteracy levels among the inmate population than among the general population (Bell et al. 1983).

A study by the U.S. Department of Justice in 1979 found that only 36 percent of inmates in state correctional institutions had completed high school. On average, inmates in federal and state prisons had completed nine years in school, but functioned two to three years below their grade level (U.S. General Accounting Office 1980). Additionally, approximately 85 percent of inmates had dropped out of school before 16 years of age (Roberts 1971). These statistics would indicate that there is a large percentage of inmates in our prisons who are learning disabled. Most of the research on treatment for learning disabilities has been conducted on children and on juvenile delinquents. Treatment for the learning disabled adult is often confined to drug therapy (Adler et al. 1995).

In an effort to understand the relationship between learning disabilities and delinquency, Bell et al. (1983) report that the U. S. General Accounting Office released a document in 1977 that states that 51 percent of institutionalized delinquents tested in Virginia and Connecticut were found to display symptoms of secondary learning problems, 25 percent were found to exhibit primary learning disabilities, with only one of this group functioning at expected grade level. Further, it was suggested that 82 percent of inmates with learning disabilities have visual or auditory deficiencies (Bell et al. 1983). The results of this study are consistent with findings of a study performed in a juvenile detention center in San Bernardino, California (Kaseno 1985).

Some learning disorders are the result of inadequate visual functioning. In the vision clinic of San Bernardino County's Juvenile Hall in California, 90 percent of the 1,000 juvenile delinquents tested were significantly deficient in visual tracking, teaming, motor skills, and perception. They were also found to be approximately six years below grade level in reading (Kaseno 1985). Physiological abnormalities associated with learning disorders have been documented through computerized tomography that indicates lateralization differences between the left and right hemispheres of the brain, asymmetry and dominance, cortical lesions, temporal, occipital and parietal lobe dysfunction, and cerebral cortex infolding variations (Schacter and Galaburda 1989; Gordon 1991; Bigler 1992; Affra et al. 1989; Semrud-Clikeman and Hynd 1990; Njiokiktjien et al. 1994).

Deficits in attention span, visual-perceptual functioning, difficulty in learning math, as well as problems in processing information associated with nonverbal communications, may represent right cerebral hemisphere dysfunction. The reading disability, dyslexia, may have coexisting deficits in cognition related to the left hemisphere (Voeller 1991). Lesions on the right hemisphere may result in learning disorders that are reflected in impaired social abilities, depression, visual and spatial relationships, and attention deficits (Denckla 1983). Brain asymmetry associated with learning disorders begins prenatally by factors affecting the growth of the embryo at varying stages of development (Schacter and Galaburda 1986).

Behavioral deficits associated with cortical asymmetry in juveniles have also been studied rather extensively. Aggressive behavior in the learning disabled has been associated with reading disabilities, as well as other socioemotional aspects of being unable to read (Cornwall and Bawden 1992). A study of antisocial behavior and its relationship to ADD found the group of delinquents in the study began life with substantial deficits in motor skills, and that academic failures resulted in antisocial behaviors that persisted and grew worse with time (Moffitt 1990). Bachara (1976) found that the ability to empathize was impaired in the learning disabled, and Bryan (1977) found that learning disabled individuals do not correctly interpret nonverbal communication, resulting in these individuals demonstrating inappropriate behavior.

As social and educational dysfunction increases in the learning disabled, self-esteem decreases, and substance abuse provides an avenue of temporary escape from feelings of frustration and social isolation (USA Educational Services Resource Center on Substance Abuse Prevention and Disability 1991). Acts of violence, driving while intoxicated, public display, and other acts considered inappropriate by criminal justice authorities and society provide the pathway to incarceration for these individuals. Traditionally, penal institutions have not addressed physiological and psychological needs of special populations, including the learning disabled. This point takes on increased significance when one considers that research has demonstrated an increased prevalence of these special populations among the incarcerated population in the United States.

It has been documented that there is a negative impact of learning disabilities, both socially and economically, relative to criminality and incarceration. Fifty percent of the learning disabled population is unemployed on a regular basis, with violent crimes increasing as the subjects' contact with the justice system increase (Bell et al. 1983). Programs that address the needs of offenders with learning disorders have been demonstrated to have had a positive impact. Rates of recidivism and acts of criminality can be reduced (Kaseno 1980).

San Bernardino's Juvenile Hall in California provides a six-month institutional program and a four- to six-month aftercare program and supervision upon release. At this juvenile center, all clients, both boys and girls, are screened for visual deficiencies, auditory impairments, and learning disorders. Therapy for visual impairments, poor tracking convergence, and fine motor skills of visual pathways is treated through sessions with monocular and binocular training, using lenses, prisms, eye-hand coordination, optometric vision therapy, and sports vision techniques. Dyslexic wards are given special training to help them understand and cope with their disabilities. The program is highly structured and focuses on teaching the juveniles to accept responsibility and accountability for personal decisions and consequent behavior. The program involves goal setting, decision-making skill development, values clarification, career education, character education, which helps develop socially productive values, and law-related education. An awareness of the impact to victims of criminal acts is taught through a program whereby the ward personally meets the victim. Vocational training and work experience are offered, together with substance abuse counseling and education. Psychological counseling for conduct disorders is also offered. Compensation for criminal acts is repaid through community service and monetary restitution (Kaseno 1980).

The rewards to society of implementing appropriate rehabilitation programs for those who commit status offenses or crimes are numerous. The San Bernardino Juvenile Hall Program documents recidivism rates for those who participated in the program at 16 percent, while those who did not participate recorded recidivism rates at 45 percent in a 24-month follow-up period. Wards repaid 100 percent of the restitution required by the courts. There were gains in the educational level of program participants, with the reading grade level average increasing from 7.8 to 9.7, and the math grade levels increase was from 8.4 to 10.2 grade level. Pre- and post-testing for victim awareness and sensitivity revealed increases in these levels on the part of the wards, with decreased antisocial attitudes exhibited by those juveniles who participated in the program. There were significant increases in emotional stability, with approximately half of the group obtaining permanent, well-paying jobs in the community (Kaseno 1980). Kaseno advises caution in interpreting these results because the study was conducted with only 45 juveniles. However, the resulting recidivism rates clearly indicate that such a program can work.

Unfortunately, there is little or no treatment available for the adult learning disabled offender. Promising treatment programs, such as the program conducted by Kaseno (1980) at the San Bernadino Juvenile Hall, are rare in adult prisons. Such treatment programs are expensive and do not offer immediate behavior change, as do some drug therapy treatments for the learning disabled, though even drug therapy is rarely used for the adult learning-disabled adult offender (Adler et al. 1995).

For example, Anna, who spent six months in a county jail before she was released to Atkins House, is a case in point. She had been diagnosed as having a substance dependence disorder and antisocial personality disorder. Treatment staff at Atkins House found ample evidence that Anna was learning disabled and had been undiagnosed and untreated for her disability. She was sent to an inpatient treatment center, where the diagnosis was confirmed, and where she was put on medication to relieve the symptoms of her disability. Rather than returning Anna to the community corrections center, her probation officer felt she was doing well enough that she no longer needed a structured living environment. After she left the inpatient treatment center, Anna did well in the community until she stopped taking the medication and began to drink again. She soon found herself back in the county prison for her aggressive behavior while she was drunk. If she had returned to the community corrections center, where the structured environment and the availability of counseling for antisocial personality disorder was available, Anna may have been able to avoid reincarceration.

CONCLUSION

The treatment approach used at Atkins House, which has an on-site treatment program, with Marie, a 34-year-old female offender, offers insight into the numerous problems counselors face in successfully treating the female offender. Marie's involvement in the criminal justice system began when she was arrested at age 12 for truancy and drunkenness and sent to a juvenile detention center. After her release, Marie ran away from home, where she was being sexually abused by her mother's boyfriend. A year later, she was once again returned to the juvenile detention center. Over the next four years, Marie was in and out of detention centers for various crimes, including retail theft of liquor from package stores, simple assault, and burglary. Drug use, starting with alcohol and marijuana, began when Marie was 7 and progressed to an active crack/cocaine addiction by the time she was 15. She had two children by the time she was 19. As an adult, Marie was arrested for prostitution, retail theft, and selling drugs. She was also charged with child neglect. She was finally sentenced to four to six years in a state correctional institution. Her daughter and son were sent to separate foster homes. Marie had repeatedly angered and frustrated correctional officers, county probation officers, and state parole officers and had been labeled as manipulative. As a final attempt to rehabilitate Marie, she was released from a state prison to Atkins House, which was located in the same community where her children were in foster care.

During intake and evaluation at the center, Marie's counselor diagnosed polysubstance dependency and antisocial personality disorder. Marie's treatment plan involved drug and alcohol counseling and a structured program to contain the antisocial personality behaviors. In addition, Marie received counseling to help her develop parenting skills and was eventually able to visit with her children. When Marie completed the program at Atkins House, she had maintained steady employment in the community and was given custody of her children, so that once again she became the sole support for them. She continued with counseling at the community corrections center on an outpatient basis and was able to remain abstinent from drugs and alcohol, maintain employment, where she was promoted several times, and continued to learn parenting skills at a community family counseling center.

Reincarceration rates for adults continue to rise. A lack of community-based treatment programs that address psychological, substance abuse, and learning problems of women offenders only helps to ensure that women who are released from penal institutions will return within a few years. As long as we consider women offenders a commodity to be housed and fed, and use the growing number of women we incarcerate as the basis for continuing to build more institutions, we will continue to fill our prisons with generation after generation of offenders.

Community-based programs that offer supervision, in addition to assessment and treatment for mental health problems, provide better possibilities for rehabilitation than incarceration. These programs can offer cooperation between caseworkers and counselors within the agency in determining the individual rehabilitative needs of the woman offender. In addition, cooperation between agency personnel and community resources personnel can offer a wide range of services that the woman offender needs to access in her effort to become a self-supporting, contributing member of the community. Because offenders live and work in, and interact with, the community in which they and their children live, they are better able to envision themselves as a part of the community. Problems of everyday living, of overcoming substance abuse or dependence, of dealing with mental health issues and of finding and maintaining employment are best addressed with the support of community-based treatment programs. Programs that focus on empowerment of the woman offender and that help her to develop a strong sense of self and personal responsibility offer hope for rehabilitation.

REFERENCES

Adler, L. A., et al. 1995. Open-label trial of Venlafaxine in adults with attention deficit disorder. *Psychopharmocology Bulletin* 34: 785–788.

Affra, S., et al. 1989. Neuropsychological profiles of children with learning disabilities and children with documented brain damage. *Journal of Learning Disabilities* 22: 635–640.

Allen, H. E., and Simonsen, C.E. 1989. *Corrections in America*. New York: Macmillan USA Publishing.

American Psychiatric Association. 1987. *Diagnostic and statistical manual of mental disorders*, 3rd ed., revised. Washington, D.C.: American Psychiatric Association.

American Psychiatric Association. 1994. *Diagnostic and statistical manual of mental disorders*, 4th ed. Washington, D.C.: American Psychiatric Association.

Bachara, G. H. 1976. Empathy in learning disabled children. *Perceptual and Motor Skills* 43:541–542.

Bell, R., et al. 1983. *The nature and prevalence of learning deficiencies among adult inmates*. A study by Lehigh University through Department of Justice grant No. 81–1J-CS-0014. Washington, D.C.: National Institute of Justice.

Bigler, E. D. 1992. The neurobiology and neuropsychology of adult learning disorders. *Journal of Learning Disabilities* 25: 488–506.

Bryan, T. H. 1977. Learning disabled children's comprehension of nonverbal communication. *Journal of Learning Disabilities* 10: 501–506.

Bunch, B. J., et al. 1983. The psychology of violent female offenders: A sex role perspective. *Prison Journal* 63: 66–79.

Cornwall, A., and Bawden, H. N. 1992. Reading disabilities and aggression: A critical review. *Journal of Learning Disabilities* 25: 281–288.

Denckla, M. B. 1983. The neuropsychology of social-emotional learning disability. *Archives of Neurology* 40: 461–462.

Gabbard, G. O. 1995. Researchers study causes and treatment of borderline personality disorder. *The Menninger Letter* 5: 1–2.

Gilfus, M. E. 1988. Seasoned by violence/tempered by love: A qualitative study of women and crime. PhD diss., Waltham, MA: Brandeis University.

Gordon, N. 1991. Specific learning disorders: The possible role of brain damage. *Brain Development* 13: 143–147.

Helzer, J. E., and Pryzbeck, T. R. 1988. The co-occurrence of alcoholism with other psychiatric disorder in the general population and its impact on treatment. *Journal of Studies on Alcohol* 49: 219–224.

Hodgins, S. 1992. Mental disorder, intellectual deficiency, and crime: Evidence from a birth cohort. *Archives of General Psychiatry* 49: 476–483.

Hoehn-Saric, R., et al. 1964. Systematic preparation of patients for psychotherapy I. Effects on therapy behavior and outcome. *Journal of Psychiatric Research* 2: 267–281.

Jordan, B. K., et al. 1996. Prevalence of psychiatric disorders among incarcerated women I. Pretrial jail detainees. *Archives of General Psychiatry* 53: 505–512.

Kaseno, S. A. 1985. Developing problem-solving skills. *Academic Therapy* 21: 99–104.

Kaseno, S. A. 1980. Treatment program for vision and learning disabilities among juvenile offenders. Funding provided by the Office of Criminal Justice Planning, State of California. Award No. TO 11. Regional Young Educational Facility: The Second Evaluation of a Short-term Intensive Program for Juvenile Court Wards from San Bernardino and Riverside Counties. Youth Authority Program Research and Review Division, February 1989.

Linehan, M. M., et al. 1994. Interpersonal outcome of cognitive behavioral treatment for chronically suicidal borderline patients. *American Journal of Psychiatry* 151: 1771–1776.

Long, P. W. 1995a. Borderline personality disorder treatment. Internet mental health. http://www.mentalhealth.com. 1/19/97 access date.

Long, P. W. 1995b. Antisocial personality disorder treatment. Internet mental health. http://www.mentalhealth.com. 1/19/97 access date.

Longabaugh, R., et al. 1994. Drinking outcomes of alcohol abusers diagnosed as antisocial personality disorder. *Alcoholism Clinical and Experimental Research* 18: 778–785.

Miller, E. M. 1986. *Street women*. Philadelphia: Temple University Press.

Mirin, S. M., et al. 1988. Psychopathology in substance abusers: Diagnosis and treatment. *American Journal of Drug and Alcohol Abuse* 14: 139–157.

Moffitt, T. E. 1990. Juvenile delinquency and attention deficit disorder: Boys' developmental trajectories from age 3 to age 15. *Child Development* 61: 893–910.

Noorani, R. 1994. Lifetime and 12-month prevalence of DSM III-R psychiatric disorders in the United States: Results from the national comorbidity survey. *Archives of General Psychiatry* 51: 8–19. http:\\psy.utmd.edu\disorder\mood\epidem\kessler.htm. 1/19/97 access date.

Njiokiktjien, C., et al. 1994. Callosal size in children with learning disabilities. *Behavioral Brain Research* 64: 213–218.

Parsons, R. 1991. Empowerment: Purpose and practice principle in social work. *Social Work with Groups* 12: 7–21.

Regier, D. A., et al. 1990. Comorbidity of mental disorders with alcohol and other drug abuse: Results from the epidemiologic catchment area study. *Journal of American Medical Association* 264: 2511–2518.

Roberts, A. R. 1971. *Sourcebook on prison education: Past, present, future*. Springfield, IL: Charles C Thomas.

Rosenhan, D. L., and Seligman, M. E. P. 1989. *Abnormal psychology*, 2nd ed. New York: W. W. Norton & Company.

Schacter, S., and Galaburda, A. 1986. Development and biological associations of cerebral dominance: Review and possible mechanisms. *Journal of American Academy of Child Psychology* 25: 741–750.

Scott, N. A., et al. 1982. Assessment of depression among incarcerated females. *Journal of Personality Assessment* 46: 371–379.

Seiter, R. P., and Carlson, E. 1977. Residential inmate aftercare: The state of the art. *Offender Rehabilitation* 1 (4): 381–394.

Semrud-Clikeman, M., and Hynd, G. W. 1990. Right hemispheric dysfunction in nonverbal learning disabilities: Social, academic, and adaptive functioning in adults and children. *Psychological Bulletin* 107: 196–209.

Sikorski, J. B. 1991. Learning disorders and the juvenile justice system. *Psychiatric Annals* 21: 743–747.

Smith J., and Fried, W. 1974. *The uses of the American prison: Political theory and penal practice*. Lexington, MA: Lexington Books.

Strick, S. E. 1989. A demographic study of 100 admissions to a female forensic center: Incidences of multiple charges and multiple diagnoses. *Journal of Psychiatry and Law* Fall: 435–448.

Tennet, G., et al. 1993. Is psychopathic disorder a treatable condition? *Medicine, Science and the Law* 33: 63–66.

Teplin, L. A., et al. 1996. Prevalence of psychiatric disorders among incarcerated women II. Convicted felons entering prison. *Archive of General Psychiatry* 53: 513–519.

USA Educational Services. Resource Center on Substance Abuse Prevention and Disability. 1991. *An overview of alcohol and other drug abuse prevention and disability.* Washington, DC.

U.S. Department of Justice. 1979. *Profile of state prison inmates: Sociodemographic findings from the 1974 survey of inmates of state correctional facilities.* Special report SD-NDS-SR-4. Washington, D.C.: Government Printing Office.

U.S. General Accounting Office. 1980. *Community-based correctional program can do more to help offenders.* Report to the Congress of the United States, GGD-80-25. Washington, D.C.

Voeller, K. S. 1991. Social-emotional learning disabilities. *Psychiatric Annals* 21: 735–741.

Washington, P., and Diamond, R. J. 1985. Prevalence of mental illness among women incarcerated in five California county jails. *Research in Community and Mental Health* 5: 83–41.

Widiger, T. A., and Hyler, S. E. 1989. Axis I Axis II interactions. In *Psychiatry,* eds. Michels, R., et al. Philadelphia: J. B. Lippincott Co.

CHAPTER 10

Female Offenders and Childhood Maltreatment: Understanding the Connections

Joyce Dougherty

Editor's Notes

At this time there is no definitive causal link between child abuse and female crime and delinquency, particularly because many victims of child abuse do not go on to commit delinquent and/or criminal acts. Yet, treatment providers working with female offenders are well aware of the fact that the vast majority of the female offenders they work with have a long history of often severe child abuse. Dougherty, the author of Chapter Ten, explores childhood maltreatment issues with respect to female offenders in depth. The chapter begins with an overview of the various types of childhood maltreatment—physical abuse, sexual abuse, emotional abuse, and neglect—and an examination of the prevalence of violence against children, particularly female children, in the United States today. Dougherty then puts those numbers into perspective by looking at the degree to which all types of child abuse typically go unreported. Next, Dougherty gives a critique of the research on the connections between childhood maltreatment and female criminality and provides suggestions regarding ways that treatment providers can find and interpret the messages of childhood maltreatment that are hidden in the official records of female offenders. Treatment providers must often read between the lines of official records where often there is no official record of maltreatment. The implications of reading between the lines means that treatment providers must be sensitive to the short- and long-term psychological, behavioral, and emotional effects of childhood maltreatment. This is a difficult challenge as far as resocialization efforts are concerned because, as alluded to earlier, clients often remain silent, most often due to the normalization of their abuse. This challenge necessitates that treatment providers explore the developmental environments within which these women and girls learned about physical, sexual, and emotional violence *before* commencing a deliberate process of resocialization.

INTRODUCTION

Many treatment providers who work with female offenders are well aware the vast majority of their clients have a long history of often severe childhood maltreatment. For some time now, researchers have theorized about the nature of the relationship between childhood maltreatment and criminality. Most agree that definitive evidence of a causal link between child abuse and adult crime and/or juvenile delinquency has yet to be found. There is, however, still some controversy regarding the significance of the link between childhood maltreatment and female offending. That fact notwithstanding, finding an effective way to deal with the impact childhood maltreatment has had in their lives often marks a critical step in the rehabilitation of female offenders. The aim of this chapter is to unravel some of the complexities of the phenomenon, and clarify the challenges that may be confronted by treatment providers who work with these women and girls.

The first section of this chapter begins with a review of the various types of childhood maltreatment, and an examination of the prevalence of violence against children, particularly female children, in the United States today. The second section then puts those numbers into perspective by looking at the degree to which all types of child abuse typically go unreported. The chapter continues with a section that attempts to make some sense of what researchers are saying about the connections between childhood maltreatment and female criminality. The next section suggests ways to find messages of childhood maltreatment hidden in the official records of so many female offenders. It also suggests how treatment providers can best understand the silence of these females about their victimization as children. The chapter concludes with a look at the challenges confronting treatment providers whose clients have normalized the violence in their lives.

THE NATURE AND PREVALENCE OF CHILDHOOD MALTREATMENT: AN EPIDEMIC OF VIOLENCE

Violence against children generally falls into four categories of maltreatment: physical abuse, sexual abuse, emotional abuse, and neglect. Typically, working definitions of physical abuse are limited to "nonaccidental, intentional injury inflicted on a child by a parent or a caregiver responsible for the child's health and welfare" (Utech 1994, p. 52). Sexual abuse commonly is defined as a sexual act forced, by a child, an adolescent, or an adult upon a child who lacks the emotional, maturational, and cognitive development needed to fully understand the experience (Sgroi 1982, p. 9). Sexual abuse usually includes incest. According to Sgroi (1982):

> Incestuous child sexual abuse encompasses any form of sexual activity between a child and a parent or stepparent or extended family member…or surrogate parent figure (for example, common-law spouse or foster parent). (p. 10)

Definitions of emotional abuse typically suggest a persistent pattern of behavior or a chronic attitude on the part of a parent or caretaker that is detrimental to, or prevents the development of, a child's positive self-image (Utech 1994, pp. 67–69). While the assaultive behavior or attitude characterizing emotional abuse is often verbal in nature (name calling, derogatory remarks, constant yelling, blaming, or scapegoating), emotional maltreatment of one kind or another almost always accompanies incidents of physical and sexual abuse (Weisz 1995, pp. 82, 88).

Child neglect generally is defined as occurring when a parent or caretaker deliberately fails to provide for basic needs that have been designated as critical to a child's physical, intellectual, and/or emotional development (Utech 1994, p. 70). Subcategories of neglect usually include physical neglect, medical neglect, educational neglect, and emotional neglect (Knudsen 1992, pp. 136–140).

Estimates of the prevalence of all types of childhood maltreatment in the United States today suggest the problem is indeed epidemic. The National Committee to Prevent Child Abuse found that in 1995 over 3.1 million children were reported to Child Protective Services as *alleged* victims of maltreatment. What this means is that in 1995, 46 out of every 1,000 American children under the age of 18 were reported as victims of some form of maltreatment. Of the more than 3.1 million official reports of alleged maltreatment, approximately 1 million ended up substantiated. The number of substantiated cases has remained constant since 1992 (Kelley et al. 1997, p. 2).

One poll found 25 million Americans—approximately 15 percent of the adult population—reported they knew of a child they suspected was being maltreated (Sagatun and Edwards 1995, p. 4). On average 25 percent to 27 percent of all reports of childhood maltreatment nationwide involve physical abuse (Kelley et al. 1997, p. 2; Myers 1994, p. 64). Edwards (1996) notes each year a *minimum* of 1.7 million children are physically assaulted by their parents or caretakers, and 5.4 million more are hit with objects (p. 995). Every year physical abuse seriously injures approximately 141,700 infants and children, and permanently disables 18,000 children (Edwards 1996, p. 1021). Fatalities among children, particularly among children under the age of five, as a direct result of physical abuse have been characterized as "tragically common and getting worse" (Myers 1994, p. 64). According to the survey by the National Committee to Prevent Child Abuse:

> During the past 10 years, more than three children died each day as a result of parental maltreatment...[Physical] abuse is the most common cause of death (48 percent), followed by [physical] neglect (37 percent) and a combination of [physical] abuse and neglect (15 percent)...The majority of victims (85 percent) are under the age of 5, and nearly half (45 percent) of the victims never reach their first birthday. (Kelley et al. 1997, p. 2)

In 1978, Gelles concluded male children are more likely to be the victims of physical abuse than are female children. However, Utech (1994) stresses that while male children are more likely to be "pushed, shoved, grabbed, slapped, or spanked" than are female children, in all other tactics of physical abuse there are no significant differences between males and females (p. 58). When it comes to physical abuse, Utech concludes, "children of all ages and both genders are subject to the violent behavior perpetrated by parents or care-takers in their homes" (1994, p. 59). In the state of Pennsylvania in 1996, 61 percent of the substantiated cases of physical abuse involved girls (Pennsylvania Department of Public Welfare 1996, p. 4).

When it comes to sexual abuse, there is little doubt that female children are far more likely to be victimized than are male children. In early studies that focused exclusively on the experiences of females (Russell 1983; Wyatt 1985), researchers found 54 percent to 62 percent of the women surveyed reported having been sexually abused before the age of 18. Faller (1990, p. 19) noted that 38 percent to 45 percent reported having been subjected to "sexual contact." While overall about one-third of all females will have been sexually abused before the age of 18, only one-sixth of all males will have suffered similar maltreatment (Weisz 1995, p. 53). In the state of Pennsylvania in 1996, 78 percent of the substanti-ated cases of child sexual abuse involved girls (Pennsylvania Department of Public Welfare 1996, p. 4). The sexual abuse of girls tends to start earlier than that of boys (Chesney-Lind 1997, p. 25), at a median age of 9.6 years (Myers 1994, p. 65). Girls are also more likely than boys to be assaulted by a family member and, as a result, the duration of their abuse is longer (Chesney-Lind 1997, p. 25). The fact is the vast majority of incest perpetrators are male and the vast majority of incest victims are female, "boys are rarely molested by their parents" (Herman 1981, p. 10).

A lack of precise social science as well as legal definitions of emotional abuse, combined with the subjective nature of the phenomenon itself, make it especially difficult to calculate accurately the prevalence of this type of violence against children. Relying solely on statis-tics based on cases of emotional abuse that are officially reported and/or adjudicated, it is easy to conclude the problem is *not* a widespread one (Utech 1994, p. 69). Weisz (1995) suggests of the 3 million or so reported cases of all types of childhood maltreatment in the United States every year, just under 13 percent of them involve emotional abuse or neglect (p. 82). Of all of the various types of maltreatment that are subject to official measurement, neglect, particularly physical neglect, appears to be the most prevalent. According to Utech (1994): "The number of child neglect reports…far exceed the combined percentages of other kinds of child maltreatment….it appears that neglect is proportionately more com-mon in the total number of cases of maltreatment than physical and sexual abuse" (pp. 70, 73). According to the National Committee to Prevent Child Abuse, of the substantiated reports of maltreatment in 1995, 54 percent involved neglect, 25 percent involved physical abuse, 11 percent involved sexual abuse, and only 3 percent involved emotional abuse (Kelley et al. 1997, p. 2). Supporting the conclusion that rates of physical neglect far exceed rates of all other types of maltreatment, a study of children placed in foster care found that 67 percent of all children had been removed from their homes because of neglect (Weisz 1995, p. 98). This same study showed that only 17 percent had been removed because of physical abuse and 11 percent for sexual abuse.

All of these numbers estimating the prevalence of the various types of childhood mal-treatment, however, can be very deceptive. They may or *may not* mean, for instance, there is more neglect going on than there is any other type of childhood maltreatment, and/or that there is relatively little emotional abuse occurring. What they may mean is cases of neglect, particularly physical neglect, are more likely to be detected, reported, and officially substantiated than are cases involving any other type of violence against children, particularly emotional abuse.

THE PROBLEM OF UNREPORTED CHILDHOOD MALTREATMENT

In spite of the adoption of mandatory reporting laws in many states, it is not unusual to find that all types of childhood maltreatment still go officially unreported. Myers (1994) suggests most physical abuse escapes official detection, and, therefore, no one can know with any degree of certainty how many children are actually being battered at any given time. Based on the findings of a 1996 Gallop poll, Edwards (1996) concludes the amount of physical abuse and corporal punishment in the United States today "is actually several times greater than what official reports indicate" (p. 984). Even the official listing of child deaths as a direct result of physical abuse are notoriously inaccurate, which makes the official numbers—61 in 1995 in the state of Pennsylvania alone—(Pennsylvania Department of Public Welfare 1996, p. 4) especially disturbing. Berman (1997) reports of the approximately 3,500 cases of children who have been officially listed as having died from SIDS (Sudden Infant Death Syndrome) every year, 2 percent of them are actually victims of physical abuse (p. A9). In cases where there is confusion over the cause of a child's death, part of the problem seems to lie with the official investigation. According to one police chief, "if you don't do a complete and thorough death scene investigation coupled with an autopsy, then the cause [of a child's death] is pure speculation" (Berman 1997, p. A9). Beyond that, the fact is many police officers are not properly trained to investigate the unique circumstances that accompany the deaths of infants in particular.

When it comes to explaining the official underestimates of nonlethal physical child abuse, another problem is with state laws that give parents and caretakers the leeway to use "reasonable" physical force to discipline children. According to Edwards (1996), all 50 states permit the use of corporal punishment to discipline children, either statutorily or through specific court decisions (p. 984). In deference to traditional child rearing practices, state laws routinely tell parents they need not "spareth the rod" when disciplining their children. The acceptance of the use of some degree of physical violence against children is indeed widespread in American society. More than 90 percent of all parent and/or caretakers in the United States today report they have used some form of corporal punishment against children of all ages at one time or another (Edwards 1996, p. 984; Myers 1994, p. 64). In 1991, Straus found 84 percent of American parents said they believed a "good hard spanking is sometimes necessary" to control their children (p. 133). Research indicates when children (particularly adolescents) are hit, it is rarely an isolated event, but rather an event that occurs quite frequently. Laws that are supposed to have been written to protect children, then, actually facilitate the routine use of this kind of violence against them by defining as acceptable the use of a "reasonable" amount of physical force.

Beyond the way laws are written, another problem when it comes to explaining the official underestimates of physical abuse, is how such laws are actually put into practice. Many unsubstantiated—thus officially uncounted—cases of physical abuse can be traced directly to how investigators routinely interpret the ambiguous boundaries of the laws. Determining whether the force a parent or caretaker has used against a child is "reasonable," in other words, deciding whether a child has been disciplined or physically abused under the law, frequently depends upon decidedly subjective criteria. In Pennsylvania, for example, the Child Protective Services Law defines "serious physical injury" as abusive. In order to fall within the parameters of legally unacceptable—"unreasonable"—physical force, a child's injury must either have caused "severe pain," have impaired a child's physical functioning (temporarily or permanently), or have been accompanied by "physical evidence of a continuous pattern of separate, unexplained injuries" (Pennsylvania Protective Services Law, section 3.4, p. 9).

One salient question with which investigators of suspected physical abuse in Pennsylvania must routinely grapple is: How can something as subjective as severe pain be objectively determined? In practice, many Child Protective Services investigators in Pennsylvania find themselves having to rely upon relatively unreliable standards like time. If a child reports he or she was in pain for 45 to 60 minutes after being struck, then the pain can be defined as "severe" and the physical injury "serious." However, if a child's word is not deemed credible by an investigator, or if a child is simply too young to comprehend the concept of time, then what? Under those circumstances, an investigator must rely completely on a physician to make the determination as to whether or not an injury caused a child severe pain. In fact, even in cases where an investigator deems a child's word to be credible, lack of a physician's verification as to the severity of pain, in the absence of impairment or evidence of a pattern of unexplained injuries, will weaken the investigator's case if it ends up in court. Thus, in practice, a doctor's assessment of *any* physical injury an investigator believes constitutes abuse becomes crucial. The problem occurs when a physician who examines a child with bruises or welts that were obviously made by a belt or wire may easily conclude, in his or her professional judgment, the injury is not serious enough to have caused severe pain. In the atmosphere of an emergency room, where the treatment of life threatening injuries has become routine, the pain caused by the kinds of bruises and welts left on a child by a parent's thrashing of a belt or wire may be determined to be relatively insignificant—certainly not "severe"—even when the child reports it as such.

It is not surprising, then, that a majority of the reported cases of physical abuse are routinely dismissed. As Weisz (1995) observes, every year "about 60 percent of the families investigated are subjects of unfounded reports [of physical abuse].... Of the substantiated reports, fewer still were brought to court and adjudicated to constitute neglect or abuse" (p. 37). In the cases of physical abuse reported by female offenders, this problem is especially troublesome. One study of girls in juvenile correctional settings found 61.2 percent of them reported they had experienced some form of physical abuse, and nearly half of those girls reported they experienced the violence routinely—11 times or more (Chesney-Lind 1997, p. 26). Many of the girls also told researchers they *had* reported the abuse, but of those girls, over 55 percent of them said after reporting it, *officials did nothing* and many said after that, the abuse got worse (Chesney-Lind 1997, p. 26).

Clearly, state laws—in theory and in practice—not only have failed to protect children against physical violence, they have condoned it. Even beyond the way the laws themselves are written and the ways that child protective service investigators put those laws into practice, there is evidence state and local law enforcement officials—specifically prosecutors—are reluctant to act in cases of suspected physical child abuse. Despite the fact statistics consistently show a significantly higher incidence of physical neglect and abuse than of child sexual abuse, a 1993 study found 91 percent of the attorneys interviewed prosecuted *fewer* physical abuse than sexual abuse cases. Eighty percent of them actually reported that they prosecuted "substantially" fewer physical abuse cases (Smith 1995, p. 1).

Determining the precise extent of sexual violence against children is particularly challenging because, as Myers (1994) notes, most cases of child sexual abuse are not reported when they happen and many are never disclosed at all (p. 65). That, of course, means these cases are never included among the officially counted cases of child sexual abuse. Faller (1990) points out the lack of disclosure in cases of sexual abuse is due in part to the fact that it is "a phenomenon that occurs in secrecy, surrounded by shame...[that] usually leaves no physical traces" (p. 16). The reporting of sexual abuse also is complicated by the variability of the contexts within which children, especially girls, are abused. Faller (1990) suggests the degree of proximity in the relationship between an offender and a victim can have a direct impact on the probability the abuse will be reported. The closer the relationship between the offender and the victim, as is the case with most female victims of child sexual abuse, the more likely it is the abuser will be concerned about the impact of disclosure. In such cases, the abuser will be more likely to use whatever means necessary to prevent the victim from reporting. While the more relationally proximate abuser initially may use psychological manipulation to engage a girl in sexual activity, when it comes to keeping her quiet about the abuse he may resort to threats of bodily harm to the victim, to other family members, or even to pets (Faller 1990, pp. 50–51). Out of sheer terror, many girls who are being sexually abused do remain silent. Those who do break their silence often find little solace. A daughter who discloses may find herself confronted by a mother who not only refuses to believe her, but actually defends the abuser and lashes out at her for lying. She also may find herself rejected by other family members who blame her for having the abuser arrested or ordered out of the home. If authorities decide to permit the abuser to stay in the home, she may find herself forced to leave, possibly even placed in foster care, essentially banished from her family for telling the truth about the abuse. It is not surprising, given the consequences, that in the rare cases when girls in proximate relationships with their abusers do disclose, they often recant their stories. Such cases, then, are counted among the officially *unsubstantiated* cases of child sexual abuse. Adult incidence studies have revealed less than half of adults who were sexually abused as children ever disclosed the abuse, and of those who did only one in five ever came to the attention of officials (Salter 1988, p. 224). Another study found 73 percent of parents whose children were sexually abused by strangers reported the assault to the authorities and 23 percent of them did so when the offender was an acquaintance, but *none* of them reported the assault when the offender was a relative (Salter 1988, p. 224). What this suggests is that it is very likely much of the sexual abuse of girls never even comes to the attention of officials.

As one attempts to assess the prevalence of childhood maltreatment, it is important to be sensitive to the fact that official statistics, as troubling as they are, vastly *underestimate* the extent of the problem. Given the complex nature of the phenomenon and of official responses to it, treatment providers who work with female offenders must be cautious not to jump to any conclusions about a client's history of childhood maltreatment based on what is found, or more importantly, what is *not* found, in her official records. Suggestions on how to read the messages of childhood maltreatment hidden in those official records will be presented below. However, as treatment providers struggle to prioritize the needs of the female offenders with whom they work, another central issue must first be addressed: What is the nature of the link between childhood maltreatment and female criminality?

UNRAVELING THE CONNECTIONS BETWEEN CHILDHOOD MALTREATMENT AND FEMALE OFFENDING

Family violence experts have struggled for years to explain the prevalence of both officially reported and unreported cases of all types of child abuse and neglect in the United States. At the same time, criminologists have been attempting to decipher the precise nature of the relationship between childhood maltreatment and criminality. In 1989, Cathy Spatz Widom concluded, "being abused as a child significantly increases one's risk of having an adult criminal record...however, the pathway from childhood victimization to adult criminal behavior is far from inevitable" (p. 266). In her study, Widom found only 29 percent of the individuals who were maltreated as children had a criminal record. Noting that females are arrested at a much less frequent rate than males, Widom (1989) still found "experiencing early childhood abuse and neglect has a substantial impact even on individuals with little likelihood of engaging in officially recorded adult criminal behavior" (p. 265). When she focused her attention exclusively on the criminal consequences of sexual abuse, Widom (1996) concluded, "the victims of sexual abuse are not more likely than other victims of physical abuse or neglect to become involved in crime" (p. 50). Thus, according to Widom's findings, while childhood maltreatment in some ways may be linked to criminality, the relationship is not as strong as is often presumed.

In regard to the specific relationship between childhood maltreatment and juvenile delinquency, Scudder et al. (1993) found "children who break the law, especially through acts of violence, often have a history of maltreatment" (p. 321). Smith and Thornberry (1995) similarly found a history of childhood maltreatment "increases the chances of involvement in delinquency" (p. 468). In 1997, Kelley et al. examined official police records and self-reports, and—controlling for the sex, race/ethnicity, family disadvantage, family structure, and mobility of subjects—concluded the following:

> Maltreated youth…displayed significantly higher prevalence rates of delinquency in terms of three measures: official records, self-reported moderate delinquency, and self-reported violence. Childhood maltreatment is a significant and nonspurious risk factor for officially recognized delinquency, violent self-reported delinquency and moderate self-reported delinquency. (pp. 5, 7)

Having controlled for sex, the implication of Kelley et al.'s findings seems to be gender is not a factor in the relationship between childhood maltreatment and delinquency. They do, however, point out that rates of teen pregnancy are significantly higher among girls with a history of childhood maltreatment, and that maltreated girls who become pregnant often exhibit a number of delinquency risk factors during adolescence such as early substance abuse and poor academic performance (1997, pp. 8, 9). Citing Dembo et al. (1995), Chesney-Lind suggests gender *does* in fact matter when assessing the relationship between childhood maltreatment and delinquency: "…girls' problem behavior commonly relates to an abusive and traumatizing home life, whereas boys' law violating behavior reflects their involvement in a delinquent lifestyle" (1997, p. 27). If gender matters, age, apparently, does not. In his 1996 study, Kakar notes *even at a very early age*, "abused children have significantly higher delinquency referral rates" than nonabused children (p. 53).

While there seems to be mounting evidence of a significant link between childhood maltreatment and delinquency, the fact remains many victims of child abuse *do not* go on to commit criminal and/or delinquent acts. As Knudsen (1992) points out, "the relationship between abuse and criminal behavior is ambiguous at best" (p. 77). In other words, while the link may be a significant one according to some researchers, it clearly is not a determinant or causal one. This fact is particularly important for those treatment providers who work exclusively with victims of childhood maltreatment, as well as for those who struggle to formulate effective policy regarding the appropriate ways to intervene in the lives of the victims of such violence. However, it may be of less importance to those who work exclusively with female offenders. Within the context of that specialized population, researchers for some time now consistently have found the percent of females with a history of some sort of childhood maltreatment is overwhelming (Silbert and Pines 1981; Chesney-Lind and Rodriguez 1983). More recently, in a study focusing on the violent victim experiences of female offenders, Lake (1993) found over 85 percent of the women in her sample claimed at least one kind of victim experience (p. 49). In another study of female offenders in prison for killing their children, Brett (1993) found *100 percent of them* had a history of "severe rejection, neglect, or abuse" (p. 27).

A history of childhood maltreatment, specifically sexual abuse, invariably has been found to be a common experience in the lives of female offenders involved in prostitution. Even Widom's (1996) findings on the criminal consequences of childhood sexual abuse supports the assumption that girls who are sexually abused, as well as those who are neglected, follow a direct path from being victimized as children, to becoming runaways as adolescents, to becoming prostitutes as adults (p. 50). In her research on prostitution and violence, O'Neill (1996) notes all of the young women she studied had "profoundly sad backgrounds: child sexual abuse; physical or emotional abuse; family breakdowns; multiple placements in care" (p. 135). Faced with the choice of enduring the violence or coping with the consequences of reporting it, many girls appear to see running away as the only way out. Chesney-Lind (1997) poignantly describes the plight of these young female runaways/offenders:

> Interviews with girls who have run away from home show, very clearly, that they do not have much attachment to their delinquent activities. They are angry about being labeled as delinquent yet engage in illegal acts....Unable to enroll in school or take a job to support themselves because they fear detection, young female runaways are forced into the streets. Here they engage in panhandling, petty theft, and occasional prostitution to survive....It is no accident that girls on the run from abusive homes...get involved in criminal activities that exploit their sexual object status. American society has defined youthful, physically perfect women as desirable. This means that girls on the streets, who have little else of value to trade, are encouraged to use this "resource." (pp. 27, 29)

For treatment providers, the background of many of the female offenders with whom they work may fit the behavioral pattern of women and girls who have been maltreated— they are, or were, runaways and have a record of multiple convictions for prostitution. They should, however, be cautious not to jump to any conclusions about a client's history of abuse since there is no causal link between female criminality and childhood maltreatment. The problem with which treatment providers must grapple, of course, is that the abuse or neglect of many of the females with whom they work may never have been officially documented. Thus while they see a behavioral pattern that indicates a history of child abuse, they can find no official record of maltreatment. For treatment providers who work with female offenders, what becomes critical is being able to identify the multitude of short- and long-term effects all types of childhood maltreatment can have on females, being able to find and interpret the messages of maltreatment hidden in the official records of their clients.

FINDING THE MESSAGES OF CHILDHOOD MALTREATMENT HIDDEN IN OFFICIAL RECORDS AND UNDERSTANDING THE SILENCE OF FEMALE VICTIMS

As the previous discussion in this chapter emphasizes, official statistics on childhood maltreatment vastly underestimate the problem. What the discussion in the preceding section establishes is that while there may be no causal link between female criminality and childhood maltreatment, having a history of often severe child abuse in a variety of forms is typical among female offenders. The problem is there probably will be no official record of those histories. What this means is treatment providers must become adept at reading between the lines of their clients' records. They can do this by becoming sensitive to the short- and long-term psychological, behavioral, and emotional effects of childhood maltreatment. Having accomplished this, however, the challenge that remains is establishing an understanding of their clients' silence about their abuse. Only then will treatment providers be able to develop effective strategies to get their clients to open up about their violent experiences. In many cases, this will mark a crucial step toward the rehabilitation of a female offender with a history of childhood maltreatment. Treatment providers, however, should be aware that it probably will be one of the most difficult steps for them to facilitate.

It has been well documented that victims of physical abuse suffer from a variety of psychological and behavioral difficulties and emotional trauma. They may exhibit signs of poor self-concept and low self-esteem, and confused dependencies. They may have difficulty trusting others and/or be generally resistant to the friendly overtures of others. Many have a history of revictimization and denial defensiveness. They may be withdrawn, isolated, and generally socially incompetent (Weisz 1995, p. 48; Knudsen 1992, p. 75). Victims of physical abuse also are at an increased risk of developing speech and language disorders, which can contribute to lower verbal and cognitive achievement levels. Beyond that, they may exhibit increased levels of depression, and lower levels of persistence and ambition (Weisz 1995, p. 48; Knudsen 1992, p. 75). While emotional abuse typically occurs in conjunction with other types of physical and/or sexual maltreatment, independently it can damage the cognitive, emotional, social, moral, and even the physical development of its victims. Emotional abuse can result in long-term fear, anxiety, and anger. It leaves many of its victims withdrawn and apathetic (Weisz 1995, p. 88). Physical and emotional neglect may result in what experts refer to as "a failure to thrive" in very young children, which is generally characterized by severe cognitive and emotional deficits (Weisz 1995, p. 100). Many physically neglected children develop subdued and inhibited personalities. The long-term effects of physical neglect also may include mental retardation, learning difficulties, and delay in language skills (Weisz 1995, p. 100). Knudsen (1992) summarizes the effects of other varieties of neglect that mirror the effects of other forms of maltreatment:

> ...difficulty in trusting others,...anger over being robbed of childhood, a sense of powerlessness,...an inability to develop satisfying interpersonal relationships...impaired social abilities, low self-esteem, and lack of negotiating, compromising, and problem solving skills. (p. 152)

Because so many more females are victims of child sexual abuse than males, it is particularly important for those who work with female offenders to have a clear understanding of the short- and long-term effects of this form of maltreatment. As noted earlier, the reporting of sexual abuse can be complicated by the variability of the contexts within which the abuse occurs. Faller (1990), however, suggests the varying degrees of proximity in relationships between offenders and victims also can have a direct impact on the characteristics of the sexual maltreatment itself (p. 50). The closer the relationship between an offender and a victim of child sexual abuse, the more problematic both the short- and long-term effects of the abuse will be (Faller 1990, p. 52). This is significant because girls are more likely to be sexually abused by someone close to them—a father, stepfather, etc.—than are boys. Also, the more proximate the relationship, the more frequent the abuse will be over a longer period of time (Faller 1990, p. 50). It has been documented that the more frequent this type of abuse is and the longer it goes, the more severe the trauma it can cause (Chesney-Lind 1997, p. 25). Some of the symptoms manifesting themselves among female incest survivors in particular include depression, dissociate episodes, emotional numbing, sexual dysfunction, intense guilt, low self-esteem, substance abuse, anxiety, somatic complaints, learning disabilities, and marital difficulties (Gelinas 1983, p. 315).

Treatment providers also should be aware that, while at greater risk of being maltreated, the daughters of battered women—whether they have been abused or not— may suffer from an array of psychological, behavioral, and emotional problems (Peled et al. 1995, p. 4). In his research on exposure to family violence, Kolbo (1996) found it was significantly related to behavioral problems, *but only in girls* (p. 123). Those problems included poor impulse control, the externalization and/or internalization of anger, absences from school, alcohol and drug use, and running away. The daughters of battered women also tend to develop little understanding of the dynamics of interpersonal violence. They often assume violence is the norm in close personal relationships (Jaffe et al. 1990, p. 28).

Those treatment providers who work with female offenders and who have sensitized themselves to the psychological, behavioral, and emotional effects of childhood maltreatment probably will find a multitude of indicators consistent with a history of child abuse and/or exposure to family violence in the records of their clients. They also are *not* likely to find any official records of those histories. Having deciphered the messages of maltreatment hidden in their clients' official records, another challenge facing treatment providers is establishing an understanding of their clients' silence about their violent experiences. For instance, the absence of a record of official reports of physical child abuse, or even a record of officially unsubstantiated reports, probably does not mean the female with whom a treatment provider is working was never the victim of physical child abuse. It is more likely the violence was never brought to the attention of the authorities or, in the case of unsubstantiated reports, the violence she suffered was deemed by officials not to have been severe enough to have crossed the legal threshold from acceptable corporal punishment to unacceptable physical abuse. In the latter case in particular, a treatment provider will be dealing with a female who may have tried to get help and who was let down by the people—school counselors, teachers, child protective services workers, etc.—she hoped might rescue her. As a direct result of the failure of others to act, the woman may have been forced to endure even more severe abuse. This kind of experience, even if it has only happened once, but particularly if it has happened more than once, can have a long-term impact on a female's attitude toward authority figures who offer help. As the impact that physical abuse can have on its victims indicates, the very act of placing trust in a stranger—reaching out for help in the first place—can be a difficult and frightening experience. When she hears, "Don't worry, you can tell us what happened. We'll help you—everything will be OK," she desperately wants to believe it. In the end, when it comes down to "We're sorry, there's nothing we can do," and she has to go home to endure the same or worse maltreatment, the issue of ever again trusting the word of a stranger who offers help will become paramount in her life. This kind of experience will have taught her to be suspicious of any authority figure that promises her a better life. When a treatment provider has found the hidden messages and suspects a history of maltreatment, despite a lack of official documentation, she must proceed cautiously and respectfully. If the provider has yet to establish a trusting relationship with her client, she very likely will get nowhere at all when she starts out by asking, "Have you ever been abused?" Understanding the nature of a client's silence about her physical abuse will enable treatment providers to recognize what needs to be accomplished in order to facilitate the breaking of that silence. The same will be true in cases where treatment providers have identified indicators of child sexual abuse, but find no official record of it.

Because female children are more likely than male children to be sexually abused by someone they know, and because the likelihood of disclosure of the abuse decreases dramatically when there is a proximate relationship between an offender and a victim, treatment providers must be prepared *not* to find much official evidence of sexual maltreatment in the records of female offenders who have in fact been sexually abused. As discussed earlier, even unsubstantiated reports of child sexual abuse—cases where girls have recanted their stories—may be more reflective of their responses to the negative reactions to their disclosures than they are genuine denials. While Faller (1990) suggests that what is known about the extent of sexual maltreatment is more apt to come "from the mouths of victims" than it is from official reports (p. 16), those who work with female offenders may have difficulty getting their clients to talk. Their silence may be rooted in fear or in a generalized lack of trust of authority figures. It also may be a consequence of emotional numbing. Many of these females have survived their abuse by erecting emotional walls around themselves, by simply refusing to reveal their pain to anyone.

A study of street prostitutes found that while 61 percent of them were victims of child sexual abuse *only 1 percent of them* reported they had ever revealed that fact to treatment professionals (Salter 1988, p. 224). Many of the women expressed feelings of helplessness and isolation, saying they believed there was nothing they could do, and there was no one that they could tell who they believed could make a difference either. As with victims of physical child abuse, when dealing with female offenders who have been victims of child sexual abuse, treatment providers will need to understand the nature of their clients' silence about their sexual victimization before they can develop effective ways of facilitating the breaking of that silence.

For many female offenders with a history of childhood maltreatment, finding a way to help them break their silence about the abuse they have endured will mark a crucial step toward their eventual rehabilitation. It will, however, likely be one of the most difficult steps for treatment providers to facilitate. What can make the task even more daunting is when treatment providers find themselves working with females who do not even recognize what has happened to them is abusive, when they have come to normalize the violence in their lives.

THE NORMALIZATION OF CHILDHOOD MALTREATMENT AMONG FEMALE OFFENDERS

One of the most formidable challenges treatment providers face when they work with female offenders with a history of childhood maltreatment, is coming to understand and then dealing with the degree to which so many of their clients have come to look upon violence in interpersonal relationships as the norm. This normalization of violence is apt to be found among females who themselves have been victimized, often multiple times and in varied ways. However, as noted earlier, it also may be found among females who have only been exposed to family violence, among the daughters of battered women. Appreciating how even the severest forms of childhood maltreatment can become normalized in the lives of female offenders necessitates abandoning traditional social service and/or legal definitions of abuse that tend to impose clear, but distinctly restrictive boundaries on what the various types of abuse entail. With no clearly defined thresholds of unacceptable violence in their lives, subtly varying degrees of abuse may be experienced subjectively by its victims in *relative* terms. In general, the term "naming" has been used to refer to the difficulty females have actually defining the violence that they have endured in their lives as abusive (Comack 1996, p. 56). Even females who have been subjected to multiple types of childhood maltreatment in varying degrees of severity may not define themselves as victims of abuse. They may actually consider the fact they are alive as proof that what they have experienced could have been worse. In relative terms, they can always imagine something much worse than what happened to them and *that* is what they are apt to define as abusive, not their own experiences. "Silencing" is the term that has been used to refer to the difficulty females have finding the appropriate language—the terminology—to talk about what happened to them (Comack 1996). A girl may describe how her father repeatedly sexually assaulted her, but she may never call it rape, sexual abuse, or incest.

Kelly and Redford (1996) suggest in general females are systematically encouraged to minimize the violence they experience in their lives, leaving them essentially unable to speak about the abuse they have suffered (p. 19). Among female offenders in particular, the problems of naming and silencing are apt to be profound. In her research on prostitutes and violence, O'Neill (1996) observed that when referring to their violent experiences—ranging from verbal abuse and threats to extremely brutal physical abuse that included being punched, kicked, battered, kidnapped, raped, imprisoned, knifed, and stoned—they talked about them "in a very matter of fact way" (p. 137). Citing the work of Hoigard and Finstad (1992, p. 63), O'Neill (1996) highlights the nature of the problem among female offenders:

I often felt that the women talked about violence in a strange way. Bluntly, without any special dramatization, they could relate kidnappings, confinements, rapes, and death threats as if these were normal occurrences…. It's possible that the women have been so exposed to violence that they have become socialized to accept violence as a part of life. (p. 137)

Treatment providers who ask females offenders who have been socialized to accept interpersonal violence as the norm, "Have you ever been physically, sexually, or emotionally abused or neglected?" must be cautious not to take the responses of these women and girls at face value. A better approach to revealing the violence these females have experienced growing up may be to ask questions more directly relating to the developmental environments within which they were socialized. How did they come to learn that physical, sexual, and emotional maltreatment are a normal part of life? Did they grow up in an environment where their parents or caretakers relied upon corporal punishment as the primary method of discipline? While overwhelmingly popular in American society, corporal punishment can teach children some very negative lessons, such as it is acceptable for those who say they love you to hurt you physically. Did they grow up in an environment fraught with what can best be described as "legal" physical abuse? This may include the routine use of a degree of physical force that is severe, but cannot be defined as abusive because it is considered "reasonable" under the law. Records of unsubstantiated reports of physical abuse may be a signal to treatment providers that this type of violence may have occurred in the life of a female offender. Legal abuse also may include more severe forms of physical maltreatment, violence that would have been officially designated illegal had it ever been detected and/or reported. It also may include the family violence that females have observed. While batterers may be held legally responsible for the harm done to their abused partners, they are rarely held accountable for the damage done to their daughters who witnessed the violence. There may be absolutely nothing in the official record of a female offender that provides even a remote clue as to whether or not she has grown up in a developmental environment within which legal abuse has occurred. What this means is treatment providers must be routinely and consistently diligent in their efforts to identify the messages of childhood maltreatment hidden in the records of their clients or risk overlooking cases that involve legal abuse.

Boulton et al. (1989, p. 18) have suggested a number of developmental environments that may subject children to what they refer to as sexual misuse (or any experience that interferes with or has the potential for interfering with the healthy development of a child's sexuality) and/or abuse. In an evasive developmental environment where the topics of sex and sexuality are avoided as much as possible, and in a developmental environment where there is a total absence of information about sexual matters, the *potential* for the misuse and/or abuse exists as girls must go elsewhere to learn about sex and their sexuality (Boulton et al. 1989, pp. 20–23). Permissive and negative developmental environments present an increased risk of misuse and/or abuse. The totally nonrestrictive attitude toward a girl's exposure to sexual matters characterizing a permissive environment usually leads her to be subjected to sexual situations that exceed her developmental capacities. What this means is she is unable to understand and/or respond appropriately to those situations. Within the context of a negative developmental environment the risk of misuse and/or abuse is increased still further as girls are taught to associate sexual feelings with shame, guilt and aversive consequences. Within this environment, girls learn that "sex is bad, evil, abnormal, harmful, a sign of moral weakness, and something to be avoided" (Boulton et al. 1989, pp. 23–25).

When female offenders have come to normalize the physical, sexual, and emotional violence they have experienced and/or observed in their lives, treatment providers who have identified psychological, behavioral, and emotional indicators of abuse must work hard to unearth the history of their childhood maltreatment. As they do this, gaining insight into the developmental environments within which these women and girls learned about all types of interpersonal violence may be beneficial. However, treatment providers should be aware that the boundaries between ideal types of developmental environments might become quite blurred in reality. For instance, as one parent or caretaker teaches a girl that sex is evil and routinely spanks her whenever she suspects the child has even held hands with a boy, the other parent or caretaker may be having intercourse with her and threatening to kill her if she tells anyone about it. Beyond that, treatment providers must be cautious as they develop strategies to help their clients define what happened to them as abusive since their primary way of coping with it has been to normalize it.

CONCLUSION

Female offenders with a history of childhood maltreatment will be women and girls who are disconnected in their relations to others. Before they can learn to build healthy connections based on mutual respect and empathy (the subject of Chapter Five), before any meaningful rehabilitation can begin, treatment providers must break down the seemingly impenetrable emotional walls these females have erected around themselves. Treatment providers will need to establish the kind of trust with their clients—many of whom will be predisposed *not* to trust authority figures who offer help—that will enable them to convince these women and girls that the maladaptive behaviors they have relied on to cope and, in many instances, to survive, can be safely abandoned. In some cases, they will need to find ways to help their clients identify their violent childhood experiences as abusive. This may necessitate exploring the developmental environments within which these women and girls learned about physical, sexual, and emotional violence, and then commencing a deliberate process of resocialization. Teaching these females that no type of interpersonal violence should be considered "normal" will mark a critical step toward effectively dealing with the impact that a history of childhood maltreatment has had in their lives and it will lay the foundation upon which the success of subsequent rehabilitative strategies may depend.

REFERENCES

Berman, T. 1997. October 3. Police are reexamining cases of infant death for possible child abuse. *The Philadelphia Inquirer*, A9.

Brett, C. 1993. From victim to victimizer. In *Female offenders: Meeting the needs of a neglected population*. 26–30. Laurel, MD: American Correctional Association.

Boulton, F. G., Jr., et al. 1989. *Males at risk: The other side of child sexual abuse*. Newbury Park, CA: Sage Publications.

Chesney-Lind, M. 1997. *The female offender: Girls, women and crime*. Thousand Oaks, CA: Sage Publications.

Chesney-Lind, M., and Rodriguez, N. 1983. Women under lock and key. *Prison Journal* 63: 47–65.

Comack, E. 1996. *Women in trouble*. Halifax, Nova Scotia: Fernwood Publishing.

Commonwealth of Pennsylvania. 1976. Child Protective Services Law. P. L. 438, No. 124. Effective April 3.

Commonwealth of Pennsylvania Department of Public Welfare. 1996. *Child abuse report '96* Publication No. 60 5/97. Harrisburg, PA: Commonwealth of Pennsylvania Department of Public Welfare.

Dembo, J.S., et al. 1995. Gender differences in service needs among youths entering a juvenile assessment center: A replication study. Paper presented at the Annual Meeting of the Society of Social Problems. Washington, D.C.

Edwards, L. P. 1996. Corporal punishment and the legal system. *Santa Clara Law Review* 36: 983–1023.

Faller, K. C. 1990. *Understanding child sexual maltreatment*. Newbury Park, CA: Sage Publications.

Gelinas, D. J. 1982. The persisting negative effects of incest. *Psychiatry* 16: 312–332.

Gelles, R. J. 1978. Violence toward children in the U.S. *American Journal of Orthopsychiatry* 48: 580–592.

Herman, J. L. 1981. *Father-daughter incest*. Cambridge, MA: Harvard University Press.

Hoigard, C., and Finstad, L. 1992. *Backstreets: Money, prostitution, and love*. Cambridge, MA: Polity Press.

Jaffe, P. G., et al. 1990. *Children of battered women*. Newbury Park, CA: Sage Publications.

Kakar, S. 1996. Child abuse and juvenile delinquency: A prospective study. *Australian and New Zealand Journal of Criminology* 29: 47–57.

Kelley, B. T., et al. 1997. *In the wake of childhood maltreatment*. NCJ Publication No. 165257. Washington, D.C.: U. S. Department of Justice.

Kelly, L., and Redford, J. 1996. "Nothing really happened": The invalidation of women's experiences of sexual violence. In *Women, violence and male power*, eds. Hester, M., et al., 19–33. Philadelphia: Open University Press.

Knudsen, D. D. 1992. *Child maltreatment: Emerging perspectives*. Dix Hills, NY: General Hall.

Kolbo, J. R. 1996. Risk and resilience among children exposed to family violence. *Violence and Victims* 11: 113–128.

Lake, E. S. 1993. An exploration of the violent victim experiences of female offenders. *Violence and Victims*: 41–51.

Myers, J. E. B. 1994. Child abuse: The response of the legal system. In *Violence and the law,* eds. Costanzo, M., et al., 63–88. Thousand Oaks, CA: Sage Publications.

O'Neill, M. 1996. Researching prostitution and violence: Towards a feminist praxis. In *Women, violence, and male power,* eds. Hester, M., et al., 130–147. Philadelphia: Open University Press.

Peled, E., et al., eds. 1995. *Ending the cycle of violence: Community responses to children of battered women*. Thousand Oaks, CA: Sage Publications.

Russell, D. 1983. The incidence and prevalence of intrafamilial and extrafamilial sexual abuse of female children. *Child Abuse and Neglect: The International Journal* 7: 133–146.

Sagatun, I. J., and Edwards, L. P. 1995. *Child abuse and the legal system*. Chicago: Nelson–Hall.

Salter, A. C. 1988. *Treating child sex offenders and victims: A practical guide*. Newbury Park, CA: Sage Publications.

Scudder, R. G., et al. 1993. Important links between child abuse, neglect, and delinquency. *International Journal of Offender Therapy and Comparative Criminology* 37: 315–323.

Sgroi, S. M., ed. 1982. *Handbook of clinical intervention in child sexual abuse*. Lexington, MA: D. C. Heath & Co.

Silbert, M. H., and Pines, A. M. 1981. Sexual child abuse as an antecedent to prostitution. *Child Abuse and Neglect* 5: 407–411.

Smith, B. E. 1995. *Prosecuting child physical abuse cases: A case study in San Diego.* NCJ Publication No. 152978. Washington, D. C.: U. S. Department of Justice.

Smith, C., and Thornberry, T. P. 1995. The relationship between childhood maltreatment and adolescent involvement in delinquency. *Criminology* 33: 451–481.

Straus, M. A. 1991. Discipline and deviance: Physical punishment of children and violence and other crimes in adulthood. *Social Problems* 38: 133–140.

Utech, M. R. 1994. *Violence, abuse, and neglect: The American home.* Dix Hills, NY: General Hall.

Weisz, V. G. 1995. *Children and adolescents in need: A legal primer for the helping professional.* Thousand Oaks, CA: Sage Publications.

Widom, C. S. 1989. Child abuse, neglect, and violent criminal behavior. *Criminology* 27: 251–271.

Widom, C. S. 1996. Childhood sexual abuse and its criminal consequences. *Society* 33: 47–53.

Wyatt, G. 1985. The sexual abuse of Afro-American and White American women in childhood. *Child Abuse and Neglect: The International Journal* 9: 507–519.

CHAPTER 11

Surviving Violence: Women's Strength Through Connection

Carolyn Swift

Editor's Notes

Dougherty, in Chapter Ten, points out that maladaptive responses to trauma include emotional numbing and normalizing violence in interpersonal relationships. Based on this reality, it is not hard to see why, among women offenders with multiple trauma histories including child abuse, domestic violence is also common to their experience. In fact, many women subjected to battering, the topic of Chapter Eleven, describe their experience as an incapacity to act, being numb. According to Swift, the author of Chapter Eleven, such major disruptions in intimate relationships, e.g., child abuse, etc., inevitably leave scars and complicate the capacity to form and maintain constructive relationships later in life. Also, according to Swift, battered women who suffered child abuse are less likely to leave their battering partners than women without this history. This fact supports the normalization phenomenon described by Dougherty in the previous chapter. Normalization, in this case, specifically refers to an increased tolerance of abuse in intimate relationships as part and parcel of life.

One purpose of Chapter Eleven is to explore the connection between female and male violence and to outline treatment approaches for battered women based on relational theory as presented in Chapter Five. A second purpose of Chapter Eleven is to consider the implications of relational theory for the education and treatment of women offenders who have a history of victimization through violence. The chapter begins with a review of some systemic causes of male violence against women. It follows with an outline of gender differences that have implications for intimate relationships: differences in the ways women and men tend to use power, resolve moral dilemmas, and gain knowledge of each other. Next is a discussion of the potential of relationships outside the batterer's world to transform the woman's experience and help her find a way out of the violence. Women's shelters are identified as safe spaces for women to recover and rebuild their lives. Their benefits in providing group support are compared with the potential for group support in women's prisons. The chapter concludes with a discussion of ways healthy relationships can help women pursue violence-free lives.

Relational theory focuses primarily on women's development in the context of their subordination in patriarchal cultures. It is closely aligned with power-belief theory (Chapter Six) inclusive of the unequal distribution of power between the sexes associated with traditional gender roles and the acceptance of the legitimacy of the patriarchal order by girls and women. Thus sex-role socialization sets up a power imbalance with males in dominant roles and females in submissive roles. These role restrictions and prescriptions, the details of which are discussed here and in Chapter Six, create situations that, according to Swift, increase the probability of abuse.

Dougherty points out in Chapter Ten that state laws give parents and caretakers the leeway to use "reasonable" physical force to discipline children. In fact, all fifty states permit the use of corporal punishment to discipline children, either statutorily or through specific court decisions. According to Swift, "Accepted practices for controlling children are readily adapted to use against women and reflect a social tolerance of interpersonal violence by the strong against the weak."

Leaving the batterer is often preceded by a transformative experience in which another person—one who stands outside the battering relationship—reflects the woman's reality in a way that enables her to acknowledge and assess her risk more objectively. From this point of view, the impact of a treatment provider in the "outside" role, and the avail-

ability of women's shelters as islands of security, support, and treatment outside the victim's battering system, is paramount. Swift emphasizes that if return visits to shelters are seen as rehearsals rather than recidivism, it should be easier for shelter workers to welcome returnees and support their efforts to practice the skills needed to live independently from the batterer. Swift's suggestion that shelter workers not count the women who make multiple visits as failures is consistent with the conceptual model of planned change presented by Hawkinshire in Chapter Four.

With respect to women offenders, Swift discusses the possibility of whether prisons could be used as treatment settings to promote relational learning and growth for women offenders much as the shelter promotes relational learning and growth for battered women. Swift states: "It is unrealistic to assume that the successful shelter experience could be extrapolated in the prison situation without attention to these (loss of meaningful access to their children, the right to make decisions about routine daily activities, and educational and counseling opportunities) and other problems none of which is easily resolved" (1987, p. 19). Indeed a strong case could be made that, in general, prisons are not places that promote healthy relationships. In fact, prisons may, depending on the institutional and staff philosophy, inhibit the development of healthy relationships. However, based on the similarities of the shelter and prison settings described, the author concludes that adapting the model of women's groups based on the relational approach holds promise for prison settings.

INTRODUCTION

Research over the last quarter century challenges traditional approaches to male violence against women, and forces a rethinking of the systemic causes of these crimes and their effects on women's lives. Although domestic abuse is a common experience that cuts across class lines, emerging research indicates that poor and homeless women (Salomon et al. 1996) and woman offenders are victims of male violence more frequently than their middle, upper class, and nonconfined sisters.

A recent study (Coll and Duff 1995) found over one-third of a sample of women at a Massachusetts prison reported living with someone other than a parent as a child. [Although women in Massachusetts continue to be but a fraction of the state's offender population (5.7 percent in 1993), this population increased 500 percent over the last decade. The women in this study "arrived in prison with multiple trauma histories, loss of parents in childhood (38 percent), child abuse (69 percent), leaving home under age 17 (70 percent), and repeated verbal, sexual, and physical abuse as adults (70 percent), both in and out of the home" (Coll and Duff 1995, p. 34). Such major disruptions in intimate relationships inevitably leave scars and complicate the capacity to form and maintain constructive relationships in later life. Whether as children or adults, whether as single incidents or a continuing cycle, most women offenders have experienced physical, sexual, or emotional abuse. Traditional approaches to treating women offenders have failed to identify their abuse histories or to analyze the effects of violence on their behavior (see Chapter Ten).

The purpose of this chapter is to explore the connection between women and male violence, to outline treatment approaches for battered women based on relational theory (see also Chapter Five), and to consider the implications of relational theory for the education and treatment of women offenders who have a history of victimization through violence. The chapter begins with a review of some systemic causes of male violence against women. It follows with an outline of gender differences that have implications for intimate relationships: differences in the ways women and men tend to use power, resolve moral dilemmas, and gain knowledge of each other. Next is a discussion of the potential of relationships outside the batterer's world to transform the woman's experience and help her find a way out of the violence. Women's shelters are identified as safe spaces for women to recover and rebuild their lives. Their benefits in providing group support are compared with the potential for group support in women's prisons. The chapter concludes with a discussion of ways healthy relationships can help women pursue violence-free lives.

NORMS SUPPORTING VIOLENCE AGAINST WOMEN

Men's physical victimization of women through the ages is well documented. What is new in this century is the collective effort by women to deliver themselves from their attackers and to protest the values and practices associated with such institutionalized violence. Feminist scholarship has established that women and men relate differently to their worlds and to each other. Failure to recognize these differences is reflected in traditional scholarship that includes women in generalizations drawn from studies based on men. New theories projecting women's development and behavior from studies of women themselves challenge conventional wisdom in the field of human behavior and cast new light on heterosexual relationships in which violence occurs.

Two major cultural norms support violence against women. The first is the unequal distribution of power between the sexes, which is associated with traditional sex roles. The second norm condones the use of physical force to resolve disputes. These norms create institutional stresses for each sex, reflected in discriminatory policies and practices. In addition, they differentially alter the quantity and quality of resources available to women and men in coping with the stresses of their daily lives, including problems in relationships.

THE UNEQUAL DISTRIBUTION OF POWER

One constant in all forms of violence between males and females is the misuse of power. The bigger, the stronger, and those with greater access to valued resources impose their will on those who are smaller, physically weaker, and have less access to resources. Finkelhor (1983, p. 18), in describing family violence, puts the principle succinctly: "The most common patterns in family abuse are not merely for the more powerful to abuse the less powerful but for the most powerful to abuse the least powerful. Abuse tends to gravitate to the relationship of greatest power differential." The most powerless victims, children under six years, suffer the highest incidence of physical abuse. The abuser in most cases is the more powerful parent, the father (Finkelhor 1983).

In our culture, major power differentials are sorted by age; by sex, with males in general commanding more social, economic, political, and physical power than females; and by ethnicity, with the white majority in our country commanding more power than other ethnic groups. When these differences are compounded abuse increases. For example, Berk et al. (1983) found that the incidence of abuse was higher among white males married to Hispanic females than in couples where both partners were white. Martin (1976) noted a similar effect for white males married to Asian women.

The traditional power imbalance between female and male heads of household sets up conditions for economic, social, and physical abuse in the marital relationship. Both sexes are burdened by discriminatory traditions that dictate the "appropriate" role of each in family life and in the world outside the family. In the context of these roles the male partner is seen as the breadwinner. His area of expertise and action is the public world, which encompasses societal institutions and the commerce between them. Women have not been expected, according to the traditional worldview, to seek fulfillment through lifetime careers outside the home, and men have not been expected to contribute major efforts to what have become known as homemaking activities or to daily child care. The female partner is assigned primary responsibility for bearing and raising children and maintaining the home. These role restrictions and prescriptions create situations that increase the probability of abuse. Sex-role socialization sets up a power imbalance, with males in dominant roles and females in submissive roles.

Evidence from cross-cultural studies supports the finding that where both male dominance and interpersonal violence are accepted, females are at high risk for victimization. In a study of 95 societies, Sanday (1981) classified 47 percent as rape free and 18 percent as rape prone. A common feature in the rape-free societies is the relatively equal balance between the sexes. The contributions of women in these societies are respected and valued, particularly their functions associated with reproduction, growth, and social continuity. Sanday found the incidence of rape in a society to be positively correlated with the ideology of machismo as well as the intensity of interpersonal violence. Interpersonal violence is rarely found in rape-free societies.

Male aggression against females, then, is neither biologically determined nor inevitable. According to Sanday, it results from social learning and from the balance between population needs and environmental resources.

In tribal societies women are often equated with fertility and growth; men with aggression and destruction. More often than not, the characteristics associated with maleness and femaleness are equally valued. When people perceive an imbalance between the food supply and a population's needs, or when populations are in competition for diminishing resources, the male role is accorded greater prestige... rape is part of a broader struggle for control in the face of difficult circumstances. Where men are in harmony with their environment, rape is usually absent (Sanday 1981, p. 25).

As Sanday writes, "The correlates of rape strongly suggest that rape is the playing out of a socio-cultural script in which the expression of personhood for males is directed by, among other things, interpersonal violence and an ideology of toughness" (1981, p. 24).

The cultural profile Sanday identifies as destructive to women is consistent with findings in our own culture. For example, Burt (1980) conducted a study of rape myths, defined as "prejudicial, stereotyped, or false beliefs about rape, rape victims and rapists" (p. 217). Rape myths condemn victims as lacking in virtue, resistance, or credibility while viewing rapists as overcome by lust, insanity, or both. The prevalence of rape myths, evident in both public and professional attitudes, contributes to a culture in which rape is common, victims are denigrated, and rapists are rarely apprehended or convicted. Surveying a random sample of adults in a midwestern state, Burt found that acceptance of rape myths could be predicted from attitudes of sex-role stereotyping and adversarial sexual beliefs (e.g., the belief that sexual relationships involve exploitation and acceptance of interpersonal violence).

THE USE OF PHYSICAL FORCE

The second factor that contributes to the prevalence of physical attacks on women is the cultural acceptance of violence to enforce compliance. Our culture has a long tradition of using physical force to resolve interpersonal conflicts. Physical discipline and punishment are commonly accepted ways for parents to control their children, and corporal punishment is still legal in most states. Accepted practices for controlling children are readily adapted to use against women and reflect a social tolerance of interpersonal violence by the strong against the weak.

SOCIAL NETWORK RESPONSE

The value of supportive relationships for healthy functioning and their role in buffering the destructive effects of stress have been extensively documented (Gottlieb 1981, 1983; Mitchell and Trickett 1980). Social networks constitute a critical variable in Albee's (Albee and Swift 1995) formula for calculating the incidence of mental and emotional dysfunction. Along with social competence and self-esteem, social networks reduce dysfunction caused by environmental stress. When the source of stress is human rather than environmental, as in male violence against women, the positive function of social networks in our society is often reversed for the victim.

Confronted with stressful life changes, most people turn for help to their spouses, other family members, friends, and neighbors. For the battered woman it is the spouse or partner who inflicts pain. She not only suffers the pain of the attack but loses the support of her primary relationship as well. Relatives and friends often side with the attacker. In these cases close network ties can perpetuate the violence. The assumption that the kin network will be opposed to violence is not necessarily correct. For example, a number of women indicated that when they left their husbands because of a violent attack, their mothers responded with urgings for the wife to deal with the situation by being a better housekeeper, by being a better sex partner, or just by avoiding him, etc. In some cases, the advice was "you have to put up with it for the sake of the kids—that's what I did!" (Straus 1980, p. 246).

Instead of countering the stress of victimization, the woman's personal and institutional support systems are likely to add to her burden. The support network reflects, through attitudes, policies, and practices, the cultural norms that denigrate a woman's role and contributions and condone interpersonal violence against her. Whether by actively blaming her for provoking the attack or by simply withdrawing customary emotional and material resources, persons and institutions in the woman's social network often have a negative impact on her capacity to survive attack.

Beyond immediate family and friends, the professional community can usually be counted on to provide assistance in most life crises. Here too women attacked by their male partners not only find little support but often encounter blame and hostile judgment instead. The church, through its clergy, is the institutional resource most frequently approached by battered women (Pagelow 1982). In a survey of Protestant clergy in the United States and Canada (Alsdurf 1985), investigators confirmed that pastors have patriarchal attitudes toward women that lead them to distrust women's accounts of family violence and to discount violence as grounds for dissolving the marriage.

One-third of the respondents felt that the abuse would have to be severe in order to justify a Christian wife leaving her husband, while 21 percent felt that no amount of abuse would justify a separation. Twenty-six percent of the pastors agreed that a wife should submit to her husband and trust that God would honor her action by either stopping the abuse or giving her the strength to endure it (Alsdurf 1985, p. 10).

Another survey of helping professionals—physicians, psychiatrists, psychologists, social workers, and clergy—found that social workers identified the largest number of abused women while physicians and clergy identified the fewest (Burris 1984). That most social workers are female and most physicians and members of the clergy are male suggest that the traditional male denial of the scope of the problem and its effect on victims accounts for this difference.

Although physicians are generally held to underestimate abuse by not identifying cases in their practice, it seems that at some level they differentiate battered women from other injured women: battered women are more likely than others to leave the emergency room with a prescription for pain medication (cited in Stark et al. 1979). Semmelman (1982) found that four times as many battered women as nonbattered women in shelters were taking psychotropic medication (21 percent vs. 5 percent). Although the medication may blunt pain, it also blunts the woman's alertness to imminent danger and reduces her ability to defend herself from attack in the short run. Over the long run, it undermines her capacity for problem solving. Stark (1984) notes that "despite its failure to 'see,' medicine responds in distinct and punitive ways to battered women ….By decontextualizing emergent social problems and treating the psychosocial consequences of abuse as an occasion for family maintenance, medicine helps stabilize families in which escalating violence is inevitable" (p. 307).

It is a function of the legal system, through its codification of crimes and social norms, to support the rights of citizens against attack. Until very recently, however, the legal system failed to protect women from their male partners' violence. The laws dealing with partner abuse and the enforcement of these laws reflected the patriarchal values of the male prosecutors, judges, and police officers who have traditionally staffed the legal system. Just over a decade ago Lerman (1986) amassed evidence that battered women were routinely discouraged from effectively registering their protests of the crimes committed against them and from seeking redress. Police filed reports in fewer than 20 percent of the domestic abuse cases for which they were called and arrested the abuser in fewer than five percent of these cases. Even when the abuser was arrested, he had roughly a fifty-fifty chance that the charges would be dismissed. Convictions in family violence cases were rare and when they did occur penalties were relatively light. Lerman concluded that "in most places prosecution is seldom an available remedy for battered women" (1986, p. 265). Although there has been progress over the last decade, Lerman's results continue to describe many jurisdictions in this country.

In the field of penology it is the certainty of punishment, not its severity, that serves as an effective deterrent to crime (Andenaes 1975; Erickson and Gibbs 1973; Tittle, 1969). In cases of violence against women the certainty principle effectively rewards the attacker and punishes the victim. Despite advances in the prosecution of the batterer, in most cases he can count on *not* being arrested, prosecuted, convicted, or punished; and she can count on *not* being protected against assault.

The new visibility of rape and battering has had two important consequences. First, though progress toward changing discriminatory institutional practices is slow, it is nevertheless occurring, as reflected in rape-law reform (Geis and Geis 1978; Loh 1981) and in greater readiness to arrest and convict rapists and batterers (Smith 1981). Second, the increased visibility of woman-targeted violence has helped women find resources and support from each other and to create relationships outside the system of violence.

GENDER DIFFERENCES WITH IMPLICATIONS FOR INTIMATE RELATIONSHIPS

A major contributor to the perpetuation of violence against women is the invisibility of women's experience. This invisibility is effectively enforced by patriarchal custom and practice. In the context of violence toward women there are three major areas in which the experiences women bring to the relationship differ from the experiences men bring:

1. the use of power
2. the resolution of ethical dilemmas
3. the perception and interpretation of information about their partner

There is evidence that males and females use power differently, resolve moral problems differently, and evaluate relational information differently.

THE USE OF POWER

An important difference between men and women involves the use of power. Issues of power, like issues of morality and knowing, tend to be viewed differently by the sexes. The discussion of power here draws heavily on the work of Jean Baker Miller (1982, 1987). Males tend to define power in terms of the capacity to effect their will, with or without the consent of those involved. Domination is a key concept in the male definition and exercise of power. Miller's definition—and one that more accurately represents women's experience of exercising power—is that power is the capacity to effect change, to move something from point A to point B. Surrey (1987) defines mutual power in relationships as the capacity to be moved by and to move another person.

In our patriarchal society women have not been viewed as needing to exercise power. In fact women do exercise power. A major gender difference is that they are more likely than men to use power in the service of others. One primary way women "empower" others is by promoting the growth and development of children in psychological, social, and intellectual spheres. Another way is by promoting their mates' growth and development. Women have traditionally provided psychological and material support to further their husbands' goals—autonomy and success in the world outside the home. For women to use their power to effect change—to move something from point A to point B—in their own self-interest threatens patriarchal values and may invoke frightening images in the women themselves.

Miller (1982) identified three fears women associate with exercising power in their own self-interest:

1. fear of being selfish
2. fear of being destructive
3. fear of being abandoned by those they care about

Enhancing one's own power in our culture is often connected with reducing the power of another. Women fear that to act in their own self-interest, as members of a subordinate group, is often to act in ways inimical to the interests of the dominant group. Such actions may in fact alter or even destroy the arrangements perpetuated by the dominant group:

> Women have lived as subordinates and, as subordinates, have been led by the culture to believe that their own self-determined action is wrong and evil. Many women have incorporated deeply the inner notion that such actions must be destructive….In most institutions it is still true that if women do act from their own perceptions and motivations, directly and honestly, they indeed may be disrupting a context that has not been built out of women's experience. Thus, one is confronted with feeling like one must do something very powerful that also feels destructive. (Miller 1982, p. 4)

The fear of being abandoned is related to the other two fears. If women do act in their own self-interest, and if these actions disrupt existing relationships, then women may suffer attack or abandonment as a consequence. Miller pointed out, "all of us exist only as we need others for that existence." Men tend to deny this view; women have incorporated it in an extreme form. "Along with it we women have incorporated the troubling notion that, as much as we need others, we also have powers and the motivations to use those powers, but if we use them, we will destroy the relationships we need for our existence" (1982, p. 4).

Women, then, are at an immense psychological as well as physical disadvantage in resolving conflicts with their male partners. First, they place the highest priority on preserving the relationship—on staying connected—when disputes arise. Second, their capacity to "know" the other in connected, empathic ways (see below) makes them the partner more likely to feel the pain of the other, even in the midst of their own suffering. Third, in abuse situations women are in a double bind in attempting to use their power in their own interest. If they save their physical selves by leaving to avoid the battering, they risk destroying their primary relationship and with it their psychological and economic security. If they act to preserve the primary relationship and their psychological and economic security they put themselves at risk of physical destruction. Women in battering situations are forced to choose which parts of themselves they will save—their physical safety and well being or their psychological and economic safety and well being. It is not surprising that many women find this a difficult choice.

ETHICS

Carol Gilligan (1982) outlined two major approaches to resolving ethical dilemmas. It is clear that both males and females have access to both approaches. It is also clear that in Western patriarchal culture males tend to use one approach predominantly, while females tend to use both. The first approach sees ethical problems as occasions for creating or enforcing rules that spell out the rights of those involved. Rules and rights are seen as necessary to define the limits of autonomy and to ensure its exercise. Autonomy in this view is a highly desired state or goal—the end of a process that begins with separation from the mother in childhood. An ethic that emphasizes rights and rules and is grounded in autonomy as the organizing principle is the predominant ethic in Western patriarchal culture.

The second approach to the resolution of ethical problems sees these problems in the context of the relationships in which they are embedded. In this approach there is an attempt to identify and assign the responsibilities of those involved in a way that maintains caring and connectedness. In our culture the ethic of responsibility, caring, and connectedness is most likely to be implemented by women. When faced with an ethical dilemma men are more likely to resolve it by asserting their rights, invoking rules, and, more often than not, preserving their autonomy. Women, on the other hand, are likely to consider the impact of various solutions on the relationship involved and to opt for assigning responsibility in such a way as to preserve these connections—in as caring a way as possible. Women tend to value relationships more highly than autonomy, whereas the opposite is true for men. This difference is extremely important for understanding the topic of family violence, because it means that women will be more devoted to preserving the relationship even through the stress of violence.

KNOWLEDGE OF THE INTIMATE PARTNER

The third area of difference between the sexes that has implications for violence toward women is the way women and men come to know their intimate partners. A number of feminist scholars have explored the ways gender roles tend to generate alternative thought paradigms for women and men. Clinchy and Zimmerman (1985) and Belenky, et al. (1986) described several approaches to knowing especially pertinent to this topic. One approach, based on Perry's work (1970, 1981), emphasizes a method of thinking that uses objective criteria to analyze new information. The analysis compares the information with what is already known, notes differences, and tests the new knowledge against established standards. This type of knowing is called "separate" in reference to the autonomous nature of the self in making comparisons and seeing differences. Another approach to knowing involves not separating the self from what is to be known, but entering into the new frame of reference in order to understand it. It is this type of knowing, called "connected" knowing, that leads to empathy.

It is the thesis of these scholars that connected knowing is more often found in women, although both sexes use both separate and connected knowing. The significance of this difference in understanding situations in which women are attacked by their male partners is that the woman is more likely to feel and relate to her partner's pain. This capacity for feeling the other's pain may contribute to the woman's lesser readiness to initiate or return violence—a position that places her at a disadvantage in protecting herself against her partner's violence.

Ruddick's (1984) illuminating account of what she calls "maternal thinking" focuses on the ways maternal practices have shaped the thought process. Although both sexes have the capacity to engage in maternal thinking, it is found more often in women because of their more intimate connection with children and their greater responsibility for bearing and rearing them. The demands of both the child and the culture are reflected in maternal practice, and they determine the priorities of maternal thinking. These priorities are to preserve life, to foster development, and to shape growth into forms acceptable to the culture at large. Confronted with responsibility for the life of another human being, the maternal parent develops an attitude Ruddick calls "holding." This attitude values keeping over acquiring. Its aims are to conserve and maintain resources to sustain fragile life. "It is an attitude elicited by the work of 'world protection, world preservation, world repair...the invisible weaving of a frayed and threadbare family life'" (Ruddick 1984, p. 217).

The foundation of maternal thought lies in the capacity to attend to and love the other—prototypically, the child. This capacity for attention and love is expressed in the question, "What are you going through?" (Ruddick 1984, p. 224) and in the empathy required to hear the response. Although maternal thinking has its roots in the mother-child relationship, the bonding of self-interest with the interests of the cared-for other is a characteristic of an intimate relationship for women.

Because maternal thinking centers on the experience of the other, because its priorities are to preserve the safety and foster the growth of the other, the maternal thinker is singularly unprepared to defend against attack from a significant other. Defense against physical attack requires an understanding of personal risk as separate from the attacker's risk. Habituated to feeling what the other is going through, the maternal thinker is psychologically unequipped to make the abrupt and sudden shift of attention from other to self needed to mobilize energy for self-defense.

Many women subjected to battering do not make this shift. Mills (1985), in a series of interviews with battered women, noted that a loss of self occurs over time. She saw this loss as taking two forms, a loss of identity and a loss of what she called the observing self. Many of the women interviewed described an incapacity to act, "like: 'being in a shell,' 'like a zombie,' 'a mechanical robot,' 'being numb,' and 'like being dead'" (p. 113). Finding their judgments and perceptions about the relationship shattered, suffering the pain and shock of attack, they have few resources—either within themselves or in the world outside—to stop the violence or restore their sense of self.

Other women victimized by battering partners react by consciously choosing not to defend themselves. For many, this strategy is calculated to heal some past wound perceived in the batterer and to create the opportunity for growth in the relationship. The following first-person accounts of battered women illustrate this strategy:

Deb: I feel he can be helped with treatment. I know he feels rejected because of all his brothers and sisters, he was the only one they gave away. So, I thought that he was trying to make me give him away just like everybody else. So, I thought if I didn't play his game, if I don't reject him, he would get over it. (Mills 1985, p. 110).

Maggie: I think a reason I got a master's in social work was to see what could be done. That's what I wrote my thesis on—how to help the men. I spent the first year trying to find out how to make it different so we could have a good marriage. (Mills 1985, p. 110).

Woman: I had the idea that I'm doing this for him. I'm coping. I'm controlling the amount of abuse I'm taking. I must be a good person. The importance I got was what I was doing for him. (Schechter 1982, p. 13).

Although the maternal thinking Ruddick describes has clear evolutionary benefits, it contributes to the physical and psychological destruction of adherents who are paired with violent partners.

A WAY OUT: RELATIONSHIPS AND RESOURCES OUTSIDE THE BATTERER'S WORLD

Why do women stay with battering partners? The question implies a freedom of choice and a multiplicity of options that do not exist for many battered women. Beyond this, it is the wrong question, even though it is the one most often asked by those dealing with domestic abuse. The more appropriate question is, "Why do men batter their intimate partners?" It has not been a priority in Western patriarchal culture to find an answer to this question. An informal literature review of psychological, sociological, family, and dissertation abstracts for the years 1982–1985 showed roughly 9 out of 10 publications on battering focused on the victimized woman, with little or no attention to the batterer. When issues concerning the batterer have been addressed the method has often involved eliciting information from his victim rather than from the abuser himself (e.g., see Walker 1984).

In the absence of significant efforts to identify the causes of battering and to prevent such behavior in men, victimized women are in need of shelter and resources to help them lead abuse-free lives. The information in studies on battered women sheds light on factors that strengthen women's abilities to help each other and to help themselves avoid male-initiated violence.

A frequent comparison made in the research literature is between women who stay with battering partners and women who leave them. Although many women leave and return more than once, those whose economic situation gives them the option of independence are more likely to leave the batterer and not return. The women who leave battering partners are more likely to be employed and have generally achieved a higher level of education than women who stay (Hilbert and Hilbert 1984; Strube 1984). Of the employed women who find themselves in battering relationships, those with higher salaries are more likely to leave. Women who suffered child abuse are less likely to leave their battering partners than women without this history (Dalto 1983). Early exposure to physical abuse may contribute to learned helplessness (Walker 1984) or to an increased tolerance of abuse in intimate relationships.

Psychological differences have also been examined. Feldman (1983) found that "leavers" had significantly higher self-esteem, had a more internalized locus of control, and subscribed to less traditional sex-role ideology than "stayers." Walker's (1984) study, based on interviews with over 400 battered women, had conflicting results. Contrary to her prediction, she found that both stayers and leavers scored significantly higher than the norm on internal locus of control measures, and both groups were more depressed than the norm.

How the woman herself perceives the relationship is a key factor. If she believes the battering is unavoidable, that she has no control over it, that the batterer does not love her or will not change, she is more likely to leave. If, on the other hand, she believes she can avoid the battering, that she is in part to blame for it, that her partner loves her or will change his battering behavior, she is more likely to stay (Butehorn 1985; Dalto 1983; Porter 1983; Strube 1984). The frequency and severity of battering also affect whether the woman stays or leaves (Gelles and Cornell 1985; Hilbert and Hilbert 1984; Kremen 1985). Daily violence has been associated with leaving and weekly violence with staying (Butehorn 1985).

The responses of those in the woman's personal network, as well as institutional response, also affect whether the woman stays with the batterer. When those in her personal network are seen as favoring a reconciliation, the woman is more likely to return to the batterer (Dalto 1983). In one study, stayers were more likely to receive feedback that their networks would not help them if they left (Butehorn 1985). Several investigators have found that leaving is associated with the responsiveness of community agencies and social institutions (Hodson 1982; Lidkea 1982). In general, helpful responses are negatively related to the length of the battering relationship. Unfortunately, as described earlier, social institutions and agencies not only have historically not been helpful to women victimized by violence but have, by their discriminatory policies and practices, added to the women's stress.

Leaving the batterer is often preceded by a transformative experience in which another person, one who stands outside the battering relationship, reflects the woman's reality in a way that enables her to acknowledge and assess her risk more objectively. Mills provides graphic examples of the impact of a therapist in the "outside" role. One woman told how she decided to leave her husband after talking with a therapist: "She convinced me that my life was in danger. I realize now that it was. I was ignoring a lot of signs even though I was in the middle of it" (Mills 1985, p. 116). The second woman described the beginnings of the restoration of her sense of self after meeting with a therapist: "One weekend I took an overdose of pills and had to go to the hospital. So, they said because I took an overdose I had to see a psychiatrist. And the funny thing about it, he said the problem was my husband and not me. He said that if I got away from him, I'd be a lot better off. I thought that was pretty good because I thought maybe I was the one that was crazy" (Mills 1985, p. 115).

BUILDING HEALTHY RELATIONSHIPS: SHELTERS AS SAFE SPACES

The availability of women's shelters and their value as islands of security and support outside the victim's battering system have proved to be critical way stations in the woman's exodus from her violent home. Research supports the conclusion that battered women use shelters to practice living on their own, apart from the battering partner. The greater the number of previous separations (Snyder and Scheer 1981), the more times the woman has returned to the shelter (Okun 1983), and the longer the duration of the shelter visit(s) (Dalto 1983; Hilbert and Hilbert 1984; Snyder and Scheer 1981), the more likely it is that the woman will leave the batterer. It is important for this information to reach the field, because shelter workers tend to count the women who make multiple visits as failures and may treat them punitively—that is, may refuse them entry on subsequent visits (Martin 1976). If return visits are seen as rehearsals rather than recidivism, it should be easier for shelter workers to welcome returnees and support their efforts to practice the skills needed to live independently from the batterer. This analysis is consistent with Hawkinshire's model of planned change (see Chapter Four).

What are the features of the shelter experience that promote the decision to leave the batterer? Data are not available to assess the relative value of the shelter's material vs. psychological resources. But it is clear from the literature that one of the most important features of the shelter experience is the opportunity it provides for women to develop healthy connections with others. Fleeing an unhealthy relationship, the battered woman finds in the shelter other women like herself who offer her understanding, who believe her story, who are committed to her safety and well-being, and who value her. A common finding is that women who form close relationships with other battered women in the shelter, or who identify with a shelter role model, are less likely to return to the abuser (Dalto 1983; Okun 1983).

Battered women receive valuable psychological resources from relationships formed in shelters. They are listened to and believed. They participate in problem solving with other women who share similar experiences. They form a more accurate picture of themselves and of the batterer. And they gain increasing confidence in their ability to live violence-free lives (Swift 1987). In sum, research indicates that women who leave battering relationships are aided in doing so by making healthy connections with persons outside the battering system. The shelter movement and the women who have left shelters to live violence-free lives demonstrate that one of the ways women survive male violence is by creating alternative ways of living, both collectively and individually.

BUILDING HEALTHY RELATIONSHIPS: CAN WOMEN'S PRISONS PROVIDE SAFE SPACES?

The woman's prison experience is very different from the shelter experience. Prison sentences are involuntary and usually much longer than shelter visits, which are voluntary. In addition to losing their freedom, offenders experience many other losses—including meaningful access to their children and families, the right to make decisions about routine daily activities, and educational and counseling opportunities. Staff within prisons have different goals and objectives than staff in women's shelters and relate differently to the women residents. Issues of safety, trust, confidentiality, informed consent, and involuntary confinement threaten the viability of women's groups inside prison walls. Could safe spaces for sharing between residents be assured in a prison setting? It is unrealistic to assume that the successful shelter experience could be extrapolated to the prison situation without attention to these and other problems, none of which is easily resolved.

The resources and public images of the two settings are also very different. Women's shelters are more likely to be located in urban settings with access to many community resources, including volunteers. Residents are viewed as victims of their battering partners, and suffer little or no stigma for their situation. Prisons are more likely to be in rural or isolated settings, with no access by public transportation. Fewer—if any—community resources are made available to women offenders, who carry the stigma of criminal status. The budgets for treatment available in the two settings reflect these realities. For these reasons, projecting treatment programs for the prison setting must take into account the lack of availability of resources. In recent decades local colleges and universities have provided counselors and therapists in training for prisons within their regions. To ensure program integrity treatment programs should have input from health and mental health professionals. In sum, there are many features of a prison setting that are problematic for the implementation of effective treatment programs.

On the other hand, the two situations share common features. In both settings the residents are women who have problems living in the outside world. Most women offenders and all shelter residents have been victimized by violence. Both settings tend to promote relationships and networks between and among residents. These similarities raise the legitimate question of whether prisons could be used as treatment settings to promote relational learning and growth for women offenders, as the shelter setting promotes relational learning and growth for battered women.

EMPOWERMENT THROUGH HEALTHY CONNECTIONS

Healthy connections grow out of human environments where interaction and discussion are encouraged, and where members share mutual respect and empathy. Over the last two decades the work of the Stone Center at Wellesley College, based on the writings of Jean

Baker Miller, has documented the characteristics of relationships that promote healthy emotional connections (Jordan 1997; Jordan et al. 1991; Miller 1987; Miller and Stiver 1997). The Stone Center's relational approach applies to both women and men, although their literature has focused primarily on women's development in the context of their subordination in patriarchal cultures. By experiencing the healing and restorative features of healthy relationships, women are empowered to live productive and fulfilling lives, and to contribute to the empowerment of those around them.

Nicolina Fedele and Elizabeth Harrington (1990) describe properties of the Stone Center relational approach that promote healing and psychological growth in group therapy. "These include validation of one's experience, empowerment to act in relationships, development of self-empathy, and mutuality" (p. 3). By sharing her painful experiences with other women who can understand and relate to her pain, the woman finds herself validated as an authentic person. The discovery that she is not alone—that other women have survived similar experience—initiates a healing process that underlies the potential for growth. The related discovery of the power of the group to stimulate movement within as well as outside the group empowers women to take action to build growth-enhancing relationships. In addition, "group therapy provides a unique forum for demonstrating the contrast between members' often highly developed capacities for empathy with others and their frequently atrophied capacities for empathy with self" (Fedele and Harrington 1990, p. 5). Finally, connections within the group that are characterized by mutuality—"an appreciation of the wholeness of the other person's experience and respect for the other person's differentness and uniqueness" (1990, p. 5)—also promote healing and growth.

Fedele and Harrington conclude that "the validating and empowering connections forged by women's group interactions have wide implications for many other types of group endeavors. The process of instilling compassion for oneself and others, and engaging in mutually satisfying and empowering relationships can enrich our understanding of women's groups for work, study, support, peer supervision, friendship, business, research activity, political action, governance, and peace keeping. For where women gather together, there exists a potentially rich relational context to foster growth" (1990, p. 10).

There is little research on the effectiveness of women's therapy or counseling groups in prison. The Stone Center recently piloted a program for staff and residents in a Massachusetts women's prison (Coll and Duff 1995). The project was based on the Stone Center's relational model and explored the implementation of a psychoeducational process group. The group—which included seven residents and three group coleaders—met for five weekly sessions, each lasting one and a half hours. Five topics were covered: relational development, healthy relationships, the depressive spiral and addiction, embracing diversity, and conflict resolution. A process evaluation was completed. Although no definitive conclusions can be drawn because of the small number of participants, results generally support the positive value of the group for residents. Feedback included suggestions to expand meeting times in frequency as well as over a more extended time period, to provide a place to examine residents' interactions with staff, and to provide a bilingual/bicultural group leader team as a model for relational differences. Hopefully this pilot program will lead to future prison programs based on the relational model using larger samples and longitudinal designs to permit tracking resident outcomes after release from prison.

The success of women's groups in providing models for relationship building and in promoting growth in members suggests these groups as powerful sources of treatment and prevention. The two residential situations considered here—women's shelters and women's prisons—although different in significant ways, are potential sites for the development of such groups. Adapting the model of women's groups based on the relational approach holds promise for prison settings. Such women's groups can create safe spaces for women who have been victimized by violence to begin to heal, to compare their experiences with those of other battered women, and to build new relationships outside the battering relationship. The transformations achieved through such outside relationships can help them build new lives, hopefully free of violence.

REFERENCES

Albee, G., and Swift, C. 1995. Introduction. In *Sexual assault and abuse: Sociocultural context of prevention.* ed. Swift, C., 1–11. New York: The Haworth Press.

Alsdurf, J. 1985. Wife abuse and the church: The response of pastors. *Response to the Victimization of Women and Children* 8: 9–11.

Andenaes, J. 1975. General prevention revisited: Research and policy implications. *Journal of Criminal Law and Criminology* 66: 338–365.

Belenky, M., et al. 1986. *Women's ways of knowing: The development of self, voice and mind.* New York: Basic Books.

Berk, R., et al. 1983. Mutual combat and other family violence myths. In *The dark side of families,* eds. Finkelhor, D., et al., 97–212. Beverly Hills, CA: Sage Publications.

Burris, C. 1984. Wife battering: A well-kept secret. *Canadian Journal of Criminology* 26: 171–177.

Burt, M. 1980. Cultural myths and supports for rape. *Journal of Personality and Social Psychology* 38: 217–230.

Butehorn, L. 1985. Social networks and the battered woman's decision to stay or leave (wife battering, women, morality, family violence). *Dissertation Abstracts International* 46105-B: 1741.

Clinchy, B., and Zimmerman, C. 1985. *Growing up intellectually: Issues for college women. Work in Progress, No. 19.* Wellesley, MA: Stone Center, Wellesley College.

Coll, C., and Duff, K. 1995. Reframing the needs of women in prison: A relational and diversity perspective. *Final Report: Women in Prison Pilot Project.* Wellesley, MA: The Stone Center for Developmental Services and Studies.

Dalto, C. 1983. Battered women: Factors influencing whether or not former shelter residents return to the abusive situation. *Dissertation Abstracts International* 44/04-B: 1277.

Erickson, M., and Gibbs, J. 1973. The deterrence question: some alternative methods of analysis. *Social Science Quarterly* 54: 534–555.

Fedele, N.. and Harrington, E. 1990. *Women's groups: How connections heal. Work in Progress, No. 47.* Wellesley, MA: Stone Center, Wellesley College.

Feldman, S. 1983. Battered women: Psychological correlates of the victimization process. *Dissertation Abstracts International* 44/04-B: 1221.

Finkelhor, D. 1983. Common features of family abuse. In *The dark side of families*, eds. Finkelhor, D., et al., 17–28. Beverly Hills, CA: Sage Publications.

Geis, G., and Geis, R. 1978. Rape reform: An appreciative-critical review. *Bulletin of the American Academy of Psychiatry and the Law* 6: 301–312.

Gelles, R., and Cornell, C. 1985. Intimate violence in families. Beverly Hills, CA: Sage Publications.

Gilligan, C. 1982. *In a different voice: Psychological theory and women's development*. Cambridge, MA: Harvard University Press.

Gottlieb, B., ed. 1981. Social networks and social support. *Sage Studies in Community Mental Health*. Beverly Hills, CA: Sage Publications.

Gottlieb, B. 1983. Opportunities for collaboration with informal support systems. In *The mental health consultation field*, eds. Cooper, S., and Hodges, W., 181–203. New York: Human Services Press.

Hilbert, J., and Hilbert, J. 1984. Battered women leaving shelter: Which way do they go? A discriminant function analysis. *Journal of Applied Social Sciences* 8: 291–297.

Hodson, C. 1982. Length of stay in a battering relationship: Test of a model. *Dissertation Abstracts International* 43/06-B: 1983.

Jordan, J., ed., 1997. *Women's growth in diversity: More writings from the Stone Center*. New York: The Guilford Press.

Jordan, J., et al. 1991. *Women's growth in connection: Writings from the Stone Center*. New York: The Guilford Press.

Kremen, E. 1985. Battered women in counseling and shelter programs: A descriptive and follow-up study. *Dissertation Abstracts International* 45/10-A: 3211–3212.

Lerman, L. 1986. Prosecution of wife beaters: Institutional obstacles and innovations. In *Violence in the home: Interdisciplinary perspectives*, ed. Lystad, M., 250–295. New York: Brunner/Mazel.

Lidkea, M. 1982. Counseling as a factor in the later incidence of wife abuse: A follow up study of the clients of Brevard Family Aid Society, Inc. *Dissertation Abstracts International* 43-12/B: 4153.

Loh, W., 1981. What has reform of rape legislation wrought? *Journal of Social Issues* 37: 28–52.

Martin, H., ed. 1976. The abused child: a multidisciplinary approach to development issues and treatment. Cambridge, MA: Ballinger.

Miller, J. 1987. *Toward a new psychology of women* 2nd ed. Boston: Beacon Press.

Miller, J. 1982. *Women and power*. In *Work in progress, No. 1*. Wellesley, MA: Stone Center, Wellesley College.

Miller, J., and Stiver, I. 1997. *The healing connection: How women form relationships in therapy and in life*. Boston: Beacon Press.

Mills, T. 1985. The assault on the self: Stages in coping with battering husbands. *Qualitative Sociology* 8:103–123.

Mitchell, R., and Trickett, E. 1980. Social network research and psychosocial adaptations: Implications for community mental health practice. In *Environmental variables and the prevention of mental illness*, ed. P. Insel, 43–68. Lexington, MA: D.C. Heath & Co.

Okun, L. 1983. A study of woman abuse: Three hundred batterers in counseling. *Dissertation Abstracts International* 44/06-8: 1972.

Pagelow, M. 1982. *Woman battering*. Beverly Hills, CA: Sage Publications.

Perry, W. 1970. Forms of intellectual and ethical development in the college years. New York: Holt, Rinehart and Winston.

Perry, W. 1981. Cognitive and ethical growth: The making of meaning. In *The modern American college*, ed. Chickering, A., 76–116. San Francisco: Jossey-Bass.

Porter, C. 1983. Blame and coping in battered women. *Dissertation Abstracts International* 44/05-B: 1641.

Ruddick, S. 1984. Maternal thinking. In *Mothering: Essays in feminist theory*, ed. Trebilcot, 213–232. Totowa, NJ: Rowman and Allanheld.

Salomon, A., et al. 1996. Patterns of welfare use among poor and homeless women. *American Journal of Orthopsychiatry* 66: 510–525.

Sanday, P. 1981. The socio-cultural context of a rape: A cross-cultural study. *Journal of Social Issues* 37: 5–27.

Schechter, S. 1982. *Women and male violence*. Boston: South End Press.

Semmelman, P. 1982. Battered and nonbattered women: A comparison. *Dissertation Abstracts International* 43/08-B: 2716.

Smith, B. 1981. *Non-stranger violence: The criminal court's response*. Washington, D.C.: National Institute of Justice, U.S. Department of Justice.

Snyder, D., and Scheer, N. 1981. Predicting disposition following brief residence at a shelter for battered women. *American Journal of Community Psychology* 9: 559–566.

Stark, E. 1984. The battering syndrome: Social knowledge, social therapy and the abuse of women. *Dissertation Abstracts International* 45/01-A: 307.

Stark, E., et al. 1979. Medicine and patriarchal violence: The social construction of a private event. *International Journal of Health Services* 9: 461–493.

Straus, M. 1980. Social stress and martial violence in a national sample of American families. *Annals of the New York Academy of Sciences* 347: 229–250.

Strube, M. 1984. Factors related to the decision to leave an abusive relationship. *Journal of Marriage and the Family* 46: 837–844.

Surrey, J. 1987. *Relationship and empowerment. Work in Progress, No. 30.* Wellesley, MA: Stone Center, Wellesley College.

Swift, C. 1987. *Women and violence: Breaking the connection. Work in Progress, No. 27.* Wellesley, MA: Stone Center, Wellesley College.

Tittle, C. 1969. Crime rates and legal sanctions. *Social Problems* 16: 409–423.

Walker, L. 1984. *The battered woman syndrome.* New York: Springer-Verlag.

CHAPTER 12

Needs Assessment and Treatment Goal Planning

Lorry Bradley

Editor's Notes

In Chapter Twelve, Bradley discusses the importance and specifics of individualized needs assessment and treatment goal planning for female offenders. Accommodating treatment to client goals, i.e., individualized goal planning, enhances the likelihood that clients will follow through with whatever suggestions and recommendations are offered. The role and characteristics of the assessor, the need for specialized training in regard to risk factors impacting female offenders, treatment goal planning recommendations, and legal and ethical considerations are presented. Real life scenarios are also presented to assist the needs assessor to learn those needs assessment strategies relevant to the environment in which he or she operates.

In Chapter Seven, Weitzman stated that the real therapeutic relationship is never free from the ordinary obstacles which relationships encounter in everyday life. From this perspective, the therapeutic relationship is not free from bias and distortion, i.e., the therapist cannot maintain a state of unbiased listening. However, Weitzman does not negate the reality that unbiased listening by therapists does take place. Bradley, in Chapter Twelve, suggests that the assessor remain objective when doing needs assessment and goal planning with a female offender. It is important to emphasize here that this state—one in which the therapist always remains present without bias even when experiencing negative reactions to the client— is clearly the idealized therapeutic situation. The point is, in the words of Weitzman, "that whatever the reaction, whatever the therapist might feel, whether or not she understands its origin, the fate of the therapeutic project depends upon her willingness to remain genuine…." This is a lofty treatment goal that the therapist or assessor should aspire to attain when working with female offenders.

INTRODUCTION

The completion of individualized assessments and treatment goal planning are arduous tasks, yet essential to ensure the success of rehabilitative efforts for female offenders. They assist in ascertaining and addressing the specific needs of the female while enhancing the provision of comprehensive services that positively affect behavioral and attitudinal changes. Studies examining the effects of accommodating treatment to clients' goals have found that clients are more likely both to enter treatment earlier and follow through with whatever suggestions and recommendations are offered. For example, drug and alcohol programs often assign clients to standardized programs with little or no regard to their own goals or individual characteristics. The result for the client is a history of poor treatment outcomes. This chapter presents clinical considerations for choosing and training an effective assessor, suggestions for developing individualized assessment protocols, and strategies for facilitating treatment goals. Scenarios, using fictitious clients, are also presented to enhance the discussion. For the purpose of continuity within these scenarios, the assessor will be referred to in the female gender.

CLINICAL CONSIDERATIONS

Completing needs assessments and treatment goal plans with female offenders can be both rewarding and frustrating for assessors. It can be rewarding when the assessor successfully develops a positive rapport fostered through unconditional positive regard by remaining open-minded and accepting of the female offender. In contrast, it can be frustrating when a client is so damaged from negative life experiences and unhealthy interpersonal relationships that developing a connection appears impossible. It is imperative the assessor be aware there is potential for this dichotomy to exist prior to working with this population. To obtain an understanding of the dynamics of female deviance, it is recommended the assessor receive formal training in the common risk factors for females that may contribute to offending behaviors. In addition, the assessor should be knowledgeable about the historical repression and objectification of females within our society (see Chapter Six) and of how to build and maintain rapport with "difficult" client types.

Training and experience in these areas will promote gender-based treatment recommendations, thereby minimizing the tendency to treat female offenders using the same methods used for male offenders. A review of the risk factors and theories of female deviance can be found within Part I of this book. The following discussion describes how to develop a rapport with female offenders.

Developing a Rapport

In *The American Heritage Dictionary, Second College Edition*, rapport is defined as a "relationship, especially one of mutual trust or emotional affinity." By definition, good rapport promotes positive growth; bad rapport leads to counterproductive outcomes. The success of an assessor in building rapport is often based on her personal qualities and characteristics. Research indicates that personal qualities can enhance or detract...and are essential (or even more essential) than specific skills or knowledge. These qualities include self-awareness, sensitivity, open-mindedness, objectivity, competence, trustworthiness, and interpersonal attractiveness (Cormier and Hackney 1987). All of these qualities are essential and often interconnected. For example, an assessor who continues to ask questions about the female offender's relationship with her father, after the female has informed the assessor that she did not feel comfortable even thinking about her father, is not being sensitive to the female's request. Ignoring the female's request may result in the female viewing the assessor as insensitive, incompetent and untrustworthy.

The assessor may have difficulty maintaining open-mindedness, sensitivity and objectivity when the female offender's behavior conflicts with the assessor's value system. Value conflicts are normal when working with populations that do not subscribe and adhere to societal norms or expectations. This is especially true when the female's offenses and/or behaviors are shocking and alarming to the assessor. Because this is often the case, prior to working with this population, the assessor should conduct a self-assessment to sense personality conflicts or personal biases that may arise with respect to her own value systems. Even after successfully working with the population, the assessor may occasionally need to ask herself whether or not she can remain objective with a particular client. The following scenario actually happened to an assessor working in a female offender day reporting program. The assessor was faced with a moral and value conflict when a female offender who previously attended the day program was re-referred for an assessment on a new prostitution charge knowing she was HIV positive. When the assessor received the new referral she became angry that the female was still engaged in prostitution—potentially infecting people with HIV. The assessor questioned whether she could remain objective due to her bias in this regard and preconceived views about the new offense and the female's "irresponsible" behavior. In this case, the assessor was able to work through this internal value conflict by discussing her frustration and anger with her coworkers during a group supervision. She was then able to complete the assessment. What should an assessor do if, after assessing the ability to remain objective, she determines that she is unable to do so? Ethically, she should refer the assessment to another staff member or to another service provider. In cases where referral out or to another staff member is not possible, it is recommended that the assessor seek clinical supervision.

The assessor's competency is enhanced through training and experience working with the population. There are many intuitive, insightful assessors that appear to have an innate ability to work with this population. As humans we are drawn to people who are kind, warm, caring, and sensitive. These qualities can be conveyed during the assessment through body language and speech patterns. For example, the assessor should not position herself across a table from the female. This will present a barrier that will be difficult to overcome. The assessor's tone of voice should be soothing and welcoming. It would be difficult for an assessor who has no effect and who uses closed body language and speech patterns to develop a rapport.

In most treatment relationships, provided the assessor possesses self-awareness, sensitivity, open-mindedness, objectivity, competence, trustworthiness, and interpersonal attractiveness, rapport can usually be developed rather quickly through unconditional positive regard, i.e., accepting the client without judgment. In any treatment relationship, the importance of fostering rapport building cannot be understated. When working with female offenders, building rapport can be complicated by the female's lack of trust or unwillingness to share any details regarding her life due to extensive histories of negative social experiences (see Chapter Nine). The female's mistrust of the assessor can be compounded if she has been referred or mandated to an agency for completion of the assessment by a criminal justice-related organization. In these cases, the female may view the assessor as an extension of a judicial system that "punished" them. It is essential the assessor be aware of the possibility of "roadblocks" to rapport building when working with female offenders. It is also important for the assessor to have strategies to divert them if presented during the interview. These strategies are presented below.

To facilitate rapport building, the interview should be conducted in a relaxed manner, giving the female a sense of trust and confidence in the assessor. The assessor should introduce herself, make the client feel comfortable through nonthreatening conversation. On occasion, clients will make offbeat comments to test, distract, and shock the assessor or because they are frustrated with their situations. Should this occur, it is a mistake for the assessor to overreact to these comments. Some clients may even attempt to elicit a negative reaction by their comments. An overreaction will provide "proof" that the assessor is judgmental and is not to be trusted. Overreaction makes rapport difficult to establish. The following example is a case in point. An assessor who interviewed individuals for welfare eligibility and other social services was required to meet with a client immediately after having an argument with her supervisor. When the assessor explained to the client, a white female, that she was not eligible because her income exceeded welfare guidelines, the woman replied, "If I were black or Puerto Rican I'd be eligible." The assessor responded, "That's right, because I'm white and hate white people, I just don't want to give you money...that's the stupidest thing I've ever heard and I refuse to talk to you anymore." The assessor left the interview, leaving the client in the room. This assessor's response was inappropriate. She may have avoided this situation by calming down and performing a self-check prior to interviewing the client. Being professional, an appropriate way to respond to this client's statement could be "I'm sorry you feel that way. I understand your frustration, however, these are the guidelines set by the federal government. Let's see if this agency can assist you in any other way."

Rapport can also be enhanced through neutral, nonthreatening dialogue during the initial phase of the assessment. Prior to asking any challenging questions, the assessor should introduce herself, give her credentials, inform the client of her experience working with female offenders, explain the reason for the female being referred for the assessment, and ask the female offender if she has any concerns or questions about the assessment process.

It is important to ask the female offender to discuss her feelings about being referred for treatment and to acknowledge these feelings by empathizing with her concerns. For example, the female may have a history of negative experiences with treatment interventions. If she verbalizes this, ask what she would have changed about the intervention(s) and what would help to make this interaction a positive experience. When an assessor discloses information about herself and allows the female to express concerns and discuss options for change, rapport is established.

LEGAL AND ETHICAL CONSIDERATIONS

Regardless of what theoretical orientation the assessor adopts, confidentiality, mandated reporter (duty to warn) requirements, and informed consent must be reviewed with the client prior to completion of the assessment.

Confidentiality

Confidentiality is mandated by the code of ethics for all helping professions as well as by most state laws. The concept of confidentiality is an ethic based on recognizing the sensitive nature of information divulged by clients within a counseling relationship. The legal aspect of confidentiality is in reference to the client's right to privacy. The premise behind confidentiality is to provide a safe environment for the client to process information. The rules protecting confidentiality are often confusing for professionals and often more confusing for clients because they vary depending on circumstances. The exceptions to confidentiality include those admissions or discussions covered under mandated reporter requirements (to be discussed later) and court subpoenaed testimony. Depending on state laws, when working with juvenile female offenders, there may also be exceptions when there is a legal duty to the parents, e.g., reports of progress or specific goals addressed. It may be advisable to give the female offender a form that explains the limits to confidentiality so they fully understand the assessor's responsibilities. When a form is used the assessor should read the document out loud to ensure the client understands the information. When mandated to complete the assessment, the referral source may require additional information about the female. When this is the case, the female must sign releases indicating the information to be divulged and the sources of the information. These releases should also indicate the purpose of sharing the information. If a mandated client refuses to sign releases, there may be a need to refer this individual back to the referral source. In all cases, the assessor should check the agency's policy for protocol in regard to confidentiality.

Mandated Reporter Requirements

Mandated reporter or "duty to warn" requirements depend on local and state statutes. Typically the assessor must report when the female is a danger to herself or others. Duty to warn requirements are based on protecting the public from harm. The legal basis for duty to warn and protect was established through the findings of Tarasoff vs. Regents of the University of California, 1976 (Knapp and VandeCreek 1990). According to the findings of this case, duty to warn is mandated when it is believed the female is dangerous to a specific person or property. The threat must be toward an identifiable target. It is also mandated when the female is a threat to herself. Threats to self include self-mutilation, suicide, and even self-neglect, such as eating disorders and severe drug abuse/use. If a female is assessed to be a threat to others under these requirements, it is necessary to take steps to protect the potential victim(s). The following example illustrates this point. An assessor interviewed a woman, Barbara, to determine if she was appropriate to participate in a women's issues class. During the assessment, Barbara reported she was going to "kill" a woman who she thought was "after" her boyfriend. Barbara indicated she worked with this woman and planned on "hurting" her "tonight." Although the assessor previously explained to Barbara the mandated reporter requirements, when Barbara made these threats the assessor informed Barbara of the need to report the threats. Barbara then stated she was not going to follow through with her plan. However, because Barbara specifically identified the target and gave supporting details about the plan she was going to implement, the assessor contacted Barbara's probation officer, the local police, and Barbara's place of employment. The assessor documented all of the activity in the case record. Ethically and legally the assessor needed to report this incident even if the report could impact the assessor's ability to build a rapport with Barbara. As illustrated in this case, the victim, local law officials, and significant contacts of the victim or perpetrator were notified and all activities were documented. These procedures are advisable under all circumstances where there is a potential threat to harm, as the protocol will help the assessor should she be subpoenaed regarding the reported incident.

The following case illustrates an example of a female threatening suicide. Jean reported, "I'm going to kill myself, life is not worth living…" while being assessed. The assessor questioned why Jean felt this way and how she was planning on harming herself. Jean reported her boyfriend left her and she did not have a place to live. Jean then stated she had a gun at home and was planning on going home and shooting herself. Because Jean reported she was going to harm herself and she had a plan, the assessor informed Jean the police needed to be called. As with threats to others, it is not the assessor's responsibility to ascertain whether or not the client will follow through with the plan. Due to the seriousness of the threat, the police were called immediately. Jean was involuntarily hospitalized for observation. Because mandated reporter requirements vary, the assessor should become knowledgeable about local statutes and agency procedures.

Informed Consent

Informed consent is a concept based on the legal doctrine *violent non fit injuria* or "no wrong is done to one who is willing." This doctrine affords clients the right to be informed of what to expect during the treatment process. It also indicates any risks involved and if the assessor adheres to a particular counseling modality. In addition, informed consent includes a disclosure of the assessor's credentials, address, availability, and experience in the field. When a female offender is mandated to the assessment, this consent should be documented in the case record because this individual is not entering into the process willingly. This is because the female cannot make an "informed" decision to participate in the process without possible consequences for noncompliance. After reviewing clinical considerations and ensuring legal and ethical standards, the assessor can begin completing the assessment.

THE NEEDS ASSESSMENT

Most assessors utilize the problem assessment, sometimes called the psychosocial assessment, as the first information-gathering tool. This assessment involves collecting information about the client's needs and experiences. With regard to female offenders, individualized assessments are necessitated by the unique confluence of risk (negative) and protective (positive) factors that impact female offenders, thereby resulting in deviant activity. Completion of an assessment is the logical way to systematically gather and sort data about these factors. The assessment also provides information relevant to the psychodynamic significance within a framework of specific domains. These domains include but are not limited to the individual, social, educational, and familial domains. The analysis of the female offender's reported current and past level of functioning within these systems assists the assessor in ascertaining risk and protective factors. This is because risk factors such as childhood abuse or drug and alcohol dependency could be mitigated by strengthening existing or building new protective factors such as the ability to "normalize" their environment, the support of nurturing caretakers and/or a positive support system. To illustrate this point, as reported throughout this book, many female offenders report childhood histories of abuse, however, not all females abused as children become female offenders. Therefore, although many females have the risk factor—childhood history of abuse—for some female offenders the protective factors neutralized the negative effect of abuse and did not contribute to or result in criminal behavior.

When completing an assessment it is essential to have a protocol that obtains useful information about the female offender regarding current and past functioning in social and personal contexts. Although the format for the assessment will vary according to the specific needs of the agency or individual conducting the assessment, an outline is provided below that can be adapted to fit the particular needs of the assessor. It should be noted that the assessment phase is not a therapeutic session, it is a data collection session. The information gathered during the assessment will be reviewed and processed during the treatment planning phase of the intake process. A suggested protocol for an assessment is presented in Exhibit 12-1.

The following is a case scenario of an assessment completed on a client named Sue. Sue, a 20 year-old Caucasian female, was referred on prostitution charges to Joan, an assessor

Exhibit 12–1 Intake Assessment Protocol

PROTOCOL FOR INDIVIDUALIZED INTAKE ASSESSMENTS

I. Demographic Information
Name
Address
Date of birth
Telephone number
Marital status
Emergency contact
Employment history: Include duration of employment and reasons for termination
Educational history: Highest grade completed, schools attended
Financial information: Source of income; monthly total
Children: Names, ages, school information
Family demographic information: Mother's name, Father's name, occupations, siblings
Information about spouse or significant other

II. Criminal History
Current charges: Date of arrest, sentencing judge, probation/parole officer, sentence
Prior record: Dates of arrest, charges, sentencing judge, sentence
Court ordered stipulations: Specific treatment recommendations, community service, costs and fines

III. Medical History
Does client have any medical problems?
Who is the primary care physician?
Is the client currently taking any medication?
Does the client have health insurance? If so, what type?
Is the client developmentally disabled?
Has the client ever been treated for a mental health issue? If so, for what? Where did the client receive services?
Does the client have suicidal ideations?
Has the client ever attempted suicide? If so, for what reason? With what mode?
Does anyone in the client's family have a mental health illness?
History of hospitalization: Place of hospitalization, circumstances, dates

IV. Substance Abuse/Use History
When did the client first begin using alcohol and drugs?
At what frequency do/did they use?
Date of last usage
Reasons for usage: Life stressors present
Does the client think their use has caused difficulty with the law, family, employment?
Was the client ever physically, verbally, or sexually abusive while using?
Was the client ever physically, verbally, or sexually abused while using?
Was the client under the influence of drugs when arrested or committing the crimes?

continues

Exhibit 12–1 continued

   V. Family Of Origin/Significant Relationships
   Residential History: Where was the client born? With whom did the client live? How
      long did the client reside at one address?
   Relationship with Mother
   Relationship with Father
   Relationship with Siblings
   Relationships with Other Significant Adults: Aunts, Uncles, Grandparents
   Description of caretakers' relationship with each other
   Is there a family history of criminal behavior? If so, who? What did they do?
   Is there a family history of abuse?
   Description of childhood peer relationships
   Description of present peer relationships
   VI. Abuse History
   Define physical, sexual, verbal, emotional abuse
   Was the client ever a victim of any form of abuse? Type, perpetrator, duration, age of
      onset
   What was client's reaction to the abuse?
   Was the abuse secret? If not, how did people react when informed?
   Has the client ever received counseling for abuse issues? If so, where? With whom?
   VII. Personal Information
   How does client spend leisure time?
   Three strengths of client
   Three weaknesses of client
   Are there any situations which make the client feel uncomfortable?
   What steps does the client plan to take to change criminal behavior?
   What kind of assistance does the client need to facilitate these changes?

for female offenders. Sue was referred to Joan by her probation officer, Joe, for an assessment to determine appropriate treatment interventions.

Introductions

Joan: Sue, my name's Joan and I'll be completing your assessment today. Did Joe tell you why you were referred to me?

Sue: No, I have no idea why and I really don't want to be here.

Joan: Well, because you're on probation he's asked that you meet with me so we can determine what may help you get off and stay off probation. How's that sound?

Sue: It sounds good. I can't stand probation.

Joan: I know how it feels to be told, "I have to do something I really don't want to do," so I'll try to make this as painless as possible. Is that a deal?

Sue: Sure, I guess so.

Joan: O.K., before we get started, I just wanted to tell you a little about myself. I've been working as an assessor at this agency for four years. I provide individual and group counseling to women in our Day Program and complete all the assessments. I have a Master's degree in Counseling Psychology and a Bachelor's degree in Psychology. I've been working as a counselor for 15 years. Before I worked here I was a counselor for women residing in a homeless shelter. Is there anything else you'd like to know about me?

Sue: Not really.

Joan: Everything we talk about here today will be confidential. Can you tell me what confidential means?

Sue: Doesn't that mean that you can't tell no one?

Joan: Kind of, according to the law it means that I can't tell anyone what you tell me unless you authorize me to do so. Now there are some exceptions to that. If you tell me you're going to hurt someone or hurt yourself, I have to report that to the police and Joe, and I do need to report to Joe the treatment goals we come up with in our session. That's why I need you to sign this release form. As you can see, the only thing I will tell him is that you showed up here today and, again, the treatment recommendations. O.K.?

Sue: All right (as she is signing the release form).

As stated previously, the importance of building rapport cannot be understated. Joan is working on building rapport by empathizing with Sue about not wanting to be assessed, and also through her self-disclosure and nonthreatening language. This language will help Sue feel more comfortable with being mandated to talk to someone she does not know.

Demographic Information

This section of the assessment assists in identifying the client and does not assist in treatment planning (see Exhibit 12-1 for suggested information to be gathered in this section). The information includes their name, address, telephone number, and who to contact in case of an emergency. Because of the nonthreatening questions asked during this portion of the assessment, Sue will continue to grow more comfortable with Joan. Next Joan questions Sue about her criminal history.

Criminal History

The purpose of completing a criminal history section is to evaluate criminal maladaptive behavior patterns. During the treatment planning phase, the length of time between offenses, consequences for criminal behaviors, treatment interventions the female offender received, and her motivation for the criminal acts will be explored.

Joan: We're all done with that section. Now I'm going to ask you some questions about your criminal involvement. Let's begin with the first offense you ever had, what was it?

Sue: When I was a kid?

Joan: Yes, how old were you and what did you do?

Sue: When I was in ninth grade I got caught stealing stuff at a store. They put me on probation for it. Isn't that stupid? I know other people who stole stuff and they just got a fine. They just didn't like me.

Joan: How long were you on probation?

Sue: Two years, they wanted me to go to some class or something and I wouldn't go, so they kept me on. I also got caught drinking at school.

Joan: Was there a fine?

Sue: No, I just had to spend more time on probation, I think.

Joan: What was your next charge?

Sue: Prostitution when I was 18. I didn't even do it, they set me up. They gave me six months probation.

Joan: O.K. the next charge?

Sue: Prostitution again, when I was 19. That time my friend and I were walking down the street and some guy called us over to his car. He asked us to give him a "b___ j__." I told him I would for $20. What the hell, it was only a "b___ j__." He ended up being a "narc," you know, an undercover guy.

Joan: So you got caught by an undercover cop, how much time did you get for that charge?

Sue: They put me on probation for a year, I think.

Joan: And your latest charge?

Sue: Prostitution and delivery charges. I was really stupid. It was my boyfriend's fault. He wanted me to make some money so we could get more weed.

Joan: So other than having to come to me for this assessment, and being on probation again, is there anything else you were mandated to do because of the new charge?

Sue: Yeah, I have to go for "pee" tests.

Joan remained nonjudgmental during this portion of the interview. She did not ask Sue to explain the motivation for her criminal activity nor did she address Sue's statements regarding her lack of responsibility for her behavior, as indicated in Sue's statements: "they set me up" and "it was my boyfriend's fault." After completing the criminal history section, Joan completes Sue's medical history.

Medical History

The purpose and function of the medical history section is to gather basic information about the female's health to facilitate goal planning and coordinate services with medical personnel if necessary. The information collected in this section includes frequency and reasons for past medical and psychological hospitalizations. It also includes questions about the female's current mental health status (see Exhibit 12-1). If the female offender is receiving outside services for medical reasons, releases should be signed. After Joan completes Sue's medical history, they continue to the Substance Use/Abuse History Section.

Substance Abuse/Use History

The purpose and function of the substance abuse/use history section is to screen for current and past abuse/use problems and assist in formulating the treatment plan. This is not a comprehensive evaluation of the female offender's drug and/or alcohol use, it is merely a snapshot of the problem. If the assessor determines the need for further analysis, the client should be referred to an experienced drug and alcohol provider for a comprehensive evaluation. It should be noted that clients will often minimize their drug and/or alcohol usage due to the shame, denial, and the possible consequences of substance use. For this reason, some creative questioning may assist in eliciting more truthful responses, as Joan's questioning will illustrate.

Joan: I'm going to now ask you questions about alcohol and drugs. How old were you when you first started drinking?

Sue: I was five. My dad let me drink his beer.

Joan: When was the last time you drank and how much did you drink?

Sue: I can't remember. Definitely before I was arrested, about a six pack and six or seven shots a day.

Joan: What made you stop drinking?

Sue: Probation.

Joan: When did you start using drugs and what drugs have you used?

Sue: When I was 10, I started smoking weed with my older brother. Then when I was 14 or 15... yeah more like 15, I started doing crack and I tried heroin when I was 16. That's it.

Joan: When was the last time you used any of those drugs?

Sue: I don't know.

Joan: Was it a week ago, a month ago?

Sue: Why do you need to know all this?

Joan: This information will help us make recommendations for your treatment plan. You said before that you have to submit urine samples, it may help to look at the patterns of your usage so you don't submit any dirty urines, right?

Sue: I guess.

Joan: As I said before, we're completing this assessment so we can come up with ways to help you to get off and stay off probation. Having clean urines will definitely help.

Sue: O.K. If I tell you something you have to keep it confidential, right?

Joan: I told you before the only thing I can report to Joe is that you showed up here today and whatever treatment recommendations we come up with.

Sue: I smoked a blunt (a cigar packed with marijuana) last week. I think Joe's going to find out because I'm sure I gave a dirty urine.

Joan: Let's talk about that later, maybe you can come up with a way to deal with that. You only smoked one blunt? How much do you usually use in one day?

Sue: It depends, sometimes I wake up smoking and go to sleep smoking. Sometimes I don't smoke at all.

Joan: Is there any reason or anything going on when you smoke all day long?

Sue: Usually it's when I get in a fight with my baby's father.

Joan: In what ways does smoking help you cope with fighting?

Sue: It calms me down, I can think better when I'm high too.

Joan: You said you used crack and heroin too, how much did you use and when was the last time?

Sue: I haven't used crack for a long time, maybe four or five years ago. I don't really like it. I just did it to stay awake when I was drinking. I didn't use much. I used heroin the night I got busted. I only use a little at a time. The most I've ever done is a bag.

Joan: Do any other members of your family use alcohol or drugs?

Sue: Yeah, all of them, my older brother died of bad heroin in Philly.

Joan: Have you ever gone to in- or out-patient drug and alcohol counseling?

Sue: I had to go to a group last time I was on probation. It was stupid! Everyone sat around talking about drugs and stuff and it made me want to use. I also had to go to two A.A. (Alcoholics Anonymous) meetings a week. They were stupid too. All these people sitting around telling you how to stay clean and sober, when half of them are still f____ing up.

Joan: So you didn't get much out of either group experience. What do you think made you stop then?

Sue: Myself, I can control when I use. If I don't want to, I don't.

Joan: Have you had blackouts or any other reactions while using?

Sue: I've passed out from drinking plenty of times but that's just falling asleep and stuff. I've never blacked out.

Joan: How would you describe yourself? Social drinker, heavy drinker, problem drinker or alcoholic?

Sue: Heavy drinker.

Joan: How would you describe yourself when it comes to drug use? Social user, heavy user, problem user, or addict?

Sue: Sometimes heavy, sometimes problem. I'm definitely not an addict because I can control it.

Joan: I know you said you can control your use. Would there be anything else that could help you out with this?

Sue: Yeah, if Bob would stop fighting with me.

Joan: Is Bob your baby's father?

Sue: Yes.

Joan did not ask "if" but "when" the first time Sue used alcohol and drugs. This was the creative questioning alluded to prior to this dialogue. Many authors of counseling textbooks would consider this leading questioning. With a female offender population however, the norm is that the female has some history of alcohol and drug use, therefore asking the questions in this manner will foster more truthful answers. Again, it is very common for female offenders to minimize or hide their usage because admitting to use may result in further criminal consequences. In those rare instances where the female has not used alcohol and drugs, she will respond that she has never used. Joan did not allow Sue to process the problem she presented, a possible dirty urine, because this will be addressed during the treatment planning phase.

Family-of-Origin/Significant Relationships

The purpose of this section is to determine the female offender's family and peer group history. Family of origin is defined as the individuals present in the household(s) in which the female offender was raised. For some females, the family structure and peer group may have changed repeatedly and the specific nature of this instability is essential to uncover. In this section, information about family members, family structure, and parental style is obtained. In addition, the situations in which the problem behaviors occurred, the antecedent events and the way significant others responded to the problem behavior are explored. From a systems perspective, as described in Chapter Three, it is important that the family-of-origin dynamics be explored because the female was once or may currently be part of a family system. Dysfunctional family and peer interactions may have negatively impacted on the female's psyche, possibly causing irreparable damage carried throughout the female's life.

Joan: When you were growing up who did you live with?

Sue: All different people.

Joan: Well let's start from your birth, when you were born where did you live, who did you live with and how long did you live in that situation?

Sue: I lived with my mom, dad, and Steve, my brother, in Allentown until I was about six.

Joan: Then where did you live and with whom?

Sue: We moved in with my grandmother because my mom kicked my dad out of the house and he kept coming back in.

Joan: Was this your mom's mom?

Sue: Yes.

Joan: How long did you stay there? Was that still in Allentown?

Sue: Yeah, in Allentown. We stayed there until I was 10.

Joan: Then where did you live and with whom?

Sue: We moved to our own apartment in Allentown when my grandmother died. Then my mom started going out with and letting a bunch of different guys live with us. There were too many guys for me to even count.

Joan: Other than these men, was it just your mother, you, and your brother?

Sue: No, by then Josh was born.

Joan: How long did you live there?

Sue: When I was 12 we went into foster care until I was 14. That's because my mom let some guy beat up Steve. It sucked! My dad tried to get us out, but Children and Youth wouldn't let him have us.

Joan: Then at 14 where did you go?

Sue: I went back to my mother's house until I was 17.

Joan: When you went back to your mother's who was living there?

Sue: Her loser boyfriend Dave, my mother, and Josh.

Joan: Where was Steve?

Sue: Steve was placed in some other home in Philly because he got caught stealing cars.

Joan: Where did you go at 17?

Sue: I got pregnant and moved in with Bob.

Joan: When your parents were together what was their relationship like?

Sue: My dad use to beat the shit out of my mom, she deserved it, though.

Joan: Is that why your mother made him leave?

Sue: She signed a Protection From Abuse against him and he wasn't allowed to come into the house. He put her in the hospital that time.

Joan: How would you describe your relationship with your mother?

Sue: Fine as long as I don't live with her. She thinks I try to steal her boyfriends.

Joan: How would you describe your relationship with you father?

Sue: Good, I get along with him better. He still lives in Allentown too.

Joan: You said before that your entire family uses drugs and alcohol. What did your parents use?

Sue: My mother used everything you can imagine. My dad just drinks.

Joan: Do either of your parents have any mental health problems?

Sue: My mother is schizophrenic. She's really out of it. My dad's O.K.

Joan: You said your dad was abusive to your mom. Was there any other abuse in your house?

Sue: My mom and dad used to hit Steve. My mom would hit me when I was bad. Some of her gross boyfriends tried to touch me.

Joan: What do you mean by touch? Physically? Sexually?

Sue: Both, most of them were scumbags.

Joan: What was your relationship like with your brothers?

Sue: Steve and I was pretty tight until he died last year. Josh still lives in Allentown with my mom. He kind of stays away from me because of my mother.

Joan: What was your relationship like with your grandmother?

Sue: Great, she would do anything for us. She was more like my mom.

Joan: Were there any other adults in your life while you were growing up?

Sue: Not really, other than my mom's boyfriends.

Joan: Other than you and Steve, did any of your family members have criminal histories?

Sue: My dad was arrested for punching a cop a couple of years ago and my mom was in jail when we were placed. I forget what they charged her with.

Joan: Now we can move on to your present relationships. You have mentioned Bob a few times. Are you still living with him?

Sue: Now we are, he just moved back in. Last year he moved out with some bitch.

Joan: How would you describe your relationship with Bob?

Sue: I love Bob and he loves me, it's special like that, no one will ever come between us.

Joan: You said before you want to smoke when you're fighting with Bob. Does that happen a lot?

Sue: Yeah, when I start bothering him. If I just let him alone we probably wouldn't fight at all.

Joan: How do you fight?

Sue: We punch each other and stuff. He only hurt me once.

Joan: How did he hurt you?

Sue: He threw me against the wall to get me away from him, I got a concussion.

Joan: When did that happen?

Sue: A couple months ago. Nothing like that has happened since then. You know because he felt really bad and stuff.

Joan: How does Bob get along with Chelsea (Sue's baby)?

Sue: O.K., he spends time with her and stuff. She just annoys him sometimes. She whines a lot and he can't stand it.

Joan: Do you have any close friends and if so what is good and bad about your relationships with them?

Sue: Bob's kind of my only friend. I can't really trust any girls, you always have to watch your back.

It took some time to obtain Sue's residential history. However, this information is essential to providing a full picture of Sue and the risk factors she experienced while a child. Joan occasionally presented questions that included information Sue reported earlier in the assessment. By doing this Sue will know that Joan is actively listening to what she has said. This will aid in increasing Sue's comfort level and Joan's ability to maintain rapport. While Sue briefly mentioned abuse issues these will not be explored until the next section.

Abuse History

Joan: This is the next to the last section, we're almost done!

Sue: Good.

Joan: You mentioned before that your mom's boyfriends tried to touch you physically and sexually. Can you define physical abuse?

Sue: When you hit someone.

Joan: Can you define emotional abuse?

Sue: When you f___ with someone's head.

Joan: Can you define verbal abuse?

Sue: It's kind of the same as emotional but you use words.

Joan: What about sexual abuse?

Sue: When someone touches you when you don't want to be touched.

Joan: Other than your mom's boyfriends you told me about before, has anyone else done any of this to you?

Sue: Bob's hit me but it's not abuse. My mom says lots of stuff that's pretty annoying.

Joan: Can you give me an example?

Sue: She always accuses me of sleeping with her boyfriends because when I was 15 Chuck wanted me instead of her.

Joan: Chuck was one of your mom's boyfriends?

Sue: Yes.

Joan: Did you have a relationship with him?

Sue: Yes, all the time. He was the first guy I was with. He didn't want my mother, he wanted me.

Joan: How old was Chuck?

Sue: Thirty something.

Joan: Would you consider what Chuck did sexual abuse?

Sue: No way, I wanted to do it. He was the first that I wanted to be with. Those other scumbags forced me.

Joan: How old were you the first time someone forced you to do something you didn't want to do?

Sue: Around 11 and it happened until I went into foster care, in foster care and after foster care until Chuck came around.

Joan: Did you tell anyone about these incidents?

Sue: I told my mother but she didn't believe me.

Joan: You're telling me this now, have you been able to talk about this with other people?

Sue: Yeah, other girls in prison and I have talked about it. But Bob doesn't know, I don't ever want him to know.

As with the substance abuse section of the intake assessment, the female offender may minimize the information presented in the abuse history section due to shame and self-blame issues. Sue's shame is evident in her statement "I don't ever want him to know," when referring to Bob becoming aware of her abuse history.

Personal Information

This final section includes questions about the female offender's likes and dislikes. The questions provide information about the female's interests, areas of and capacity for pleasure and achievement, and quality of interpersonal relations. This information provides a closing for the assessment portion of the intake process and sets up the treatment goal planning phase.

Joan: Sue, this is it. Just a few more questions. How do you spend your free time?

Sue: I spend it with Chelsea and Bob. Chelsea's out of control so I'm always chasing her around.

Joan: What are three things you like about yourself?

Sue: I don't know, I'm pretty, I take care of Bob, and I take care of Chelsea.

Joan: What are three things you dislike about yourself?

Sue: I'm dumb, I don't have a GED (General Equivalency Diploma), and I'm a prostitute.

Joan: Are there any groups of people or situations that make you feel uncomfortable?

Sue: I hate groups. I don't like it when girls are after Bob.

Joan: The last and final question, what are three things that you plan to change about your lifestyle?

Sue: I already have, I'm not using and stuff.

Joan: O.K. reword that. Maybe keep staying clean and sober is one.

Sue: Oh, well then to continue to not use, get along with Bob, and be a good mother to Chelsea.

Closing

After completing the needs assessment, it is beneficial to schedule a second appointment to complete the treatment goal plan. This will allow time for the assessor to review the information provided and to develop specific questions for the female offender that can facilitate treatment planning.

TREATMENT GOAL PLANNING

Briefly, treatment goal planning can be described as the summarizing and prioritizing of the information gathered during the needs assessment interview. This is the problem definition phase. This is also a time for the female offender to determine which specific behaviors she would like to change. This process allows the female offender to identify the most problematic areas of her life that can be addressed through treatment interventions. She will receive recommendations for treatment and perhaps referrals to outside agencies during this phase. For this reason, as explained in Chapter Nine, community-based programs are more suited to treatment needs. In developing treatment goals, the assessor must allow the client to identify the relevant social domains or systems in which the problematic situation is rooted, i.e., family, peer, community, etc. Further, treatment is both more effective and more efficient when client goals are accepted at face value. The assessor should not reformulate the goals along formal lines because these goals determine the focus and structure of the intervention process. The treatment goal plan is a working plan that will continuously change during the counseling relationship. It is a tool used to chart the course of treatment. Again it is imperative that the female offender play the lead role. If the assessor determines the goals of treatment, the plan may be flawed by the assessor's projections. To avoid frustration, it is also essential to remember female offenders may choose to continue maladaptive behaviors because they are not ready or able at the assessment or treatment planning stages to change them. Their intent is to keep their life exactly as it is. (See Chapter Four for further information regarding the multiphased treatment process.)

The treatment plan can be formatted in many different ways; there is no universally accepted style. The following format is an example of what is typically included in a treatment goal plan. Sue's completed goal plan is presented in Exhibit 12-2.

Problem Definition

During the problem definition portion of the treatment plan, the female offender and assessor identify three to five problem areas that the client would like to change. One of these goals should be the presenting problem. The presenting problem is what brought the assessor and the client together. If the client is referred or mandated, the presenting problem may be indicated by the referral source. It is interesting to note that female offenders referred by a third party usually have very different evaluations of their social situations and problems than their referral source. In Sue's situation, she and Joan reviewed the assessment information and identified four problem areas that could be addressed through treatment interventions. Sue identified her presenting problem as "being on probation." The problem identification was facilitated through reviewing the assessment. Joan asked specific questions to obtain a clear picture of Sue's reality. For example, when reviewing the criminal history the following conversation occurred:

Joan: When discussing most of your offenses you stated someone else was responsible. Why do you think you always end up being the victim?

Sue: I didn't say I was a victim.

Joan: You did say when you were arrested for shoplifting you received probation when other people received fines. You also said you were wrongly accused of prostitution and that your boyfriend was responsible for this last arrest. Well that sounds like you're usually the victim doesn't it?

Sue: Yeah, I just get myself in the wrong place at the wrong time.

Joan: Sounds like maybe some problem solving skills may be helpful. What do you think?

Sue: I'm not very good at thinking before I do anything. That might be a good idea. Yeah let's put that down.

It should be noted that although Joan made this suggestion, she allowed Sue to make the decision as to whether or not this would be a goal.

Goal Planning

The client and assessor define both long-term goals and short-term objectives. The goals should be based on the problems identified. The objectives should be task based and bring

Exhibit 12–2 Planning Treatment Goals

TREATMENT GOAL PLAN

Client: _____ Sue _____   **Date:** _____ 1/1/98 _____

Assessor: _____ Joan _____   **Referral Source:** _____ Joe _____

Goal 1:   To be Released From Probation

Objective: Submit urines one time per week until 6/30/98

Objective: Attend the female offender day reporting program for 15 weeks

Objective: Meet with probation officer one time per week until 6/30/98

Goal 2:   To Learn Problem Solving Skills

Objective: Meet with Joan on a weekly basis for individual counseling until 3/31/98

Objective: Write down three examples of positive problem solving and three examples

of negative problem solving by 1/15/98

Objective: Use and list five examples of positive problem solving situations

between 1/1/98 and 6/1/98

Goal 3:   To Learn New Parenting Skills

Objective: Research local parenting classes and enroll in a class by 2/1/98

Objective: Complete parenting classes by 6/1/98

Objective: Research and attend a parent support group by 3/1/98

Goal 4:   To Stay Clean and Sober

Objective: Attend two A.A. meetings per week until 6/30/98

Objective: Complete a 10-page report on alcohol and drug use by 3/1/98

Objective: Submit clean urines on a weekly basis until 6/30/98

Client Signature: _____ **Counselor Signature:** _____

---

the goals to concrete, measurable levels with specific dates of completion. During goal planning the client's reported strengths and limitations should be reviewed to determine any roadblocks or maladaptive coping skills that may impede or facilitate goal attainment. One of Sue's goals was to be released from probation in six months. The short-term objectives were to report to submit urine samples once per week for six months, attend individual counseling once per week for a minimum of three months, and meet with Joe a minimum of once per week for six months.

Treatment Recommendations

The assessor and female offender determine appropriate interventions to be used to assist in goal attainment. The assessor takes the lead during this phase, making recommendations for addressing the client's identified problems. For this reason, if the agency is in a community-based setting, the assessor needs to be aware of community resources including treatment resources. Joan recommended that Sue attend the local day reporting program for 15 weeks. The day reporting program includes individual and group counseling, life skills classes, and GED classes.

RESPONSIBILITIES

The final step of developing a treatment plan requires a division of responsibilities. The assessor and client assign tasks, who is responsible for what, by what date and when the treatment plan will be reviewed and updated. After conducting the treatment goal plan the assessment phase is complete.

CONCLUSION

Female offenders have a multitude of risk factors impeding their ability to become and remain law abiding citizens. Through the completion of individualized needs assessments and treatment goal planning these factors can be identified and processed with the female offender. The ability of an assessor to successfully facilitate these procedures can be hindered by clinical, legal, and ethical barriers. Moreover, the female offender's life experiences can also impede the process of completing needs assessments and treatment goal plans. With training in reference to female offending populations, awareness of personal and societal biases about female offenders, and the assessor's innate ability to build rapport with difficult client types, successful completion of needs assessments and treatment goal plans can be attained.

REFERENCES

Cormier, L.S., and Hackney, H. 1987. *The professional counselor: A process guide to helping.* Needham Heights, MA: Allyn & Bacon.

Knapp, S., and VandeCreek, L. 1990. *Pennsylvania law and psychology.* Harrisburg, PA: Pennsylvania Psychological Association.

PART III

The Program Perspective

It should now be apparent that the rehabilitative needs of female offenders are far too complex for any one agency to handle alone. For this reason, female offenders often need services and treatment provided by noncriminal justice agencies. Further, because they are often on the caseloads of one or more human service providers when they become involved with the justice system, integrated systems of community-based service delivery are particularly important in successfully intervening with them. A comprehensive, interdisciplinary approach dramatically increases the efficacy of prevention and intervention efforts with female offenders while reducing duplication of services.

Interestingly, many practitioners, researchers in criminal justice, treatment providers, and others *do* advocate the integrated approach with a spectrum of graduated sanctions and treatment options. At the same time, they are often disappointed with the results. One reason for the disappointment is the perception, discussed in Chapter Four, that "nothing works" because female offenders are an intractable population. Another reason is the perception that women offenders are involved in less serious crimes and, therefore, receive lower risk assessment scores. As a result they are typically under supervision for too brief a time to benefit fully from broad-based interventions. In Chapter Thirteen, Velasquez suggests that the failure of the integrated approach is due predominantly to the fact that the various entities in the criminal justice system, irrespective of the approach they espouse, continue to operate as independent entities. These entities include those that serve the correctional system: education and public behavioral health, inclusive of social welfare systems. The result is, in effect, a single focus approach to service provision that targets one risk factor alone, e.g., substance abuse.

The reality is that these entities have distinct functions and different missions. Additionally, because they have so much to do, there is usually not enough time or effort expended to learning about or integrating fully with other components across service delivery systems. It is suggested here that human service providers should aspire to go beyond providing a single focus treatment response that tends to be incident-oriented and crisis-oriented. This response cannot comprehensively address the root causes of female offenders' maladaptive behaviors. While service integration efforts can take a variety of forms, to be truly effective in meeting female offenders' rehabilitative needs, the integration cannot continue to occur on a superficial level only.

In Chapter Thirteen, "An Integrated Systems Approach to Program Development and Implementation," Velasquez presents a practical integrated approach to effective program development and implementation for female offenders. This approach requires the organization of key community leaders around the principle of viable programs that address the rehabilitative needs of female offenders. These programs should encompass gender-specific and culturally competent services inclusive of the female offender's individual, complex health, educational, and social needs. This chapter is aimed at community or institutional correctional administrators and others who are interested in comprehensively addressing the multiple needs of the female offender population.

In Chapter Fourteen, "Programs that Work: Self-taught Empowerment and Pride: A Multimodal/Dual Empowerment Approach to Confronting the Problems of African-American Female Offenders," Henriques and Brown discuss the Self-Taught Empowerment and Pride (STEP) program, an institutional and aftercare program for incarcerated, soon-to-be and recently released female offenders in New York City. The program offers counseling, job search skills, coping and parenting skills, and referrals to relevant community resources. The STEP program offers these services within a dual empowerment treatment model and has proven to be particularly useful with African-American offenders. This model focuses on women gaining power over their own lives and learning to support and assist in the empowerment of others.

In Chapter Fifteen, "Programs that Work: Mothers," Zaplin and Dougherty describe the realities faced by institutionalized mothers. The authors review selected examples of institutional programming for mothers and present a community-based program that is comprised of three components: an eight-week parenting class, an ongoing parent support group, and an eight-week "Working With Emotions" curriculum. Implicit in this model program is the assumption that simple cognitive interventions such as parent education classes are not sufficient to change behavioral outcomes for the offenders who participate. Also implicit in this model program is the logic that if the sources and causes of the female offender's criminal behavior are addressed, a female offender eventually can develop responsibility and independence as a woman and a mother.

In Chapter Sixteen, " Programs that Work: Working With Prostitutes," Bradley and Moschella explain the dynamics of prostitution by presenting an historical overview of prostitution and an overview of prostitution as it is seen today. They describe the steps taken to develop a program for prostitutes. They then describe Regaining Esteem Stopping Prostitution by Education and Continued Treatment (RESPECT), a program for prostitutes.

In Chapter Seventeen, "Evaluation of Programs for Female Offenders," Kendall examines program evaluation with women and girl offenders. The chapter identifies elements of successful programs for them. The emphasis on recidivism and actuarial methods as measures of program success is questioned within the context of a broader debate over program effectiveness. Examples are then provided of both quantitative and qualitative evaluations and research in order to identify the strengths and limitations of each. The chapter concludes with a brief exploration of some possible unintended consequences of correctional evaluation research.

It should be emphasized here that the model programs described, while geared to the needs of each subpopulation addressed, will be successful to the extent that they truly incorporate the broad-based approach presented and to the extent that they are theoretically grounded and outcome-driven.

CHAPTER 13

An Integrated Systems Approach To Program Development and Implementation

Angela Velasquez

Editor's Notes

In Chapter Thirteen, Velasquez provides community and/or institutional correctional administrators with a practical approach to program development and implementation for female offenders. Specifically, the author discusses: (1) traditional "barriers" to developing effective programming; (2) the benefits afforded by implementation of community-based female offender programming; and (3) a planned learning strategy culminating in an integrated systems approach to program development and implementation. The implementation consists of a comprehensive strategic plan for achieving the integrated approach developed.

The traditional barriers to both gender-specific and holistic, system-wide program development and implementation for female offenders are, according to Velasquez, largely the result of widely held myths that perpetuate incorrect information about female offenders in particular and crime in general. Velasquez contends that the real reason that it appears "nothing works" with female offenders is, in addition to these myths held by both the general public and politicians, the current human service delivery system, inclusive of justice, education, and public behavioral health, is not well integrated. The author contends that the current single focus approach to service delivery is both ineffective in terms of client goal attainment and costly to tax payers. Velasquez describes, in detail, a model for effectively integrating human service delivery on both a policy and functional level and the methods for implementing the model. The integrated model of service delivery focuses on four primary functions: assessment/diagnostic, supportive services, educational services, and custodial services. Effective integration of these functions among all entities in the human service delivery system will ensure that the rehabilitative needs of female offenders are holistically addressed. By moving from the single focus approach to program development that historically has produced only marginal impacts on the rate of female offending, to the integrated system approach to program development and implementation, greater positive outcomes can be achieved both programmatically for the female offender and for the community at large in terms of permanently reduced crime rates and less money spent for crime interventions.

INTRODUCTION

It is clear from previous chapters that female offenders have specific needs in terms of programs. That is, programmatic options for female offenders must holistically address both the risk and protective factors specific to their gender, factors that define their treatment needs. Specifically, female offenders exhibit the following risk factors: physical, sexual, and emotional abuse, negative body image, emotional stress and resultant depression, suicidal tendencies, and pregnancy. Conversely, the protective factors are inclusive of improved self-esteem, the ability to be self-aware when expressing feelings and ideas or responding to praise and approval, and increased knowledge of limitations, boundaries, and good health practices. Given the typical risk factors of the female offender, the task of developing and implementing holistic, gender-specific rehabilitative programs that address needs can be frustrating and appear overwhelming to many practitioners. The clear frustration of practitioners lies in where to begin to address the multiple dysfunction of female offenders from a holistic and cost effective point of view, while at the same time ensuring the following Balanced and Restorative Justice (BARJ) principles: (1) community protection, (2) accountability, and (3) competency development (Umbreit 1997). For example, in one intermediate punishment program (THE PROGRAM for Women and Families 1997) during the first half of 1997: 79 percent of the female offenders mandated by the Judiciary had at least one (1) prior criminal conviction with the average number of prior convictions being 2.5; 61 percent were not high school graduates, with educational testing level averages between the 6th and 8th grade reading level and the 4th and 6th grade math level; 24 percent possessed a General Equivalency Diploma (GED); 80 percent were drug-related addicts; 76 percent were single heads of household, with an average of 2.5 children; 45 percent had no work history and no knowledge in terms of work ethics or of securing or maintaining employment; 44 percent had a sporadic work history with the average length of employment being 2 months; and 74 percent had a history of abuse (physical, sexual, or emotional), with 63 percent of the abuse reported as sexual.

Given the general characteristics of female offenders, never before in the history of institutional and community corrections has the challenge to develop effective programmatic options been more critical to reducing the rate of criminality in females. The fact is, these same females are fast becoming, or are already, the heads of households in our community and the custodial parents of our youth. If society continues to respond by developing programming that does not holistically address their risk/protective factors, societal impacts will continue to be: (1) a continued escalation in the incidence of crime committed by females; and (2) intergenerational criminality. If society seeks to reduce the likelihood of maladaptive behavior in our future youth, we need to begin by rehabilitating, or perhaps more appropriately stated, by "parenting the parent."

This chapter will present a practical approach to effective program development and implementation for female offenders. It is aimed at community or institutional correctional administrators and others who are interested in comprehensively addressing the multiple needs of the female offender population. Specifically, the chapter will present (1) traditional barriers to developing effective programming; (2) the benefits afforded by implementation of community-based female offender programming; and (3) a planned learning strategy, culminating in an integrated systems approach to program development.

BARRIERS TO PROGRAM DEVELOPMENT

Traditional barriers to both gender-specific and holistic program development and implementation for female offenders are largely the result of myths, which perpetuate incorrect information about the female offender. These myths include:

- Holistic, gender-specific programming cannot be fiscally justified due to the relatively small number of crimes committed by females in terms of the total criminal population.
- Females who commit crimes do so as the result of moral turpitude requiring institutionalization to provide for their "moral correction."
- The public favors "lock 'em-up" solutions to crime regardless of the nature of the crime committed.
- The public and political sentiment of "nothing works" appears justified by the human service delivery systems' marginal effectiveness in meeting human needs.

These myths, repudiated below, have resulted in costly, marginally effective, gender-specific programming in response to the female offenders' holistic rehabilitative needs.

Myth 1: Holistic, gender-specific programming cannot be fiscally justified due to the seemingly small number of crimes committed by females in terms of the total criminal population

The fact that the female criminal population is seemingly small in relation to the total criminal population, resulting in lower numbers of crimes committed by females than males, is a significant barrier that misleads the community and its leaders, of the importance of developing and implementing holistic, gender-specific programming. This problem is exacerbated by the media, which highlights violent crimes committed largely by males. The result is the exclusion of gender-specific programming and/or the development of programs for female offenders largely as afterthoughts or extensions of the male offender programs based on research directed and driven in response to male crime.

To counteract and correct these responses this myth must be dissipated. This can be accomplished through systematic public education. This education will cultivate an understanding that although the female crime rate is low compared to the overall crime rate, the impact of female crime is significant in terms of societal impact. The community and its leaders will come to appreciate that failure to address crime committed by females will have long lasting societal impact, as these girls and women are, or are rapidly becoming, the heads of households and the primary custodial parents of our youth.

Myth 2: Females who commit crimes do so as the result of a lack of moral turpitude, requiring institutionalization to provide for their "moral correction"

The myth that females commit crime due to moral turpitude has contributed to both the increasing numbers of institutional placements of female delinquents into public/private behavioral health residential facilities and the incarceration of women offenders into penal institutions. These responses, while they may provide immediate relief so often sought by the community, result in marginal, long-term effects in regard to reduction of female crime and delinquency.

To counteract and correct these responses, understanding within the community must be cultivated through diffusion of this myth. Again, education of the community should promote understanding that females, in general, do not commit crime as a result of "lacking morals," but predominately as a means for survival. The need of these females to survive emotionally and economically in society manifests itself in behavioral responses that can be identified as risk factors. Once the community develops an understanding of this it will come to appreciate that the programmatic response for female offenders must be inclusive of measures specifically designed to confront risk factors and secure survival of the female in society (Chesney-Lind 1997). The community will then embrace holistic, gender-specific measures. Ideally, these holistic, gender-specific measures should incorporate the three following components in the least restrictive environment possible: (1) counseling directed toward core issues of abuse; (2) building career and vocational skills directed toward self-sufficiency; and (3) developing empowerment and self-efficacy.

Myth 3: The public favors "lock 'em-up" solutions to crime regardless of the nature of the crime committed

The myth that the public favors "lock 'em-up" solutions to crime, regardless of the seriousness of the offense, is a significant barrier to holistic, gender-specific program development for female offenders. Belief in this myth has resulted in the costly provision of "immediate relief," through escalating institutionalization of female offenders; again, with only marginal long-term impact upon the reduction of female crime and delinquency. Ultimately, the community and its leaders must be educated to the following fact:

> If severe punishment and incarceration were effective, America should be one of the safest societies in the world. Despite the common perception among many citizens that the United States is too lenient on criminals, the fact is that more Americans are locked up in prisons, per capita, than any developed nation in the world. In a similar vein, sentences in the U.S. are far in excess of other democratic western nations. The U.S. is the only developed nation to routinely advocate and use capital punishment. (Umbreit 1997, p. 22)

DiMascio (1995) states that, "Americans have become more and more concerned about the problem of crime, and increased incarceration often seems like a solution. But studies have shown that when the public is made aware of the possible range of punishments, and given information about how and with whom they are used, they support alternatives to incarceration, including punishments administered in the community" (p. 43). As indicated by national crime statistics, female crime and delinquency is predominately self-destructive and nonviolent in nature. It is, therefore, largely represented by drug offenses, theft, violations of sex crime codes, and status offenses for juveniles, unlike their male counterparts whose crimes are significantly more externally directed toward society and violent in nature. It stands to reason, as these women and girls are not as likely to jeopardize public safety, moving dollars from institutional settings to the public community-based sector, best suited to meet the holistic, gender-specific needs of the female offender population, would better serve to alleviate their escalating crime rates. This would allow society to break the cycle of criminality in women and girls instead of having it perpetuate intergenerationally.

Myth 4: The public and political sentiment of "nothing works" is justified by the human service delivery systems' marginal effectiveness in meeting any population's human needs

The political and public sentiment of "nothing works" may be the greatest barrier to be overcome when attempting to develop and implement holistic, gender-specific programming for female offenders. This sentiment has been fueled by the marginal success of the human service delivery system, inclusive of justice, education, and public behavioral health, to effectively meet the comprehensive needs of *any* criminal population. The principal reason for their marginal success is due to the fact that the current human service delivery system approach is not a coordinated effort—that is, it is fragmented due to a single system approach to service provision. This approach leads to costly, ineffective prevention and intervention efforts, because of significant gaps in service delivery. In short, the "nothing works" sentiment is the result of the inadequacy of the current human service system to integrate effectively on both a policy and functional level. The faults of the single system approach are elaborated upon below, with the remainder of the chapter focusing on how to remedy this situation.

Single System Approach To Program Development and Delivery

Consider that historically, businesses unable to meet their stated goals, e.g., meet profit margins, do not survive. Conversely, human service providers, whose goals are not profit-driven, have traditionally been permitted to define service need and service delivery effectiveness by merely providing the public with assurances that they are producing adequate results. Furthermore, they have been unable, and in some cases unwilling, to provide consumers with realistic, measurable service delivery goals and objectives, for which they could be held accountable. This state of affairs has been possible because the general public, with a limited understanding and/or interest in the use of public financial resources, is easily convinced that problems are being effectively addressed when in fact they are not. In other words, public service providers have traditionally not been held accountable by the public in terms of their goal attainment and use of financial resources. The problem of accountability is further exacerbated because the community at large is not required to take ownership of its social problems. Thus, when no one entity—the human service system or the community— is held accountable for failures, the "nothing works" sentiment seems justified.

Attempts to provide gender-specific programs that meet the holistic rehabilitative needs of female offenders have been largely unsuccessful because there has been little coordination and, in some cases, outright competition among the systems that necessarily serve the female offender,. As illustrated in Figure 13-1, the single system approach has limited effectiveness for the following reasons: (1) it is client-centered—each system provides largely independent services, resulting in duplication, fragmentation, and service gaps; (2) it is not directed by a common goal—each system has differing goals for the female offender; and (3) it is unable to evaluate the success of the intervention in terms of the total service provision to the female offender as a whole.

The net result of the singular focus of each system, on its policy and functional levels, is that it precludes, due to the lack of coordination, efficient and effective program service delivery to female offenders as they are shuffled between systems. In essence, this fact sets the female offender up to fail. Consider the following illustration. The daily expectations of a seemingly "normal," nonoffending, educated, professional, single working mother, with a an effective network of support are that she: (1) provide for the care—physically, emotionally, and developmentally—of herself and her children; and (2) secure the financial means to accomplish this level of basic care. This requires her daily to assume simultaneously the roles of teacher, nurturer, chauffeur, banker, employee, food service provider, and cleaning and maintenance worker. Are these expectations realistic? Yes. Are they difficult to accomplish on a daily basis? Yes. Now, consider the female offender, who is undereducated, unskilled, and lacks a support system. Add to her daily tasks: acquire education for herself, receive counseling for herself and children, attend an addictions self-help group, submit to a urine test for the detection of controlled substances, and attend a visit with her probation officer. She is expected to meet all of the expectations of the seemingly "normal" female

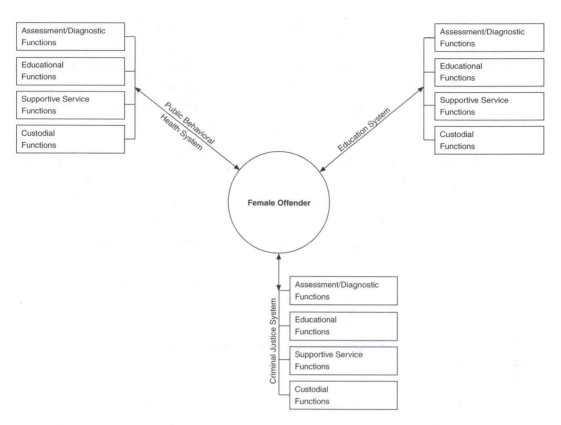

Figure 13–1 A single systems approach to program development and implementation for female offenders

and more as a result of her offending behavior. She must fulfill her obligations at multiple locations and at differing times that are not always conveniently synchronized. In many cases, often due to her lack of financial means, she is without reliable transportation and adequate childcare. The likelihood of her being successful is minimal at best. It is, however, important to stress that the female offender must learn to function in these roles and accomplish these additional tasks that are due to her offending behavior in order to become a productive, contributing member of the community. Yet the current human service delivery system is actually designed to encourage failure, not success, through its multiple— often conflicting—expectations, and multiple service delivery sites with multiple treatment goals. Even the "normal," nonoffending female probably could not negotiate this situation successfully.

Fortunately, although their motives are sometimes unclear and often tainted by their belief in the myths discussed above, elected officials, the media, and the public are starting to become much more demanding about accountability and receiving quality services in return for tax dollars and donations. The use of an integrated systems approach—an approach to program development and delivery that is concerned with meeting public expectations and maximizing the positive impact on female offenders for which the systems are responsible—is clearly needed. Such an approach makes a conscious effort to link all of the systems that deal with female offenders to a common goal. Adopting this integrated system approach is the only way to diffuse the political and public sentiment of "nothing works," while at the same time, effectively addressing the risk and protective factors of the female offender.

The community must be educated that the opportunities afforded by developing and implementing programs for female offenders utilizing an integrated systems approach will:

- require a "community" commitment to program development and delivery, thereby holding the community accountable for its success or failure;
- require shared resources by all human service entities;
- hold all program entities accountable for the achievement of measurable goals;
- reduce duplication, fragmentation and service gaps; and
- produce cost effective long- and short-term positive impacts on female crime and delinquency.

INTEGRATED SYSTEMS APPROACH TO PROGRAM DEVELOPMENT AND DELIVERY

As previously stated, an integrated systems approach to program development and delivery for female offenders is based on the premise that programming results in measurable change on the part of the individual and is more cost effective when provided through an integration of existing human service delivery systems to include, at a minimum, education, criminal justice, and public behavioral health. It is important to emphasize here that this integrated approach encompasses far more than current practices of establishing coalitions, networks, or collaborating service delivery efforts while, at the same time maintaining different organizational missions. An integrated systems approach is concerned with system change through a comprehensive integration of human service entities on both the policy and functional levels. This type of integration is the mechanism for change from a single system service focus to a holistic service focus, an integration that provides the greatest potential for success for both the individual system and the community it is designed to serve. The approach is based on general systems theory as described in detail in Chapter Three of this book.

Interestingly, examination of the independent operations of the education, criminal justice and public behavioral health systems reveals similarity in goals and functions. A common goal of all three is to assist the community in actualizing the fullest potential of all of its members. Additionally, all three systems have four primary functions in common: (1) assessment/diagnostic, (2) supportive services, (3) educational, and (4) custodial. Effective integration of these functions will ensure that program development and delivery for female offenders can provide gender-specific services for the female offender population and improve the community quality of life by reducing costs in terms of wasted resources and human potential.

Function Integration

Currently, each primary function—assessment/diagnostic, supportive service, educational, and custodial—is performed in the manner prescribed by the individual system, even though these functions are designed to accomplish a common goal of assisting the community in actualizing the fullest potential of all of its members (refer to Table 13-1).

Precisely what makes each system unique is what compels the need for functional integration in order to address holistically the needs of the individuals they each are designed to serve. For example, in order to actualize the fullest potential of the female offender, the diagnostic/assessment function must be inclusive of an educational assessment of the offender, a judicial, social assessment of the offender, a mental health/substance abuse and physical health assessment of the offender. All too often, each system compiles this information separately, with little information sharing. The result is conflicting treatment plans, duplication of services, and manipulation and frustration, and inability on the part of the female offender in meeting multiple expectations at multiple service locations. The administration of the assessment/diagnostic function, and the other three functions is less likely to result in negative impacts when the organizational structure of each system is integrated according to function across all systems. As previously stated, this implies more than simply sharing the individual findings of each system, *it means determining the findings as one functional unit*, fully integrated across all the systems. The integrated systems approach to program development and delivery described in Figure 13-2 details the composition of each functional unit across all three human service systems.

This integrated approach to service delivery establishes a balanced approach to service provision capable of meeting the needs of the female offender. This approach allows for coordinating and sharing responsibilities across all community systems in terms of staff resources, expertise, and budgets in order to attain the targeted treatment goal(s). This approach also requires the community—to whom the individual systems answer—to assess impact because of the focus on attaining a common goal(s). Based on systematic assessment of existing resources, the community can then determine those services that are best able to achieve the common goal(s). This assessment is best accomplished by following a strategic learning plan, the steps of which are described below.

STRATEGIC LEARNING PLAN FOR A COMPREHENSIVE COMMUNITY STRATEGY

When developing and implementing programs for female offenders, it is critical a strategic learning plan be followed. Use of a strategic plan will avoid costly mistakes, both in terms of valuable community resources and human potential. The strategic learning plan

Table 13–1 Functional objectives by individual system

Individual Community System / Primary Focus	Functional Objectives			
	Diagnostic/Assessment	Supportive Service	Educational	Custodial
Education System: Primarily concerned with building competency within the individual directed toward self-sufficiency	• Learning ability • Competency attainment assessments	• Guidance: Primarily internal resource referral • Advocacy: Individual	• Formal academic • Career/vocational	• Safe learning environment • Monitoring/tracking for individual and community accountability
Criminal Justice System: Primarily concerned with individual competency development directed toward social responsibility and accountability	• Social needs assessment • Community risk potential	• Guidance: Primarily external resource referral • Advocacy: Community Individual	• Life skills • Social responsibility and accountability	• Community safety • Monitor/tracking for individual accountability

Public Behavioral Health System: Primarily concerned with maximizing the individual's mental and physical health directed toward maintaining self dignity	• Mental health assessment
	• Physical health assessment
	• Substance abuse assessment
		• Therapeutic counseling
		• Directed self-help
		• Medical intervention
			• Psycho-education
			• Prevention education
				• Safety
				  Individual
				  Community
				• Monitoring/tracking for service delivery

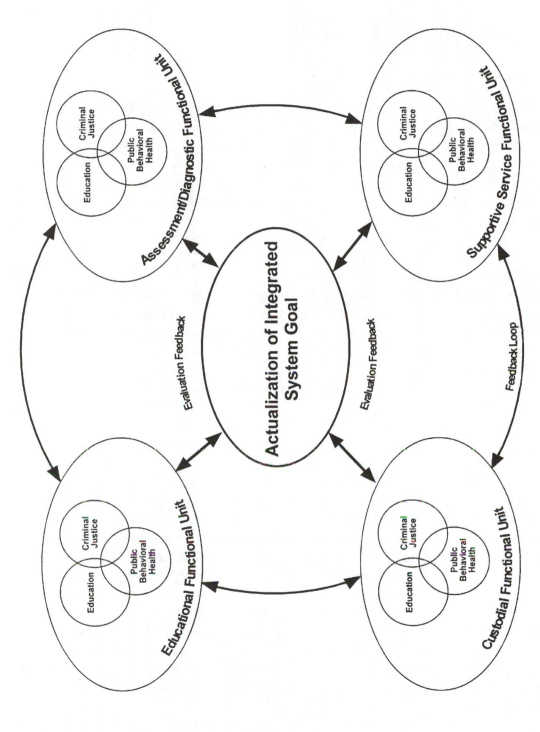

Figure 13–2 An integrated systems approach to program development and implementation for female offenders

must be inclusive of the following steps: (1) convening stakeholders; (2) designing an integrated system program; (3) implementing the program; and (4) evaluating the program (President's Crime Prevention Council 1995).

Convening the Stakeholders

The first step in developing and implementing holistic, gender-specific programming for female offenders is to seek and select a Key Leader who possesses: (1) an understanding of the risk/protective factors of female offenders and is able to communicate these factors effectively to the community; (2) the respect of and access to the community's key opinion leaders, e.g., a community leader known to multiple public and private Boards; and (3) the knowledge required to oversee and guide the implementation of an integrated systems approach.

The Key Leader will have two primary functions: (1) to establish a working Board of Community Stakeholders, and (2) to regularly convene and guide the Board of Community Stakeholders toward the defined purpose.

In terms of establishing a Board of Community Stakeholders, the Key Leader should make every attempt to establish a diversified Board including: (1) high level policy makers from the community's educational, criminal justice, and public behavioral health systems; (2) local, high level corporate and business leaders; (3) local community interest group representatives, e.g., victim rights, clergy, and service organizations; and (4) representatives of the population to be served, e.g., a female offender and a family member of the female offender.

In establishing the working Board, the following two critical factors must be considered by the Key Leader. First, it is important the Board be inclusive of persons with differing viewpoints—those that would view the initiative as favorable, as well as those who would oppose it. Those in opposition of the initiative may have been influenced by the pervasive myths surrounding female offenders as discussed earlier in this chapter. The inclusion of representatives in opposition of the initiative will afford the opportunity to dispel myths, and hopefully, generate additional support for the initiative. Second, it is important to determine if there are existing Boards within the community to address human service issues. For example, many communities have established Community Advisory Councils, Intermediate Punishment Boards, or Family Service System Boards. Logically, the Key Leader should first seek to convene and educate an existing Board in terms of the needs specific to the female offender population and explore the feasibility and willingness of the existing Board to develop and implement gender-specific programming designed to holistically meet their rehabilitative needs. If an existing Board is to be used, the Key Leader must ensure all community factions are represented by that Board and, if they are not, require their inclusion.

The primary function of the Board of Community Stakeholders is education and assessment. Specifically, the Board is responsible for educating their respective employees and the general public about the needs of female offenders and about how the integrated systems approach can meet the rehabilitative needs of this population. Further, the Board is responsible for establishing a systematic approach for assessing the existing system-wide program resources. Once assessed, gaps in services can be identified and provisions made to fill these service gaps, maximizing the impact of gender-specific programming designed to holistically meet the needs of the female offender population.

Designing the Integrated Systems Program

Once the Board of Community Stakeholders has evaluated the existing resources and identified and addressed service gaps, it is their task to provide and be responsible for the completion of specific program design tasks. The primary design task that must occur during this stage is the development of both an allocation and reallocation of resources plan. In other words, the Board must ensure that each individual human service system learns how to share "the community sandbox" rather than compete for resources. The individual hierarchical organization must now make the shift to a horizontal organization structure in order to integrate individual staff and fiscal resources across *all* system boundaries into functional units for the delivery of service that effectively meets the rehabilitative needs of female offenders.

Once the allocation and reallocation plans are completed and adopted by the Board of Community Stakeholders, an implementation plan must be developed. This plan must be inclusive of the specific program protocols for all systems involved with the female offender population and the educational needs of the community. Additionally, the plan must clearly define the out reach strategies to be implemented for the clients to be served.

Implementing the Integrated Systems Strategy

The purpose of the implementation stage is to transfer the designed program from "planned learning" to "planned doing." During this stage, the implementation plan is enacted. Additional staff are hired if necessary and all direct service staff are trained and developed to maximize the coordination and communication among all of the systems involved to positively affect attainment of the targeted overall goal(s).

The training and development of staff and implementation of the program should be completed gradually. This gradual implementation is described by Garvin (1993) as "Crawl, Walk, Run." During the crawl stage, employees of all systems involved "should focus on asking questions and familiarizing themselves with the various elements of the innovation. They should then progress to bringing the innovation on-line gradually, starting with the simplest tasks and advancing to the most difficult" (Garvin 1993, p. 9). For example, all four functional units—assessment/diagnostic, educational, supportive, and custodial—may meet to perform a mock enactment of the program components with a fictitious client, allowing for communication protocols to be refined between units. During the

Walk stage, "the innovation should be completely operative but functioning at slow speed. Increasing emphasis should be placed on quality" (Garvin 1993, p. 9). For example, during this stage, the program services may only be provided to a pilot subpopulation of female offenders, referred from one source, such as one criminal court. Finally, during the Run stage, "the innovation should be completely operative, functioning at full-speed, full-volume, and at the highest quality standards" (Garvin 1993, p. 9).

The integrated systems approach described allows for the development and implementation of programs for female offenders on a more comprehensive level and proves very cost effective because many of the services already exist on differing levels in the individual systems. With the efforts now combined instead of being offered separately, enhanced service delivery and financial resources become available because there is less duplication.

Evaluation of the Integrated Systems Programs

The greatest benefit that results from the implementation of programs using an integrated systems approach is feedback. This system is designed to provide constant feedback loops among the various functional units in terms of needed modification at the earliest point possible. This is possible because the program will be continually analyzed and modified on all functional levels to provide for common goal attainment (see Figure 13–2). The approach requires constant communication of all functional units, with breaks in communication immediately noticed and corrected. Evaluative feedback should be constantly transmitted back to the functional units based strictly on the assessed ability of the female offender to meet the established measurable goal(s). Newly determined services are easily infused into the program model across all functional levels once the integrated systems model is operational.

CONCLUSION

It is critical that community response measures be developed that will prove effective in reducing female crime by more holistically meeting the gender-specific, rehabilitative needs of the female offender. Failure to do so will result in a continued escalation in the number of females who commit crime, further resulting in an intergenerational perpetuation of the cycle of criminality. These measures must be developed holistically in direct response to female-specific risk and protective factors.

The current human service delivery system inhibits coordination and communication among community systems because of its single system approach to service delivery. The continued development of programs with separate goals will decrease the quality of human life, at great financial and human potential cost to the community. Instead, an integrated systems approach must be used when developing and implementing programs for female offenders. This approach will: (1) allow for holistic, gender-specific programming designed to address the rehabilitative needs of female offenders, and (2) improve the community quality of life by reducing costs in terms of wasted resources and human potential.

Two factors are critical in order to achieve success with programs aimed at the female offender population: (1) education of the community, especially in terms of the myths surrounding female offenders, and (2) the need for an integrated systems approach. This education, coupled with the implementation of a strategic learning plan for a comprehensive community strategy, will allow for program development and implementation before committing ever shrinking, valuable financial resources. Most important, it will result in a balanced approach—the shared and equal responsibility of all entities and factions within the community to determine and respond to the needs of its members.

REFERENCES

Chesney-Lind, M. 1997. *The female offender:Girls, women, and crime.* Newbury Park, CA: Sage Publications.

DiMascio, W. M. 1995. *Seeking justice: Crime and punishment in America.* New York: Edna M. McConnell Clark Foundation.

Garvin, D. 1993. Building a learning organization. *Harvard Business Review.* July–August 1993:80.

President's Crime Prevention Council. 1995. *Preventing crime and promoting responsibility:50 programs that help communities help their youth.* Washington, D.C.: Author.

Umbreit, M. S. 1997. Restorative justice: What works? *The ICCA Journal on Community Corrections* 7 (4):21–24.

CHAPTER 14

Self-Taught Empowerment and Pride: A Multimodal/Dual Empowerment Approach to Confronting the Problems of African American Female Offenders

Zelma Weston Henriques and Delores Jones-Brown

Editor's Notes

Chapter Fourteen presents an illustration of a model program designed to ease the female offender's re-entry into society. The authors, Henriques and Jones-Brown, discuss the Self-Taught Empowerment and Pride (STEP) program, an institutional and aftercare program for incarcerated, soon-to-be and recently released female offenders in New York City. The program has proven to be particularly useful with its targeted population, African American women. The dual empowerment model presented emphasizes both individual and community empowerment by focusing on women gaining power over their own lives and, consistent with the tenets of relational theory presented (see Chapters Five and Eleven), learning to support and assist in the empowerment of others.

In addition to discussing the multimodal/dual empowerment approach that STEP takes to correction, the authors suggest that such an approach is necessary and effective in providing the comprehensive treatment required for long term desistance from crime. Background information is presented to support this argument. The chapter begins with an overview of why African American women are typically incarcerated and the special needs of the African American adult female offender.

The systems perspective is apparent in the STEP mission statement, which reads, "Through teamwork, the total environment is a reflection of both the individual human system and the larger social system, in that, it must be responsive to physical, emotional, social, cognitive, and spiritual growth needs." The systems perspective is also apparent in the integrated model of service delivery utilized. The STEP program is a collaborative effort between The Rose M. Singer Center, New York City Department of Corrections, John Jay College of Criminal Justice, City University of New York, Division of Special Programs, and South Forty Corporation, an agency that provides job placement services to persons who have been involved with the criminal justice system. This is a unique partnership that allows incarcerated women to maintain and cultivate connections with the outside world that they can continue to utilize once they are released.

It is important to note that compared to White women in jail, for example, incarcerated African American women are less likely to be high school graduates, more likely to be single mothers, less likely to have ever had a job, more likely to be on welfare, and more likely to have been raised in father-absent, welfare families. Thus, while the factors discussed in this chapter are contributing factors in the incarceration of all women, they have been found to be particularly acute among African American women.

INTRODUCTION

In 1991, the New York City Department of Corrections recognized that re-entry to society without having adequately addressed issues leading to incarceration was a main cause of recidivism among its jail population; and, that recidivism was a major contributor to the population's size and persistence. In efforts to reduce recidivism and thereby reduce operating costs, the Self-Taught Empowerment and Pride (STEP) Program was developed and implemented. Although the STEP program was initially set up for men, the goal of STEP for female offenders is to "attempt to empower women to live independent and productive lives in the community" (STEP 1995, p. 1).

This chapter focuses on New York City's STEP program. The uniqueness and promise of STEP lies in its currently successful attempt to provide holistic treatment to female offenders who have multiple needs. STEP is a program designed to help women develop decision-making and other skills that they can use continuously to construct and reconstruct lives and relationships conducive to law-abiding existences, even within contexts that are not ideal for achieving that end.

In addition to discussing the multimodal/dual empowerment approach that STEP takes to correction, this chapter argues that such an approach is necessary and effective in providing the comprehensive treatment required for long-term desistance from crime. Background information is presented to support this argument. The chapter begins with an overview of the factors typically leading to the incarceration of African American women and an overview of the special needs of the African American adult female offender.

This chapter is dedicated to Deputy Warden Joseph Patrissi, the STEP Program staff, and STEP program participants past and present.

AFRICAN AMERICAN WOMEN, DRUGS AND CRIME

Like male offenders, the majority of female offenders are poor, disproportionately African American or Hispanic, under-educated, unemployed, and unskilled (Pollock 1997; Wellisch, et al. 1993, p. 18). Of the 431,278 admissions to state prisons in 1992, African Americans comprised 47 percent and Hispanics 19 percent of all new court commitments. Together, these two minority groups comprised 66 percent of all new state court commitments to prison (Perkins 1994, p. 7; Merlo 1997). However, of all demographic groups, African American women have experienced the greatest increase in criminal justice control (Free 1996, pp. 130; Kline 1993, p. 6; Binkley-Jackson et al. 1993, p. 66). In fact, their rate of criminal justice supervision rose by 78 percent in the five years from 1989–1994 (Mauer 1995).

Pollock (1997, pp. 220-221) notes that African Americans have always represented a disproportionate number in our nations prison's, meaning that their numbers far exceeded the roughly 12 percent of the general population that they represent. Now, however, they are not just disproportionately represented, they form the majority of the prison population, comprising 50.8 percent (Bureau of Justice Statistics 1995). Justice Department statistics indicate further that, between 1980 and 1993 African American females showed the single largest increase in imprisonment at 343 percent compared to the White females' increase of 327 percent (Bureau of Justice Statistics 1995; Pollock 1997, p. 221).

While the difference over a 13-year period may not seem so dramatic at first, consider that in 1992 alone the incarceration rate for Black females was 143 per 100,000 residents while for White females it was 20 per 100,000 White residents (Gilliard and Beck 1994, p. 9; Merlo 1997, p. 57). These figures only pertain to prison incarceration. When jail incarceration figures are included, the differences become even more extreme. For 1994, in state and federal prisons and local jails, there were 435 incarcerated Black females per 100,000 Black females in the general population and 60 White females per 100,000 of such residents (Gilliard and Beck 1994, p. 9; Merlo 1997, p. 57; Bureau of Justice Statistics 1995).

Consistent with the nationwide findings, demographic data profiling women detained at the New York City Correctional Institution for Women on Rikers Island suggest that drug use and a more aggressive criminal justice policy on drug offenses are the primary cause of the drastic increase in the incarceration rates of women at that facility (Richie 1996, p. 123). This is particularly so for African American women who make up 59 percent of the Rikers Island population.

Specifically, Mauer (1995) highlights the impact of mandatory sentencing as well as other sentencing policies and the way in which law enforcement concentrates its efforts on minority communities, as disproportionately impacting on women and minorities.

Many federal and state mandatory sentencing laws require prison terms for certain offenses, e.g., drug offenses, and such laws stipulate a minimum number of years the offender must serve before being released (DiMascio 1995, p. 19). In practice, the current policy has tended to treat Blacks more severely than Whites (Mauer, 1995). For example, within the federal corrections system, a 100:1 disparity in sentencing of defendants in drug possession cases was created by legislation enacted by Congress in 1986 (Wren 1997). Sentences for selling crack were equal in length to sentences for selling 100 times that amount of powdered cocaine (Bureau of Justice Statistics 1993). The racial impact of such sentencing guidelines becomes clear when we consider that the U.S. Sentencing Commission reported in 1995 that 88 percent of offenders sentenced for crack cocaine offenses were African American and 4.1 percent were White (DiMascio 1995). Recent changes in the sentencing legislation has reduced the ratio of disparity; however, the racial impact remains. Specifically with reference to women, the Commission reports that in 1994 Black women represented 82 percent of women sentenced for crack cocaine offenses. For drug offenses overall, the percentages were: Black, 50 percent, White, 7 percent, and Hispanic, 5 percent (see Stuart 1997). [Note: The term "Black" is the racial category used in the official statistics, while the current authors use the term African American to cover persons in the United States of Black racial identity. These may include not only Black people born in the United States but also Blacks of Caribbean and other African ancestry.]

Rather than the punitive approach that has been adopted by the government, Mauer (1995) suggests that the necessary response for confronting these enormous disparities in sentencing lies in addressing long-term social and economic issues. The logic of Mauer's suggestion is apparent when it is considered that more than half of all prison and jail inmates had a reported income of less than $10,000 before their arrest (DiMascio 1995, p. 13).

There is an abundance of evidence that suggests that drug involvement is but a single manifestation of more complex problems for African American women. Richie (1996, p. 2) has observed that poor African American battered women in society are "increasingly restricted by their gender roles, stigmatized by their racial/ethnic and class position, and constrained by the competing forces of tremendous unmet need and very limited resources." Richie (1996) uses a theoretical paradigm called "gender entrapment" to address the contradictions and complications in the lives of African American battered women. She uses the model to illustrate "how gender, race/ethnicity, and violence can intersect to create a subtle, yet profoundly effective system of organizing women's behavior into patterns that leave them vulnerable to private and public subordination, to violence in their intimate relationships and, in turn, to participation in illegal activities" (Richie 1996, p. 4).

In Richie's view (1996), even before African American women's official detention, they are imprisoned at different points in their lives in other, more symbolic ways. "They are confined by social conditions in their communities, restrained by their families' circumstances, severely limited by abuse in their intimate relationships, and forced to make hard choices with very few options. (p. 5)"

Thus women in general, and African American women in particular, enter the criminal justice system with a host of unique medical, psychological, and financial problems and needs that distinguish them from male offenders (Wellisch et al. 1996; Austin et al. 1992, pp. 3–4). Traditional prison and jail programs for women have, however, failed to address these primary factors leading to their incarceration (Wellisch et al. 1993) and have ignored the acute needs of women of color.

THE SPECIAL NEEDS AND PROBLEMS OF AFRICAN AMERICAN WOMEN

Henriques (1995, p. 68) notes that, "the lives of African American women continue to be impacted by racial oppression, sex discrimination and class stratification on a constant basis." Citing Gordon (1987) she notes that, hence, African American women are victims of a "trilogy of oppression." This trilogy has led to her historical and current sexual exploitation and her over-representation among those who are victims of multiple forms of psychological and physical abuse.

A sense of perpetual oppression is enforced by the fact that never has the African American woman been "placed on a pedestal" or viewed as "pure" in social imagery. Hence the negative images of her that stem from the time of slavery have never been countered (Henriques 1995). Instead, the reality of her life is that she has a substantial likelihood of death (or serious injury) at the hands of an intimate partner (See Chapter Eleven and National Victimization Surveys). Should she avoid this fate, the likelihood of a long-term partner of comparable social standing, if she falls within the professional (middle) class, is slim (Staples and Johnson 1993). Because she is significantly more likely than her White counterpart to be a single head-of-household with more than one child (Gilliard and Beck 1994; Staples and Johnson 1993; Bureau of Census 1992; Bresler and Lewis 1983), the more likely scenario is that, absent some form of intervention, she and her children will live in poverty.

The consequences of living in poverty are that she and her children are, therefore, substantially more likely to spend their entire lives in substandard housing within crime ridden neighborhoods (Sampson and Wilson 1995; Bickford and Massey 1991; Sampson 1987; Wilson et al. 1988; Wilson 1987). She is more likely to lose a child to infant mortality. And, she is significantly more likely than her White counterpart to lose a son to homicide (Sampson and Wilson 1995; Fingerhut et al. 1991; Fingerhut and Kleinman 1990).

Many of the conditions that afflict African American women by virtue of history, culture, and skin color, undoubtedly are also endured by Hispanic/Latina women by virtue of history, culture, immigration status, and language (most notably, the racial prejudice experienced by some Spanish-speaking women with dark complexions). Lest someone be inclined to argue that the conditions under which African American women find themselves living are solely or primarily of their own making, a detailed discussion of a few important factors is being included here.

African American Women and Economic Opportunity

While a combination of legislation and court prohibitions against discrimination have provided some protection for the employment status of women, African American women continue to occupy the bottom of the socioeconomic ladder in comparison to other gender/ race groupings (Henriques 1995, p. 73). This is true despite the fact that in the decade of the 1980s most of the Black gains in the area of education, occupations, income, health, and literature were achieved by African American women as compared to African American men (Staples and Johnson, 1993).

For reasons that will be discussed more fully in the next section, African American women must often bear the economic responsibility of raising children alone or with little help (Henriques 1995; Rothenberg 1988). In 1991, for example, estimates indicate the 54.8 percent of all African American households were headed by females as compared to 16 percent of White households (U.S. Department of Commerce 1992). One reality of the single-parent female-headed household is that such families are significantly more likely than others to live below the poverty level. One estimate indicates that the poverty rate for families maintained by women with no husband present is as much as six times higher than that for two-parent families. It is estimated further that as many as 78 percent of poor Black families live in households maintained by a woman (U.S. Department of Commerce 1992).

While the stereotypical image of the African American female head-of-household is that of welfare recipient, in actuality, the African American woman has a long history of participation in the workforce (Henriques 1995; Malveaux 1988). However, annual labor force statistics indicate that African American women must work harder than other groups to stay out of poverty because they are amongst the lowest paid wage earners.

Figures for 1991 indicate that African American females earned an average of $8,816 compared to $10,721 for White females. This translates into 82 cents paid to the African American women for every dollar earned by White women (U.S. Department of Commerce, 1992; see also Henriques, 1995). This disparity in wages illustrates the economically disadvantaged status of African American women in the labor market. The economic situation for her male counterpart is equally disparate and has been cited as a major contributor to the problem discussed next.

African American Women and Potential Male Partners

Official statistics indicate that a majority of African Americans are not married or living in traditional nuclear family units. Data from the Bureau of Census (1992) indicate that in 1991 only 30 percent of adult African American females were married and living with a spouse. Henriques (1995) notes that the low percentage of married African American females does not necessarily imply a devaluation of the marriage institution. The low marital rate is often a function of limited opportunities for African American women to find acceptable individuals in an increasingly restricted and small pool of potential partners (Staples and Johnson 1993).

Several factors contribute to the lack of potential partners. The first is the limited number of Black/African American men. Of that number, the pool of desirable partners is reduced by factors such as imprisonment, drug use and abuse, and death at early ages due to violence. In addition, economic issues have had a significant impact on the formation and maintenance of stable African American male-female unions. The lower earning capability of African American males as compared to White males, and in some instances, as compared to African American females, has had significant implications for the African American family. Staples and Johnson (1993) note that while African American women made some gains in education, occupations, and income during the 1980s, Black men lost ground. This loss of economic ground by African American men has exacerbated potential relationship problems between the pair. In fact, where marriages exist, lack of a job or sufficient money has been cited as the most frequently reported explanation of marital instability (Staples and Johnson 1993).

Employment discrimination is still an inescapable American reality (Staples and Johnson 1993). Hence, the African American male's best efforts for preparing for the job market do not necessarily assure him equal employment opportunity (Henriques 1995). On the other hand, while on average she earns less than her White female counterpart, for whatever reason, the African American women has been more readily accepted (than African American men) into the mainstream labor market particularly at the professional levels. This has resulted in a mismatch of eligibility. That is, African American women of middle-class status have an even more limited opportunity than others to find a mate (of equal social status). Consequently, it is not unusual to find African American women with professional standing married to African American men who work in semiskilled blue collar jobs (Staples and Johnson 1993). While on the surface, this match is not in and of itself detrimental, there are various tensions that may develop within and from these unions. The tensions may then contribute to a host of behaviors detrimental both to the partners themselves and the children that they raise.

Already mentioned is the potential destabilizing impact of questionable financial status. Feelings of financial or status inadequacy may engender feelings of powerlessness or incompetence in African American male partners. High levels of such feelings may manifest themselves in any number of problem behaviors (such as drug or alcohol abuse or chronic infidelity), the worst of which would be physical abuse.

Staples and Johnson (1993) note another potential source of tension in blue-collar/white-collar marriages. That is, that such marriages are more likely than dual-career families to organize family household duties around traditional lines, with women assuming the full-time social roles of wife, mother, and worker. The extent to which the female partner may then feel overtaxed by familial demands may push her into similar problem behaviors as mentioned with reference to her male partner. The level of palpable acrimony that is possible under the wrong circumstances is certain to be viewed and perhaps experienced by any children in the household. The potential for negative impact on those children is enormous.

Rather than function as a dysfunctional dual-parent family, many African American women of all social statuses opt to remain or return to being single. They do, however, continue to consider their relationship with men to be an important part of their lives

(Henriques 1995; Staples and Johnson 1993). The scarcity of eligible/desirable men eventually creates a situation in which many women faced with a choice would rather stay in an abusive relationship than not have a mate (Henriques 1995, p. 69).

African American Women and Experiences of Abuse

Relational theory, discussed in Chapter Five of this textbook, notes a tendency for western societies to push males into a "power/dominance" mode of socialization and females into a "love/empathy" mode (Jordan 1993, p. 234). This dual socialization may have particularly problematic implications for the lives of African American women. As described to a limited extent in the preceding paragraphs, there are a number of economic and other social factors that may intersect to make African American males feel powerless, leaving them susceptible to inappropriate means of power exercise.

Henriques (1995) notes that African American women appear to endure unnecessary abusive relationships. One explanation is that, perhaps due largely to a sense of guilt flowing from their slave experience, Black women are socialized to "stand by their man." According to Henriques (p. 76), "Many African American women who silently suffer as victims of battering and sexual abuse at the hands of African American men do so because they need to show solidarity with their men in the White majority society." Consistent with this notion, African American women from the South were often socialized into the mindset that, "an old piece of man is better than no man at all."

Hence, Staples and Johnson (1993), among others, note that despite the physical violence and sexual aggression that African American women experience in relationships, they continue to consider their relationships with African American men important to sustain. Research by Joseph (1997), however, indicates that reasons for remaining in abusive relationships may have both an emotional and economic motivation.

In her study of battered women, Joseph (1997) found that 45 percent of battered Black women were still living with the abuser, although all of the women had left the batterer at least once. Of that 45 percent, she found that 21 percent returned between one and four times, 44 percent returned between five and seven times, 11 percent returned between eight and ten times, and 13 percent returned over ten times. The majority of all the battered Black women (61 percent) returned for economic reasons; 30 percent returned because of emotional attachment to the batterer; and 9 percent because they were fearful of the batterer (as cited in Henriques 1995, p. 69). Thus, despite the reality of being physically abused by men, the relationships with those men were sufficiently important to the women to warrant multiple attempts at maintaining them.

As noted previously, continuation in such relationships have a strong potential for negatively impacting children. In many cases the children may themselves become targets of abuse and/or learn to model the abusive behavior. Thus, these children are significantly more likely to become involved in the justice system as either victims or victimizers. Continuation in the relationships also significantly raises the possibility of the women becoming defendants in the justice system.

Feeling otherwise powerless to escape the relationship, a woman may kill or seriously injure the abuser in an effort to protect herself or her children. Such an outcome may take place under circumstances that do not meet the legal technicalities of self-defense. Or in the alternative, women who are powerless to escape the control of their abusers may also be more prone to succumb to involvement in the abusers' other illegal activities. Hence they are often accomplices, or otherwise involved as co-defendants in their abusers' criminal charges (Richie 1996).

The foregoing information about abusive relationships is not necessarily unique to African American women. It is the case, however, that the circumstances that push women into abusive relationships and those that cause them to return to such relationships are substantially more acute within poor and minority communities. Much like the traditional view of the convicted woman, the women who survive within abusive relationships are often misunderstood and deemed undeserving of assistance. It is their children, however, who must bear the brunt of their mothers' social circumstances, whether those circumstances be by choice or accident of birth.

Profile of African American Women Who Are Incarcerated

Free (1996, p. 131) notes that studies from the 1980s suggest that African American women in prison tend to be younger than incarcerated White women and tend to have less formal education (French 1983). They are also more likely to have been reared in a father-absent family and to be on welfare or to be employed in a low-paying job requiring few skills (Bresler and Lewis 1983). Similar findings have been made regarding African American women in at least one jail (San Francisco). For example, compared to White women in jail, incarcerated Black women are less likely to be high school graduates, more likely to be single mothers, less likely to have ever had a job, more likely to be on welfare, and more likely to have been raised in father-absent welfare families (Bresler and Lewis 1983).

A similar profile emerges from 1991 data on women in state prisons (U.S. Department of Justice 1994). A comparison of the family backgrounds of African American and White women in state prison in 1991 corroborates the earlier data. African American women were more likely than their White counterparts to have lived in a single-parent family headed by the mother (46.1 percent vs. 29.3 percent of all White women). And, consistent with other studies cited throughout this chapter, African American women were somewhat more likely than White women to have lived with their nonadult children before incarceration (U.S. Department of Justice 1994, pp. 5–6). Given the likelihood that African American women will be raising children without a partner, it therefore is very important that, despite their own backgrounds, they learn to become self-reliant. Self-reliance requires skills that can only be gained through education in its broadest and narrowest sense.

Successful programs must provide opportunities for gaining knowledge and skills to find and maintain legitimate gainful employment. Such programs must provide guidance in parenting, general life skills, stress management and self-awareness. Importantly, the programs must also provide concrete information about available community resources (for example, employment services, legal assistance, shelters, and health care).

The road to self-reliance leads away from abusive relationships, chemical dependency, and other dysfunctional behaviors and toward law-abiding lifestyles, despite less than optimal life chances and conditions. The self-taught empowerment and pride approach utilized within the STEP program is particularly necessary for the rehabilitation of African American women, because given the social challenges they face, African American women must become self-reliant or risk mental breakdown, incarceration, or death.

STEP: A PROGRAM THAT WORKS

Contrary to the Martinson (1974) conclusion that "nothing works" in prison treatment programs, there is significant promise that the STEP program is having an impact on recidivism rates among incarcerated women. Currently, STEP is being used to reduce the sentence length served by City-sentenced female inmates through the New York City Conditional Release Commission and the Parole Commission. Since 1991, the program has served approximately 2,000 women.

A national survey of female offenders conducted by the American Correctional Association (ACA) noted that one of the greatest hindrances in designing jail programs to meet the perceived needs of the female offender is the time that one has to actually work with an inmate. The survey results indicate that, on average, there is approximately one month to work with jail program participants. Given the time constraints within jail settings, the ACA recommends short-term programs with an emphasis on returning the offender to the community. In addition, the ACA suggests that the success of programs for female offenders directed toward return to the community depends on an affirmative link between institution and community (ACA 1990).

Consistent with this line of thought, the STEP program is composed of a short-term institutional component and an ongoing aftercare component. Both components provide a variety of programs and activities designed to enable women to make a smooth transition from prison to the community.

STEP Mission Statement

The following mission statement summarizes the essence of what STEP is designed to achieve and how it goes about achieving it:

The Self-Taught Empowerment and Pride Program is designed to promote positive involvement of the participants in an environment that has as its focus successful societal reintegration. Members participate in program management to show their capacity to make informed, responsible decisions. The program is designed to be a total learning environment. This approach fosters involvement, self-direction and individual responsibility.

The Mission Statement goes on to note, however, that:

> Through teamwork, the total environment is a reflection of both the individual human system and the larger social system, in that, it must be responsive to physical, emotional, social, cognitive, and spiritual growth needs. Positive behavior that supports individual and community growth is expected, while negative behavior is confronted and targeted for change. (STEP Orientation Booklet, p. 2)

Collaborative Effort

The STEP program is a collaborative effort between The Rose M. Singer Center, New York City Department of Corrections, John Jay College of Criminal Justice, City University of New York, Division of Special Programs, and South Forty Corporation, an agency that provides job placement services to persons who have been involved with the criminal justice system. This is a unique partnership that allows incarcerated women to maintain and cultivate connections with the "outside world" that they can continue to utilize once they are released.

Institutional Component

Both the institutional and aftercare components of the STEP program incorporate a three-step empowerment process that teaches women to:

1. Assume responsibility for self through positive skill, attitudinal and value development;
2. Gain a basic understanding of personal "roadblocks" that hinder the ability of women to live healthy, successful lives; and
3. Become instrumental and supportive in the empowerment of others.

Reflected within the three-step process are empowerment-based themes of motivation, self-discipline, self-awareness, self-sufficiency, teamwork, and positive change. These themes are integrated and reinforced throughout the program cycle. These themes are particularly important given research that indicates that traditionally the incarceration experience for women may tend to de-emphasize self-sufficiency.

According to Clark (1995, p. 315) [traditionally] the prison—represented by officers, staff, and administration—acts as a "parent," imposing rules and sanctions, much like the model of a punitive parent who seeks to control the child through sanctions and punishments. Yet, while men's prisons also operate on rules and sanctions, the dynamic in women's prisons according to Humphrey (1990), is often different because it is intertwined with infantilization and the emphasis on remolding attitudes and relationships. (For instance, women describe instances when they have angered authorities and have consequently been moved from choice living units or jobs, but were told that these punitive actions were "for their own good.")

Rather than providing women with a means of becoming self-sufficient, programming in such prisons tends to act as an immediate means of control, and thereby virtually ensure future control of these women by men or social service agencies promising financial support, or perpetual control via the criminal justice system.

By contrast, empowerment theory is based on the assumption that the capacity of people to improve their lives is determined by their ability to control their environment, connect with needed resources, negotiate problematic situations, and change existing social situations that limit human functioning (Gibson 1993).

Empowerment, then, is a way of increasing an individual's autonomy in various areas of one's life. As discussed throughout this chapter, the empowerment of women is a very important need that must be addressed in order to prevent their re-incarceration. Absent empowerment, Austin et al. (1992, p. 4) note that addiction, poverty, unemployment, physical and sexual abuse, and homelessness trap women in a recurring cycle of hopelessness and crime. As demonstrated previously, for numerous reasons, African American women are particularly susceptible to this cycle.

The institutional component of the STEP program offers assistance to empowerment within a 10-week highly structured and intensive learning/training environment for 100 city-sentenced women and/or parole violators (per 10-week session). Empowerment as a treatment model constitutes the underlying framework for the entire STEP program, thus, empowerment principles are utilized in both the institutional and aftercare components of the program.

It is considered critical that participants understand what they are learning and how to practically apply newly acquired information into their daily lives upon their release to the community. To facilitate this effort, before release, soon-to-be releasees attend the aftercare support group as preparation for release. The group-centered approach utilized by both the institutional and aftercare components of STEP incorporates aspects of social learning theory that recognizes that criminal behavior is learned through a process of social interaction with others. It should be noted that the STEP program designers used Travis Hirschi's social control theory and William Glasser's control theory as a structural framework for the program (STEP 1995, p. 4). Thus, prosocial behaviors must be learned to replace deviant behaviors (through a similar process) (Wexler et al. 1988, pp. 25, 27). "Unlike traditional social service providers which assisted women by teaching coping and stress management skills designed to enable clients to better *endure* their stressful life circumstances, STEP provides the behavioral and skills training necessary for participants to change, rather than merely cope with difficult life situations." (STEP 1991)

While some may contend that inmate-directed therapy groups have not had a record of success, STEP and other recent programs show a great deal of promise. By contrast, behavioral programs that are simply imposed without inmate input into their development and operation have proven to be unsuccessful (given recidivism rates). Many of these programs fail to neutralize or utilize the inmate's peer group and fail to sustain continuity of care after release from prison (Wexler et al. 1988, pp. xi, 7). They also (1988, p. 7) criticize such programs as tending to focus on antisocial rather than prosocial behaviors. Such a focus may as a result give undue attention and reinforcement to negative behavior. As will be discussed in subsequent sections, the approaches utilized by STEP allow for learning through both group confrontation and celebration.

STEP represents an improvement over other "unsuccessful" programs because it neutralizes the potential for negative peer group influence through careful selection of participants and then utilizes the peer group to develop, reinforce and build positive knowledge and behavior within the individuals who are a part of the group. Group members who are doing well become credible role models for others. Despite the "nothing works" mentality, research findings continue to accumulate that the approaches utilized by STEP and similar programs have been successful in reducing recidivism. Wexler et al. (1988, p. 7) note that self-help groups, family therapy, contingency contracting, role playing and modeling, and successful therapeutic communities (like STEP), all have several things in common. These include: (1) authority structures that clearly specify rules and sanctions; (2) anticriminal modeling and reinforcement of prosocial behavior; (3) pragmatic personal and social problem-solving assistance; (4) program staff knowledgeable about the use of community resources; and (5) relationships between staff and clients that are empathetic and characterized by open communication and trust.

The use of ex-offender addict counselors to serve as credible role models of successful rehabilitation is another characteristic that successful programs have in common. This is true of STEP, primarily in the aftercare component where STEP program graduates frequently attend and/or lead the support group meetings. There are also a number of program graduates who visit the institutional program to give inspirational and/or warning messages to women who are still confined.

Through a combination of group-centered activities and individual counseling, the STEP program's approach to empowerment and change represents an interesting mixture of supportive and disciplinary measures. Within the institution, correction officers are the main facilitators of the program. While maintaining order is a necessary part of the officers' responsibilities, the corrections officers, along with a small number of civilian staff, are responsible for helping program participants understand and achieve the three-step process, both through formal instruction and through modeling appropriate behaviors. Corrections officers are also responsible for instilling program participants with a sense of discipline and an orientation toward teamwork.

The correctional staff who work within the STEP unit at Rikers are carefully selected to fit the attributes described by Wexler et al. (1988). Rather than the traditional hierarchical relationship that typically exists between "the keepers" and "the kept," the relationship between the staff and STEP program participants is "empathetic and characterized by open communication and trust." Working with STEP program inmates is a privilege for correctional staff because the women who are selected to participate in STEP generally tend to be easier to work with than are other inmates. They tend to be self-motivated and are less likely than other inmates to present discipline problems. For women inmates, the closed environment of the STEP program unit affords them better living conditions, a safer environment, early release consideration, and an opportunity to possibly change their lifestyles. A violation of these qualities of the relationship is grounds for termination from the program for both staff and inmates alike. The potential for loss of the privilege of involvement with the STEP program serves as an incentive for cooperation (rather than apathy or confrontation) between program staff and the women inmates who are selected to live in the STEP therapeutic community unit.

The STEP program emphasizes community and teamwork. The program operates under a premise of reciprocal empowerment—that is—individual empowerment enhances community empowerment and community empowerment enhances individual empowerment. Every member of the STEP community is expected to be involved in the process. For example, all uniform and civilian staff of STEP are expected to act as role models for participants. All staff are expected to support and abide by the Community Philosophy and Community Standards (See Exhibit 14–1) and a uniform and civilian staff code of conduct. The designers of the STEP program note that, "STEP staff cannot demand performance levels from participants that participants cannot, in turn, demand from STEP staff. Staff and participants are both responsible for maintaining all facets of the community."

The program is also designed such that staff are required to constantly demonstrate how each activity promotes successful community living. Toward that end, the STEP program and STEP staff demonstrate two other attributes of Wexler et al.'s (1988) characteristics of successful programs. Staff members are "knowledgeable about the use of community resources" and they represent, "authority structures that clearly specify rules and sanctions." The intensity of the integral relationship that exists between staff and program participants has as its primary goals: "anti-criminal modeling and reinforcement of pro-social behavior" and the development of "pragmatic personal and social problem-solving assistance."

While the goals of the STEP program may appear to some to be overly ambitious, interviews with program participants indicate that to a large extent these goals are being met. Both STEP graduates and dropouts indicate that they enjoyed a strong, caring, informative reciprocal relationship with all levels of program staff. Staff indicate that they gained additional knowledge from their interactions with program participants. The overall atmosphere in the STEP unit is one of constructive cooperation and criticism when necessary.

Before continuing with a separate discussion of the main components of the institutional STEP program, excerpts from various STEP program literature contained in Exhibit 14–2 helps to give a fuller picture of what STEP seeks to achieve and how.

Exhibit 14–1 The STEP Program

STEP PHILOSOPHY

STEP Is:

A positive caring community where a woman learns to help herself and other women identify and practice behaviors and skills that lead to self-discovery, independence, and a healthy community living.

A highly structured community where a woman has a chance to change, confront mistakes, accept responsibility, set goals, and take control of her life and well-being.

ROSE M. SINGER CENTER
SELF-TAUGHT EMPOWERMENT AND PRIDE PROGRAM

Community Standards

1. I will support the Program philosophy and facility rules and regulations.
2. I will refrain from the use of violence and/or threats of violence.
3. I will not use drugs and/or alcohol.
4. I will demonstrate respect, care, concern and support for all community members.
5. I will remain attentive and participate in all community activities at all times.
6. I will speak the truth with compassion.
7. I will manage my time effectively by adhering to the Program schedule.
8. I will speak and act in an appropriate manner, maintaining a positive attitude at all times.
9. I will practice good hygiene and maintain a neat, well-groomed appearance at all times.
10. I will maintain all physical areas of the STEP Program in a neat and orderly manner.
11. I will confront behaviors and situations that have a negative effect on me and negotiate for a resolution.
12. I will strive to achieve all personal and group goals.

Courtesy of Self-Taught Empowerment and Pride Unit, City of New York Department of Correction, East Elmhurst, New York.

Exhibit 14–2 STEP Empowerment

Important Aspects of the STEP Empowerment Process

- Standards of behavior expected from all community members have been developed, tested and refined by staff and participants. This results in participants taking responsibility for the quality of their (own) lives.

- It is the objective of STEP to create a program environment that reflects the **rigors** of professional and personal life. Thus the program philosophy, standards and rules reinforce the central program theme of empowerment, and connote values, attitudes, behaviors, and skills acceptable for continued program participation and successful community **re-integration**.

- The STEP program is a learning lab, intentionally designed to provide members with the tools (and information) necessary to both exert control over their personal lives and to constructively effect attitudes and behaviors of others, STEP staff operate under the assumption that all members inherently have this potential.

- In order to make responsible decisions, individuals must consider their own wants and needs, the effect that these decisions have on others, and how they contribute to the variables of the situations in which they find themselves. Emphasis is on individual and social responsibility.

- In recognizing one's responsibility to others, it is important that one not discount the abilities of others to think and act. **Responsibility** to others is not responsibility **for** others. **Many participants have developed unhealthy dependency relationships with others.** These relationships have been detrimental, both to the inmates and to those whom they involved. While participating in the program, individuals learn how to create and sustain **growth-producing** relationships. Participants learn supportive confrontation skills via group sessions. **They learn to give and receive feedback about behavior that inhibits their progress toward stated goals.**

- **Empowerment is seen as a continual and progressive process of growth and change (from powerless to empowerment).**

- Responsibility for oneself implies that a person must be aware of personal goals and have the skills necessary to enable fulfillment of these goals. Program participants learn skills in self-assessment, decision-making and communication for clarifying and actualizing their goals.

- **Program Philosophy**

  Reflects empowerment-based themes of:
  –Motivation
  –Self-discipline
  –Self-awareness
  –Self-sufficiency
  –Teamwork
  –Positive change

  These themes are integrated and reinforced throughout every program cycle.

continues

Exhibit 14–2 continued

- Participants learn to evaluate the effects of their attitudes and behaviors in a variety of situations and learn new behaviors to deal with situations in which they have problems. They learn that they have choices and learn what some of those choices **are** within their control.

- Life within the learning environment (the facility) provides a range of opportunities for practicing positive behaviors. These positive habits that the participants **practice** such as: **work, study, the use of leisure time, relationships with family and friends, and even spiritual development**, help with their reentry back into society.

- A sense of self-worth and personal pride are the foundation of living a responsible lifestyle. STEP communities are structured to foster respect for self and others and to focus on positive self-images.

- Emphasis is on both learning and practicing behaviors and skills essential to overcoming adverse socio-economic forces traditionally hindering women from successful community living.

- Each program component is designed to support the STEP Program Philosophy and Community Standards to which all members must fully adhere.

- Empowerment as a treatment model constitutes the underlying framework for the entire STEP Program. Every facet of the program reinforces empowerment. **It is designed to counteract feelings of powerlessness. Within the context of the STEP program powerlessness refers to the inability of STEP participants to direct the course of their lives due to societal conditions and power dynamics, lack of skills, or lack of faith that they really can change their lives.**

- A highly structured network of program activities includes:
  –Academic and vocational education
  –Substance abuse intervention (or other addictions)
  –Independent living skills workshops
  –Psychodrama journal writing
  –Individual and group counseling and discharge planning

- Performance evaluations include:
  –Pretests, midtests, and posttests in education, substance abuse intervention, and independent living skills,
  –A self-esteem assessment
  –Daily housing area inspections
  –Daily personal hygiene inspections, and
  –An individual and group performance evaluation system.

- There is also a community service/restorative justice aspect to the STEP program, in that Communities throughout New York City are provided with approximately 700 hours of community service monthly. The services include feeding the homeless at Missions, working at the Partnership for the Homeless, and Project 'In Touch' [which] involves informing adolescents in the New York City Public School System about the consequences [of] criminal behavior.

Courtesy of Self-Taught Empowerment and Pride Unit, City of New York Department of Correction, East Elmhurst, New York.

The institutional component of STEP is facilitated by individual STEP workbooks. These workbooks demonstrate the true extent to which STEP is intended to be a total community. The workbooks cover a variety of topics including the following:

- Program requirements and protocol
- The twelve steps of Narcotics Anonymous
- A listing of substance abuse programs
- A section entitled "I am lovable and capable" (IALAC)
- Five steps to decision-making
- Tips to achieving your goals
- Herbal remedies
- Stress management
- Relaxation techniques
- Sexually transmitted diseases
- A sexuality workshop
- Parenting
- Family/domestic violence
- Issues related to life on the outside.

Academic Education

Participants who are accepted into the STEP program must attend school daily. Rosewood Alternative High School provides academic training for participants. Offered are courses in basic education and GED preparation; English as a second language (ESL); Exit Counseling; Family Counseling; and Aftercare follow-up programs (for graduates). At the conclusion of the institutional portion of the program there is a graduation ceremony where certificates are awarded to those who successfully complete the education programs. A basic College Prep program is sponsored by the John Jay College of Criminal Justice Inmate Education Program. It is designed to give college level instruction to those inmates who have graduated from high school, received their General Equivalency Diploma (GED), have taken technical college classes, have some college credits or have graduated from college. Useful current vocational programs are also offered.

Vocational Education

One way in which the vocational component of the STEP program works to rectify the prison/jail program practices of the past is by providing both traditional and nontraditional occupational training. Even in areas that may be thought of as traditionally "women's work," STEP provides training in areas that can produce significant income. For example, there is much available training in the nursing field (as nurses' aides) and training as paralegals; however, there are external forces that may adversely impact the offender's ability to work in those fields. Home Economics courses are offered, however they may serve more as a means of improving skills related to parenting rather than as viable employment opportunities. Courses offered in nontraditional, potential moneymaking fields, include training for working with computers and handling audiovisual equipment.

Because economic inequality and a lack of social mobility are conditions of life confronting a growing number of the urban underclass, female offenders are at an additional disadvantage, due to their criminal label. The label "convict" multiplies the already overwhelming dilemmas confronting these women and increases the risk of unfavorable outcomes. It is important, therefore, that incarcerated women are guided in their efforts to identify and address issues related to economic and gender inequality as well as the potential consequences of having a criminal label. In this circumstance, it may indeed be true that to be "forewarned is to be forearmed." It is important, also to encourage and facilitate women ex-offenders' participation in aftercare programs, especially programs that address drugs and other related issues.

Substance Abuse Intervention

Substance abuse intervention is a major component of the STEP institutional program. Wexler et al. (1988, p. 6) notes that "Although criminal justice sanctions alone may have uncertain value in reducing the criminality of drug involved offenders, those sanctions can serve a powerful role by facilitating effective drug treatment." The Violent Crime and Law Enforcement Act of 1994 authorizes programs to support treatment of drug abusing offenders. The Residential Substance Abuse Treatment (RSAT) for State Prisoners Formula Grant Program, created by Subtitle U of the Act, addresses the treatment goal by providing funding for the development of substance abuse treatment programs in state and local correctional facilities. Under this federal legislation, states are encouraged to adopt comprehensive approaches to substance abuse treatment for offenders, including relapse prevention and aftercare services.

While there is some indication that women's access to programs in jails is significantly worse than it is in prisons, (Gray et al. 1995; Hughey and Klemke 1996, p. 40), the Substance Abuse Intervention Division (SAID) of New York City's STEP program is run by experienced counselors who interview inmate participants regarding their substance abuse history (in order to better serve their needs), facilitate group discussions, and keep order in the housing areas. The counselors also assist inmates in their discharge planning process and referrals.

As one possible explanation of STEP's success, Wexler et al. (1988, p. 6) note that in-prison substance abuse programs that offer better conditions than those available to the general population are substantially better able to recruit participants than those that do not. They also note that although these offenders may not be completely sincere at admission, there is an opportunity for the program to engage them in an effective treatment experience. In short, "the threat of substantial sanctions (for arrestees) or the promise of better in-prison conditions (for those in custody) can operate as extremely useful incentives for treatment...."

THE STEP AFTERCARE COMPONENT

The STEP Aftercare program component has been in existence only since 1994. Women who have participated in the institutional component of the STEP program are encouraged (but not required) by the staff to participate in the aftercare component of the program after their release. The purpose of the aftercare component is to provide recently released female offenders with the necessary resources and support to continue their empowerment. It is designed to provide the women with a range of alternatives to crime and violence. The goal is to continue the work that was begun with them while they were incarcerated. Individual counseling and group encounters are the main vehicles used in the aftercare aspect of the STEP program. In group sessions, their reasons for engaging in crime and criminal behaviors are discussed and analyzed. Attendance at the group sessions varies because women are in constant transition with respect to their release and incarceration.

The Aftercare component facilitates a positive, caring community in which women can help themselves and each other to identify and practice behaviors and skills that lead to self-discovery, independence and a healthy community life. The Aftercare group meets at the South Forty Corporation. At these weekly group meetings individual counseling and group support is available. Program participants, especially those who have remained drug free and who have not re-offended after their release, participate and serve as role models for new program participants who are nearing their release from prison or jail. Without this "STEP Sisters" support group, after their release from prison, most of these women would be basically on their own.

SELF-REPORTED BENEFITS OF STEP

Women who participate in the Aftercare component of the STEP program consider their participation to be important because it enables them to interact with other STEP program participants who are also in recovery. [Note that the word "recovery" here is not limited to recovery from substance abuse, but includes recovery from all of the negative influences leading to and involved with being incarcerated.] They emphasize that participating in the STEP Aftercare meetings enables them to see and interact with soon-to-be released inmates and educate and prepare them for the reality of life on the outside. Institutional program participants attend Aftercare meetings dressed in institutional garb and are accompanied by institutional staff. These women serve to remind those who have been released from where they came, as well as to what they might return. In addition, the STEP Aftercare program provides women with a sense of structure and commitment because meetings are held weekly and women are encouraged to attend.

For most women, however, STEP meetings provide a medium through which they may share their pain, anger, frustration, and failure, as in the case when a woman relapses into drug use; or, their successes and good fortune in the outside world. The pain, anger, or frustration may include the discovery that a woman is HIV positive. The shared success or good fortune may include regaining legal custody of one's children, securing an apartment, obtaining employment, or being readmitted to college.

In a sense, the group also functions as a surrogate family, with group members referring to themselves as "sisters," and acting as sisters toward each other, through the sharing of experiences, as well as the love and concern that they express toward one another. During STEP meetings it is not uncommon for participants to cry and be comforted and/or address issues in a caring but sometimes confrontational manner. There is also applause for the sharing of information regarding a happy or successful event, positive undertaking, or positive change. The group provides a safe place where women can share their private and personal activities. Women appear willing to listen to each other and willing to consider suggestions given regarding the need for change, especially when the information shared is by someone with similar experiences.

PROGRAM OUTCOMES

Hepburn (1996) states that "success" may be viewed in one light by the criminal justice system and in quite another by treatment specialists. He states that for the criminal justice system, the objective of treating the drug-using offender is to prevent future criminal activity, especially theft, fraud, and other crimes related to drug use. Treatment professionals, on the other hand, may feel they have accomplished their goal if they can extinguish the offender's use of drugs, regardless of subsequent criminal behavior. Moreover, the treatment professionals know that most drug users will relapse occasionally as part of their recovery (see Chapter Four), so the occurrence of a relapse is not a sign of failure as long as the offender continues with the treatment program. Yet these same sporadic and intermittent episodes may be defined by criminal justice professionals as instances of recidivism and the treatment is considered a failure (Hepburn 1996, pp. 176–177).

While no formal evaluation of STEP has taken place, unofficial estimates of recidivism range from 17 to 20 percent. However, the intangible improvements in the lives of the women who have been involved with the program defy any attempts at "objective" measurement.

CONCLUSION

It is important to examine the phenomenon of female criminality with respect to programs that will effectively help in the process of their rehabilitation. Corrections, as a system, must encompass all aspects of rehabilitative service, including mental health, employment services, education, and social service. The success of programs designed for female offenders, directed toward their return to the community, must be based on an affirmative link between the institution and the community (ACA 1990, p. 23). STEP achieves this goal by maintaining collaborative links to multiple support systems within the New York City and surrounding community.

STEP as a multimodal approach to treatment of female offenders has the greatest potential for the reduction of recidivism because the various components of STEP attempt to address all of the areas noted above. Over time, these areas have been emphasized by the

Wickersham Commission, President Johnson's Task Force on Corrections, and the various state task forces that continue to be established in our attempt to find solutions to the problem of crime in today's society.

Over time these same areas have proved to be critical areas of need for minority women, especially African Americans. STEP's attention to these critical areas along with its emphasis on empowerment, self-reliance, and positive change, rather than mere coping, holds the promise of being a particularly effective mechanism for building or rebuilding stable, productive, and law-abiding lives among African American (and other, including Latina) women who have been incarcerated. By empowering women to gain control over their own lives, STEP provides women offenders with the ways and means to avoid repeat "entrapment" into criminality and repeat cycling through the correctional system.

REFERENCES

American Correctional Association 1990. *The female offender: What does the future hold?* Washington, D.C.: St. Mary's Press.

Austin, J., et al. 1992. *Female offenders in the community: An analysis of innovative strategies and programs.* Washington, D.C.: National Institute of Corrections, U.S. Department of Justice.

Bickford, A., and Massey, D. 1991. Segregation in the second ghetto: Racial and ethnic segregation in American public housing, 1977. *Social Forces* 69: 1011–1036.

Binkley-Jackson, D., et al. 1993. African American women in prison. In *Women prisoners: A forgotten population,* eds. Fletcher, B., et al., 65–74. Westport, CT: Praeger Publishers.

Bresler, L., and Lewis, D. K. 1983. Black and white women prisoners: Differences in family ties and their programmatic implications. *The Prison Journal* 63: 116–123.

Bureau of Census 1992. *Marital status and living arrangements: March 1991.* Washington, D.C.: U.S. Government Printing Office.

Bureau of Justice Statistics 1993. *Sentencing in the federal courts: Does race matter?* Washington, D.C.: Department of Justice.

Bureau of Justice Statistics 1995. *Prison and jail inmates 1995.* Washington, D.C.: Department of Justice.

Clark, J. 1995. The impact of the prison environment on mothers. *The Prison Journal* 75 (3): 306–329.

DiMascio, W. 1995. *Seeking justice: Crime and punishment in America.* New York: Edna McConnell Clark Foundation.

Fingerhut, L., et al. 1991. Firearm mortality among children, youth, and young adults 1–34 years of age, trends and current status: United States, 1979–1988. *Monthly Vital Statistics Report* 39 (11):1–6. Supplement.

Fingerhut, L., and Kleinman, J. 1990. International and interstate comparisons of homicide among young males. *Journal of the American Medical Association* 263: 3292–3295.

Free, M., Jr. 1996. *African Americans and the criminal justice system.* New York: Garland Publishing Co.

French, L. 1983. A profile of the incarcerated black female offender. *The Prison Journal* 63: 80–87.

Gibson, C. 1993. Empowerment theory and practice with adolescents of color in the child welfare system. *Families in Society* 747: 387–396.

Gilliard, D., and Beck, A. 1994. Prisoners in 1993. *Bureau of Justice Statistics Bulletin* June: 1–11. Washington, D.C.: U.S. Department of Justice, U.S. Government Printing Office.

Gordon, V. 1987. *Black women, feminism and black liberation: Which way?* Chicago: Third World Press.

Gray, I., et al. 1995. Inmate needs and programming in exclusively women's jails. *The Prison Journal* 75: 186–202.

Henriques, Z. 1995. African American woman: The oppressive intersection of race, class and gender. *Women and Criminal Justice* 7: 67–80.

Hepburn, J. 1996. Classifying drug offenders for treatment. In *Drugs and crime: Evaluating public policy initiatives,* eds. MacKenzie, D., and Uchida, C., 172–187. Thousand Oaks, CA: Sage Publications.

Hughey, R., and Klemke, L. 1996. Evaluation of a jail-based substance abuse treatment program. *Federal Probation* 604, 40–44.

Humphrey, E. 1990. *Review of the literature on female security issues*. New York: Department of Correctional Services, Division of Program Planning, Research and Evaluation.

Jordan, J. 1993. The relational self: Implications for adolescent development. In *Adolescent Psychiatry*, 227–239. Chicago: University of Chicago Press.

Joseph, J. 1997. Woman battering: A comparative analysis of black and white women. In *Out of the Darkness: Contemporary perspectives on family violence*, eds. Kantor, G, and Jasinski, J. 161–169. Thousand Oaks, CA: Sage Publications.

Kline, S. 1993. A profile of female offenders in state and federal prisons. In *Female offenders: Meeting needs of a neglected population,* ed. American Correctional Association, 1–6. Laurel, MD: American Correctional Association.

Malveaux, J. 1988. Ain't I a woman: Differences in the labor market status of black and white women. In *Racism and sexism: An integrated study*, ed. Rothenberg, P., New York: St. Martin's Press.

Martinson, R. 1974. What works? Questions and answers about prison reform. *Public Interest* 35: 22–54.

Mauer, M. 1995. Disparate justice imperils a community. *Legal Times* October 16.

Merlo, A. 1997. The crisis and consequences of prison overcrowding. In *Prisons today and tomorrow,* ed. Pollock, J., 52–83. Gaithersburg, MD: Aspen Publishers, Inc.

Perkins, C. 1994. National corrections reporting program. *Bureau of Justice Statistics Bulletin,* October. U.S. Department of Justice, Washington, D.C.: Government Printing Office.

Pollock, J., ed. 1997. The social world of the prisoner. In *Prisons: Today and tomorrow,* 218–269. Gaithersburg, MD: Aspen Publishers, Inc.

Richie, B. 1996. *Compelled to crime: The gender entrapment of battered black women*. New York: Routledge.

Rothenberg, P., ed. 1988. The feminization of poverty. In *Racism and sexism: An integrated study*, 80–84. New York: St. Martin's Press.

Sampson, R. and Wilson, W.J. 1995. Toward a theory of race, crime, and urban inequality. In *Crime and inequality*, eds. Hagan, J., and Peterson, R., 37–54. Stanford, CA: Stanford University Press.

Sampson, R. 1987. Urban black violence: the effect of male joblessness and family disruption. *American Journal of Sociology* 932: 348–382.

Self-Taught Empowerment and Pride Program 1991. *Overview*. East Elmhurst, NY: New York City Department of Correction.

Self-Taught Empowerment and Pride Unit 1995. Pamphlet. Elmhurst, NY: City of New York Department of Correction.

Self-Taught Empowerment and Pride Unit. *Orientation booklet*. East Elmhurst, NY: City of New York Department of Correction.

Staples, R. and Johnson, L. 1993. *Black families at the crossroads*. San Francisco: Jossey-Bass Publishers.

Stuart, R., 1997. Behind bars. *Emerge* Special Report on Black Women in America 85, March: 44–48.

U.S. Department of Commerce 1992. *Money, income of household, family and persons in the United States, 1991*. Washington, D.C.: U.S. Government Printing Office.

U.S. Department of Justice 1994. *Women in Prison: Survey of State prison inmates, 1991 Office of Justice Programs*. Washington, D.C.: Bureau of Justice Statistics.

Wellisch, J., et al. 1993. Numbers and characteristics of drug-using women in the criminal justice system: Implications for treatment. *The Journal of Drug Issues* 231: 7–30.

Wellisch, J., et al. 1996. Needs assessment and services for drug–abusing women offenders: Results from a national survey of community-based treatment programs. *Women and Criminal Justice* 81: 27–60.

Wexler, H., et al. 1988. *A criminal justice system strategy for treating cocaine-heroin abusing offenders in custody*. Washington, D.C.: National Institute of Justice, U.S. Department of Justice, Office of Communication and Research.

Wilson, W. J., et al. 1988.The ghetto underclass and the changing structure of American poverty. In *Quiet riots: Race and poverty in the United States,* eds. Harris, F., and Wilkins, R., 123–154. New York: Pantheon Books.

Wilson, W. J. 1987. *The truly disadvantaged: The inner city, the underclass and public policy.* Chicago: University of Chicago.

Wren, C. 1997. Reno and top drug officials urge smaller gap in cocaine sentences. *The New York Times* July 22: A1, A12.

CHAPTER 15

Programs That Work: Mothers

Ruth T. Zaplin and Joyce Dougherty

Editor's Notes

Most women who become institutionalized are mothers. Before their institutionalization, they were the sole caretakers of young children. During their institutionalization they will have to deal with the trauma of separation from their children, a trauma that is usually compounded by other forms of trauma that precede the institutionalization. And, when the terms of their institutionalization are ended, most of these mothers, even if they have not been ideal parents, will return to their children as the sole caretaker. For this reason, Zaplin and Dougherty suggest that it is vitally important to both enhance the parenting capability of the institutionalized mother and maintain the integrity of the family whenever possible.

Chapter Fifteen is a review of the plight of institutionalized mothers and their children including the retention of parental rights and the mother's shame related to their children's awareness of their criminal involvement. Selected examples of institutional programming are presented. A comprehensive, model program designed to nurture the mother-child relationship is described. Based on the premise that simple cognitive interventions like parenting programs alone are not sufficient to promote feelings of parental worth or profound behavioral change, the model program described is comprised of three components: an eight-week parenting class, an ongoing parent support group, and an eight-week "Working With Emotions" curriculum. This model program is also based on the premise that continuing contact between parent and child is perhaps the most significant predictor of family reunification after institutionalization. Continuing contact is largely an untenable situation when the mother is institutionalized a considerable distance from her children. This is due to the fact that women's prisons are often located in rural areas far from urban centers where the family members generally reside, and they are often inaccessible by public transportation (Gabel and Johnston 1995). Thus, when children do visit their mothers in prison, contact may be quite limited, and usually not enough to nurture the parent-child relationship. For this reason, the model program described is community-based.

Last, but not least, Zaplin and Dougherty strongly echo the words of Bloom and Steinhart (1993, p. 63) who advocated that the first priority for policymakers should be "to recognize the need to support the incarcerated mother's relationship with her children and the need to avoid unnecessary incarceration when safe and reasonable alternative dispositions can protect the mother-child relationship and meet the fundamental parenting needs of the child."

REFERENCES

Bloom, B., and Steinhart, D. 1993. *Why punish the children? A reappraisal of the children of incarcerated mothers in America.* Washington, D.C.: National Council on Crime and Delinquency.

Gabel, K., and Johnston, D., eds. 1995. *Children of incarcerated parents.* New York: Lexington Books.

INTRODUCTION

The vast majority of female offenders in this country today are also mothers. This chapter examines some of the issues related to incarcerated mothers and their children. What is revealed is the degree to which the contact between imprisoned mothers and their children is woefully limited and how detrimental this is to both the mothers and their children. Conventional programs (some of which are briefly described in this chapter) have responded to this problem by developing ways to *maintain* the mother-child relationship while the mother is behind bars. This chapter introduces an innovative program grounded in the assumption that the mother-child relationship must be *nurtured*, not just maintained.

Placing a high priority on the importance of nurturing the mother-child relationship necessarily leads one to question the wisdom of relying so heavily upon the institutionalization of female offenders. Most female offenders would benefit enormously by being sentenced to community-based programs structured to accommodate their special needs as mothers. Significantly, the program introduced in this chapter is a community-based one. The hope is that what is presented here will stimulate policymakers and treatment providers alike to question their reliance on the incarceration of nondangerous female offenders, and serve as a catalyst for the development of urgently needed community-based services for these mothers and their children.

INSTITUTIONALIZED MOTHERS: DOING TIME ON THE INSIDE

Since the mid-1970s, the number of females imprisoned in the United States has risen dramatically. The vast majority of these incarcerated females are mothers. In 1986, 76 percent of institutionalized females were mothers according to a report by the United States Department of Justice. In a study of women in California prisons, Bloom and Owen found 80 percent of their respondents were mothers (Bloom 1995, p. 21). Most female offenders have children who are under the age of eighteen and most retain primary responsibility for child rearing. As Bloom (1995) suggests, more often than not mothers, not fathers, are the ones who serve as the sole economic *and* emotional support for their children before their incarceration. According to Johnston (1997), "jailed and imprisoned mothers are half as likely to be married as incarcerated fathers, three times as likely to have lived with their children before arrest, and half as likely to be satisfied with their children's placement" (p. 1). A mother also is more likely than a father to have difficulty arranging and maintaining a secure placement for her children while she is serving time. If a father has custody of his children, he usually can depend on the fact that the children's mother will provide for them during his imprisonment (Belknap 1996, p. 34). Families, then, are much more likely to be disrupted by the institutionalization of their mothers than they are by that of their fathers.

What can make the burdens of motherhood even worse for these females is the fact that most of them have very limited contact with their children while they are incarcerated. Mothers who lived with their children before their arrest are almost twice as likely to see their children while they are in prison than are mothers who were not living with their children before their arrest (Bloom 1995, p. 25). However, given the vital nature of such mother-child contact, the overall visitation rate is still relatively low—only 54 percent. The reality is, the primary way most institutionalized females keep in touch with their children is by letter or by telephone (Bloom 1995, p. 25). But even this kind of limited mother-child contact can be hampered by correctional institutions. For example, if telephone privileges are restricted—as they typically are—to "mutually exclusive systems of collect calls...or telephone credits," the calls that mothers can make to their children will be severely limited, especially if the mothers are indigent (Johnston 1997, p. 3).

This is not to suggest that prisons in the United States today do not permit mother-child visits. The high no-visitation rate is explained most often, not by restrictive institutional policies, but rather by the fact that most children (upwards of 60 percent of them) live more that 100 miles from the correctional institutions where their mothers are being held (Bloom 1995, p. 25). To make matters worse, the rural locations of most female facilities typically leave them inaccessible by public transportation. Beyond the basic, often insurmountable problem of finding a way to get children to the places where their mothers are being held, Bloom (1995) suggests the following as yet another explanation for low mother-child visitation rates:

> Reluctance of the child's caregiver to allow visitation...[is] another reason for lack of mother-child contact....Some foster parents are reluctant to assist children in maintaining contact with their imprisoned mothers due to concern about the mother's "fitness" as a parent or fear of losing their own relationship with the children. (p. 25)

Further, Bloom (1995) contends some females simply do not want their children to visit them in prison because they may harbor feelings of shame or embarrassment about their children's awareness of their criminal activity. Also according to Bloom (1995), some mothers simply choose not to tell their children they are in prison at all, and the "extent of powerlessness experienced by some mothers…is so severe that they sever their emotional ties to their children [completely] out of sheer self-preservation" (p. 25).

There is little doubt, that the responsibilities of motherhood add considerable stress to the already stressful lives of incarcerated female offenders, particularly teenage mothers institutionalized largely because community-based alternatives are unavailable. Not only are these women and, increasingly, girls dealing with whatever brought them into the criminal and juvenile justice systems in the first place (i.e., substance abuse problems, the consequences of their criminal activities, repeated incarcerations, etc.), they are struggling to deal with the additional burdens of motherhood. Simply put, incarceration for these females is doubly agonizing because they are confronted by the fact that their children are suffering too—doing time on the outside while they are doing time on the inside (Dowling 1997, p. 84).

The emotional toll this can take on a mother is graphically illustrated in the following excerpt from a case study of a 52-year-old former female offender as she reflected upon her years in prison:

> My children were 18, 15, 12, and 9 when I left for four years. My grandson was 1 1/2 years old. You call as often as you can to keep up with all the aspects of their lives. You write a lot. I missed two graduations from high school, the looking for colleges, birthdays, first days of the new school year, holidays. The 9-year-old was asked to draw a family picture in art class. His mother was missing. His picture had a blank spot where I should have been. Visits are exciting and also can be very hard because they end. Sometimes it takes days to get over the emotion of having a visit. If the visit does not have to end you would feel better. But they leave and you are again all alone and wondering what they will be doing. The first two years my children came for a visit about every month. The last two years I was moved to another prison and I did not have a visit from my children as I was too far away for them to see me. They did send me a lot of pictures. You look forward to visits, phone calls, and mail. You have children going through puberty, starting to date and drive and you aren't there for them when they need to talk and need their mother. When my son graduated from high school he made a video and I got permission for him to send it in. I was called to the library and the video was shown. There was not a dry eye in the library as every woman who was in the library was allowed to watch. It was wonderful. At the end of the video was a message from my children and grandchild in their own words. You do a lot of thinking about when you go home. You are not sure what it will be like. Things are changed. You cannot go back to the way things were. If your child gets sick it

is terrible. You cannot take care of him. My son got pneumonia and they did not tell me at first. You feel as if everything is your fault and your children will hate you for being away.

Adding to this emotional toll is the fear many incarcerated mothers have of losing legal custody of their children. Indeed, those fears are not unfounded, especially for mothers whose children are in foster care. As Bloom (1995) points out: "Upon incarceration, many women prisoners face losing custody of their children" (p. 26). According to Johnson (1997), incarcerated female offenders seem to be far more likely to have child custody problems, and are at greater risk of losing their parental rights than are their male counterparts (p. 1):

No studies specifically examine the extent of loss and retention of parental rights among female offenders, however, some evidence exists that terminations occur disproportionately among women offenders. The Center for Children of Incarcerated Parents has found that about 25 percent of women offenders whose children participate in Center therapeutic programs have lost parental rights to at least one child (Johnston 1997). Also, national samplings of court data on terminations of parental rights in black families have revealed that 12 to 18 percent of all terminations occur among incarcerated parents (National Black Child Development Institute 1989). (Johnson 1997, p. 2)

Some states have termination-of-parental rights or adoption statutes that explicitly pertain to incarcerated parents. According to Bloom (1995):

The current foster care system is poorly equipped to deal with the growing population of incarcerated mothers who are serving lengthy sentences. This time-driven model of foster care placement simply cannot handle the situation of an imprisoned mother who has a relationship with her child but is unable to resume physical custody for many years. (p. 27)

In point of fact, mothers with long prison terms, or more typically, repeat offenders, are often forced to give up custody of their children to ensure the continuity of their children's care. Thus, the rates at which incarcerated mothers are permanently separated from their children are rising (Johnston 1997, p. 3), and with it the emotional anxiety from which many females suffer as the result of such separation.

Fear of losing custody of their children can take the greatest emotional toll on pregnant females who deliver their babies while incarcerated. Approximately 8 percent to 10 percent of female offenders are pregnant when they enter prison. The standard practice in most states is for females to be transferred to designated medical facilities to deliver their babies. They are then allowed to remain with their babies in those facilities for a recovery time of usually only two days. After that they are taken back to prison without their infants (Bloom 1995). With few exceptions, correctional facilities do not allow newborns to stay with their mothers. Instead, babies are taken from their mothers' arms and, if the mothers have been able to make such an arrangement before their child's birth, handed over to relatives or friends who have agreed to care for the babies. When no such arrangements have been made, however, the babies are taken into custody by the child welfare system where they eventually end up in foster care. It has been suggested that these standard practices not only interfere with the essential bonding between a mother and her newborn, they also have serious implications for the likelihood that a positive mother-child relationship will be possible in the future (Bloom 1995, p. 24).

Not surprisingly, if they have managed to retain legal custody of their children, female offenders often express feelings of inadequacy about resuming parental authority upon their release from prison. The issue of reunification with their children is paramount in the lives of incarcerated mothers. As Bloom (1995) observes: "Imprisoned mothers face enormous obstacles...in reunifying with their families once they are released...[because they] are forced to navigate through a number of complex governmental and social service agencies in order to receive court-mandated reunification services" (p. 27). According to Bloom (1995):

> Continuing contact between a parent and child is a significant predictor of family reunification after parental incarceration. Child welfare laws provide for termination of parental rights...if the incarcerated mother...has failed to sustain an adequate relationship with her child....In addition...incarcerated mothers do not have access to the resources they need to meet other reunification requirements imposed by the court such as parent education, counseling, drug treatment, and job training. (p. 26)

Incarcerated mothers whose children have been placed in foster care face even more daunting obstacles when it comes to reunification with their families upon their release. According to requirements established by the 1980 Adoption Assistance and Child Welfare Act, a caseworker must make a concerted effort either to reunify the family upon a mother's release (i.e., remove the children from their foster care homes), *or* provide the children with an alternative permanent care plan. The law also mandates specific case plans be developed and implemented. These so-called permanency plans require, among other things, regular contact between a mother and her children's caseworker (Bloom 1995, p. 26). If a mother fails to maintain this requisite contact with her children's caseworker, her parental status may be jeopardized. Bloom (1995) points out the difficulties many incarcerated mothers have with these requirements:

> Various authorities...have suggested that contact between caseworkers and mothers is strained and infrequent and that mothers are uninformed about their legal status and responsibilities. Beckerman (1994) confirmed these perceptions in a recent study that found that the prerequisite conditions deemed necessary for a mother's involvement in permanency planning—including frequent interaction

and collaboration between caseworker and parents of children in foster care—are not present among imprisoned women." (p. 27)

Reunification with their families is a trying process for all incarcerated mothers. As they struggle with their own anxieties about resuming a parental role full-time, they also must struggle to overcome the legal and bureaucratic obstacles that threaten to derail reunification. In the midst of all of these struggles, these mothers are left to agonize over the impact their imprisonment may have had on their children and over how that impact may complicate their efforts to reestablish a relationship with their children.

THE CHILDREN OF INSTITUTIONALIZED MOTHERS: DOING TIME ON THE OUTSIDE

It has been estimated that there are at least 1.5 million children of incarcerated parents living in the United States today (Bloom 1993, p. 15). Like other children who experience some form of parental separation (e.g., the children of divorced or deceased parents), these children typically become distressed. Signs of this distress may include such things as depression, aggression, poor school performance, and truancy. According to Bloom (1993), the immediate and sometimes long lasting psychological harm done to the children of incarcerated parents can be substantial (p. 16). A 1992 study conducted by the Center for Children of Incarcerated Parents concluded children can in fact be traumatized by the events relating to parental crime, arrest, and institutionalization (Bloom 1993, p. 16).

When a mother is arrested, childcare arrangements may have to be made hastily. A grandparent most commonly is asked to assume care of the children. Many grandparents do not contemplate having to take responsibility for the full-time care of their grandchildren at this stage in their lives. Even if they have anticipated such a turn of events, many simply are not physically or financially able to provide the ideal level of care their grandchildren need. If a grandparent cannot, or will not, take responsibility for the children, other family members may agree to care for them. Frequently those relatives have their own children whose needs understandably take priority over the needs of the children whose mother is incarcerated. Children not cared for by relatives may go to friends with similar priorities if they have their own children. If all else fails, the children of incarcerated female offenders will be taken into custody by child welfare and placed with a foster family. Wherever the children go, the mother-child relationship will be jeopardized, and, as decades of studies have shown, this means jeopardizing a bond that is vitally important to children's healthy development (Bloom and Steinhart, 1993). This is particularly true when it comes to the development of very young children. A 1996 report by the U.S. Department of Health and Human Services on child development suggests routine nonmaternal care in a child's first year of life may have a direct impact on the security of that infant's attachment to his or her mother in later life (Boudouris 1996, p. 1). According to Bourdouris (1996): "The assumption is that [mother-child] bonding is critical for healthy development and emotional growth, and that its absence has many undesirable consequences for the child" (p. 1).

A reliable measure to assess the risk that children of incarcerated mothers face in regard to their becoming involved in the juvenile justice system currently is not available. There is, however, a growing body of evidence suggesting the children of incarcerated parents are more likely than the children of parents who are not incarcerated to end up behind bars themselves at some point in their lives. A 1987 U. S. Department of Justice survey of youth in custody found about one third of the children reported at least one of their parents had been institutionalized at some time. A survey of female offenders by the American Correctional Association found that 48 percent of the women and 64 percent of the girls reported they had other family members who had been incarcerated (Bloom 1993, p. 70). Girls whose mothers are incarcerated and who lack a stable home life are also more likely to become pregnant as teenagers. In short, like their mothers, the children of incarcerated female offenders are exposed to a multitude of factors that can propel them toward at-risk behavior.

INSTITUTIONAL PROGRAMS FOR MOTHERS AND THEIR CHILDREN

Given the importance of the mother-child relationship to healthy child development, many correctional facilities for females have instituted programs that facilitate better contacts between incarcerated mothers and their children. While these programs may be seen as a step in the right direction, their focus tends to be on finding ways to *maintain* the mother-child relationship and not on finding ways to *nurture* that relationship. What follows is a brief description of some of these types of programs.

The prison MATCH (Mothers And Their Children) program was first established in 1978 at the Federal Correctional Institution at Pleasanton, California. Instead of having infants at the institution, this original MATCH program called for strengthening the mother-child bond by improving conditions for visiting, improving inmate training in parenting and early childhood education, and improving prenatal care and referrals for other social services (Boudouris 1996). In 1989, another MATCH program was established at the San Francisco County Jail with components similar to those found in the original Pleasanton program. The San Francisco program, however, did call for less involvement of the incarcerated parents in the administration of the program. The components of a model MATCH, as described in Boudouris (1996, p. 22) include:

- Children's Centers where prisoners and their children—from infancy to fifteen years of age—can develop "parent-child bonds through play and learning activities";
- Supportive social services and referrals to assist the parents with foster care and child custody issues, and crisis intervention;
- Parenting classes where mothers learn parenting skills by interacting with and observing volunteer staff, and other parents and their children;
- A human services training program designed to teach paraprofessional skills that would enable inmates to work with children and their families;

- A program called "Breaking the Intergenerational Cycle of Addiction," which includes supportive services such as individual and family counseling, postrelease planning, referrals, and follow-up.

Jails and prisons across the country have implemented programs similar to MATCH, such as the Mother-Offspring Life Development program (MOLD) and the Parents And Their Children at Home program (PATCH). In the Nebraska Correctional Center, the MOLD program, which is used as a reward for good behavior, allows inmates to visit with their children who are between the ages of one and nine years for up to five days every month. One of only two states with established prison nurseries, Nebraska modeled its visitation program after one begun at the Bedford Hills Correctional Facility in New York. Some of the various special visiting programs in place at Bedford Hill are described below:

> *The Summer Program* is when children can visit for five days in a row during one of 10 weeks between June and August. Children either live with host families in the neighborhood or they are picked up as far as an hour and a half away in New York City, and driven back and forth each day by volunteer drivers…
>
> [The success of the Summer Program led to the development of] the *Weekend Visiting Program,* in which the children can come one weekend each month for two days in a row. They stay overnight with host families, often the same ones that took them over the summer…
>
> Finally, the *Family Reunion Program,* run by the Department of Correctional Services, allows mothers to visit with their children for 48 hours in mobile homes situated in a fenced-off area on the prison grounds. Eligibility is determined after thorough investigations. This program allows for an even greater exchange between mothers and children. (Boudin 1997, p. 61)

Girl Scouts Behind Bars is a program that involves mothers in their daughters' lives through a unique partnership between a youth services organization and state and local corrections departments. In addition to increased visiting time, one aim of the program is to enable incarcerated mothers to assume parental responsibility and develop organizational skills. With Girl Scout staff support, the mothers are expected to plan some of the mother-daughter meetings. In general, the focus of these meetings is parental training. When the mothers return to the community, they are encouraged to continue to participate in the community-based program (Moses 1997).

Programs such as the ones described above attempt to promote the maintenance of family ties. However, as Bloom (1995) points out, conditions of confinement typically found within correctional facilities—the institutional primacy of security—can have a negative impact on the experiences of the visiting children. The institutional environment of a prison itself, then, actually may reproduce some of the same destructive relational dynamics for children that they do for their incarcerated mothers (Clark 1995). According to Boudin (1997), while many prison programs may attempt to promote the "importance of independent thinking and responsibility among inmates, qualities necessary for both mothering and inmate initiative," the institutions themselves "by their very nature foster dependence and passivity" (p. 57).

It is apparent the environment within correctional institutions is neither logistically nor programmatically ideal when it comes to the development of programs that strive, not just to maintain but to nurture the mother-child relationship. In the words of Superintendent Elaine Lord:

> If we are ever going to effectively intervene in the intergenerational connections of crime, abuse, drugs, and incarceration, we must recognize that these are families at risk. To effect change and enhance the healthy nurturing potential of these mother/child relationships, we must face that this can occur only in the context of consistent relationships and cannot occur in isolation. These relationships cannot thrive on two hours a week or month, and they cannot thrive on one week a year—they cannot thrive in prison. Everything that we are doing in prison to address family issues we can do better in free society and at considerably less cost. (Boudin 1997, p. 81)

A MODEL COMMUNITY-BASED PROGRAM FOR MOTHERS

It is important to emphasize that the model community-based program for female offenders and their children described in this section should be incorporated with other holistic programmatic efforts, such as the ones mentioned below and described in more detail throughout this book. Such efforts should be aimed at addressing the intersecting needs of these females, as well as at matching subgroups of these females to treatment and services based on their individual needs, e.g., females with children, females with little education, etc. (Koons et al. 1997). Beyond that, programs designed around this model should help foster personal growth and development. In a supportive and nurturing environment, these programs must provide clients with structure. However, they also must teach clients parenting and emotional management skills, and basic life management skills. Positive role models should be provided, as should health and mental health counseling, drug and alcohol education, and job readiness training. Without these kinds of skills, treatment, knowledge, and training, female offenders have little hope of developing the strength they need to stand up against the pressures that got them into trouble with the law in the first place. When implemented effectively, these programs should provide female offenders with what they need to become not just better mothers, but self-reliant and self-supporting individuals.

Phase One: Parenting Classes

Parenting is not an instinct with which humans are born. It is a skill that is learned, primarily within the family-of-origin. Given the negative family-life experiences of most female offenders, their parenting skills typically are lacking in the extreme. Phase One of this program consists of an eight-week parent education class that explains the developmental stages of children, as well as the appropriate types of discipline to be used during each specific developmental stage. This, of course, is basic knowledge all parents need. However, the curriculum for a population of female offenders should include discussions about how a parent's negative behavior can impact upon the family unit. Then what must be emphasized is that individuals do have the ability to change these negative behaviors. Classes should be offered in one-and-a-half-hour increments on a weekly basis. The participants should be given pre- and posttest measures to determine knowledge gained regarding the curriculum as outlined in Exhibit 15–1. If deemed necessary, control groups may be utilized to further evaluate the effectiveness of the class.

Phase Two: Parent Support Groups

After learning in the classroom setting what is developmentally normal for their children, a support group that focuses on specific issues impacting female offenders should be offered. This support group should include discussions on how criminal behavior may impact children and affect family interactions. Exhibit 15–2 outlines a 16-week program with specific suggestions for focus topics of discussion.

The parent support group should be held in conjunction with a child support group. The child support group should encourage the children to explore their feelings about their parent's deviance and to learn what they can do as children to protect themselves. Time also should be made in the schedules of both groups for a structured parent/child activity to promote family bonding.

Phase Three: Working with Emotions

The need for female offenders to deal with their emotions was discussed in Chapter Three. That chapter emphasized that the untreated—even unacknowledged—childhood trauma caused by abuse, combined with serious economic, social, and emotional deprivation can create tremendous emotional stress. The term *stress* as it is used here refers to the overarching context within which all difficult, uncomfortable emotions fall. This phase of the program should be designed to address female offenders' emotional deficits and inability to manage stress. Specifically, this phase should encompass the teaching all of the following competencies critical to management of emotions:

- Learning and accepting the concepts of emotional management, identifying individual deficits, and learning stress management strategies;
- Identifying, expressing, and managing feelings and building a vocabulary for them; learning to recognize if thoughts or feelings are ruling a decision and coming to understand the links between thoughts, feelings, and reactions; identifying patterns in one's own emotions and recognizing similar patterns in the emotions of others;
- Examining actions and knowing their consequences; learning the difference between feelings and actions and learning to make better emotional decisions by first control-

Exhibit 15–1 Parenting Class Curriculum—Phase One

Phase One: Eight-Week Parenting Class Outline

WEEK 1:   *Introduction*
Expectations/Rules/Pretest
Satisfactions and Frustrations in
   Being a Parent

WEEK 2   *Infancy: Birth–12 months*
What Children Need
Trust vs. Mistrust
Being in Charge and Involved
Goals of Misbehavior

WEEK 3   *Toddler: 1–3 years old*
Group Building Exercise
Autonomy vs. Self-Doubt
Self-Concept

WEEK 4   *Preschool: 4–5 years*
Preschooler's Relationship with
   the World
My Relationship with My Child

WEEK 5   *Elementary*
Next Time I Will Worksheet
Good or Responsible Parent

WEEK 6   *Discipline*
Discipline vs. Punishment
Natural and Logical Conse-
   quences
Making Rules and Setting
   Limits

WEEK 7   *Adolescence*
Today Poem
Missing Assignment Activity
Maslow's Hierarchy of Needs
Identify vs. Role Confusion
Toddler vs. Adolescent
Parent, Adult, Child

WEEK 8   *Wrap-up*
Parenting Poem
Communication
Posttest/Evaluations/Certificates

Courtesy of THE PROGRAM for Women and Families, Inc., Allentown, Pennsylvania.

---

ling the impulse to act, then identifying alternative actions and their consequences before acting;

- Learning the value of stress reduction; becoming aware of chronic functional sources of stress including poor posture and breathing, restricted movement, and speech patterns, etc.;
- Practicing guided imagery and relaxation methods specifically designed to discipline participants to manage emotions;
- Talking about feelings effectively; learning how to take the perspective of others and respecting the differences in how other people feel about things; learning to be a good listener and question asker, and understanding what behavior is acceptable in a situation; learning the value of openness and trust building in a relationship; knowing when it is safe to risk talking about private feelings;
- Taking responsibility; recognizing the consequences of decisions and actions, accepting feelings and moods; following through on commitments (e.g., to stay off drugs);
- Learning to distinguish between what someone says or does and one's own reactions and judgments; being assertive rather than angry or passive and learning the arts of

Exhibit 15–2 Parenting Class Curriculum—Phase Two

Phase Two: Sixteen-Week Parent Support Group Outline

WEEK 1 *Introduction*
Group Rules
Class Expectations with
Anticipated Outcomes
Pretest

WEEK 2 *How Parental Deviant Activity*
Impacts Children
Performing a Self-Check
The Impact of Parent's Devi-
ant/Criminal Involvement

WEEK 3 *Reasons for Becoming Parents*
Planned vs. Unplanned
Parenting

WEEK 4 *Satisfactions and Frustrations*
of Parenting
Self-Reflection
Brainstorming

WEEK 5 *Parenting: A Learned Behavior*
An Evaluation of our Parent's
Parenting Styles
What Did We Like/Dislike

WEEK 6 *Parenting Styles*
Authoritative
Assertive
Permissive

WEEK 7 *Developmental Stages and*
Normal Expectations
Erikson's Psychosocial Stages
of Development

WEEK 8 *Basic Needs of Children*
Maslow's Hierarchy of Needs
Parent's Responsibilities

WEEK 9 *How the "Wants" of Parents*
Can Negatively Affect
Children
Unhealthy Interpersonal
Relationships
Quantity vs. Quality Time

WEEK 10 *Personal Characteristics*
Associated with Positive
Parenting
Developing a Positive Self-
Concept
Substance Abuse/Use Free
Parenting

WEEK 11 *Fostering Self-esteem in*
Children
Developing a Child's Positive
Self-Concept
Leading by Example

WEEK 12 *How Children Learn*
Natural and Logical Conse-
quences
Making Rules and Setting
Limits

WEEK 13 *Communication: What Is It?*
Basic Communication
Roadblocks to Communication
Perceptions

WEEK 14 *Communication: Skill Building*
Transactional Analysis: Parent,
Adult, Child
Active Listening
Removing Barriers

WEEK 15 *Effective/Appropriate Disci-*
pline
Discipline vs. Punishment
Being in Charge and Involved

WEEK 16 *Group Closure*
Review
Post Test
Group Closing

Courtesy of THE PROGRAM for Women and Families, Inc., Allentown, Pennsylvania.

cooperation, conflict resolution and negotiating compromise; knowing when and how to lead, and when to follow.

The specific objectives of this phase of the program should be to teach female offenders first how to identify the sources of their stress that result in their high risk behaviors, thereby reducing the likelihood that their impulsive behavior will be based on emotions and second, the program should teach stress reduction and emotional management techniques and provide female offenders with a supportive environment in which to practice these newly learned techniques. Ultimately, in terms of parenting, the curriculum for this phase should help mothers:

- Correct maladaptive and habitual ways of relating to their children;
- Apply more adeptly the knowledge learned from the parenting education and parent support group *because of the new ability to step out of conceptual limitations and identify new solutions to unhealthy conditioned responses to children*;
- Teach their children to talk about *their* feelings in a positive way.

The curricular structure of this phase of the program is outlined in Exhibit 15–3.

Ideally all phases of this model program should operate in an environment that is as least restrictive as possible and in close proximity to the children. It should be an environment that is open and receptive for children to help minimize their trauma. According to Koons et al. (1997), an open and receptive environment for children depends on at least two factors being present: program staff members who are caring and environments in which women and children feel comfortable. The following factors are essential to creating this kind of environment:

> ...the maintenance of certain physical (e.g., equipment, space, technology) and social environments (e.g., peer support, open communication, isolation from the general population, "homey" atmosphere) that benefit program participants by creating places in which women feel comfortable, are open to learning from staff and other participants, and feel they can take risks in changing their lifestyles. For example, in one community-based program, participants supported one another and viewed the program as a "family." (Koons et al. 1997, p. 525)

Finally, for this model program to succeed in nurturing the mother-child relationship, it must be based on a systems approach. As Bloom and Steinhart (1993), point out, "the overall cost burden to the taxpayer could well be reduced by consolidating the costs of imprisonment and foster care into one, cost-effective alternative placement for the mother and her children" (p. 49), such as the one suggested by this community-based program. In order to accomplish this task, however, the adoption of a systems approach is critical.

CONCLUSION

A major theme throughout this book has been on the importance of adopting a systems approach when working with female offenders. Chapter Thirteen actually provides the sce-

Exhibit 15–3 Parenting Class Curriculum—Phase Three

Phase Three: Working with Emotions

WEEK 1: STRESS, EMOTIONS, AND THE BODY

- Understanding stress and the role of emotions in stress
- The effects of negative and positive emotions on health and well-being
- The physiology of stress: fight or flight
- Introduction to mindfulness; what it is and how it can be used to help discover the inner working of stress and stressful emotions as they occur
- Self-awareness and recognition of emotion as it occurs
- Start with body—gross, physical level—it is easier to learn and has an immediate impact
- Learn to recognize/discriminate difference between the body in varying degrees of tension and relaxation
- Bringing together relaxation with awareness (Relaxation is usually associated with "flopping" into sleep or an unaware state. Awareness is often associated with being "hyper" or in an agitated state.); learning to discriminate between unaware, dull relaxation, and aware relaxation
- Deep diaphragmatic breathing; the Body Scan progressive muscle relaxation; Stop and Breathe technique to use throughout the day to reduce stress or emotional escalation, especially when under stress

WEEK 2: TAKING RESPONSIBILITY TO CHANGE

- Cultivating nonjudgmental awareness and acceptance of things/events/sensations as they are
- Taking responsibility for one's own stress
- Understanding how one's attitude/perception of an event to a large degree determines our stress
- The stress "reaction": automatic (habitual), unconscious reactions experienced in form of thoughts/emotions/physical sensations
- Learning to discriminate exactly what happens to one when "stressed" or emotionally upset; what happens to body, thoughts, emotions, awareness
- Introduction to sitting mindfulness of breathing: using the breathing to train the mind to be present-centered, nonjudgmental observation and monitoring of bodily sensations, thought patterns and emotional states

WEEK 3: RESPONDING VS. REACTING

- Discriminating between the external event and one's reaction to it
- Discriminating between external stress (event) and internal stress (thoughts about the event)
- Learning to respond vs. react to stress
- Mindful stretching exercises

WEEK 4: YOU ARE NOT YOUR THOUGHTS

- The role of thoughts in stress/emotions; self-defeating thought patterns

---

continues

Exhibit 15–3 continued

- Objectifying the thought process through mindfulness; moving from being caught up in the contents of thoughts to seeing the overall process of thoughts as they occur
- Using the cognitive labeling technique of noting thoughts as they arise to interrupt/disengage from random thoughts, self-talk, negative self-talk, worrying, angry thoughts, etc.
- Questioning automatic, unconscious assumptions
- Recognizing/questioning, reversing negative habitual thought patterns
- Confronting cognitive distortions

WEEK 5: EMOTION-FOCUSED COPING

- Learning to discriminate between the stress (internal or external) and the emotional reaction to the stress
- Learning to recognize and self-monitor feelings as they occur
- Discriminating between thoughts and feelings and emotions
- Learning to self-manage stress/emotions using mindfulness of breathing and bodily sensations to de-escalate and restore physiological balance in the midst of stressful feelings
- Emotion-focused coping skills
- Empathy training

WEEK 6: PROBLEM-FOCUSED COPING

- Learning to identify the problem which is the cause of one's stress
- Learning to see the problem apart from personal feelings about the problem
- Self-inquiry regarding possible actions one could take to help solve/alleviate the problem
- Learning to break the problem down into smaller pieces
- Learning coping skills to apply to the problem
- Taking action as self-empowerment and movement toward resolution

WEEK 7: COMMUNICATION SKILLS

- Building listening skills and identifying blocks to effective listening
- Empathic listening
- Learning to modulate: pacing and speed
- Using complete "I messages"—not putting others in a defensive position
- Assertiveness as a way to take action rather than anger or passivity

WEEK 8: HOW TO PROCEED

- Conclusion and review
- Planning how to proceed without the structure of the program

Courtesy of THE PROGRAM for Women and Families, Inc., Allentown, Pennsylvania.

nario of integrating a community's educational justice and public behavioral health systems. There are organizations that can provide the range of community-based services female offenders and their children need to break intergenerational cycles of involvement in crime. The systems approach, however, suggests that one critical question must be asked:

What will serve the best interests of the family as a whole? Ideally, treatment providers within a coordinated system of services should be able to make decisions *with* the mothers, not *for* them. As it stands now, the educational justice and public behavioral health systems inclusive of the child welfare system, as well as independent systems of service providers act autonomously, each with separate responsibilities. Each of these systems serves a distinct function, often with little information about or coordination with the other systems. The single system approach to service delivery precludes the efficient and effective treatment of female offenders and their children. If the goal is not just to maintain the relationship between female offenders and their children but to nurture it, then adoption of a systems approach is absolutely vital.

REFERENCES

Belknap, J. 1996. Access to programs and health care for incarcerated women. *Federal Probation* 60: 4, 34–39.

Bloom, B. 1995. Imprisoned mothers. In *Children of incarcerated parents,* eds. Gabel, K., and Johnston, D., 21–30, New York: Lexington Books.

Bloom, B., and Steinhart, D. 1993. *Why punish the children?* San Francisco: National Council on Crime and Delinquency.

Boudin, K. 1997. The Children's Center Programs of Bedford Hills Correctional Facility. In *Maternal ties: A selection of programs for female offenders,* ed., Blinn, C., 55–86, Lanham, MD: American Correctional Association.

Boudouris, J. 1996. *Parents in prison: Addressing the needs of families.* Lanham, MD: American Correctional Association.

Clark, J. 1995. The impact of the prison environment on mothers. *The Prison Journal* 75, 306-329.

Dowling, C. G. 1997. Part one: Women behind bars. *Life Magazine* October: 77-84, 807-90.

Johnston, D. 1997. Developing services for incarcerated mothers. In *Maternal ties: A selection of programs for female offenders,* ed., Blinn, C., 1–8, Lanham, MD: American Correctional Association.

Koons, B. A., et al. 1997. Expert and offender perceptions of program elements linked to successful outcomes for incarcerated women. *Crime and Delinquency* 43: 4, 512–532.

Moses, M. 1997. The girl scouts beyond bars program: Keeping incarcerated mothers and their daughters together. In *Maternal ties: A selection of programs for female offenders,* ed., Blinn, C., 35–49, Lanham, MD: American Correctional Association.

U.S. Department of Justice 1991. Women in prison (Report No. NCJ-127991). Washington, D.C.: Bureau of Justice Statistics.

CHAPTER 16

Programs that Work: Working with Prostitutes

Lorry Bradley and Lori Moschella

Editor's Notes

In Chapter Sixteen, Bradley and Moschella argue that within patriarchal societies, consistent with the tenets of power-belief theory discussed in Chapter Six, prostitution is a male-dominated activity that perpetuates and maintains sexist oppression and exploitation of women. This chapter provides information to support this argument, to assist in understanding the dynamics of prostitution, and to provide treatment options that work for this subpopulation of female offenders. Specifically, the authors present an historical overview of prostitution, prostitution as it is today, and the steps taken by the staff of THE PRO-GRAM For Women and Families, an agency that provides community-based and in-prison services to female offenders in northeast Pennsylvania, to develop a psychoeducational program in conjunction with and for prostitutes. The authors discuss the Regaining Esteem Stopping Prostitution by Education and Continued Treatment (RESPECT) program developed. The 12-hour program described consists of four modules: HIV/AIDS, Sexually Transmitted Infections/Contraception, Gender Roles/Societal Norms, and Sexuality/Sexual Expectations.

INTRODUCTION

Prostitution, the world's oldest profession or the world's oldest example of the objectification and repression of women in society? The latter appears to be a more accurate description. This is true for several reasons. (1) Historically, the majority of prostitutes have been women. In some societies male prostitution and prostitution of children occurs, however, even these individuals have less power than the dominant male culture. (2) In general, prostitutes are from lower societal classes and have relatively little political power because they are women. Therefore, it is argued that within patriarchal societies (see Chapter Six), prostitution is a male-dominated activity that perpetuates and maintains sexist oppression and exploitation of women.

Antiprostitution sentiments and attempts to regulate the behavior of prostitutes date back to the Old Testament. Prostitution is condemned by Christian theology within the seventh Commandment, "Thou Shalt Not Commit Adultery." Therefore, controversy over prostitution began with the earliest forms of the industry and continues today. Some argue about the ills of prostitution while others question these ills citing the prostitute's ability to choose this profession to earn a living. The proprostitution arguments epitomize the mark of female oppression; they reaffirm and reinforce a sexist male-dominated culture.

There are six primary reasons for working with females involved in prostitution:

1. The practice perpetuates a detrimental power differential between men and women.
2. The act is currently against the law in most states, therefore, there are criminal consequences for the behavior.
3. Many prostitutes are drug abusers who use prostitution as a means to pay for their habit.
4. Most of these women have low self-concepts and/or undiagnosed mental health disorders (see Chapter Nine); intervention can assist in addressing these issues.
5. Many street prostitutes report they have been victims of violence while prostituting, thus intervention may save their lives.
6. A large percentage of these women are at-risk for contracting and spreading HIV and other sexually transmitted infections (STIs).
7. Many women report family histories of sexual abuse. Their continued participation in the practice continues the exploitation of their bodies that began in childhood.

These reasons will be elaborated on further within this chapter.

To assist in understanding the dynamics of prostitution and providing treatment options that work for this subpopulation of female offenders, this chapter will present an historical overview of prostitution, prostitution as it is today, the steps taken to develop a program for prostitutes, and a presentation of Regaining Esteem Stopping Prostitution by Education and Continued Treatment (RESPECT), a program for prostitutes.

THE HISTORY OF PROSTITUTION

Prostitution is an ancient institution that has flourished throughout the ages. The origin of the word "prostitute" comes from the Latin "prostitutus" meaning "up front" or "to expose." This term was used because Roman women covered their faces, whereas the faces of prostitutes were uncovered or exposed. This differentiation stigmatized the women involved in prostitution. They became deviants in the eyes of society because they would not conform to the norms of a patriarchal society. Ironically, although they were outcasts, they were free from the control of Roman men. Even during Roman times the age-old battle of the sexes existed.

The earliest form of prostitution, "temple prostitution" existed in the Ancient Near East, India, and Southeast Asia. Temple prostitution was a religious duty for women associated with the temples of love and fertility. In Babylon, this duty included openly prostituting themselves on the steps of the temple. The proceeds of these services were donated to the temple; therefore, this was considered a religious duty.

In ancient Greece, there were several classes of prostitutes: the brothel prostitutes, the street prostitutes, the auletrides, and the hetaerae. In 600 B.C., Solon established state brothels in Athens, the employees of which came from the lower social strata. Later street prostitutes emerged. The street prostitutes were women who were unmarried and often destitute. Many street prostitutes became involved in the sex industry either through forcible recruitment or as the only alternative to unemployment. The third class of prostitutes, the auletrides, were dancers, acrobats, and musicians. They were attractive and sensual and hired themselves out to perform at orgies and other social events. Along with their entertainment skills, they often provided sexual gratification for their clients. Finally, the hetaerae were the highest ranking prostitutes who associated with the most powerful men in Greece. These women were showered with gifts and other benefits. According to Grolier Encyclopedia, in order to reach the hetaerae level, in addition to being beautiful, the women "had to have achieved the highest social graces and have learned to read and write." For these women, prostitution was "occasional and contingent, as the hetaerae relied upon a much larger repertoire of salable skills for their livelihood."

In ancient Rome, prostitutes were primarily slaves, and they were licensed and taxed. These female slaves were often sold to brothels for the purpose of prostitution. Women who performed—dancers, entertainers—were able to freely sell their sexual services without regulations. Male prostitutes were numerous in Rome. Like their female counterparts, they were controlled by the dominant male culture.

In the fourth century through to the Reformation there was a tolerance for prostitution. The prostitutes mentioned in the Bible influenced prostitution sentiments during this time period. For example, Mary Magdalene, a harlot who was redeemed, was a role model for a number of prostitutes. Many prostitutes became holy women. Some even became saints. Throughout the Middle Ages, prostitution flourished under the protection and regulation of municipal governments. Restrictions against prostitution eventually appeared in early modern Europe. The advent of these restrictions coincided with the outbreak of a syphilis epidemic. Additionally, a repressive stance toward sexuality developed during the Reformation, which fostered an antiprostitution sentiment.

During the sixteenth century there were several attempts to restrict and regulate prostitution. Protestants banned prostitution in countries that adopted Lutheran and Calvinist codes. Parisians banned all prostitutes and promised to brand them with hot irons if they did not leave the city. In 1566, the Pope banned all prostitutes from Rome. However, he rescinded this request when 25,000 people were prepared to move from the city. In the end, none of these efforts slowed prostitution, and the practice prospered under limited regulations until the nineteenth century (Perkins 1991).

In modern Europe, even when the practice of prostitution was condemned and strictly regulated, it continued to flourish. During the nineteenth century, the English Vagrancy Act of 1822 included the term "common prostitute." By adding prostitution to this act, it enabled police to overlook formalities in arrest procedures concerning prostitutes. The Contagious Diseases Acts of 1864, 1866, and 1869 presented the notion that prostitutes, not their customers, were spreading contagious diseases. These acts gave judicial and police agents the power to arrest and detain any women suspected of having a venereal disease. The rationale of these laws, holding the prostitute, not the customer, liable for spreading diseases, was pervasive in English legislation until 1985 (Hatty 1992). This was also the case in the United States. For example, as late as 1995 a woman arrested for prostitution in the Commonwealth of Pennsylvania was charged with a misdemeanor while a "john" (customer) was charged with a summary offense.

Throughout history prostitution has primarily been a profession where females provide a service for male clients. Within our society today there continues to be a power differential between women and men that perpetuates female prostitution. This will be discussed further in the program development section of this chapter.

PROSTITUTION TODAY

Same Old Song and Dance

An old saying can be used to describe the difference between prostitution today and the ancient forms of the profession: *the more things change, the more they stay the same*. Not much has changed concerning the dynamics of prostitution. Prostitutes continue to be separated into classes, often by social ranking. As ancient Greece set standards for different forms or levels of prostitution, so does contemporary society.

- Nevada has legal brothels or prostitution houses that are monitored by local officials. Licensure of the brothels "ensures" safety because the women are tested for diseases. Ensuring safety is beneficial, however, legalizing prostitution merely perpetuates the repression of women.
- There are still street prostitutes who are seen as unworthy of concern. Most females involved in this form of prostitution are drawn from economically marginalized segments of society and therefore have relatively little power. Many street prostitutes rely on prostitution as their primary source of income. Typically, they left their families during adolescence and as a result, have limited skills (see Chapter Two). Therefore it is common for runaway adolescents to resort to street prostitution as their only means of survival. Being the most visible form of illegal prostitution, these street prostitutes are often arrested and treated as public nuisances. This is not unlike the experiences of the uncovered, exposed prostitutes of ancient Greece.

- The auletrides are comparable to the pornography workers, massage parlor workers, and nude dancers of today. These women are to provide entertainment but often cross the legal line by providing sexual gratification to customers. In these professions, women are presented as continually available to provide sexual services to men. The women involved are dehumanized, not regarded as persons with feelings or opinions. Women are seen as commodities, something to buy, existing only to please the consumer. This belief is detrimental to women in society because it allows women to be viewed as objects.

- The hetaerae are equal to the escort services of today where wealthy clients pay for attractive, cultured companions. These women provide leisure and entertainment services. They are not often stigmatized like the other levels of prostitution because of their social status. Although true, their profession continues to perpetuate the subordinated status of women in our society. It is evident that some of these services are illegal while others are legal. As stated previously, in the United States, prostitution is illegal in 49 states. Nevada provides the exception to the prostitution rule, and there is no rational explanation as to why this discrepancy exists.

When looking at prostitution, we need to ask not, "Why do women do it?" but, "Why do men buy the services?" Why have men throughout history felt it necessary to have unlimited access to women's bodies for their sexual pleasure? The way males are socialized contributes to this problem. Within our society, males are led to believe that sexual behavior confirms manhood. "Men are supposed to be ever ready for sex, constantly seeking sex, and constantly seeking to escalate every encounter so that intercourse will result" (Kimmel 1993). Risk taking is synonymous with male sexuality. Sex is about excitement, risk, danger. Therefore, it is not shocking that some men solicit prostitutes.

Most antiprostitution proponents today continue to focus on religious teachings and moral "shoulds" for why prostitution needs to be eradicated. In addition, there are concerns about prostitutes spreading infectious diseases. These concerns have been compounded by HIV. All this being true, there is clearly a reason to work with prostitutes.

STEPS FOR PROGRAM DEVELOPMENT

The following is a description of the steps taken to develop the RESPECT Program, a psychoeducational program for female offenders, primarily prostitutes, in Northeastern Pennsylvania.

Step One

Because there were no treatment programs exclusive to prostitutes or those at-risk for involvement in prostitution in Northeastern Pennsylvania, the staff at THE PROGRAM for Women and Families, Allentown, Pennsylvania, thought there was a need for a program.

Research was needed prior to taking on the task. A clear understanding of the common risk factors or root causes of prostitution needed to be obtained. This was essential so that a program could be developed that would adequately address the specific needs of the population. In addition to a review of relevant research, the experience of staff members who worked with female offenders and sexual abuse victims was helpful in determining these risk factors. It should be noted the primary risk factor evident in the backgrounds of many women involved with prostitution is sexual abuse. Research on the backgrounds of female offenders indicates a connection between childhood victimization and criminal behavior (Chesney-Lind 1989 and Chapter Two of this book). In a study conducted by Chesney-Lind and Rodriquez (1983), virtually all of the respondents reported a history of physical and/or sexual abuse. Furthermore, more than half of the respondents reported being sexually abused and about half reported being sexually assaulted as adults. In Chapter Ten, Dougherty notes that "a history of childhood maltreatment, specifically sexual abuse, invariably has been found to be a common experience in the lives of female offenders involved in prostitution." Other risk factors presented in this population are similar to those evident for other female offenders.

Step Two

Based on the primary risk factors for prostitution identified, the next step was to schedule meetings with women involved in prostitution to obtain perceptions of their reality. This was imperative because the target population should always be involved in the program development phase. This enabled THE PROGRAM staff to ascertain what the women thought were the most significant areas to be addressed. A small sample of approximately ten were selected to participate in in-depth, nonstructured interviews (THE PROGRAM for Women and Families runs programs for female offenders). Because the women were already working with the staff they were extremely verbal regarding what they thought should be included in the program. Although these interviews were nonstructured it is advisable to use an interview guide whenever possible to ensure the collection of consistent data. The women interviewed, like staff, expressed the need for a program exclusive to prostitution because there were no programs that dealt with this issue. When questioned about the information they thought would be helpful, their primary requests were for information about AIDS and other STIs, basic information about sexuality and normal sexual behavior, and discussion about interpersonal relationships. The positive and encouraging responses received from the women interviewed confirmed for staff the need for a program targeting prostitutes.

Step Three

A list of possible program topics presented by the women during the interview process was developed. This list was narrowed to four areas of concentration by process of elimination, i.e., all of the women interviewed consistently reported the need for the four topic areas. These four areas provided a conceptual framework for program development. The program was named Regaining Esteem Stopping Prostitution by Education and Continued Treatment (RESPECT), because it was to be a program geared towards eradicating prostitution. It was determined RESPECT would be conducted in four modules addressing the focus topic areas identified by the women interviewed: Module 1, HIV/AIDS; Module 2, STIs/Contraception; Module 3, Gender Roles/Societal Norms; and Module 4, Sexuality/Sexual Expectations.

Step Four

Evaluation of effective programming has shown there are several elements that promote successful program outcomes. The most important is the inclusion of activities that enhance self-efficacy. Self-efficacy is defined as the confidence an individual has in specific areas. Often prostitutes have high self-efficacy in areas pertaining to their ability to provide prostitution services, however, do not have high self-efficacy in areas that can help to stop the offending behavior. For example, a woman involved in prostitution may have high self-efficacy in her ability to perform oral sex; however she may have low self-efficacy in her ability to stop using drugs. Self-efficacy in socially acceptable skills is strengthened by the infusion of personal and social skill development within the curriculum. Important skills to be addressed with participants are communication, decision making, assertiveness, risk reduction, and goal setting.

1. Communication skills enable women to openly express feelings, actively listen, and give clear messages regarding their needs.
2. Decision-making skills enhance the ability to solve problems, analyze, and review their options.
3. Assertiveness skills enable the female to resist negative influences.
4. Risk-reduction skills are essential to positive coping with life circumstances.
5. Goal setting skills provide the female the ability to clarify realistic goals based on her needs and interests.

These concepts were incorporated into the RESPECT curriculum.

Step Five

Because the subject matter presented in the curriculum could be considered sensitive in nature, it is imperative to create an environment in which the female offender feels safe. A safe atmosphere is essential for the female to openly express opinions and feelings. Therefore, consideration needed to be given to the format that the concepts would be presented. The format selected included brainstorming, class discussion, group activities, self-assessment, surveys, and inventories.

Step Six

After six months of program development, the program was piloted to the female day reporting program participants at THE PROGRAM in August of 1994. This population was used as a test population, and it should be noted that not all of these women were found guilty of prostitution, however, all had risk factors for involvement. The female day reporting program is a daily intermediate punishment program—an alternative to incarceration—for women in Lehigh County, Pennsylvania. The response to the curriculum was overwhelmingly positive. What follows are descriptions of the modules and the reasons for their inclusion in the curriculum.

RESPECT

An outline of the RESPECT Curriculum can be found in Exhibit 16–1.

Module 1: HIV/AIDS

The need for a discussion about HIV/AIDS when working with women involved in the sex industry cannot be overstated. By nature of their activities, these women are at-risk for HIV infection. In a study of 1,963 female prostitutes in New York City, 653 were found to be HIV positive (Weiner 1996). That equates to approximately one-third of the individuals studied.

Many of the women attending the RESPECT Program have not been educated about HIV transmission. They are often misinformed about the likelihood of contracting the virus from interpersonal relationships. Some women report safe sex practices with clients but do not practice safe sex with intravenous (IV) drug using partners. Given education about the potential of contracting HIV through unprotected sex with clients, many prostitutes changed their risk behaviors. In a 1990–91 study, after receiving HIV education, 95 percent of the 280 prostitutes sampled reported using condoms with every client. Conversely, in a 1985–86 study of 436 prostitutes who had not received education, 70 percent reported consistent use (Perkins 1992). Therefore, basic education about HIV and other STIs, further discussed below, as it relates to their interpersonal relationships is essential and is the basis for continued prevention.

During this module the participants complete pretests to determine their knowledge base prior to attending the program. Goals and objectives of the program and class rules are discussed. The activities in this section provide information about HIV transmission. The myths and facts about the virus are explored. One activity that has a strong impact on the participants requires them to respond yes, no, or unsure to questions such as, "Have you ever had unprotected sex?", "Have you had more than one sexual partner?", and "Have you ever had unprotected sex with a man who has had sex with another man?" Participants are taught that if there are yes or unsure answers to any of the 15 questions, they are at-risk for

Exhibit 16–1 RESPECT Curriculum Outline

RESPECT OUTLINE

Module #1—HIV/AIDS

1. Introduction
2. Outline
3. Class Rules
4. Pretest
5. Warm-Up
6. Video
7. History of HIV Lecture
8. HIV Risk Activity
9. HIV Risk Ranking
10. Value Statements
11. Personal Risk Assessment
12. Safe Sex Activity

Module #2—Sexually Transmitted Infections/Contraception

1. Sexually Transmitted Infections/Contraception Quiz
2. Female and Male Anatomy
3. Reproduction
4. Contraception Lecture
5. Sexually Transmitted Infection Activity
6. Sexually Transmitted Infection Lecture
7. History of Contraception
8. Condom Exercise

Module #3—Gender Roles/Societal Norms

1. The Rape of Mr. Smith
2. Societal Expectations of Men and Women
3. 1950s Expectations of Women
4. Gender Role Lecture
5. Video
6. Objectification in the Media Discussion
7. Magazine Exercise
8. Codependency Activity

Module #4—Sexuality/Sexual Expectations

1. Sex Versus Sexuality
2. Sexuality Lecture
3. Sexuality Activity
4. Physical/Sexual Boundaries
5. Perceptions of Female Sexual Responsibilities
6. Posttest
7. Instructor Evaluation
8. Closure

Courtesy of RESPECT, an AIDSNET-funded program facilitated by THE PROGRAM for Women and Families, Inc., Allentown, Pennsylvania.

HIV infection. The activities in this module are designed to educate the women and raise their consciousness level about their participation in high-risk behaviors.

Module 2: STIs/Contraception

In the New York City study cited earlier, of the 1,963 women studied, 60 percent of the women reported a history of STIs. In addition, more than two-thirds of these women had at least one child (Weiner 1996). Thus, there is a need to not only educate these women about

HIV/AIDS, there is also a need to discuss STIs and contraception. Many of the women in the RESPECT Program reported they were not aware they had a STI until they were examined while incarcerated. The need for basic education about STIs warranted by the women's high-risk behavior cannot be overstated.

A portion of this module is devoted to a basic discussion of the female and male anatomy. This is because many women involved in prostitution are misinformed about their bodies. Most of the women report no one ever educated them about reproduction. In fact, most learned incorrect information from their life on the streets. For example, one woman stated a way to prevent pregnancy is to stand up after having sex. She reported her boyfriend told her semen could not travel upwards when a women is standing. This woman was given factual information about reproduction and now can make informed decisions about her sexual behaviors. A discussion of the history of contraception and a lecture demonstrating how to use contraceptives is also presented in this module.

Module 3: Gender Roles/Societal Norms

This module can be described as an overview of society's sexuality. The repression and objectification of women within society is presented. The goal of this module is to help participants develop insight and awareness into how different systems—individual, peer, family, community—have shaped how they feel about being female. In addition, the concepts of codependency and victimization are explored. These issues are important to discuss because many of these women continue to become involved in unhealthy interpersonal relationships. Finkelhor and Bowne (1985) report that women who are abused as children consistently experience revictimization as adults. This cycle of repeat victimization is especially evident in the women's choice of abusive partners. During this module the facilitators describe the cycle of victimization and encourage the women to discuss the reasons for this phenomenon.

Module 4: Sexuality/Sexual Expectations

The final module includes a discussion of sex, sexuality, and sexual responsibilities. These issues are especially important to explore because many prostitutes possess a distorted perception of sexuality due to sexual abuse histories. A study of 200 juvenile and adult female prostitutes found 60 percent were sexually abused by an average of two people and two-thirds were sexually abused by father figures. Moreover, 70 percent of these women reported "that the sexual exploitation definitely affected their decision to become a prostitute" (Silbert and Pines 1981). Finkelhor and Bowne (1985) present a model that postulates that "the experience of sexual abuse can be analyzed in terms of four trauma-causing factors," what they call "traumagenic dynamics" —traumatic sexualization, betrayal, powerlessness and stigmatization. The traumatic sexualization dynamic can be used to describe the female prostitute's tendency to have distorted perceptions of sexuality. This dynamic occurs when a child's sexuality is "shaped in a developmentally inappropriate and interpersonally dysfunctional fashion as a result of sexual abuse." The female learns to use sexual behavior to obtain affection, attention, money, and gifts (Finkelhor and Bowne 1985). Most of the women attending the RESPECT Program have not thought of the connection between abuse issues and their involvement with prostitution. The presentation of this connection often promotes catharsis and positively affects behavioral and attitudinal changes.

At the end of the program the women complete a posttest. The posttest score is compared to the pretest score to determine the amount of knowledge the women gained from participating in the RESPECT Program. Since the inception of this program the average knowledge gained has been 30 percent. Referrals for further treatment are provided at the class closure.

CONCLUSION

Why Does This Program Work?

The female offender's input into the design of the RESPECT Program is the primary reason for the success of the curriculum. Whenever possible, the planned target population should be involved in the design and implementation of a new program. Well-meaning professionals may think they know what the client needs; however, the best source of determining need is interviewing the target population. The second reason this program works is it is a program designed by women for women. Adhering to feminist theory (see Chapter Five), women require gender-specific interventions because they experience and process life differently than men. Although this is true, sadly, there are few gender-specific treatment interventions available for female offenders.

The RESPECT Program 1997

Since 1994, the RESPECT Program has grown. In 1996 the program's name was changed to Respect, deleting the acronym, because other female offenders expressed interest in attending the program. These women stated the Respect curriculum contains information that is important for all women to know, not just women involved in prostitution. A good indicator of a program's success is when a "difficult" population requests to participate in the program. The Respect Program is now being facilitated in Pennsylvania in Berks, Lehigh, and Northampton County Prisons and at other locations within these regions. The services have expanded to include ongoing support groups for women who have completed the 12-hour program and individual mental health counseling for HIV positive clients. Until women and men are treated equally within a society there will be a need for interventions like the Respect Program.

REFERENCES

Chesney-Lind, M., and Rodriguez, N. 1983. Women under lock and key. *Prison Journal* 63: 47–65.

Finkelhor, D., and Bowne, A. 1985. The traumatic impact of child sexual abuse: A conceptualization. *American Journal of Orthopsychiatry* 55: 530–541.

Hatty, S. E. 1992. The desired object: Prostitution in Canada, United States and Australia. *Sex Industry and Public Policy* 14: 71–83.

Kimmel, M. S. 1993. Clarence, William, Iron Mike, Tailhook, Senator Packwood, Spur Posse, Magic …and Us. In *Transforming a rape culture,* eds. Buchwald, E., et al., 119–138. Minneapolis: Milkweed Editions.

Miller, E. 1986. *Street woman*. Philadelphia: Temple University Press.

Perkins, R. 1991. *Working girls: Prostitutes, their life and social control.* Canberra: Australian Institute of Criminology.

Perkins, R. 1992. Sexual health and safety amongst a group of prostitutes: At work and in their private lives. *Sex Industry and Public Policy* 14: 147–154.

Silbert, M., and Pines, A. 1981. Sexual child abuse as an antecedent to prostitution. *Child Abuse and Neglect* 5, 407–411.

Weiner, A. 1996. Understanding the social needs of streetwalking prostitutes. *Social Work* 41: 97–102.

CHAPTER 17

Evaluation of Programs for Female Offenders

Kathleen Kendall

Editor's Notes

While there is no "holy grail" in terms of program evaluation methods, the importance of systematically evaluating the outcome measures of programs for female offenders cannot be overemphasized if there is to be any impact on the escalating rates of female crime. The intentions of an organization to reduce female offending, no matter how lofty an endeavor, are simply not good enough. Nor is it good enough for organizations to assume that they are achieving the results they desire, and based on this belief, determine that it is not important to formulate outcome measures and evaluate the results of services provided. Simply put, entities dealing with female offenders, regardless of whether they are penal institutions or private organizations, should be able to demonstrate the impact of services provided through systematic program evaluation of key performance areas and goals. The evaluation methods should capture both agency and structure as described in Chapter Seventeen. Unfortunately, the evaluations that do exist on programs for female offend-

ers are, according to Kendall, the author of Chapter Seventeen, often poorly designed, nonempirical, and selectively ignore the diversity among female offenders.

Kendall critically examines program evaluation issues with respect to women and girl offenders. The author identifies elements of successful programs for them including staff characteristics such as a caring attitude and personal experience with criminal activity, and specific skills training relevant to women's family responsibilities and/or work among others. The emphasis on recidivism and actuarial methods as measures of program success is questioned within the context of a broader debate about program effectiveness. Specifically, Kendall discusses the problems in utilizing recidivism as an indicator of program success because of the complexities that encompass criminal statistics. For example, is recidivism determined by actual offenses, arrests, or convictions? According to Kendall, "It is likely the case that people re-offend but do not get caught. They would be included in official measures of recidivism and despite their criminal involvements would be counted as instances of program success. Additionally, someone may offend less often or less seriously than they did previously. Would this count as success? (p. 20)" Issues related to recidivism, considered failure, were raised in Chapter Four by Hawkinshire. They are discussed here in the context of evaluation of programs for female offenders. After the discussion of recidivism as an indicator of program success, examples of both quantitative and qualitative evaluations and research are reviewed in order to identify the strengths and limitations of each. Kendall argues that quantitative and qualitative approaches should both be used in evaluation research as they each measure different aspects of programs and tell us different things about them. The chapter concludes with a brief exploration of some possible unintended consequences of correctional evaluation research.

The qualitative studies reviewed suggest that it is crucial to consider the context within which programs operate and social interaction. According to Kendall, the contradictions inherent in corrections, particularly prisons, compromise program effectiveness. For example, short-term benefits of programs for female inmates may include: a sense of autonomy, control over one's life, positive connections with other people, and practical assistance. Thus, programs offering these components appear to be of value to women while imprisoned. However, these benefits are continually compromised by the broader prison context, which generally removes autonomy and control, disrupts relationships, and hinders practical assistance. It is this paradox, central to the female institutionalization experience, which programmers and evaluators must consider. Only then can the effectiveness of programs in both the short- and long-term be realistically evaluated.

INTRODUCTION

This chapter critically examines program evaluation with women and girl offenders. It begins by recognizing that while there is a paucity of evaluations developed specifically for females, there have been attempts to identify elements of successful programs for them. These elements are then considered. Next, the emphasis on recidivism and actuarial methods as measures of program success is questioned within the context of a broader debate over program effectiveness. Examples are then provided of both quantitative and qualitative evaluations and research in order to identify the strengths and limitations of each. Studies of girls' and women's lawbreaking are then examined. Research here emphasizes the importance of contextualizing offending within structures of oppression. It is argued that program providers and evaluators must recognize the ways in which structural oppression limits the power of offenders to act and to change their circumstances. Without acknowledging this, we may overestimate the power of programs to rehabilitate and further perpetuate inequalities. The chapter concludes with a brief exploration of some possible unintended harmful consequences of correctional evaluation research. The main argument throughout is that qualitative and quantitative methods should both be used in program evaluation, as they each capture different aspects of the program. In recognizing the complexities and contradictions in women's programming and offending, this chapter emphasizes that evaluators must consider both female offender's agency and the structures that impose on them.

ELEMENTS OF EFFECTIVE PROGRAMMING FOR FEMALE OFFENDERS

As previous chapters have indicated, there are very few programs designed specifically for female offenders. It is therefore unsurprising that evaluations of programs for these groups are similarly scarce. While most correctional programs are neither evaluated nor informed by evaluations (Coulson and Nubrown 1992), this neglect is most evident for female offenders. For example, in their 1986 review of North American programs for female offenders, Ross and Fabiano conclude that researchers largely ignore evaluations of female offender programs. They add that the existing evaluations are typically poorly designed, nonempirical, and selectively ignore the diversity amongst offenders. More than a decade later, the situation appears to remain unchanged. In their recent study of promising correctional programs, Koons et al. (1997) found that of the 67 programs identified as effective for women offenders, only 12 incorporated specific outcome measures. Only six of these programs included measures of drug use and/or recidivism, and of these six programs, none considered which particular components were correlated with success. They recommend that future evaluations be designed to ascertain which specific program elements are associated with positive outcomes. Koons et al. note that service delivery, including such aspects as program staff and the physical environment, should also be considered. Austin et al. (1992) found that none of the community programs for female offenders they studied had undergone rigorous evaluation. They suggest that it is crucial to compare gender-specific and co-ed programs for effectiveness. Perhaps the most neglected offender population is girls and young women. Here, Lyon (1996) and Schwartz and Orlando (1991) write that long-term follow-up studies are especially needed to determine what works. Lyon adds that culture and "race" must be considered in assessing the appropriateness of programs.

Despite the dearth of program evaluations, a number of writers have identified what appear to be elements of effective programming for female offenders. For example, based on the impressions and experiences of program administrators, correctional administrators, and program participants, Koons et al.(1997) found a general convergence of opinion regarding attributes of effective programs for incarcerated women. These include: staff characteristics such as a caring attitude and personal experience with criminal activity; female staff; specific skills training relevant to women's family responsibilities and/or work; nontraditional job skills training; treatment to overcome codependent relationships; a safe and comfortable environment; and peer interactions. Feedback also suggested that successful programs appear to employ a comprehensive and holistic strategy aimed at addressing women's multiple needs in a continuum of care.

After their analysis of innovative strategies and programs for female offenders in the community, Austin et al. (1992, p. 22) conclude that the best programs "combined supervision and services to address the specialized needs of female offenders in highly structured, safe environments where accountability is stressed." They add that the most promising programs appear to be multidimensional, deal specifically with women's issues and provide skills that will help women achieve emotional and economic independence. Other important aspects included a continuum of care design; clearly stated program expectations, rules and possible sanctions; consistent supervision; ethnically diverse staff including ex-offenders; coordination of community resources; and aftercare.

The Correctional Service of Canada is in the process of implementing a program strategy for federally sentenced women (women serving sentences of two years or more). The strategy was initially informed by a Task Force report that identified five basic principles for effective programming: empowerment, meaningful and responsible choices, respect and dignity, supportive environment, and shared responsibility (Task Force on Federally Sentenced Women 1990). The Task Force report further recommended that for increased effectiveness, programs should be holistic and women-centered, in order to "reflect the social realities of women and respond to the individual needs of each woman" (Federally Sentenced Women Program 1995, p. 1).

Six additional components have since been recognized as essential to all programs: (1) women-centered principles, (2) principles of women's education, (3) diversity, (4) analytical approach, (5) program structure, and (6) program process. Each of these components is comprised of subcomponents. Women-centered principles consist of the following: contextual analysis, cooperative, challenging, connection, and agency. Principles of women's education include, recognize, and value the unique learning styles of participants, diversity in pedagogical tools, experiential, modeling, and humor and social interaction. The subcomponents of diversity are: reflecting diversity, appropriate to participant diversity, diversity is recognized and valued and sensitive to individuals. The analytical approach, which should be woven throughout all programs, consists of problem solving, values, creative thinking, critical thinking, and social skills. Program structure incorporates a supportive environment, programs that fit participant's needs, program integrity, accessibility, and intensity and duration. The program process is comprised of a screening process, group rules, monitoring, reporting, and evaluating. For a more detailed description, readers are directed to the *Correctional Program Strategy for Federally Sentenced Women* (Federally Sentenced Women Program 1994).

Qualities of an effective program provider are also outlined and include knowledge of and commitment to the aforementioned principles, training and experience in facilitation or counseling techniques, exceptional interpersonal skills and empathy (Federally Sentenced Women Program 1995). Finally, the strategy supports the implementation of four core programs geared toward the following:

1. Living skills (e.g., cognitive skills, anger management, and parenting)
2. Survivors of abuse/trauma
3. Literacy and continuous learning
4. Substance abuse

The Correctional Service of Canada has also constructed a Healing Lodge. This is a separate facility for Aboriginal women, where programs and services are designed to meet their specific needs. Program emphasis is placed upon healing from trauma and substance abuse through reconnection with Aboriginal culture(s) (Federally Sentenced Women Program 1995).

These core programs are recognized as fundamental to meeting women offender's criminogenic needs. Needs are defined as "criminogenic" because they are characteristics that are linked with offending. Therefore, it is assumed that when these needs are addressed, recidivism will decline. This is known as the "needs principle." The criminogenic needs of female offenders include the following (Hannah-Moffat 1997, p. 226):

- Low self-esteem
- Dependency
- Suicide attempts
- Self-injury
- Substance abuse
- Poor educational and vocational achievement
- Parental death at an early age
- Foster care placement
- Constant changes in foster care
- Residential placement
- Living on the streets
- Prostitution and parental responsibilities

NEEDS, RISK, AND RESPONSIVITY PRINCIPLES

The notion of criminogenic need is informed by a tide of current correctional research (see for example Andrews 1996; Andrews et al. 1990; Andrews et al. 1990; Cullen and Gendreau 1989; Coulson and Nubrown 1992; Gendreau and Goggin 1996). This research further suggests that criminal activity can be predicted by identifying risk factors. High risk factors include antisocial associates, antisocial cognitions, antisocial personality complex, and a history of antisocial behavior. Minor risk factors include lower-class origins, personal distress, and biological and neurological factors (Andrews 1996). This distinction is important because it is argued that treatment works best with higher-risk offenders. It is therefore advocated that more intensive programming be targeted to higher-risk subjects. This is known as the "risk principle." Finally, the "responsivity principle" maintains that offenders reap the greatest benefits from the most appropriate type of service. In this regard, services that are deemed most suitable or effective for offenders are based on behavioral strategies (such as social learning, skill building, or cognitive behavioral), are highly structured, located in the offender's natural environment, multimodal, individualized, and provide continued assistance and aftercare. Appropriate program implementation factors include a program director with professional credibility, a strong curriculum, staff training, and program evaluation. These principles have been largely informed by meta-analyses, although narrative reviews, experimental studies, and clinical knowledge have been drawn on as well (Gendreau and Goggin 1996).

Meta-analysis is simply a study of other studies. It assesses the effectiveness of different correctional programs by coding each study on different variables such as the type of treatment and subject characteristics. By combining and reanalyzing existing studies, this method attempts to control for various factors such as subject characteristics and poor research design (Logan and Gaes 1993). Thus it is claimed that meta-analysis can determine the most effective treatment programs. Meta-analysis is also used to determine the risk factors associated with offending. Here, studies of risk factors are combined, and an average result is then computed for each risk factor. This provides the degree of association between offending and a particular risk factor (Simourd and Andrews 1994).

It is argued that overall, programs for offenders reduce recidivism by approximately 10 percent. Nonetheless, it is believed that programs adhering to the needs, risk, and responsivity principles have potential for much greater impact. Unfortunately, the studies on which these principles have been based have predominantly relied on male subjects; therefore, their applicability to female offenders is unknown. Still, some researchers suggest that they can be generalized to females (see for example; Blanchette 1997; Losel 1996) and many of the components identified as effective coincide with those described above as effective for programming with female offenders. However, as Blanchette (1997) concludes, there is little or no evidence that institutional programming contributes to a reduction in recidivism with female offenders. To remedy the situation, she recommends the more intensive use of actuarial measures to determine program effectiveness, specifically for female offenders. These measures are quantitatively based, typically employ an experimental design, and enhance the determination of statistical association, such as meta-analysis. There appears to be a growing trend toward the use of actuarial methods in correctional research and programming, including program evaluation. For example, it would appear that currently the most credible measure of program effectiveness is a reduction in recidivism. Yet, sole reliance on such methods is misguided. Before addressing the limitations of actuarial methods, it is important to address the historical context in which their use arose.

NOTHING WORKS?

In the 1970s there was a wave of evaluation studies claiming that no one type of correctional programming appeared to be more effective than any other type. Thus, community corrections was claimed to be no more or less successful than incarceration; incarceration no more or less effective than alternatives such as fines; and the specific type of program (e.g., educational, vocational, therapeutic) did not seem to matter (Greenberg 1975; Logan 1972; Robison and Smith 1971). Martinson (1974) is the most widely cited of these evaluation studies. His analysis of the impact of different correctional treatment on recidivism indicated that nothing worked. Others countered these claims by criticizing Martinson's methodology and developing their own more sophisticated quantitative measures (Gendreau 1981; Clarke and Sinclair 1974). The quest for a more rigorous evaluation tool has led to the current usage of meta-analysis. As discussed above, a number of researchers using this technique profess to have discovered the most effective methods of correctional treatment. However, still others using meta-analysis refute these assertions with their own, echoing Martinson's claims that nothing appears to work (Lab and Whitehead 1990). These two camps are likely to continue battle *ad infinitum*. However, it is important to consider the central assumption that underlies the debate. Current correctional evaluation appears to be driven by a belief that program effectiveness can ultimately be determined through greater scientific precision. This has translated into an emphasis on actuarial measures. More specifically, these measures are used to assess the influence of programs on recidivism. As discussed by Hawkinshire in Chapter Four of this book, the use of recidivism as a measure of program effectiveness is inadequate and misguided. Hudson (1987) argues there are problems in using recidivism as an indicator of program success because of the complexities that encompass criminal statistics. For example, is recidivism determined by actual offenses, arrests, or convictions? It is likely the case that people re-offend but do not get caught. They would not be included in official measures of recidivism and despite their criminal involvement would be counted as instances of program success. Additionally, someone may offend less often or less seriously than she did previously. Would this count as success? Furthermore, failure to reduce recidivism does not mean that they have no value, only that whatever value they may have has not been considered in the calculations. Finally, the fact that someone has not recidivated tells us very little about his or her circumstances. As Ross and Fabiano (1986) indicate, despite no further arrests or convictions, many ex-offenders continue to live marginally, in conditions of poverty and violence. Thus, recidivism can tell us nothing about the quality of life.

Similar kinds of methodological and theoretical considerations haunt all evaluation research and to date, there is no agreement on the best measure or set of measures to determine program effectiveness. However, there is reason to be concerned about the current emphasis being placed on actuarial methods. While they are useful in recognizing general patterns, they are in themselves insufficient. This is because they measure what appears to work for offenders as a whole, rather than determine what works best for specific offenders in particular circumstances and why. That is, they generally strip away the context within which programs and offending occur and do not typically offer an explanation for either program success or failure (Pawson and Tilley 1997). Additionally, actuarial methods tend to pathologize and individualize women's law breaking rather than contextualize it.

QUANTITATIVE EVALUATIONS OF FEMALE OFFENDER PROGRAMS

An evaluation of THE PROGRAM for Female Offenders will be considered in order to illustrate the problems that arise through decontextualization (Russell 1995). The PROGRAM, located in Pittsburgh, Pennsylvania, is a community-based provider of residential services for women and children. It emphasizes independence through employment and family stability. Training and employment opportunities are provided for participants through its telemarketing business. The program includes a variety of other services such as life-skills training, substance abuse treatment, parenting education , general equivalency diploma (GED) preparation, and aftercare (Austin et al. 1992). A dataset was constructed from client records in order to examine recidivism rates statistically as well as specific variables associated with recidivism such as age, marital status, and income. A control group comprising a random sample of female offenders from the County Court Common Pleas records was also employed. While it was found that the recidivism rate of PROGRAM participants compared favorably (15 percent) to the control group (26%), some of the control group members (25 percent) had some form of contact with the PROGRAM. This throws some doubt on the validity of comparing these two groups.

However, analysis of the relationship between various PROGRAM participant variables and recidivism yielded some interesting findings. The recidivists tended to be single and younger, and have informal custody arrangements with their children, they often had four or more children and a monthly income of less than $210. The single greatest indicator of recidivism was involvement in retail crime. The author of the evaluation report recommends that program staff consider explanations for these differences. While the study highlights some relationships between offender characteristics and recidivism, it cannot provide us with details sufficient enough to consider the mechanisms through which these variables may operate.

The Stay'n Out program is another example. This therapeutic community drug-treatment program is often recognized as a success because it has been shown to decrease recidivism. In their evaluation of Stay'n Out, Wexler et al. (1992) employed a large-scale, long-term quasiexperimental design using two types of comparison groups: inmates who volunteered for the program but did not actually participate and inmates who participated in other types of prison-based drug abuse treatment programs elsewhere. By including the subjects who volunteered but did not participate (they were on waiting lists) the evaluators assumed that the design controlled for self-selection bias. The study included both male and female prisoners and as outcome variables considered arrest, time until arrest, and parole/revocation. Data was procured from Division of Parole computer statistics. It found overall differences between the three groups for the males but none for the females. For example, the male results showed that when compared to the controls, the Stay'n Out program was substantially more effective in reducing the percent arrested. However, while the female Stay'n Out program was found to be significantly more effective in reducing the percent arrested than the other substance abuse groups, there was no statistical difference when compared to the no-treatment group. Likewise, while it was found that the females in the Stay'n Out program had a significantly higher percent who were positively discharged from parole than the no-treatment group, there was no significant difference between the Stay'n Out and the other treatment group. Unfortunately, the study provided no explanation for the gender differences or for the variation among the female groups, except for noting that the small sample size of the no treatment group may have influenced the statistics. An examination of the differences would provide a deeper understanding of the program effects and its appropriateness for females. Because the study relies on official statistics, it does not allow for this kind of nuance.

The study did, however, find that for males the amount of time in prison was correlated with recidivism rates. For example, the success of the Stay'n Out program increased as the time in prison increased, but after 12 months the effect diminished. While there was a similar pattern for females, it was not as vivid. Additionally, the multivariate analysis used in associating time in prison to other factors could not be carried out with the female population because of the small number. Nonetheless, the authors found the effects of time in prison on recidivism to be of considerable interest and therefore spoke to program staff about it. Staff suggested that the finding might be explained by the nature of the program, which emphasizes promotion in a hierarchy through achievement. The 12-month slump may occur because after this period of time there are no further status levels to which one can aspire. Prisoners thus denied parole after 12 months may become disillusioned and withdraw from the program. This suggestion highlights the fact that programs do not occur in a vacuum but within a particular context. As Palmer (1995) suggests, nonprogrammatic aspects need to be taken into account. Evaluations must consider these if they are to reach a better understanding of program effectiveness. While quantitative methods indicate general patterns, qualitative methods can consider these more closely.

A study of a women's boot camp by Camp and Sandhu (1995) further stresses the importance of context. Similar to the evaluations cited above, the authors compared recidivism among participants of the Female Offender Regimented Treatment Program (FORT) at the Dr. Eddie Warrior Correctional Center, Taft, Oklahoma, to a control group using a computerized data set. Statistical analysis of the data found that there was no statistically significant difference in recidivism among the two groups; 35 percent of the FORT participants recidivated while 37 percent of the control group did. However, surveys were conducted with FORT graduates who had been released into the community, and interviews were held with FORT recidivists as well as with probation and parole officers. This part of the evaluation suggested that post-release difficulties constrained long-term program success. The program graduates maintained that while they appreciated the program, they found it very difficult to integrate back into the community, due to such factors as peer pressure, job discrimination, and the availability of drugs and alcohol. Another important factor was aftercare—the more involved a woman was with aftercare, the more likely she was to remain free from arrest. The probation and parole officers interviewed reached similar conclusions. This study illustrates the way in which program effectiveness can be subverted by new contexts and stresses the necessity of looking beyond individual characteristics and program elements to include the larger social environment. Other research demonstrates that women encounter a myriad of difficulties on prison release (Shaw et al. 1991; Kendall 1993a; Sobel 1982). It would be naïve to believe that any program or programs could entirely overcome these problems.

One might expect that women who are HIV positive and women with AIDS would encounter the greatest barriers post-release. In recognition of this, Rhode Island Correctional Facility established an AIDS Education and Management Program. This program includes education, counseling, and health care management both in the prison and the community. The Prison Release Program aims to link HIV positive prisoners to primary medical care, substance abuse treatment, and psychosocial support on release. When requested, the program also attempts to provide women with housing and financial assistance. Comparison with two control groups (HIV positive women who did not participate in the program and HIV negative women not enrolled in the program) showed that the recidivism rate was significantly decreased by 50 percent. However, it is not known which elements of the program are most responsible for the decrease. The authors indicate that future research plans include an exploration of this question. This evaluation illustrates the value of quantitative measures of recidivism, as it demonstrates the program's impact on recidivism. Clearly, something is working. However, it also points to the limitations of this type of method, as it cannot determine which elements within the program are having an effect or why. Thus, evaluations are best achieved when quantitative and qualitative measures are used together. Furthermore, they must consider the specific context not only in which programs operate, but also in which offenders and ex-offenders live.

QUALITATIVE EVALUATIONS OF FEMALE OFFENDER PROGRAMS

Examinations of the broader environment within which programs operate suggest the importance of their consideration in any evaluation. For example, Juda (1984) reports that a group he facilitated with co-ed inmates collapsed due to intrusions by prison staff and administration. He concludes staff and institutional support is vital for program success. This is especially true for peer support programs (Pollack 1993; Clark and Boudin 1990). Kendall (1993b) notes that a range of factors can impact on institutional programs, such as personal hostilities between inmates and/or inmates and staff, family visiting days, "lock ups" or "lock downs," and communication breakdowns. Program evaluators must be aware of the prison culture as well as facility rules, schedules, and procedures in order to establish how these may influence the program.

For example, in their evaluation of an intensive short-term psychodidactic support program for sexually and/or physically abused female inmates, Sultan and Long (1988) found that prison procedures reversed the progress on two measures of program effectiveness. The program was designed to increase self-esteem, perceived personal control, and trust-in-others, and reduce alienation. Improvements in these were assessed through scales specifically designed for their measure. The scales were applied before the first meeting and every four weeks afterward for a total of five administrations. It was found that three out of four measures reached statistical significance and the fourth measure approached significance (personal control). However, there was a reversal of progress in alienation and control in week 12 of the program. The evaluators concluded that this was precipitated by a lengthy search of prisoners' belongings and living quarters the evening before administration of the measures. Thus, the women's growing independence and confidence was undermined by this procedure.

A program evaluation of therapeutic services conducted by this author at a federal Canadian women's prison demonstrated that the prison environment can create even greater impediments to program effectiveness (Kendall 1993a). The evaluation was qualitative in design and included observations, interviews, and document analysis. Preliminary interviews were conducted with seventy-two inmates, prison staff and program providers in order to determine key questions and concerns. Issues identified in the first phase of the evaluation were then explored in subsequent interviews with 20 staff and 40 prisoners. The evaluation showed that there were conflicting views about therapeutic services among prisoners, staff, and program providers. Staff acknowledged that these programs contributed positively to the prison environment through crisis prevention and management, by calming prisoners and helping them to adjust. However, many were also concerned that the programs, particularly individual counseling, were causing prisoners to self-injure, attempt suicide, and become volatile. Indeed, some speculated that recent suicides were a consequence of an increase in the number and availability of therapeutic programs in the prison. Staff felt that the therapies were pushing prisoners into confronting issues before they were ready to deal with them. In effect, a "Pandora's Box" of painful memories was being opened. It was felt that given the already volatile environment, the box was better left closed.

When confronted with this theory of "Pandora's Box," inmates denied it, declaring instead that they only worked on issues with which they felt comfortable. Rather, they reported that their negative feelings and expressions were overwhelmingly associated with the rigid control imposed over them. They described the prison experience as being stripped of their own identities. Extreme control, combined with an arbitrary enforcement and application of rules, left the women feeling that their lives were unpredictable and that they were powerless. As numerous writers have identified, prisons generally eliminate whatever autonomy women have left by governing almost every aspect of their lives: movement, space, schedule, activities, and communication (Eaton 1993; Faith 1993; Wilfley et al., 1986). Studies have linked this profound power over prisoners with self-injury, suicide, and prison violence (Heney 1990; Liebling 1992, 1994; Mandaraka-Sheppard 1986). Additionally, more harm than good may occur if women gain a sense of autonomy and control in programs but are unable to act on them or are punished for their expression (Griffith 1984). The dissonance created by this paradox may cause long-term damage to a prisoner's sense of control and to future learning.

When the prisoners were asked what it was about the programs that they found to be most helpful, they replied assistance in taking control over their own lives, space to just be themselves, and the opportunity to be both of value to and valued by others. Yet they recognized that these same elements were ones that prison denied by its very nature. Thus, benefits gained through programming were continually being sabotaged. The women also stressed that mutually respectful relationships among staff and prisoners underscored the value and benefit of everything else. Again, the potential for such relationships to develop was greatly inhibited because prisons are constructed on an unequal distribution of power between staff and inmates.

The prisoners emphasized that for programs to work, they had to be voluntary. Nonetheless, they claimed that program involvement could never be completely voluntary because they often felt pushed into programs by their case management workers and they perceived participation to be a requirement for a positive parole recommendation and other rewards. As Shaw (1994) notes, treatment is more effective if entered into voluntarily, yet prisons often require mandatory participation in treatment programs. She suggests that this situation has intensified in recent years with the emphasis on needs and risk. Similar concerns around staff-offender relationships and compulsory program involvement have been identified in community corrections (Kendall 1993a; Shaw et al. 1991).

An important aspect of prison culture the evaluator should be aware of is the inmate code. In his study of discipline among male and female prisoners, Lindquist (1980) identified how prisoners must negotiate incongruities in role expectations. On the one hand, prisoners gain respect among one another by doing time with dignity, by acting without deference to staff, and by never placing other prisoners in jeopardy. On the other hand, staff punish lack of deference and encourage prisoners to inform them of improprieties by other inmates. Thus, inmates must paradoxically adhere to both the formal rules enacted by staff and the code expected by fellow prisoners. Correspondingly, Lindquist found that inmates' lack of deference accounted for a large proportion of prison violations resulting in sanctions. He also noted that women were punished for more minor incidents than were men. This finding is confirmed by other researchers (Mandaraka-Sheppard 1984; Pollock-Byrne 1990).

Shaw (1995) suggests that prison violations and consequent sanctions are not simply reflections of the inmate code, but are often indicators of how prisoners perceive the legitimacy of prison. She argues that prisoners will engage in violent disruptions and other serious violations when they feel that either the prison or prison staff are acting illegitimately; that is, when they feel they are being unfairly and unjustly treated. She emphasizes that in such circumstances, the actions of prisoners should be regarded as rational responses rather than as character flaws.

Taken together, these qualitative studies suggest that it is crucial to consider social interaction and the context within which programs operate. The contradictions inherent in corrections, particularly prisons, compromise program effectiveness. As Hannah-Moffat (1997) writes, cultural sensibilities, mentalities, and material structures seriously constrain program ideals. Punishment, discipline, and security continue to underscore corrections. Pawson and Tilley (1997) argue that the social conditions in which programs operate are most often ignored in evaluation research. Likewise, the authors maintain that evaluations tend to neglect a prisoner's volition. Prisoners are not simply "acted upon" by the prison structure and others, they are active, creative, and make choices. However, their agency is enacted in conditions of constrained and limited choice. Evaluators must consider the complex relationship between structure and agency. In this regard, studies of women's and girls' lawbreaking is informative.

STUDIES OF WOMEN'S AND GIRLS' LAWBREAKING: IMPLICATIONS FOR PROGRAM EVALUATION

The relationship between structure and agency should also be considered in any research into women's and girls' lawbreaking activities. As Maher (1997) cogently argues, most accounts of women's and girls' crime either over- or under-endow women with volition. In her ethnographic study of 200 women drug users in three Brooklyn neighborhoods, Maher challenges the victim/volition dichotomy. By considering women's subjective understandings and the broader cultural and economic structures encompassing them, she demonstrates how structure and agency form a dialectical and mutually constitutive relationship. This framework informs her interpretation of women's lawbreaking as instances of resistance to structural and interpersonal oppression. That is, Maher conceives of women's criminal activities as a rational and creative means of coping with and challenging gender, race, and class inequalities. Women's actions, including their illegal activities, are thus circumscribed by the social, political, and economic context. While such activities may be ultimately self-defeating, they are logical rather than pathological.

Arnold (1990) reaches similar conclusions in her study of young African American women who end up imprisoned. She argues that female African American offending must be understood in the context of victimization by economic marginality, racism, patriarchy, family violence, and miseducation (see Chapter Fourteen). Within such a framework, their pre-criminal activities can be understood as resistances to victimization. For example, running away is a means to escape family violence, and truancy can be a way of avoiding racism within the classroom. However, these responses may lead young women to become "structurally dislocated" from two key socializing institutions: the family and education. As a result, many of these young women are also marginalized from legal occupations and so turn to crime for survival. Arnold argues that without an understanding of the context within which African American females are located, their survival strategies become criminalized.

As described in Chapter Fourteen, Richie's (1996) study of African American female prisoners who had been battered reaches similar conclusions. Through life-history interviews she constructs a "gender entrapment" model to account for women's crime. Gender entrapment refers to the way in which the women in her study were lured into crime by their racialized and gendered social positions. That is, Richie argues that the women's sense of their own agency, their marginalized positions, and their actual activities (including criminal), were constructed by race and gender oppression as well as interpersonal violence. Thus, while Richie acknowledges women's subjectivity and agency, she places them within the social environment, thus highlighting the complex dualism in which women are at once victims and survivors, engaged in and acted on.

By discerning the complexities surrounding agency and structure, or the individual and society, the dynamics of women's and girls' offending are better articulated. Messerschmidt (1997) calls such an analysis "structured action theory." He maintains that structure and action are inextricably linked together through gender, race, and class relations. Thus, crime can be understood as activity that occurs under "specific social structural constraints" (Messerschmidt 1997, p. 6). In this way, analysis moves away from a view of crime as irrational, pathological, and centered on individual personalities toward a dynamic approach that considers crime to be a product of both structure and agency. This approach challenges the liberal notion of free will that posits that criminal actions are freely chosen. Instead, it suggests that criminal actions are often responses to structural constraints such as racism, classism, and sexism. This argument further suggests that the actual power of female offenders to effect change is limited by oppressive structures. This last point is crucial for corrections programming and evaluation. To be realistic, programs and program evaluations must not underestimate the ways in which structural oppression limits the power of women and girls to change their circumstances. Programs and evaluations that focus entirely on women's and girls' personalities as the cause and cure of crime obscures the impact of structure and overestimates the potential of programs to rehabilitate and prevent crime. A structured action perspective suggests that crime prevention measures must target both the structure and individuals. It also suggests that effective programs are ones that assist women in challenging and even changing their structural location. Finally, structured action theory helps us to see the multiple and contradictory ways in which programs can be subverted or enhanced.

QUANTITATIVE AND QUALITATIVE METHODS: TWO ARE BETTER THAN ONE

While principles such as criminogenic need, risk, and responsivity may point to general patterns, they cannot comprehend the complex relationship between structure and agency nor account for the variety of influences on program effectiveness. This does not mean that quantitative measures should be dismissed, but that their limitations should be recognized. Likewise, the shortcoming of qualitative methods must be acknowledged. While there are many problems, only the key ones will be addressed here. First, because the numbers are typically small, it is difficult to make generalizations. Second, there are rarely comparison groups to act as controls. Third, qualitative methods generally do not involve long-term assessments. Fourth, they cannot capture general patterns. Fifth, it can be argued that qualitative approaches are more open to subjective interpretation and thus to bias. On this last point, however, it could be argued that *all* methods are open to interpretation and that it is impossible to be entirely value-free. Indeed, the way in which we design our program evaluations will be informed by our own theory about what counts as knowledge, or our epistemology. That is, the kinds of methods we use to evaluate programs depend on the kind of information we regard as valuable. For example, if we believe that subjective experience is important, we may conduct open-ended interviews with offenders for their own accounts of a program. If, on the other hand, we do not think that subjective experience can tell us much, we may instead evaluate the program through actuarial measures such as recidivism.

As with other disciplines, program evaluation is characterized by an epistemology rooted in positivist science. Such an approach assumes a linear view of causality, devalues subjectivity, and emphasizes universality (universal laws about social behavior and the social world). Arguably, this perspective has contributed to a misguided search for the "holy grail" of evaluation methods. It is assumed that the best technique is the most empirically sophisticated, allowing for the highest level of objectivity, prediction and control, and the greatest scope for statistical analysis. However, this amounts to naïve quantification that strips away the context. As argued earlier in this chapter, consideration of the context within which criminal actions occur and programs operate is essential. Instead of prioritizing one approach over another, quantitative and qualitative methods should both be used in evaluation research as they each measure different aspects of the programs we study and tell us different things about them. Unfortunately, qualitative methods appear to be less valued because they are regarded as unscientific. It is hoped that this chapter has illustrated their importance within correctional program evaluation.

UNINTENDED CONSEQUENCES OF CORRECTIONAL PROGRAM EVALUATION

Before concluding this chapter, it is important briefly to consider some possible unintended consequences of programming and program evaluation within correctional environments. As with any type of social research, evaluations may have unanticipated effects. Given the fact that female offenders are in correctional settings by coercion rather choice, the need to consider such effects is paramount. Numerous studies have shown that various mechanisms of social control operate to subordinate women and girls. Institutions such as the family, education, and the media work to ensure that women and girls conform to the status quo. Arguably, female offenders have fallen through this net of control and landed in another one —the criminal justice system. Correctional institutions, and prisons in particular, are the ideal type of social control. However, control is not exerted solely through physical and overt means but also through softer and covert means. For example, Foucault (1977) argues that social control now operates largely through what he calls disciplinary power. Disciplinary power is exercised by various humanities and social sciences including criminology, psychology and social work. Scientists' gather information about individuals and populations by monitoring, observing, and regulating them within institutions such as prisons, schools, hospitals, workplaces, and social service agencies. The knowledge produced from information gathering is then used to establish "norms" to which people are compelled to fit. Ultimately, disciplinary power operates through individual's own agency as she regulates herself in order to match the norm.

Treatment programs for female offenders are examples of disciplinary power. As Young (1994) argues, the goal of treatment is often to alter the behavior, even the very self of women and girls, in order to fit in with the norm. Programs frequently encourage offenders to see themselves as the entire source and cure of their problems. Such an approach contradicts the structured action theory discussed earlier that contextualizes offenders' actions within the social structure. Young acknowledges that most program providers do not consciously aspire to exert disciplinary power. However, she insists that unless program providers are conscious of the ways in which social norms are reproduced in their work and actively resist this from occurring, programs will inevitably duplicate structures of oppression. However, the good intentions of program providers are not enough. What is required, Young proposes, is to structure programs in such a way that they become empowering to program participants. Toward this end, Young recommends that programs be designed to establish greater equality between providers and participants and to connect participants with the wider community. She also suggests that some group sessions be developed on a model of "consciousness raising" where members are encouraged to locate themselves and their actions within structural relations of power and inequality. Such an approach counters individualization and depoliticization of offending. Young (1994, p. 52) further recommends that programs "include structured client participation and evaluation of the program." For example, clients would participate in making the program rules and be actively encouraged to formally evaluate the program and program providers.

Program evaluators must be aware that evaluations are means through which disciplinary power works. Thus, programs may serve to control rather than assist women prisoners. Given the historical abuses of women and girl offenders under the mantle of rehabilitation, and particularly with ethnic and "racial" minorities, such a possibility must be seriously considered (see for example, Dobash et al. 1986; Sim 1990; Howe 1994). Yet, if we reject the rehabilitation model, it is likely that a punishment model will become dominant, and response to offenders will be more punitive. Hudson (1987) has shown how disillusionment with rehabilitation after the "nothing works" debate led to a shift away from rehabilitation toward more repressive penal measures. Additionally, as Young suggests, programs and evaluations can serve progressive rather than oppressive purposes. For example, Clark (1995, p. 309), herself a prisoner, has noted that many inmates claim that prison "saved them." This is mainly because prison allows time away from outside pressures and provides them with resources they would not otherwise have, including a variety of programs. Numerous prisoners take the opportunities offered in prison and other correctional facilities and make positive changes *despite* the limitations imposed on them by the prison structure.

This dilemma has divided feminist writers. On one hand, Carlen (1990) recommends that researchers use their knowledge in the development of progressive penal policy and politics. Accordingly, she proposes a "woman-wise penology," arguing that because women prisoners comprise a relatively small population, progressive penal reform can begin with them. On the other hand, Smart (1989) is skeptical that any research, especially that which is policy-driven, has the potential to challenge rather than legitimate the social order. This debate will not be resolved here. What is important, however, is to recognize that there *is* a debate and that evaluators do not operate outside of it. For better or worse, the evaluations we produce have implications. Fundamentally, we must acknowledge that whether or not we carry out evaluations, women and girls will continue to experience the pain of punishment and we must not neglect them.

CONCLUSION

This chapter argues that program evaluations must consider the complexities and contradictions surrounding lawbreaking correctional programming for women and girls. This means developing methods that capture the dialectical relationship between agency and structure. Toward this end, it is recommended that both qualitative and quantitative methods be adopted. It is also suggested that evaluators consider the potential unintended consequences of their work. Only if all of these aspects are taken into account will programs offer the potential for positive change and realistic program evaluations.

REFERENCES

Andrews, D. A. 1996. Criminal recidivism is predictable and can be influenced: An update. *Forum on Corrections Research* 8: 42-44.

Andrews, D. A., et al. 1990. Classification for effective rehabilitation: Rediscovering psychology. *Criminal Justice and Behavior* 17: 19–52.

Andrews, D. A., et al. 1990. Does correctional treatment work? A clinically relevant and informed meta-analysis. *Criminology* 28: 369–404.

Arnold, R. A. 1990. Processes of victimization and criminalization of Black women. *Social Justice* 17: 153–166.

Austin, J., et al. 1992. *Female offenders in the community: An analysis of innovative strategies and programs*. Washington, D.C.: National Institute of Corrections, National Council on Crime and Delinquency.

Blanchette, K. 1997. Classifying female offenders for correctional intervention. *Forum on Corrections Research* 9: 36–41.

Camp, D., and Sandhu, H. S. 1995. *Evaluation of female offender regimented treatment program (FORT)*. Unpublished paper.

Carlen, P. 1990. *Alternatives to women's imprisonment*. Milton Keynes, England: Open University Press.

Clark, J. 1995. The impact of the prison environment on mothers. *The Prison Journal* 75: 306–329.

Clark, J., and Boudin, K. 1990. Community of women organize themselves to cope with the AIDS crisis: A case study from Bedford Hills Correctional Facility. *Social Justice* 17: 90–109.

Clarke, R.V.G., and Sinclair, I. 1974. Towards more effective treatment evaluations. *Collected Studies in Criminological Research* 7: 55–82.

Coulson, G. E., and Nubrown, V. 1992. Properties of an ideal rehabilitative program for high-needs offenders. *International Journal of Offender Therapy and Comparative Criminology* 36: 203–208.

Cullen, F. T., and Gendreau, P. 1989. The effectiveness of correctional rehabilitation: Reconsidering the 'nothing works' debate. In *The American prison: Issues in research and policy*, eds. L. Goodstein and D. L. Mackenzie, 23–44. New York: Plenum Press.

Dobash, P.R., et al. 1986. *The imprisonment of women*. London: Blackwell Publishers.

Eaton, M. 1993. *Women after prison*. Buckingham, England: Open University Press.

Faith, K. 1993. *Unruly women: The politics of confinement and resistance*. Vancouver, B.C.: Press Gang Publishers.

Federally Sentenced Women Program 1994. *Correctional program strategy for federally sentenced women*. Ottawa, Ont.: Correctional Service of Canada.

Federally Sentenced Women Program 1995. *Overviews: Correctional Service of Canada regional facilities for Federally Sentenced Women*. Ottawa, Ont.: Correctional Service of Canada.

Foucault, M. 1977. *Discipline and punish: The birth of the prison*, trans. Sheridan, A. London: Allen Lane.

Gendreau, P. 1981. Treatment in corrections: Martinson was wrong. *Canadian Psychology* 22: 332–338.

Gendreau, P., and Andrews, D. A. 1990. Tertiary prevention: What the meta-analyses tell us about "what works." *Canadian Journal of Criminology* 32: 173–184.

Gendreau, P., and Goggin, C. 1996. Principles of effective correctional programming. *Forum on Corrections Research* 8: 38–41.

Greenberg, D. F. 1975. Problems in community corrections. *Issues in Criminology* 19: 1–34.

Griffith, J. 1984. Evidence of unidimensionality of locus of control in women prisoners: Implications for prisoner rehabilitation. *Journal of Offender Counseling, Services and Rehabilitation* 9: 57–69.

Hannah-Moffat, K. 1997. *From Christian maternalism to risk technologies: Penal powers and women's knowledges in the governance of female prisons*. PhD diss., Centre of Criminology, University of Toronto.

Heney, J. 1990. *Report of self-injurious behaviour in the Kingston Prison for Women*. Kingston, Ont.: Correctional Service of Canada.

Howe, A. 1994. *Punish and critique: Towards a feminist analysis of penality*. London: Routledge.

Hudson, B. 1987. *Justice through punishment: A critique of the "justice" model of corrections*. Houndmills, England: Macmillan Publishing.

Juda, D. 1984. On the special problems in creating group cohesion within the prison setting. *Journal of Offender Counseling, Services and Rehabilitation* 8: 47–59.

Kendall, K. 1993a. *Program evaluation of therapeutic services at The Prison for Women*. Ottawa: Correctional Service of Canada.

Kendall, K. 1993b. *Literature review of therapeutic services for women in prison. Companion volume I to program evaluation of therapeutic services at The Prison for Women*. Ottawa: Correctional Service of Canada.

Kim, J., et al. 1997. Successful community follow-up and reduced recidivism in HIV positive women prisoners. *Journal of Correctional Health Care* 4: 1–9.

Koons, B. A., et al. 1997. Expert and offender perceptions of program elements linked to successful outcomes for incarcerated women. *Crime and Delinquency* 43: 512–532.

Lab, S. P., and Whitehead, J. T. 1990. From "nothing works" to "the appropriate works": The latest stop on the search for the secular grail. *Criminology* 28: 405–417.

Liebling, A. 1992. *Suicides in prison*. London: Routledge.

Liebling, A. 1994. Suicide amongst women prisoners. *Howard Journal of Criminal Justice* 33: 1–9.

Lindquist, C. 1980. Prison discipline and the female offender. *Journal of Offender Counseling, Services and Rehabilitation* 4: 305–318.

Logan, C. H. 1972. Evaluation research in crime and delinquency: A reappraisal. *Journal of Criminal Law, Criminology and Police Science* 63: 378–387.

Logan, C. H., and Gaes, G. 1993. Meta-analysis and the rehabilitation of punishment. *Justice Quarterly* 102: 245–263.

Losel, F. 1996. Effective correctional programming: What empirical research tells us and what it doesn't. *Forum on Corrections Research* 8: 33–37.

Lyon, J. 1996. Introduction: adolescents who offend. *Journal of Adolescence* 19: 1–4.

Maher, L. 1997. *Sexed work: Gender, race and resistance in a Brooklyn drug market*. Oxford: Clarendon Press.

Mandaraka-Sheppard, A. 1986. *The dynamics of aggression in women's prisons in England and Wales*. London: Gower.

Martinson, R. 1974. What works? Questions and answers about prison reform. *Public Interest* 35: 22–45.

Messerschmidt, J.W. 1997 *Crime as structured action: Gender, race, class and crime in the making*. Newbury Park, CA: Sage Publications.

Palmer, T. 1995. Programmatic and nonprogrammatic aspects of successful intervention. New directions for research. *Crime and Delinquency* 41: 100-131.

Pawson, R., and Tilley, N. 1997. *Realistic evaluation.* Newbury Park, CA: Sage Publications.

Pollack, S. 1993. *Opening the window on a very dark day: A program evaluation of the Peer Support Team at The Kingston Prison for Women.* Masters thesis. Ottawa: Carleton University School of Social Work.

Pollock-Byrne, J. 1990. *Women, prison and crime.* Pacific Grove, CA: Brooks/Cole.

Richie, B. 1996. *Compelled to crime: The gender entrapment of battered Black women.* New York: Routledge.

Robison, J., and. Smith, G. 1971. The effectiveness of correctional programs. *Crime and Delinquency* 17: 67-80.

Ross, R., and Fabiano, E. 1986. *Female offenders: Correctional afterthoughts.* Jefferson, NC: McFarland & Company.

Russell, T. 1995. *An analysis of recidivism among clients of THE PROGRAM for Female Offenders, Inc., Pittsburgh, Pennsylvania.* Unpublished report.

Schwartz, I. M., and Orlando, F. 1991. *Programming for young women in the juvenile justice system.* Ann Arbor, MI: Center for the Study of Youth Policy, University of Michigan.

Shaw, M. 1995. Session on Managing Risk and Minimising Violence. Phase II: Session on Managing Risk and Minimising Violence. *Proceedings of the Commission of Inquiry into Certain Events at the Prison for Women in Kingston.* November 21. Kingston, Ont.: Unpublished transcript.

Shaw, M. 1994. Is there a feminist future for women's prisons? Paper presented at the Prisons 2000 Conference: International Conference on the Present State and Future of the Prison System, University of Leicester, England, April.

Shaw, M., et al. 1991. *The release study: Survey of Federally Sentenced Women in the community.* Ottawa: Solicitor General Canada.

Sim, J. 1990. *Medical power in prisons: The prison medical service in England 1774–1989.* Milton Keynes: Open University Press.

Simourd, L., and Andrews, D.A. 1994. Correlates of delinquency: A look at gender differences. *Forum on Corrections Research,* 61, 26-31.

Smart, C. 1989. *Feminism and the power of law.* London: Routledge.

Sobel, S. 1982. Difficulties experienced by women in prison. *Psychology of Women Quarterly* 72, 107-118.

Sultan, F. E., and Long, G. 1988. Treatment of the sexually/physically abused female inmate: Evaluation of an intensive short-term intervention program. *Journal of Offender Counseling, Services and Rehabilitation* 12: 131–143.

Task Force on Federally Sentenced Women 1990. *Report of the Task Force on Federally Sentenced Women—creating choices.* Ottawa: Ministry of the Solicitor General.

Wexler, H. K., et al. 1992. Outcome evaluation of a prison therapeutic community for substance abuse treatment. In *Drug abuse treatment in prisons and jails,* eds. Leukefeld, C. G., and Tims, F. M., 156-75. Rockville, MD: National Institute on Drug Abuse.

Wilfley, D., et al. 1986. Angry women offenders: Case study of a group. *International Journal of Offender Therapy and Comparative Criminology* 30: 41-51.

Young, I. M. 1994. Punishment, treatment, empowerment: Three approaches to policy for pregnant addicts. *Feminist Studies* 20: 33–57.

PART IV

Future Directions

Female offenders, as part of their rehabilitative process, need to be empowered with confidence in their capacity to deal with the larger social world. This is not an easy task. Multiple trauma histories create multifaceted problems. From a systems perspective, multifaceted problems require a holistic, multifaceted response in terms of rehabilitative programming and opportunities designed to address them. Designing effective, multifaceted programs for female offenders that promote a sense of well being, ability to take action, and increase self-worth in participants, also requires creativity. Specifically, it requires that the staff designing these programs maintain a systems perspective incorporating the relevant management principles, the focus of the last chapter of the book.

The heart of the approach to management suggested is that the effective and responsible organization be designed so that it can learn from its own experience and is therefore able to manifest constant growth in the quality of the services it delivers. Such an organization, including institutions, has the highest probability of delivering those services that will ultimately integrate the female offender into society as a contributing member. Organizations that are oriented in this way are organized as horizontal systems of racially and ethnically diverse individuals, rather than as vertical systems of racially and ethnically homogeneous individuals, so common in hierarchically structured management organizations.

Horizontal, systems-oriented agencies enable team members to manifest a commitment to constant growth and learning. Toward this end, both teamwork and the taking of individual initiatives are stressed. In point of fact, one cannot maintain a systems perspective as an individual, not because systems thinking is so difficult, but because good results in a complex system depend on bringing in as many perspectives as possible (Senge et al. 1994). Team members are encouraged to take responsibility, to propose and implement crossfunctional solutions, and to be the inspiration for the organization. The result is that team members on the front line are constantly refining existing services and implementing new projects and new directions of development with community-wide support and resources.

Although this might seem to some an idealistic and impractical requirement, in practice, experiences with such organizational structures are quite positive. Such organizations increase the likelihood that the female offender will receive those rehabilitative services guided by a policy framework that ultimately inspire her to acquire the skills and take advantage of the opportunities that she needs to be successful in reintegrating into society.

REFERENCE

Senge, P. M., et al. 1994. *The fifth discipline fieldbook.* New York: Doubleday.

CHAPTER 18

Looking Toward the Future

Ruth T. Zaplin

There is much that is known with respect to female offending. For example, we now know that status and minor offenses do not necessarily lead to more serious crimes (Barnett et al. 1987). There is also much that is still unknown with respect to female offending. For example, it is still not completely known what factors lead women and girls to criminal activity, and how interventions can be designed to mitigate these factors effectively. It seems clear from this book that the courses of adult criminal convictions can be traced back to childhood. However, it is still not possible to differentiate between what factors make one young girl from a poor neighborhood with high rates of single-parent households who is sexually and physically abused enter the juvenile and eventually the criminal justice system and another young girl with the same background not enter these systems. The literature reveals impressive correlations in findings about the variables of abuse, class, and crime; but it is quite another matter to establish causality among these variables. Beyond questions of causality, other questions remain unanswered. Why do some female delinquents become career criminals while others do not? What are the effects of disproportionate representation in corrections programs? What are the most effective ways to respond to female offenders' failures? And which sanctions are truly the most effective in producing desired behavioral changes such as the ability to maintain employment over time and improved parenting skills? While many questions remain, hopefully, practitioners who work in the criminal justice system, treatment providers, researchers, and policymakers alike, will be guided by the themes presented in this book and restated below, that are designed to rehabilitate and empower female offenders.

- The importance of adopting a rehabilitative perspective rather than a punitive perspective when working with female offenders. This approach does not preclude the use of rules and restitution for crimes committed.

Source: M.B. Straus. *Abuse and Victimization Across the Life Span.* pp. 153–169. © 1990. The Johns Hopkins University Press.

- The importance of adopting a broad-based perspective to treatment that addresses the core issues of the female offender's maladaptive behaviors as opposed to a single focus approach that targets one risk factor alone, e.g., substance abuse.
- The importance of adopting a broad-based perspective to program development and implementation in order to institute comprehensive, interdisciplinary service delivery across justice, education, and public behavioral health systems.
- The importance of developing programs that are both grounded in theory that is relevant to female offenders and outcome driven. A program must be outcome driven in order to demonstrate impact of services provided through systematic program evaluation of key performance areas and goals.
- The importance of gender-specific services. These services are not possible if program development efforts focus exclusively on providing the same programs to both males and females—what Chesney-Lind in the Foreword to this book calls, "equality with a vengeance."
- The importance of being culturally sensitive to the rehabilitative needs of female offenders. Like male offenders, the majority of female offenders are disproportionately African American or Hispanic.
- The importance of developing and implementing comprehensive long-term aftercare as part and parcel of rehabilitative efforts based on the reality that planned change is neither linear or short-term in nature.
- The importance of doing all of the above, if possible, while the offender is in a community-based setting, preferably in the least restrictive environment possible. The reality is that girls and women are institutionalized overwhelmingly for nonviolent offenses and therefore pose far lower institutional risks than males.

This information and the management considerations presented below, taken together and applied skillfully, can significantly reduce the incidence of female offenders being institutionalized and then recidivating upon their release.

An underlying cause of female offenders' errant behavior, as discussed in Chapter Seven, is rooted in the belief in their own powerlessness that manifests in low self-esteem and lack of basic confidence, a condition that is often exacerbated by the broader prison context that removes autonomy and control. Throughout this book, it has been emphasized that to effectively correct errant behavior, the rehabilitative needs of female offenders must be addressed. It is emphasized here that if the organization or institution that provides services to female offenders has, as part of its mission, to deter crime by correcting behavior through rehabilitative services, the only course advocated in this book, then the first step is to treat them as worthwhile human beings—as customers. Specifically, what this attitude means is that the female offender is equal to the service providers themselves, while at the same time being subject to rules, regulations, and laws (Mintzberg 1996). From this point of view, the notion of female offenders as customers is extremely useful.

To adopt the attitude of female offender as customer requires that those who deliver services to female offenders be responsive to their needs. This requires more flexibility, greater innovation, and more attention to where customers' needs are heading in the future (Drucker 1993). It involves organizational tasks related to facing the challenge of innovation, and managing growth, change, diversity, and complexity. Concurrently, it involves staff at all levels developing new competencies and working collectively. The design, structure, and relationship of the individuals performing the work are key to not only getting desired outcomes accomplished but to serving as role models for the customers they serve. The new ways based on this attitude involve management strategies and considerations related to tapping into the knowledge, experience, resources, and imagination of the people who comprise the organizational system to accomplish quality program outcomes with and for female offenders. While a comprehensive discussion of the ideas related to this attitude and the new ways of accomplishing organizational tasks are beyond the parameters of this book, suffice it to say here that applying what we now know about addressing the rehabilitative needs of female offenders in a productive way requires that organizations, including institutions, must, in the future, cultivate the learning potential of the individuals delivering the services to them. That is to say, they need to become learning organizations.

The systems perspective is a core perspective of the learning organization. According to Kofman and Senge (1993),

> In learning organizations, people are always inquiring into the systemic consequences of their actions, rather than just focusing on local consequences. They can understand the interdependencies underlying complex issues and act with perceptiveness and leverage. They are patient in seeking deeper understanding rather than striking out to "fix" problem symptoms—because they know that most fixes are temporary at best, and often result in more severe problems in the future. (p. 33)

Simply put, learning organizations develop and adopt learning strategies. These strategies engage people in confronting the challenges that face them, adjusting their values, changing perspectives, and learning new approaches to work. Specifically, "Learning organizations are skilled at five main activities: systematic problem solving, experimentation with new approaches, learning from their own experience and past history, learning from the experiences and best practices of others, and transferring knowledge quickly and efficiently throughout the organization" (Garvin 1993, p. 81).

The leader of a learning organization must have values that are compatible with learning as well. This is not about managers creating solutions to organizational problems. It is about managers instilling confidence in people so that they have the courage to act based on their own special knowledge within a framework of collective responsibility or shared vision toward the customer.

Although becoming a learning organization might seem to some an idealistic and impractical requirement, it is not. Consider that organizations are not made up of bricks and mortar. They are not made up of technology. Their efficiency is not based on treating people as machines, an idea that originated early in the twentieth century with the pioneer of scientific management, Frederick Taylor. They are made up of people who want to learn, want to be satisfied with what they do, and want to believe in an organizational mission. As Weitzman said in Chapter Seven, "Every human being, at some point in her life, aspires to a heroic ideal (p. 16)." Further, in an effective learning organization, they are made up of people who are predisposed to share the organization's vision and strategy.

The methods for staffing an organization with these "vital strategic resources" (Bartlett and Ghoshal 1995, p. 142) and how to retain them encompasses issues related to diversity, not in terms of identity-group representation, but in terms of bringing in varied perspectives and approaches to work. With respect to the concept of the female offender as customer, this issue is extremely important. Female offenders come from many backgrounds. Diversity in those that deliver services to them will serve the customer better and foster legitimacy with them. This may, in turn, result in making the world of work more attractive to the female offender, thereby making her maladaptive behaviors that will not serve her in the world of work less attractive.

Addressing the multifaceted rehabilitative needs of female offenders also requires innovation. How, after all, can the problem of a single focus approach utilized by most entities working with female offenders be solved without innovation? Essentially, innovation is about members of the organization taking responsibility and not accepting complacency for the situations that face them at work. Otherwise, they will repeat habitual patterns and innovation will be temporary at best. Innovation is essential if learning is to take place.

Based on new knowledge and insights, shared vision and organizational strategy emerge; what the organization stands for itself and what it seeks to become in partnership with other entities. Shared vision is necessary in order to develop organizational strategy. A first step in that process has to do with clarifying organizational realities and values. Strategy is part and parcel of shared vision. Shared vision means shared beliefs and values, which are a component of what Collins and Porras (1996, p. 66) call "core ideology." For example, it is recommended here that an organization decide for itself to hold the "female offender as customer" as a core ideology. In turn, this ideology becomes the "glue" holding the organization together. The vision is held by the people who are committed to each other and to the common goals of the organization.

It is important to emphasize here that people who share the same vision and organizational strategy do not necessarily all think or look the same, especially in organizations that celebrate diversity. According to Heifetz and Laurie (1997, p. 128), "Different people within the same organization bring different experiences, assumptions, values, beliefs, and habits to their work. This diversity is valuable because innovation and learning are the products of differences. No one learns anything without being open to contrasting points of view." What matters is whether a team can integrate its members in order to capitalize on the value of these different perspectives and use one another as resources to problem-solve to address the rehabilitative needs of female offenders. Effective teams become the medium for creating the conditions within the organization for diverse groups to talk to one another. And, according to Heifetz and Laurie (1997), "Giving a voice to all people is the foundation of an organization that is willing to experiment and learn (p. 129)."

The importance of teamwork in this regard cannot be overstated. Teamwork implies a focus inward and a focus outward. The focus inward involves building a credible staff through intra-agency methods of organizing, addressing work teams and knowledge work as well as obstacles to achieving structural change within the organization. The focus outward involves integrating teamwork and making it happen across boundaries, to other entities that work with female offenders. According to Garvin (1993, p. 91), "Boundaries inhibit the flow of information; they keep individuals and groups isolated and reinforce preconceptions. Opening up boundaries…ensures a fresh flow of ideas and the chance to consider competing perspectives." Only when boundaries are open is a truly integrated systems approach, described in Chapter Thirteen, achievable.

These management considerations and the themes presented in this book, taken together and applied skillfully, can significantly reduce the incidence of female offenders being institutionalized and then recidivating upon their release. They will result in organizations increasing the likelihood that the female offender will receive those rehabilitative services guided by a policy framework that ultimately inspire her to acquire the skills and take advantage of the opportunities that she needs to be successful in reintegrating into society.

REFERENCES

Barnett, A., et al. 1987. Probabilistic models of youthful criminal careers. *Criminology* 25: 83–107.

Bartlett, C. A., and Ghoshal, S. 1995. Changing the role of top management beyond systems to people. *Harvard Business Review* May-June: 132–142.

Collins, J. C., and Porras, J. I. 1996. Building your company's vision. *Harvard Business Review* September-October: 65–77.

Drucker, P. F. 1993. *The five most important questions you will ever ask about your nonprofit organization,* Participant's workbook. San Francisco: Jossey-Bass Publishers.

Garvin, D. A. 1993. Building a learning organization. *Harvard Business Review* July-August: 78–91.

Heifetz, R. A., and Laurie, D. L. 1997. The work of leadership. *Harvard Business Review,* January-February: 124–134.

Kofman, F., and Senge, P. M. 1993. Communities of commitment: The heart of learning organizations. In *Learning organizations,* eds. Chawla, S., and Renesch, J., 15-43. Portland, OR: Productivity Press.

Mintzberg, H. 1996. Managing government, governing management. *Harvard Business Review* May-June: 75-83.

Taylor, F. W. 1947. The principles of scientific management. In *Scientific management.* New York: Harper and Row.

Index